Internal Models and Solvency II

Internal Models and Solvency II

From Regulation to Implementation

Edited by Paolo Cadoni

Published by Risk Books, a Division of Incisive Media Investments Ltd

Incisive Media
32–34 Broadwick Street
London W1A 2HG
Tel: +44(0) 20 7316 9000
E-mail: books@incisivemedia.com
Site: www.riskbooks.com
www.incisivemedia.com

ISBN 978 1 78272 093 5

British Library Cataloguing in Publication Data
A catalogue record for this book is available from the British Library

Publisher: Nick Carver
Commissioning Editor: Amy Jordan
Associate Editor: Alice Levick
Managing Editor: Lewis O'Sullivan
Designer: Lisa Ling
Copyeditor: Laurie Donaldson

Typeset by Mark Heslington Ltd, Scarborough, North Yorkshire
Printed and bound in the UK by PrintonDemand-Worldwide

Contents

About the Editor

Paolo Cadoni is a technical head of department in the Prudential Policy Division leading the Prudential Regulation Authority's input into EIOPA's Solvency II committees and the International Association of Insurance Supervisors' (IAIS) Solvency and Actuarial Issues Subcommittee. Since March 2013, he has been the chair of the IAIS ComFrame Field Testing Task Force, and he has chaired the EIOPA Internal Models Committee since 2009. Before that, Paolo was responsible for the FSA's policy development and implementation of the IMM for counterparty credit risk for banks and investment firms, and represented the FSA on the Basel Committee and led their work on QIS5. He has a PhD in finance from the ICMA Centre and an MSc in econometrics from Southampton University.

About the Authors

Markus Bellion works in the cross-sectoral department of risk modelling at BaFin, where he coordinates policy activities with respect to quantitative aspects of Solvency II internal models. He is a member of the EIOPA Internal Models Committee and is also actively involved in the EIOPA informal supervisory meetings of European modelling experts. Since the beginning of the internal model pre-application phase, Markus has been responsible for issues in accumulation risk modelling, in particular of natural catastrophes, and carried out numerous on-site inspections of catastrophe models at major European insurance and reinsurance groups. He holds a PhD in theoretical physics from Saarland University.

Ravi Bharos has worked at the De Nederlandsche Bank (DNB), the Dutch central bank, as a member of the Solvency II internal model team. He joined DNB in 2000 as a banking supervisor and switched to insurance supervision in 2004, working mainly with large internationally active financial institutions. Before joining DNB, Ravi worked as a public auditor for several audit firms and as an internal auditor with ING. He is a Dutch qualified auditor, graduated in law at Leiden University and is studying psychology at the Open University, Heerlen.

Dean Buckner has worked in the financial services industry for 27 years since just before the 1987 stock market crash. He worked as a trader and hedge fund manager before moving into risk management and risk systems design, and also had two spells in regulation, working at the Financial Services Authority in the banking sector on capital model recognition until 2007, and is now working at the Prudential Regulation Authority, reviewing data quality and data governance of Solvency II capital models. Dean has a PhD in philosophy and an MSc in computer science.

Andrew Candland works at the EIOPA in Frankfurt, where he has set up the Centre of Expertise in Internal Models. He also led the modelling team for Prudential's UK business, before he moved to the group head office to head up their work on regulatory and economic capital modelling. In 2010, Andrew joined the Financial Services Authority to lead an internal model assessment team. He read maths at the University of Cambridge before joining Prudential Plc, where he qualified as an actuary.

Ben Carr works in group risk at Aviva, where he is responsible for the development of their economic capital modelling methodology. He joined Aviva in August 2011, having spent several years at the Financial Services Authority in the UK leading their Solvency II internal model approval process. Before that, Ben worked as a seconded national expert at the European Commission on the development and negotiation of the Solvency II framework directive. He holds a PhD in pure mathematics from the University of Warwick.

Christopher Chappell is a London-based actuary and risk management professional, with over 20 years within the financial services industry. He has significant experience in risk management through responsibilities as a group chief actuary and chief risk officer. Christopher has worked with boards to design and embed enterprise risk management frameworks that provide strategic value, insight and solutions for the business. He is a fellow of the Institute and Faculty of Actuaries (FIA) and a Chartered Enterprise Risk Analyst (CERA).

Ishtiaq Faiz works in the general insurance risk specialists department at the Prudential Regulation Authority (PRA), where he is responsible for the internal model review of various insurance entities. Before joining the PRA in May 2010, he spent several years at Suncorp-Metway in Australia working on pricing and capital models. Ishtiaq holds a bachelors degree majoring in actuarial science from the University of New South Wales.

Agnieszka Groniowska is chief specialist in the Risk Monitoring Department of the KNF, the Polish Financial Supervision Authority, where her responsibilities include dealing with Solvency II issues at

European and national level. She is a KNF representative in the EIOPA Financial Requirements Committee and Group Solvency Subgroup of Insurance Groups Supervision Committee. Agnieszka was also a member of Internal Models Committee and CEIOPS QIS5 Task Force, and was an EU short-term expert in a technical assistance project for the Russian insurance sector. She graduated from the Warsaw University and holds a PhD in economics at Warsaw School of Economics.

Perrine Kaltwasser has been head of a banking supervision division within the ACPR, part of the French central bank, since 2011. She has worked in the supervision of financial institutions spans for over a decade, and covers both the banking and the insurance sector, at a national and international level. Perrine joined the French Embassy economic services in Washington in 2004, before moving to the French insurance supervisor in Paris, where she was heavily involved in Solvency II negotiations. In 2009, Perrine accepted a policy position at the EIOPA in Frankfurt, where she dealt with topics such as QIS5. She studied at the École Polytechnique and ENSAE ParisTech, and is an actuary.

Christian Kerfriden is a policy associate at the Prudential Regulation Authority, with a focus on Solvency II internal models. Before joining the Financial Services Authority in 2010, he spent over 10 years in the reinsurance industry with positions in pricing and risk management. Christian gained a masters in economics from the University of Toulouse.

Åsa Larson is the executive director for supervision of insurance at Finansinspektionen, the Swedish Financial Supervisory Authority. She joined Finansinspektionen in 2010 to set up an internal models team, and has led their insurance risk supervision department since 2012. Åsa was the vice chair of the EIOPA Internal Models Committee in 2012–13, and has also held various actuarial positions in the insurance groups Folksam and Skandia, focusing on actuarial governance and business modelling. Previously, she worked at the Swedish Society of Actuaries, representing and chairing the society in the AAE and the IAA committee work for many years.

Christopher Lotz heads ups the department for cross-sectoral risk modelling at BaFin, where he covers quantitative aspects of internal risk models across banks and insurance companies. In his previous roles at BaFin, he carried out on-site inspections for market, credit and operational risk models. Christopher has also participated in several international working groups and was actively involved in the EIOPA Internal Models Committee. Prior to joining BaFin in 2004, he worked at Deutsche Bank in the areas of market risk management and risk control. Christopher graduated in mathematics and received his PhD in economics from the University of Bonn.

Juan Lumbreras is a senior expert in Solvency II at EIOPA, where he is responsible for its Internal Models Expert Group, providing technical advice to the European Commission on the Solvency II delegated acts, drafting the pre-application for internal models preparatory guidelines and working on the final guidelines for internal models. He joined CEIOPS in 2008 to work on the Solvency II project, occupational pensions and cross-sectoral work streams. Prior to this, Juan worked for the Direccion General de Seguros y Fondos de Pensiones in Spain. He holds a degree in economics and business from the Universidad Autonoma de Madrid.

Dermot Marron is an actuarial consultant for Allied Risk Management. He was previously at the Central Bank of Ireland, where he was Ireland's representative on the EIOPA Solvency II Internal Model Expert Group, and headed the documentation working group. Prior to that, Dermot held a number of senior positions in the insurance/reinsurance industry, including as chief actuary of Atradius Reinsurance. He has a PhD in pure mathematics from the Queen's University of Belfast, and is a fellow of the Society of Actuaries in Ireland and a fellow of the Institute of Actuaries. Dermot has a diploma in regulatory management from the Irish Management Institute, and is studying to be a Chartered Enterprise Risk Actuary.

Peter Müller works in the cross-sectoral department risk modelling at BaFin, where he coordinates the activities in the pre-application phase for internal models of major European insurance and reinsurance groups, and is responsible for modelling premium and reserve risk. Since 2008, he has carried out numerous internal model on-site inspections in all risk categories, participated in several international working groups and was actively involved in EIOPA informal supervisory meetings of European modelling experts. Peter began his career as a scientific assistant at the University of Hamburg, after graduating in mathematics at Dresden University of Technology. He holds a PhD in mathematics from the University of Hamburg.

Stefano Pasqualini works in the Supervisory, Regulation and Policy Department at IVASS, the Italian insurance supervisor, which he joined in 2000. He spent several years in the Prudential Supervision Department, mainly working on stochastic loss reserving methods. As a member of the EIOPA Internal Models Committee, Stefano participated in the technical work of the committee, helping to manage and finalise advice to the European Commission on the procedure for approval of an internal model and the pre-application process for internal models. He holds a BSc in actuarial science and statistics and an MSc in insurance risk management from the University of Rome, and is a member of the Italian Actuarial Association.

Vesa Ronkainen is a chief risk expert at the Financial Supervisory Authority in Finland, where he is in charge of internal models and research. In various roles, he has been closely involved in the Solvency II project for over a decade, which included a secondment to the European Commission and long-standing participation in EIOPA's Internal Models Committee. Previously, Vesa worked at life and pension insurance companies in Finland. He holds a PhD in statistics from the University of Eastern Finland.

Elliot Varnell is head of enterprise risk management at Pension Insurance Corporation. Before that, he worked at Milliman providing economic capital and market risk advisory and models to life assurance companies, and at KPMG, where he led economic capital internal model reviews for major European multinational insurers. Elliot has also held roles at Barrie & Hibbert and at Deloitte, and is a fellow and an elected member of the governing council of the Institute and Faculty of Actuaries. He has in-depth knowledge of the

Solvency II framework and has advised both EIOPA, CEIOPS and key stakeholder trade associations on how models would be used in Solvency II.

Coomaren Vencatasawmy works as a technical specialist in the insurance supervision department of the Prudential Regulation Authority (PRA), where he is responsible for IMAP and ORSA reviews for UK groups and subsidiaries. He joined the PRA in 2009 to work in the policy department, and previously spent several years working at Aviva and Groupama Insurance. Coomaren also gained experience in developing econometric models for the Swedish and Mauritian governments, and has a research focus on large datasets from satellite images in applications such as agriculture, geology and marine. He holds a PhD in statistics from the University of Sheffield and an MBA in risk management from Heriot Watt University.

Régis Weisslinger is development director at Milliman in Paris, where he is responsible for the development of innovative offers and takes part in various actuarial consulting projects with clients, including some related to Solvency II. Prior to joining Milliman, he worked for Towers Watson as a non-life senior consultant. Régis began his career as an insurance supervisor at French prudential authority, ACPR, and is a qualified actuary. He studied at the École Polytechnique and ENSAE in Paris.

Foreword

Solvency II will bring about a transformation of insurance supervision in Europe. It will replace an outdated and fragmented regulatory regime with a harmonised approach based on sound core principles that will increase policyholder protection.

Internal models play an important role in Solvency II. Through them, the same modern developments in risk management and actuarial science, tailored to the risk profile of an individual company, can be used to calculate regulatory capital and make decisions in running a company.

Internal models must necessarily be as complex as the risks they are seeking to quantify, but this must not be at the expense of transparency and responsibility. Solvency II rightly sets high standards for any company wanting to gain approval to use its internal model to calculate regulatory capital requirements.

For all but the most advanced insurers, internal models have been something of a new world. As with any new place, it takes a while to become familiar with the surroundings, to discover pitfalls and dangers that may not be evident at first, and to find shortcuts that can save time. A book that shares the knowledge of experienced practioners and allows others to accelerate their learning is most welcome.

WHO COULD WRITE SUCH A BOOK?

The world of insurance capital models is vast. As well as insurance risks on the life and non-life side, covering the insurance of everything from motor vehicles to large engineering structures, death and health, there are the risks that are also familiar in banking circles (market, credit and operational risk). Unlike banking, however, an insurance model can include all these risks under one roof. Solvency

II emphasises the importance of qualitative as well as quantitative standards. The governance of the model and wider risk management framework are as important as the statistical techniques used in the model. The data used to calibrate the model's parameters matters as much as the choice of mathematical models to represent the underlying risks.

No one person could write a book that covered all such areas. In *Internal Models and Solvency II*, each chapter has been written by experts in the topic, individuals with hands-on experience of designing, validating, reviewing and using models. They share their experience here, and bring alive the requirements of Solvency II through practical insight.

Combining the work of so many experts in such diverse disciplines is no small challenge for the Editor. I have known Paolo Cadoni for 10 years, and he is well-suited to the role. Having trained as an economist, he worked as a model builder before moving to the UK Financial Services Authority (now part of the Bank of England). After several years working on Basel II, he moved into insurance policy and has represented the UK on EIOPA's Internal Models Committee since 2005, and as its chairman from 2009 onwards. He has led the committee in grappling with every one of the topics in this book as it drafted advice to the European Commission and EIOPA's Guidelines. Paolo also chairs the ComFrame Field Testing Task Force of the International Association of Insurance Supervisors (IAIS).

Whatever your role in the world of internal models, I trust this book will help you.

Gabriel Bernardino
Chairman of the European Insurance and Occupational Pensions Authority, Frankfurt
March 2014

Introduction

Since the early 1990s, we have witnessed remarkable advances in financial engineering and financial innovation. These innovations in financial products have also given rise to some new challenges for market participants and their supervisors. Risk-sensitive capital standards, the development of improved risk management practices and the greater role that a firms' own internal model for the measurement and management of risk in the definition of capital requirements – in both insurance and banking – are examples of this shift. More specifically, internal models have also been used increasingly for external purposes, such as in communicating information about an institution's risks to creditors, shareholders, regulators and rating agencies.

The 2007–08 financial crisis has led to questions about the use of internal models for the calculation of regulatory capital both in banking, where they are widely used, and in the forthcoming European insurance regulatory regime that is Solvency II.[1] The financial crisis exposed the limitations of banking models and the way they failed to measure extreme financial events, capture all risks to which firms were exposed to and overstated the effect of risk mitigation, diversification and fungibility of capital.

In fact, in 2008 the financial markets experienced extreme movements beyond the range of internal models "predictions" and expectations. This showed up in changes both in the volatility of individual market risk factors and in correlations between risk factors. As co-dependencies under a stressed scenario are different from a non-stressed scenario, historic relationships between markets ceased to hold. Models were not calibrated to cater for these severe scenarios and/or did not cover all relevant risks. Firms experienced significant losses on positions that (based on historical experience) were deemed to bear immaterial risks. These "immaterial" risks were often modelled by simplified methods or omitted.

The effects of risk mitigation were often overstated. As a result, when needed, management actions could not be implemented. In other cases, counterparty risk was not taken properly into account. Moreover, market liquidity dropped sharply, making it impossible to price certain assets, as well as calibrate internal models.

The financial crisis also heightened concerns about the fungibility of capital within groups, particularly as some regulators restricted the flows of internal dividends to protect local interests. As a response, management at firms tried to release the level of prudence embedded in models to reduce capital requirements, further exacerbating supervisory concerns about the use of models.

SHOULD INTERNAL MODELS STILL FEATURE IN A REGULATORY FRAMEWORK?

As mentioned, evidence from the use of models in the banking regime seems to indicate that internal models are of dubious utility and should not feature in a regulatory framework. It has often been argued[2] that internal models have become so complex that firms themselves do not adequately understand them. Therefore, their use within a regulatory framework should not be allowed without appropriate safeguards. To this end, the Basel III reforms[3] have introduced a simple, transparent, non-risk-based leverage ratio to act as a supplementary measure to the risk-based capital requirements that firms would have to meet in addition to the capital requirement calculated by the internal model.

CAN THE SAME ARGUMENTS BE USED FOR INSURANCE INTERNAL MODELS?

The answer to this question is not so straightforward. It would be fair to say that the history, and indeed meaning, of approaches designated by the emotive label "internal model" is quite different in insurance from that in banking. In particular, the label "internal model" is not used in insurance to refer to the same thing under the Basel framework as it is for Solvency II.

An insurance internal model need not be based on complex mathematics. It may simply be a formula adapted to the specificities of a particular specialist type of insurance, often with the same or similar formulas used for the whole of an insurance sub-sector. It may also be a set of more or less standard stress tests applied, such as of specified natural or man-made disasters, or changes in macroeconomic variables (eg, interest rates, general equity prices, inflation).

The focus of non-life insurance models tends to be on the probability and severity of possible future seismic, metrological, epidemiological and industrial events. The focus of life insurance models tends to be on demographic (mortality and morbidity) events and macroeconomic shocks. Therefore, insurance models – with the exception of life insurers' economic modelling – do not contain the same sort of "feedback loops" or drive the same sort of behavioural change as banking models, principally because the existence of the model does not drive change in the nature of the phenomena being modelled.[4] This means there is less potential for insurance models to give rise to systemic risk. They also tend to concentrate on low probability but high-impact events, and have to take into account much less complex hedging structures. Even where insurers are exposed to similar sorts of risks to banks (such as market risk), behaviours are likely to be different, as asset allocation is driven principally by the need to match assets to liabilities, rather than by a desire to optimise their capital position under a model.

Insurers have therefore been using models for many years[5] to manage the non-economic factors that drive their business, and these have generally proved robust in the face of actual experience. Life insurers' modelling of risks to their balance sheets arising from economic shocks is more recent, only gaining significant momentum after, and due to, the 2003 equity values crisis. These models are almost all based on one of four external models, and are susceptible to non-model comparison to simple stress tests.

It should also be noted that an internal model regime allows for a much greater degree of supervisory judgement than a standardised one, in that it allows for wider discussion of what is acceptable and what is not. For example, under the Solvency II standard formula, all European Economic Area (EEA) sovereign debt attracts a capital charge of zero, whereas an internal model compliant with Solvency II must "cover all material risks to which insurance companies are exposed",[6] and supervisors might therefore take a different view from that implied by the standard formula where the impact is deemed material. More generally, this means that an internal model regime gives supervisors much more flexibility to respond to issues that directly threaten firms' viability than is the case under the standard formula.

SO, WHAT CAN WE CONCLUDE? CAN WE IGNORE WHAT HAPPENED ON THE BANKING SIDE?

Certainly not . . . However, the Solvency II internal modelling framework was developed during the financial crisis and has already benefited from lessons learned during that period. Examples of this shift are a stronger emphasis on the governance (eg, policy for model changes) and validation of the internal model. It is important to recognise that there are no "correct" models, only appropriate or inappropriate models. Deciding on the appropriateness of a model is in the end a judgement call by the supervisor. Supervisors should only approve the use of models to calculate the capital requirements if they are satisfied that the systems for identifying, measuring, monitoring, managing and reporting risks are adequate and, in particular, if the model fulfils the tests and standards set out in the Solvency II framework.

WILL THIS BE ENOUGH?

No, having a good regulatory framework where lots of emphasis is placed on striving to ensure that only appropriate models are approved for use is a necessary, but insufficient, condition for an appropriate internal modelling regime. For example, while the supervisory authorities and firms focus is on the work needed to review/submit an internal model application, it is important to use the knowledge and learning gained during the model development/review process to develop systems that would enable both firms and supervisors to monitor the ongoing appropriateness of a firm's internal model post-approval. This is often forgotten, and leads to a risk that standards of solvency deteriorate over time. Following approval, firms are responsible for ensuring the ongoing appropriateness of the internal model by ensuring that the internal model meets the tests and standards, and reflects the firm's risk profile. Supervisors need to be assured that firms have put in place systems that ensure that the internal model operates properly on a continuous basis. Supervisors also need to be confident that the controls put in place are adequate and effective at all times, including stressed market conditions or crises. At a market level, it is important that supervisors monitor the movement of insurance sector capital over time.

To avoid nasty surprises during turbulent times, it is in the interest of supervisors and senior management at firms to ensure that a suite of tools that can help them to ensure that, after approval, internal models and capital requirement's calculation remain appropriate on an ongoing basis at both a firm and system level, and are developed and used as a "sense check" for the results of the internal models.

To be effective, these tools should capture the risks to which the firm is exposed to from a different perspective than the one used in the internal model. Namely, they should be based on metrics that are independent from the internal model calculations, not based on the firm's modelled capital requirement.[7] This calls for tools that are simple in their construction, calibration and application, avoiding complexity and, if breached, trigger an immediate response both by the firm and the supervisor. This is the path that several supervisory authorities are following and is, in a nutshell, what will be illustrated by this book.

WHO IS THIS BOOK FOR?

Insurance firms and groups are preparing for the implementation of Solvency II, with some following the internal models pre-application process, as structured by their supervisory authorities. The intention of *Internal Models and Solvency II* is to present the reader with a near exhaustive spectrum of topics on internal models for insurers.

This book deals with these issues in detail, with the aim of providing the building blocks for an appropriate development, review and monitoring of an internal modelling framework. To this end, it provides a unique insight regarding the spirit and rationale of the requirements for the use of internal models to calculate the capital requirements under Solvency II. This is complemented by practical solutions to daily challenges that both practitioners and supervisors face when developing, implementing, monitoring and reviewing models for internal and regulatory purposes.

The views reflected in the book come directly from people that contributed to the development of the Solvency II internal modelling framework, on both the supervisory and/or the industry/practitioner side.

The legislative material on internal models is not easily accessible or digestible for non-regulators; therefore, this book will give practitioners (actuaries and quants) and senior executives a practical interpretation of the internal modelling requirements. It will also provide support to managers charged with implementing the internal modelling framework at firms. Insurance supervisors who review a company's application for the use of internal models for the calculation of capital requirements will find the book useful when looking for clarifications of the requirements, and practical solutions to challenges faced during the review work. Finally, the book is for those interested in gaining a better understanding about the use of internal models for regulatory purposes, as well as their history, challenges, philosophy and future prospects.

The book looks particularly at the application of internal models for Solvency II purposes (ie, Europe). The principles developed in this framework build on what should be good practice, and this applies to any internal modelling framework. As Solvency II is an emerging standard for insurance supervision that is inspiring modernisation of the regulatory regimes of several jurisdictions (South Africa, Israel, Mexico, China, etc), the book should be helpful to both supervisors and practitioners working in these countries.

ORGANISATION OF THE BOOK

The book starts with a look at basic internal model principles, before moving on to more complex concepts, supporting explanations with examples that illustrate the challenges faced both by firms and supervisors during the development, implementation, review and monitoring of internal models. It stresses the need for firms to seek to go beyond a simple regulatory "box-ticking" exercise, reflecting internal management priorities and covering all material aspects of the internal model environment. The internal model approval process aims not only to assess how the internal model meets the Solvency II requirements in isolation, but also considers any potential interrelation between these requirements. The review process should therefore include the necessary steps and tools to ensure supervisory authorities are able to satisfy themselves that these requirements are met. It is essential that the methodologies, components and inputs used by firms are appropriate for the internal model and its use, and enable them to identify, measure, monitor and report risks adequately. Complying with the internal models standards is not a one-off exercise. Standards have to be met on an ongoing basis, and the bar should be raised over time to take into account both internal and external developments. To this end, an ongoing dialogue between firms and regulators is not required, but essential.

Chapter 1 lays out the foundations for the Solvency II internal modelling framework. It provides a high-level review of the Solvency II balance sheet, and illustrates how assets and liabilities are to be valued under this framework. It explains the role of the solvency capital requirement (SCR), and describes how it should be derived as a difference between the net asset values of the balance sheet at the valuation date (pre-stress) and one year forward (post-stress). It also defines an internal model in the Solvency II context, discussing the potential costs and benefits arising from its development and use for both supervisors and firms. Finally, the concept of proportionality and how it applies to internal models is explored.

In Chapter 2, Juan Antonio Lumbreras provides details about the Solvency II partial internal modelling regime. He defines the scope of application of a partial internal model, and compares and contrasts the use of partial internal models in Solvency II and the Basel/CRD framework. The concept of the major business unit is explained, and a number of examples of partial internal models are provided. The specific provisions that apply to partial internal models, the rationale for these measures and the use of transitional plans to extend the scope of the models are also discussed. Finally, firms' challenges to capture those risks that are not explicitly covered by the standard formula are covered.

In Chapter 3, Stefano Pasqualini presents an overview of the procedure to be followed for the approval of an internal model. Particular attention is paid to internal models' application for groups, where cooperation between different national supervisory authorities is critical for the effective review of the application. The chapter also highlights the importance of firm's contingency plans, were the internal model's application to be unsuccessful.

In the next chapter, Christian Kerfriden describes the policy for model changes, and highlights its role within the overall governance of the internal model. Chapter 4 also discusses the elements that need to be covered by the policy, including the changes and sources of changes. The practical issues faced by firms when setting and implementing the policy are discussed, as well as the classification of changes between minor and major. Finally, the supervisory approval of major changes to the model is examined.

In Chapter 5, Agnieszka Groniowska, Perrine Kaltwasser and Regis Weisslinger discuss the challenges faced by the implementation of the group internal modelling regime. They explain the option provided by Solvency II to calculate the group solvency and, in particular, the implications and challenges raised by the accounting consolidation or deduction and aggregation methods; the treatment of entities located outside the EEA is also considered. The challenges of home and host supervisors, as well as the role of the supervisory college and EIOPA during the review and assessment of applications for the use of an internal model for groups, are considered. Finally, the chapter considers the application of the concept of materiality in a group context.

Following that, Christopher Chappell, Elliot Varnell and Coomaren Vencatasawmy describe the Solvency II requirements for the use test. Chapter 6 proposes a case study that discusses the challenges related to its implementation (eg, governance, alignment of business metrics), and includes some practical solutions on how to evidence the requirements.

In Chapter 7, Markus Bellion, Christopher Lotz and Peter Müller look at the internal model statistical quality standards in the light of the implementation efforts of both firms and supervisors as observed during the internal model pre-application phase. The main statistical quality standards implementation challenges and issues are presented. The examples are specific to a particular risk category or model component, although the approach used can be easily transferred to other internal modelling areas.

In the next chapter, Dean Buckner explores some of the common confusions surrounding data governance, as well as some of the common traps and pitfalls to avoid. These include the difficulties of distinguishing data governance from the science of information technology, the problem of measuring and controlling data quality, and the purpose of a data directory. Chapter 8 identifies two serious obstacles to successful data governance, namely the fragmentation of systems caused by the growth of end-user computing in the late 20th century and the failure to recognise common principles of data governance, leading to failure to develop it as a discipline in its own right. The examples relate to asset risk management, longevity risk management and catastrophe risk management.

In Chapter 9, Ishtiaq Faiz and Paolo Cadoni introduce the Solvency II internal model calibration's standards. They clarify the purpose of these often-misunderstood requirements and how they apply to firms that are calibrating their internal models using different risk measures (eg, tail value-at-risk, VaR) and time horizons from those set out in the Solvency II directive. They go on to provide an insight on how both supervisors and firms are dealing with these requirements during the internal models' development, implementation and review.

In Chapter 10, Andrew Candland and Christopher Lotz describe the profit and loss (P&L) attribution process. They present examples of the results of P&L attribution exercises, and examine the prerequisites for a successful P&L attribution. The chapter also explains its use in model validation and risk management, and the issues and challenges around P&L attribution.

Following that, Ravi Bharos, Christian Kerfriden and Vesa Ronkainen provide a regulatory perspective on model validation in Chapter 11. The authors explain the importance of an appropriate model validation process, its governance, and the planning and execution of the model validation activities. Examples of some of the tools that can be used to validate a model and the reporting of the outcome of the model validation activities are also provided.

In Chapter 12, Ben Carr presents an industry perspective on model validation. He offers an industry interpretation of the Solvency II validation requirements, illustrated by an example of how the regular cycle of model validation could be organised by an insurance company to ensure the model validation process is implemented pragmatically and add real value to the company.

In Chapter 13, Dermot Marron provides a critical analysis of the Solvency II internal model documentation's requirements. The chapter explains the importance of the scope, form and review of documentation, and gives examples of how firms should go about documenting the outputs of the model, its methodologies, expert judgement and external models. This is complemented by other examples of how firms should document the validation process and its outcomes and, most importantly, how documentation should be validated.

In the next chapter, Åsa Larson proposes a definition for external models. Chapter 14 explains the typology of external models, the principles to be applied when reviewing data and external data for use in the internal model, the requirements and challenges from a supervisory and firm perspective (eg, use test, statistical quality standards, calibration, P&L, validation, documentation and confidentiality), and the interface between internal and external models.

In Chapter 15, Paolo Cadoni and Christian Kerfriden introduce a paradigm to deal with internal model's limitations, present an illustration of the typical sources of limitations and stress the importance of a good governance framework to identify potential issues and manage them appropriately. They explain how to deal with the ongoing monitoring of internal model performance, and describe those instances, post-approval, where the use of the internal models stops satisfying the Solvency II requirements. Finally, they provide an illustration of the internal models' supervisory reporting and public disclosures requirements.

I hope that, after reading this important book, the reader will have a broad and clear perspective on the relevant issues and thinking on internal models, and of how these leading authors see the practice evolving in the future.

Paolo Cadoni

1 For further details, see European Parliament and the Council of the European Union (2009).
2 For further details, see Haldane and Madouros (2012).
3 For further details, see Basel Committee on Banking Supervisions (2013).
4 Thus, the presence of a model that seeks to understand such phenomena (eg, equity risk) could drive decisions around asset allocation, hedging strategies, etc, which in turn change the underlying nature of the risk itself. By contrast, a model that seeks to understand the impact of natural catastrophes or shifts in mortality patterns might drive changes in a company's exposures to those risks, but would not give rise to changes in the nature of the risk itself.
5 For instance, the use of some modelling to estimate technical provisions was introduced in the UK by the Assurance Companies Act 1909. Historical modelling has mainly been on the liability side of the balance sheet (eg, mortality tables, which essentially are simple models), whereas the use of models for the derivation of capital requirements is relatively new and still being tested.
6 For further details, see Article 121 of the European Parliament and the Council of the European Union (2009).
7 It is worth mentioning that this does not mean being independent from the risks borne by the firm.

REFERENCES

Basel Committee on Banking Supervision, 2013, "Revised Basel III Leverage Ratio Framework and Disclosure Requirements", consultative document, June.

CEIOPS, 2005a, "Answers to the European Commission on the 'First Wave' of Calls for Advice in the Framework of the Solvency II Project", June.

CEIOPS, 2005b, "Answers to the European Commission on the 'Second Wave' of Calls for Advice in the Framework of the Solvency II Project", October.

European Parliament and the Council of the European Union, 2009, "Directive 2009/138/EC of the European Parliament and of the Council of 25 November 2009 on the Taking-up and Pursuit of the Business of Insurance and Reinsurance (Solvency II) (recast)".

Haldane, A. G. and V. Madouros, 2012, "The Dog and the Frisbee", paper delivered to the Federal Reserve Bank of Kansas City's 36th economic policy symposium, Wyoming, August.

1

Balance Sheet, Capital Requirements and Internal Models

Paolo Cadoni

Prudential Regulation Authority, Bank of England

This chapter will lay out the foundations for the Solvency II internal modelling framework. The first section provides a high-level review of the Solvency II balance sheet, illustrating how assets and liabilities are to be valued under this framework. The following section explains the role of the solvency capital requirement (SCR), describing how it should be derived as a difference between the net asset values of the balance sheet at the valuation date (pre-stress) and one year forward (post-stress). In the absence of an explicit definition, the third section then attempts to define what an internal model is in the Solvency II framework, while the next two sections analyse the potential costs and benefits of an internal modelling approach for both firms and supervisors. The concept of proportionality is then discussed, with an assessment of what this means for firms intending to use internal models. Finally, we draw some conclusions.

A PRIMER ON SOLVENCY II

Solvency II, which will come into effect from January 2016, is fundamentally redesigning the capital adequacy regime for European insurers and reinsurers. The new rules continue the trend, placing demanding requirements on firms' risk management. It establishes a solvency system better matched to the risks of each (re)insurance firm than current regulations.

Fundamental shifts introduced by the new framework are:

- its principle-based approach;
- the emphasis put on the proportionality principle;
- forward-looking and three-pillar structure;
- total balance-sheet approach;
- two-level approach to capital requirements – the supervisory ladder of intervention and the use of internal models;
- the introduction of the "prudent person principle";
- requirements on the system of governance, the own risk and solvency assessment (ORSA) and the supervisory review process (SRP); and
- importance given to supervisory reporting and public disclosures.

Solvency II is structured around the three-pillar architecture of Basel II, with each pillar governing a different but complementary aspect of the regime. The pillars are not discrete and should be considered together. The first pillar sets out the quantitative requirements that insurers must satisfy to demonstrate they have sufficient financial resources. These encompass the valuation of assets and liabilities, the calculation of the Solvency II capital requirements and the assessment of eligible own funds. The second pillar covers the qualitative requirements, and aims to supplement the first one. Central elements of the second pillar include:

- demonstrating an adequate system of governance, including effective risk management system and prospective risk identification through ORSA; and
- the SRP – the overall process conducted by the supervisory authority in reviewing insurance and reinsurance undertakings, ensuring compliance with the directive's requirements and identifying those with financial and/or organisational weaknesses susceptible to producing higher risks to policyholders.

The third pillar completes the framework, and deals with supervisory reporting (report to supervisors, RTS) and public disclosures (solvency and financial conditions report, SFCR). Supervisory reporting requirements aim to support the risk-oriented approach to insurance supervision, while public disclosure requirements, on the other hand, have the objective of reinforcing market mechanisms and market discipline by acting as a strong incentive to undertakings to conduct their business in a sound and efficient manner. This includes an incentive to maintain an adequate capital position that can act as a cushion against potential losses arising from risk exposures.

This new regime uses a total balance-sheet approach, considering both assets and liabilities, and aims to improve risk management and reward good practice. Solvency II establishes two levels of capital requirements:

- a lower-level minimum capital requirement (MCR) – ie, the threshold below which the authorisation of the (re)insurance firm shall be withdrawn; and
- an upper level (the SCR) – ie, the level below which an insurer will be subject to much heightened supervision.

An important innovation introduced by Solvency II is that, to calculate the SCR, insurers can use either a standard formula or their own full internal model as approved by the relevant supervisory authorities. Solvency II also allows firms the option of using a partial model, with some components of the standard formula (module or submodules; all, or only major business units) replaced by results from an internal model. Compared to the banking regime – ie, the Basel II/Capital Requirements Directive (CRD) framework – Solvency II allows significant design freedom in the choice of methods, assumptions and calculation of dependency structure for internal models.

Solvency II is also set to remove many of the limits on the nature and extent of admissible assets. The existing rules on admissible assets (ie, the list of qualifying asset types) will be replaced by the prudent person principle (ie, the requirement to invest so as to ensure the security, quality, liquidity and profitability of the portfolio as a whole), with the requirement that assets covering technical provisions must be invested in the "best interests" of policyholders. This concept has been largely borrowed from the EU Reinsurance Directive, although it applies to all assets, not just those backing technical provisions. The prudent person principle effectively places responsibility on the insurer to act in the best interests of their policyholders. Insurers have to decide whether the nature of any investment is appropriate, and have an obligation to show that they have appropriate systems and controls to hold and manage any such investments. In practice, this may require insurers to give their investment managers greater detail about the type of investments permitted.

Moreover, Solvency II strives to ensure that effective risk management and policyholder protection are embedded into the governance, operations and decision-making of the business. Mechanisms include:

- ❑ the requirement for firms to complete an ORSA of overall solvency needs, taking into account their risk profile and approved risk tolerance; the results of the ORSA must be incorporated into the firm's strategic decision-making and disclosed to the regulator; and
- ❑ the SRP, which could lead to sanctions, including capital add-ons.

The ORSA is an internal risk assessment process that aims to ensure senior management have conducted their own review of the risks to which they are exposed, and that they hold sufficient capital against those risks. The ORSA must reflect the firms' own risk appetite. The ORSA will also provide supervisors with an early indicator of the firm's solvency position, as the insurer may breach its economic capital target level before it breaches its regulatory capital requirement. The ORSA should enable the supervisor to draw conclusions regarding the ability of the insurer to review its own risks.

Although detailed requirements for the internal modelling framework have not been finalised and agreed,[1] the principles contained in the Solvency II directive[2] are already clear.

THE STARTING POINT: THE BALANCE SHEET

Both Solvency I and II use the balance sheet of insurance companies as a starting point for the solvency assessment. While Solvency I is mainly based on statutory figures reported in the financial statements and focuses on liabilities, Solvency II aims to capture the economic value of balance-sheet items. This approach is independent of statutory accounting, and considers not just the liabilities but also the asset side of the balance sheet.

To this end, Solvency II sets out a total balance-sheet approach, where the determination of an insurer's capital that is available and needed for solvency purposes is based upon all assets and liabilities, as measured in the regulatory balance sheet of the insurer and the way they interact. Implications of this approach are that:

- available solvency capital is given as the difference between the market-consistent values of assets and liabilities; and
- solvency capital requirements are calculated based on a comprehensive analysis of risks, taking into account the interaction between assets and liabilities, risk mitigation and, where applicable, diversification.

An economic approach has several advantages, as it:

- can be calibrated to provide a better balance between protection to policyholders and encouraging the efficient operations of companies;
- is more transparent and limits arbitrage opportunities;
- leads to a closer alignment of regulatory capital requirements with good practice internal risk management processes;
- is more able to cope with changing market circumstances and practices (eg, increasingly sophisticated product design and capital markets innovation); and
- is likely to limit the double counting of risks and capital requirements.

Valuation of assets and liabilities

Under Solvency II, assets and liabilities are to be valued on a market-consistent basis. The fair valuation of assets and liabilities is based on the amount for which the asset or liabilities could be exchanged between knowledgeable willing parties in an arm's-length transaction.

Wherever possible, the fair value of assets is to be based on a mark-to-market approach, using readily available prices in orderly transactions that are sourced independently. Where this is not possible, mark-to-model procedures should be used. Mark-to-model is defined as any valuation that has to be benchmarked, extrapolated or otherwise calculated as far as possible from a market input. The application of mark-to-model approaches will require systems and controls sufficient to give senior management and supervisors the confidence that their valuation estimates are appropriate and reliable.

Liabilities are divided into: technical provisions (or insurance liabilities), ie, obligations relating to policyholders and beneficiaries of insurance contracts; and non-insurance liabilities (other liabilities), ie, other obligations such as amounts payable, tax liabilities (current and deferred) and employee benefits or wholesale funding obligations, including senior and subordinated debt securities or other loan arrangements.

Technical provisions will be valued using a "current exit value" approach. The general approach to working out the value of technical provisions requires the calculation of the sum of two components: the best estimate and a risk margin. Both components should be valued separately. The best estimate is equal to the expected value of future cashflows, taking into account the time value of money. The risk margin represents the cost of capital that a market participant taking over the liabilities would need to hold until run-off. The risk margin calculation is based on the cost of holding regulatory capital for risks considered non-hedgeable ("cost of capital" methodology).

However, where future cashflows associated with insurance or reinsurance obligations can be replicated reliably (ie, they are hedgeable) using financial instruments for which a dependable market value can be observed, the value of the technical provisions associated with those future financial cashflows shall be determined on the basis of the market value of those financial instruments (ie, calculation of the technical provision as a whole). An illustration of the Solvency II opening balance sheet is provided in Figure 1.1.

FROM THE BALANCE SHEET TO THE SCR

Insurers hold capital for a number of reasons, not necessarily just for regulatory purposes. The capital structure of insurers is determined partly by departures from Modigliani and Miller's world[3] – for example, expected costs of financial distress, taxes, transactions costs, signalling behaviour and agency problems arising from asymmetric information between shareholders and policyholders and between owner and managers. The insurer's objective is to attain an optimal level of insolvency risk that balances the marginal benefits[4]

Figure 1.1 Solvency II opening balance sheet

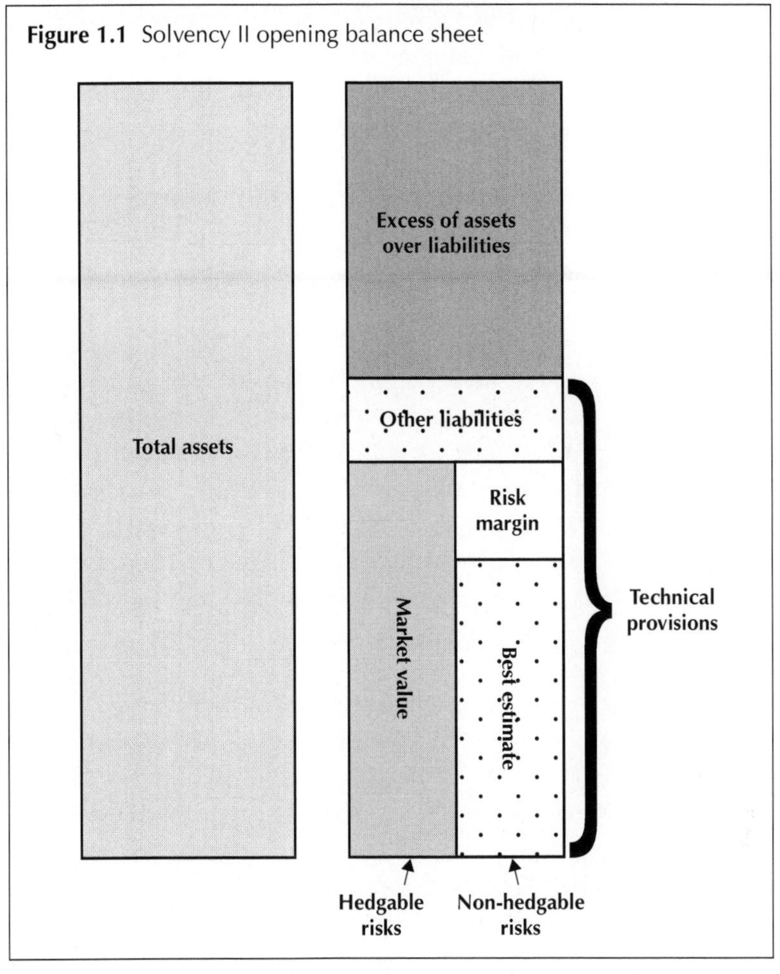

and costs[5] of holding equity capital. Hence, insurers do not hold sufficient capital to eliminate insolvency risk; rather, insurers maintain market-driven "safe" or "adequate" levels of capital. Therefore, capital is a buffer to protect insurance firms against the risk of unexpected losses, to finance growth or to take advantage of unexpected profitable opportunities. In essence, in managing their own solvency position, insurers consider their own private costs and benefits but typically do not consider any potential implications to the wider financial system. Setting adequate solvency standards through regulatory capital requirements aims to mitigate these risks and protect the economy from negative externalities caused by insurer's failures.

As described earlier, Solvency II capital requirements are split into two levels: the higher SCR and the lower MCR.[6] The SCR is defined as the level of capital that enables an insurance firm to absorb significant unforeseen losses over a specified time horizon, and gives reasonable assurance to policyholders that payments will be made as they fall due. In Solvency II, this is set out to correspond to the value-at-risk (VaR) of the basic own funds of a (re)insurance firm subject to a confidence level of 99.5% over a one-year period. The SCR must cover all the quantifiable risks that are borne by the firm. The capital assigned to each risk should be proportionate and risk-based, and should cover, at a minimum, insurance, market, credit and operational risks.

It is also worth pointing out that the SCR must be calculated on the basis that the business is a going concern – ie, that it will continue to be operational and will not be liquidating its assets or winding up. The SCR must take account the uncertainty in the results of business currently on the insurer's books, but also the business that the insurer expects to write in the following year. The effect of risk mitigation techniques should be considered when calculating the SCR; however, firms need to ensure that any counterparty risk and other risks arising from these techniques is properly reflected in the SCR calculation.

The calculation of the SCR follows a dynamic approach looking at the balance sheet at two points in time: the current balance sheet (pre-stress) and the balance sheet at the end of the year (post-stress). The SCR for each individual risk is determined as the difference between the net asset value (NAV) in the unstressed balance sheet (NAV_0) and the NAV in the stressed balance sheet (NAV_1). The overall SCR is then calculated by combining these separate risk charges, allowing for diversification by means of correlation matrices or other methodologies. Figure 1.2 illustrates the Solvency II balance sheet at the valuation date (pre-stress) and one year forward (post-stress). As described, the SCR is the difference between the current NAV_0 and the post-stress scenario NAV_1.

WHAT IS AN INTERNAL MODEL?

When dealing with internal models, it is useful to distinguish between: internal models in a narrower, quantitative, statistical sense (ie, the calculation kernel);[7] and internal models in a broader sense of

Figure 1.2 From the balance sheet to the SCR

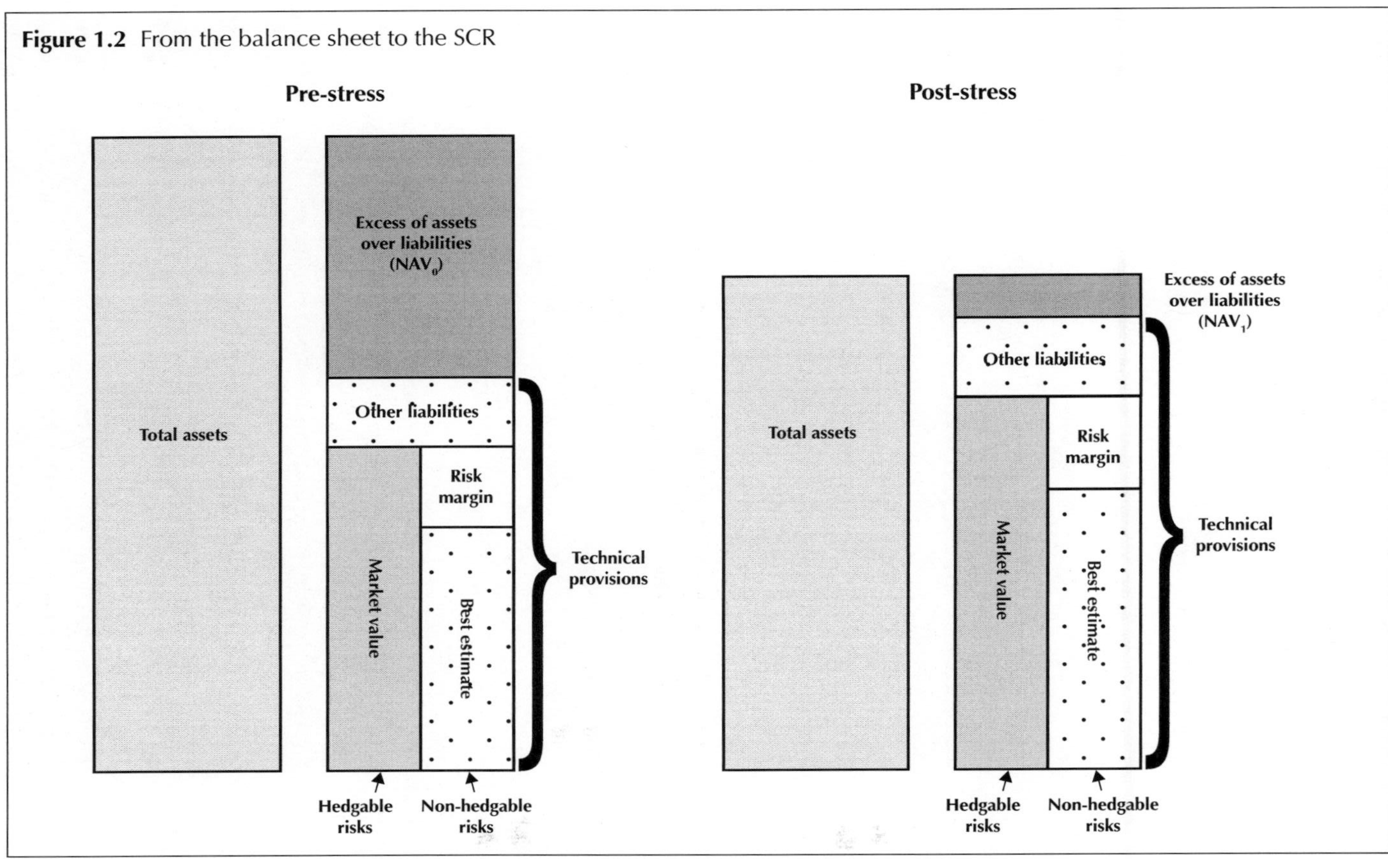

being an integral part of firms' enterprise risk management framework.

To this end, it is very helpful to compare and contrast the definitions provided by the International Actuarial Association (IAA)[8] and the CEA-Groupe Consultatif.[9] According to the IAA, an internal model is defined as a "mathematical model of an insurer's operations to analyse its overall risk position, to quantify risks and determine the capital to meet those risks". According to the CEA/GC, on the other hand, an internal model is defined as "a risk management system developed by an insurer to analyse the overall risk position, to quantify risks and to determine the economic capital required to meet those risks".

While these two definitions share some important characteristics (ie, the analysis of the overall risk position, the quantification of risks and the determination of the capital to meet these risks), the scope, coverage and integration of the two types of models is rather different. The narrower, mathematical or actuarial view of the internal model is the system that transforms risk exposure data (how many contracts of which type are written) and risk-driver data (historic information on the likelihood of certain events) to forecasts of profit and loss (P&L) distributions. In practice, a firm may use a collection of models that make predictions for the P&L at different levels of aggregation.[10]

However, this narrower view imposes some constraints. To produce a social optimum from the regulator's point of view, the interests of the market and the regulator need to be closely aligned. The only effective way to achieve this objective and reduce regulatory arbitrage is to align regulatory capital requirements more closely to firms' own assessment of economic risks by providing them with the right incentives to employ models in a prudent manner. Therefore, from a regulatory perspective, the internal model should be more than this mechanistic process and much closer to the definition of internal models in a wider risk management sense. It should also encompass the way in which the mathematical or actuarial model is integrated with the internal risk management system. Integration demonstrates that the actuarial model is genuinely relevant to the management of the business and has not been developed simply to satisfy regulatory requirements. The approval of the internal model applies in this broader context, rather than focusing

Figure 1.3 Internal modelling framework under Solvency

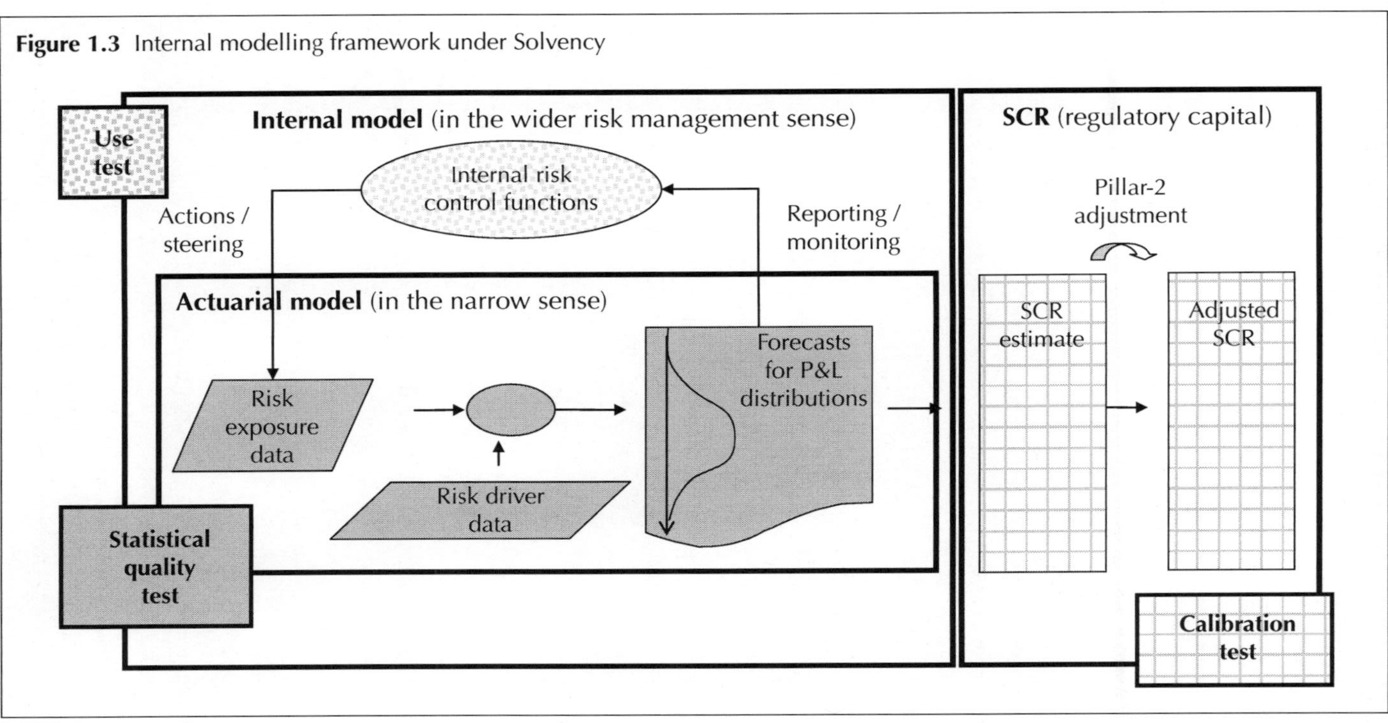

solely on the mathematical and/or actuarial techniques to arrive at the forecast distributions or the single regulatory capital number (see Figure 1.3).

The Solvency II directive does not provide a definition for an internal model, it only sets the requirements that a (re)insurance firm has to satisfy to be able to get its internal modelling framework approved for use to determine its capital requirements. While at first sight this may be perceived as a deficiency of this new regulatory regime, it should rather be interpreted as an advantage. In line with the philosophy of Solvency II, this allows for a higher degree of flexibility, encouraging (re)insurance firms to define and tailor their internal modelling framework in accordance with their needs, risk profile and potential uses.

To this end, it becomes extremely important that (re)insurance firms think carefully about the scope, coverage and integration of their internal modelling framework within their risk management before submitting their application for approval to their supervisory authorities. As will be explained, while a correct a definition of the scope and coverage of the internal modelling framework may enhance the ability of the (re)insurance firm to operate in the market, an incorrect one, on the other hand, may impose significant constraints.

WHAT ARE THE EXPECTED BENEFITS OF AN INTERNAL MODEL UNDER SOLVENCY II?

The development of internal models can potentially deliver a wide range of benefits to supervisors, firms and, ultimately, policyholders. For example, while the Solvency II standard formula may be appropriate and easy to implement for (re)insurance firms without complex or highly unique risks, it cannot by definition reflect all the characteristics specific to any (re)insurance firm operating within the European Economic Area (EEA). Internal models can overcome some of the drawbacks related to the standard formula, but require expertise and resources for parameterisation, model building, validation, interpretation and communication. Integrating an internal capital model into key enterprise business processes can turn what is perceived to be a regulatory burden into a competitive advantage.

First, an internal modelling framework integrated into the risk management system and tailored to the needs, risk profile and uses of (re)insurance firms allows for an improved risk sensitivity of the SCR. This leads, among other things, to a more adequate modelling of non-standard (especially non-linear) contracts, a better evaluation of the company's risk profile and related reinsurance and investment strategies in the context of the firm's risk appetite. Consequently, this could bring an evaluation of returns on risk-adjusted capital for individual business segments, a deeper understanding of the relative contribution of the major categories of risk (non-catastrophe losses, catastrophes, reserve, credit and market) to the company's risk profile and, ultimately, a better allocation of capital.

Moreover, the high degree of modelling freedom allowed by Solvency II not only strives to achieve a better alignment of regulatory capital to economic capital reducing the regulatory burden on firms, but, more importantly, also aims to encourage the innovation of risk measurement and continuous improvement of management methodologies – leading again to an enhanced assessment of the (re)insurance firm's risk profile and capital allocation. This, in turn, if appropriately implemented, is likely to translate into an improvement of policyholder protection.

The use of an internal model may also lead to a more effective Pillar 2-type discussion with the supervisor. For example, (re)insurance firms that apply the standard formula are likely to follow a sequential approach. They first calculate the Pillar 1 capital requirements by applying the standard formula, and then proceed to accurately identifying the risks they are exposed to through the ORSA process. On the other hand, (re)insurance firms that have opted for the internal modelling route are bound to follow a different process. The design and development of an internal model requires a deeper understanding of the (re)insurance firm business and risk profile at inception. First, they need to identify the risks they are exposed to, before, through the modelling activities, proceeding to measure and quantify them.

Overall, this may lead to a better realisation of cost efficiencies through re-use of risk modelling infrastructure for discussion with other external parties, such as supervisors, rating agencies, analysts and shareholders.

WHAT ARE THE POTENTIAL COSTS/DRAWBACKS OF AN INTERNAL MODEL UNDER SOLVENCY II?

Despite the benefits, it is important not to underestimate the challenges of developing, reviewing, monitoring and maintaining an internal model so that it gains approval for use while remaining compliant with the Solvency II requirements. In particular, the timing, cost, resource implications, complexity and risks involved should not be dismissed.

To meet their tight timetables and project plans, both companies and supervisors need to be adequately resourced, which is difficult. Developing, reviewing monitoring and maintaining internal models at firms and supervisors requires multi-disciplinary teams. Responsibilities cannot be delegated just to actuaries, mathematicians and physicists. Business, legal and finance experience are essential, and the skills and expertise of econometricians, behavioural scientists and psychologists are highly desirable. Acquiring and retaining these skills and resources is a big challenge, both for firms hoping to achieve and maintain internal model approval and supervisory authorities in charge of the reviews of internal model's applications. People who have the right skills and knowledge of the companies and the Solvency II requirements are very much in demand. These skills are both scarce and costly.

Another challenge is firms' over-reliance on models. This over-reliance is obviously dangerous, as there are no "correct" models; they are, by definition, imperfect representations of reality and no replication is truly accurate. However, models can be either appropriate or inappropriate.

The use of models depends on the firm's risk culture and invariably presents model risk. If the risk culture is not appropriate, model's results are likely to be unreliable. For example, there can be a tendency to disregard internal model's results if they get in the way of carrying out business that generates short-term profits.

Model risk, on the other hand, can lead to financial loss, poor business and strategic decision-making, or damage to a firm's reputation. Model risk occurs primarily for two reasons: (i) a model may have fundamental errors (eg, data, assumptions and parameterisation), and produce inaccurate outputs when viewed against its design objective and intended business uses; and (ii) a model may be used incorrectly or inappropriately, or there may be a misunderstanding about its limitations and assumptions. Model risk increases with greater model complexity, higher uncertainty about inputs and assumptions, broader extent of use and larger potential impact.

For instance, in some cases, model assumptions (implicit and explicit) and parameterisation are based on "wishful thinking" rather than on a realistic assessment. Internal model's parameters are calibrated to the expected case using only historical data, or adjusted (consciously or unconsciously) so that the results correspond to expectations. In some others, models are developed and calibrated to capture what is easier to model, rather than what is necessary or relevant.

Lack of understanding of the limitations of the model can lead to inappropriate reliance on the results of the model (eg, misuse of ratings). A guiding principle is that managing model risk involves the "effective challenge" of models: critical analysis by objective, knowledgeable parties that can identify model limitations and produce appropriate changes. Effective challenge depends on a combination of incentives, competence and influence. However, it is often the case that once results are obtained they are not subjected to challenge, or worse, where data, assumptions and models are obtained from a third-party (eg, vendor, regulator, rating agency and accounting framework), responsibility is ignored.

Finally, deciding on the appropriateness is a judgement call by the supervisor. The need for supervisory judgements is the major difficulty in the approval of models. The major danger lies in the wish of many supervisors to base the model review on objective checklists rather than on subjective judgements. It is important to avoid situations where the assessment of the internal model application by the supervisor focuses on what is easy to review rather than what is relevant (eg, too much focus on processes and documentation).

GENERAL CONSIDERATIONS REGARDING THE PROPORTIONALITY PRINCIPLE FOR INTERNAL MODELS

Solvency II and proportionality

The Solvency II framework is designed for insurers and reinsurers of all sizes and complexities. Although the same general principles apply to large and small insurers alike, Solvency II is designed to be "proportionate" in the demands placed on insurers.

The proportionality principle applies throughout the new

solvency framework,[11] and is linked to the nature, scale and complexity of the risks inherent in the business. This implies that the size of an undertaking on its own is not the only relevant criterion. In fact, on one hand, the new regime takes account of the specificities of the insurance sector and allows for a range of methods to be used to meet those principles, tailored to the nature, scale and complexity of the risks borne by the insurer. On the other hand, insurance supervision has to be carried out in a proportionate manner.

As proportionality is a two-way concept, when assessing what is proportionate, the focus must be on the combination of all three criteria to arrive at a solution that is adequate to the risk an undertaking is exposed to. This means that simpler and less burdensome ways of meeting requirements for low-risk-profile portfolios are allowed. At the same time, for more complex risk portfolios, more sophisticated approaches are likely to be required.

It should be clear that proportionality does not exempt insurers from any of the requirements of Solvency II, but that depending on the nature, scale and complexity of the risks borne by a company, the process for meeting these requirements may be simpler than for others.

Different approaches for the calculation of the SCR

As described, according to the Solvency II framework,[12] firms may calculate their SCR either in accordance with the standard formula or using a full or partial internal model, as approved by the supervisory authorities.

Within the standard formula, and subject to supervisory approval, Solvency II also allows (re)insurance firms to use their own data to calibrate some of the parameters in the underwriting risk modules (ie, insurance risk modules) for the calculation of the SCR. Non-life insurers and health insurers (providing health insurance is conducted similar to non-life insurance) may replace the standard risk factors for the premium and reserve risk with their own parameters. For life insurance companies and health insurers (where health insurance is similar to the life business), the choice is limited to the factor for the sustained rise in pension benefits in the revision risk.

The Solvency II framework also provides simplification with respect to the calculation of the standard formula SCR. For example, among other life risks (mortality, longevity, disability, expenses, permanent lapses, catastrophe, etc), health risks (expenses, mortality, longevity, disability, etc) spread risks on bonds and loans, risk-mitigating effects for reinsurance arrangements or securitisation, and risk-mitigating effects for proportional reinsurance arrangements.

The use of one of these options for regulatory purposes has to be coherent with the risk profile and the size of the insurance firm, and its availability constitutes *per se* a direct application of the proportionality principle. An illustration of the different approaches for the calculation of the SCR is set out in Figure 1.4.

Proportionality and internal models

By its nature, the concept of an internal model is strictly linked to proportionality. Its design and functionalities should be driven directly by its intended use, and the nature, scale and complexity of the risks borne by the (re)insurance firm. Implicitly, one might also see this principle as relating to the level of complexity of the mathematical approach used to calculate the level of regulatory capital, and therefore to the application of internal models to assess this requirement.

As it will be explained in more detail in Chapter 7, Solvency II does not prescribe the use of any specific modelling approach for the calculation of the "probability distribution forecast".[13] Overall, a

Figure 1.4 Proportionality and the calculation of the SCR

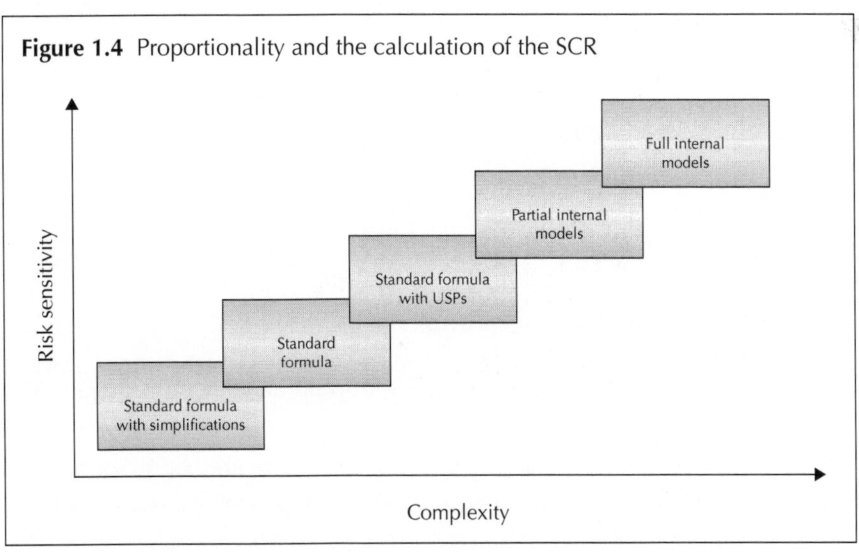

balance has to be struck between the avoidance of unnecessary complexity of the internal model and the objective that firms' obligations are met as they fall due. Irrespective of the modelling approach chosen, the calibration standard of 99.5% VaR confidence level over a one-year time horizon is the target criterion to meet. This level of safety represents one of the core components of the new solvency regime, and is part of the necessary conditions to guarantee a level playing field among insurers within the EU.

The adequacy of a chosen internal modelling approach, if also used to compute the regulatory capital requirement, has to be evaluated considering simultaneously the nature, scale and complexity of the risks borne by the company. In fact, choosing the internal model option does not necessarily imply a highly complex mathematical approach. Simple internal modelling approaches can be appropriate for some risk profiles, and sometimes be more, or at least as, appropriate at capturing risks as more complex approaches. For example, a company writing only short-term pure endowment policies would be expected to use a less complex internal model than one selling long-term life insurance contracts with discretionary participating features, embedded options and other complementary guarantees (such as the risk of disability). This does not mean, however, that an insurer using a simpler approach to modelling is exempted from any of the requirements set out in the Solvency II framework.

Moreover, as stated earlier, proportionality is a two-way concept. For firms that are using internal models, proportionality must not be solely understood as a possible reduction of the required complexity of the approach but also as a due supervisory requirement for an appropriately elaborated modelling approach, where necessary due to the nature, scale and complexity of risks. This also applies to the frequency of calculations. For example, an insurer with a more complex, dynamic and/or less stable risk profile would be expected to compute its economic and regulatory capital requirement at a higher frequency than an insurer with simpler and/or more stable one.

The dynamic nature of internal models and insurers' assets and liabilities also implies that what is proportionate is likely to change over time. For instance, the introduction of the new solvency regime will enable both firms and supervisors to collect more information and data relevant to internal models. This may facilitate the use of a variety of approaches and also make it easier to demonstrate that simpler models are good approximations for more complex ones. Moreover, the appropriateness of a modelling approach used by a firm changes over time as the nature, scale and complexity of its portfolios and lines of business varies.

Lack of resources can never be an excuse for an inappropriate internal modelling approach. Appropriate resourcing can be achieved by using both in-house and external resources (outsourcing). Firms may resort to external models and data (vendor models), or to any other knowledgeable third party, whatever the risk profile or the size of the company. However, as will be explained in Chapter 15, the use of external models and data does not exempt a firm from meeting the Solvency II internal models requirement. The onus is on the firm (not the vendor) to demonstrate that the requirements are met.

The proportionality principle does not only apply to the quantitative aspects of the internal model, but also to its qualitative aspects – such as the use test, its governance and controls, and documentation.

Any internal model should be embedded into a strong governance framework. As is generally the case with other risks, materiality in the light of the nature, scale and complexity of the risks borne by the firm is an important consideration in model governance. If, within a firm, the use of models is less pervasive and has less impact on its financial condition, then this firm may not need as complex an approach to model governance to meet supervisory expectations. However, where models and model output have a material impact on business decisions, including decisions related to risk management and capital and liquidity planning, and where model failure would have a particularly harmful impact on the firm's financial condition, a firm's model risk management framework should be more extensive and rigorous.

Moreover, as meeting the internal models requirements is not a one-off exercise (ie, limited to the time of submission of the application), as a part of its governance an insurer needs to develop and maintain a robust framework to monitor the performance of its internal model, whereby it regularly re-assesses the appropriateness of data, assumptions and methodologies used. The proportionality principle does not exempt any insurer from complying with this requirement and/or taking any necessary action to remedy to internal models deficiencies. However, the effort required will depend on the nature, scale and complexity of the risks to which the firm is exposed.

As regards the "validation function", Solvency II does not consider that each company must have this task fulfilled by independent staff. As will be explained in Chapter 11, what supervisors are looking for is an effective validation, for which an objective challenge is essential. In this spirit, ensuring the structural independence of the validation function can be a means to that end. When deciding who will perform this task, it is important that firms pay due consideration to the nature, scale and complexity of the risks that the insurer faces and to the firm's internal organisation and governance system. The right balance must be struck between any potential conflict of interest that might arise in the course of the cycle of internal model validation on the one hand, and a disproportionate level of segregation of duties on the other hand. Moreover, it is also essential that the individuals performing the validation possess the appropriate skills, knowledge, expertise and experience. For this purpose, the Solvency II framework also allows for the outsourcing of these activities, and some other critical operational functions, subject to predetermined set of criteria.[14]

Documentation is also a crucial tool for the firm to demonstrate to the supervisor that it understands and has mastered the internal model it is using. This represents a key assessment element in the supervisory approval process. To this end, it is important to observe that proportionality does not exempt any insurer from adequately documenting its internal model. Documentation of all internal models (both partial and full internal models) must be thorough, detailed and complete enough to allow third parties to replicate the internal model. For simpler internal models, this might result in smaller amounts of documentation. However, this should be a consequence of the level of complexity of the model, and not of the thoroughness of its documentation.

CONCLUSION

This chapter has discussed the foundations for the Solvency II internal modelling framework, and provided some clarification of expectations in light of its implementation in 2016. It explained how the development of internal models can potentially deliver a wide range of benefits to supervisors, firms and, ultimately, policyholders. It also assessed the challenges arising from developing, reviewing, monitoring and maintaining an internal model. On one hand, it stressed the need for firms to pay particular attention to the internal model's regulatory requirements and seek to go beyond a simple regulatory "box-ticking" exercise, reflecting internal management priorities and covering all material aspects of the internal model environment. On the other hand, it highlighted the need for supervisors to take responsibility in expressing judgements in the internal model approval process – ie, avoiding the indiscriminate use of objective checklists rather than expressing supervisory judgements. Finally, the internal model approval process should also aim to assess any potential interrelation between the internal model's requirements. Proportionality plays an important role in model development and review, but it should never be an excuse for failing to satisfy the requirements. Complying with the internal models standards is not a one-off exercise. Standards have to be met on an ongoing basis, and what is appropriate does change over time to take into account both internal and external developments. To this end, an ongoing dialogue between firms and regulators is not required, but essential.

The views expressed in the chapter are those of the author and not necessarily those of the PRA, Bank of England

1 Adoption of the Level 2 Delegated Acts is expected in July/August 2014.
2 For further details, see European Parliament and the Council of the European Union (2009).
3 See Modigliani and Miller (1958).
4 Holding capital provides marginal benefits because safer insurers command higher prices, and because insurers risk losing customers if insolvency risk is perceived as excessive.
5 Holding capital in an insurance company is costly due to the regulatory costs, agency costs from unresolved owner–manager and owner–policyholder conflicts, the costs of adverse selection and moral hazard in insurance underwriting and claims settlement, corporate income taxation and other market frictions.
6 The MCR is calibrated to the value-at-risk of the basic own funds of an insurer subject to a confidence level of 85% over a one-year period.
7 The technical model used for the quantification of capital requirements for all risk categories can be seen as the calculation kernel. As the quantification covers all risk categories, it will include elements that are not necessarily statistically modelled.
8 For further details, see IAA (2008).
9 For further details, see CEA-Groupe Consultatif (2007).
10 For further details, see CEIOPS (2006).
11 For further details, see CEIOPS (2008).
12 For further details, see Articles 100 and 110 of European Parliament and the Council of the European Union (2009).

13 For further details, see Article 121.4 of European Parliament and the Council of the European Union (2009).

14 For further details, see Article 29 of the European Parliament and the Council of the European Union (2009).

REFERENCES

Basel Committee on Banking Supervision, 2013, "Revised Basel III Leverage Ratio Framework and Disclosure Requirements", consultative document, June.

Cadoni, P., 2009, "Using Internal Models to Determine the Solvency Capital Requirement: The Regulatory View", in Marcelo Cruz (Ed), *The Solvency II Handbook* (London: Risk Books), pp 75–112.

Cadoni, P., 2009, "Validating Internal Models Under the Solvency II Directive", *Journal of Regulation and Risk North Asia*, I(2), pp 59–65.

Cadoni, P. and P. Sharma, 2008, "Why Do Supervisors Want the 'Use Test' and How to 'Measure' It?", Forum Financier, *Revue Bancaire et Financier*, 8, pp 454–58.

Cadoni, P. and P. Sharma, 2010, "Solvency II: A New Regulatory Frontier", in C. Kempler, M. Flamée, C. Yang and P. Windels (Eds), *Global Perspective on Insurance Today: A Look at National Interest Versus Globalization* (New York: Palgrave MacMillan), pp 53–68.

CEA-Groupe Consultatif, 2007, "Solvency II Glossary".

CEIOPS, 2005a, "Answers to the European Commission on the 'First Wave' of Calls for Advice on the Framework of the Solvency II project", June.

CEIOPS, 2005b, "Answers to the European Commission on the 'Second Wave' of Calls for Advice on the Framework of the Solvency II project", October.

CEIOPS, 2006, "Consultation Paper 20: Draft Advice to the European Commission in the Framework of the Solvency II Project on Pillar I issues – Further Advice".

CEIOPS, 2008, "Advice to the European Commission on the Principle of Proportionality in the Solvency II Framework Directive Proposal".

European Parliament and the Council of The European Union, 2009, "Directive 2009/138/EC of the European Parliament and of the Council of 25 November 2009 on the Taking-up and Pursuit of the Business of Insurance and Reinsurance (Solvency II) (recast)".

IAA, 2008, "Guidance Paper on the Use of Internal Models for Risk and Capital Purposes by Insurers".

IAIS, 2008, "Guidance Paper on the Use of Internal Models for Regulatory Capital Purposes".

Keller, P., 2009, "Internal Model Review", presentation to the CEIOPS Internal Model Expert Group, January.

Modigliani, F. and M. Miller, M., 1958, "The Cost of Capital, Corporation Finance, and the Theory of Investment", *American Economic Review*, June, pp 261–97.

2

Partial Internal Models

Juan Antonio Lumbreras

EIOPA

The Solvency II framework allows (re)insurance firms, both solo entities and groups, to calculate the solvency capital requirement (SCR) using either the standard formula or, subject to supervisory approval, their own internal model (either full or partial). Partial internal models can be used to model one or more of the standard formula risk modules or sub-modules, the capital requirements for operational risk or for the loss-absorbing capacity of technical provision for either the whole business or one or more business units.

From a firm's perspective, choosing whether to opt for an internal model (either full or partial), or adopt the standard formula is an important and relevant consideration. For some firms, the decision is fairly clear-cut, as a partial model approach may offer an attractive solution that fits their risk profile while optimising the cost of capital. For others, the balance between the advantages and disadvantages is harder to assess, particularly given the various options between the standard formula and the internal model.

Taking into account firms' difficulties in meeting internal model approved standards for all risks, legal entities and major business units in all territories in time for day one approval, the right choice for a particular firm could also vary over time. For example, full internal model approval may not be essential in the first wave, when the Solvency II regulatory regime comes into force, but it may be a longer-term or strategic aim. To add a further complication, what is typically described by firms as a full internal model for part of their business, from a supervisor's perspective often boils down to a partial internal model.[1]

This chapter will provide background on the evolution of the regulators thinking on the Solvency II partial internal modelling regime, and shed light on the expected benefits of this new framework. It provides evidence of challenges that both supervisor and firms face when developing, reviewing and maintaining partial internal models. More specifically, the next section defines the scope of application of a partial internal model, and compares and contrasts the use of partial internal models in Solvency II and Basel/CRD framework. The third section defines the concept of "major business unit", explaining how it relates to partial internal models, before a number of examples of uses for partial internal models are examined. We follow that with a description of the specific provisions that apply to partial internal models, including the rationale for these measures. The next section explains the concept of a transitional plan to extend the scope of the internal model, followed by a look at the challenges to capture risks that are not explicitly covered by the standard formula.

PARTIAL INTERNAL MODELS: SOLVENCY II VERSUS THE BASEL/CRD FRAMEWORK

The Solvency II internal modelling framework for insurers differs from the Basel/Capital Requirements Directive (CRD) internal modelling framework for credit institutions and investment firms in several respects. These differences include model coverage, calibration and modelling freedom.

Model coverage

The Basel/CRD framework does not allow for full internal models covering all the risks borne by a credit institution or an investment firm. However, the Basel/CRD framework does allow firms to use partial internal models or approaches for the calculation of the minimum required capital for certain types of risks – for example, credit risk, market risk and operational risk.

Calibration

As opposed to Solvency II, where the SCR must be calibrated using a value-at-risk (VaR) measure with a 99.5% confidence level over a one-year period, the Basel framework does not prescribe a single confidence level across risks. Each one of the four above-mentioned frameworks is calibrated to a different standard and a different time horizon.[2]

Modelling freedom

A different level of modelling freedom also characterises the Basel/CRD modelling approaches. The Basel/CRD framework only allows a full internal model approach for market risk (internal models approach, IMA) and operational risk (advanced measurement approach, AMA). For example, the internal ratings-based (IRB) approach for credit risk falls short of full-blown portfolio credit risk modelling. Under this approach, firms' ability to model is limited to the estimation of the probability of default (PD), loss given default (LGD) and exposure at default (EAD). On the other hand, the modelling freedom allowed in Solvency II for partial internal models is higher. This flexibility aims to ensure that a firm is able to design its internal model to better reflect its risk profile and fit it to its specific business uses and needs. To this end, a firm may model:

- one or more risk modules of the standard formula SCR;
- one or more risk sub-modules of the standard formula SCR;
- the capital requirement for operational risk; and
- the adjustment for the loss-absorbing capacity of technical provisions and deferred taxes.

In addition, partial modelling may be applied to the whole business of firms, or only to one or more major business units. Some practical examples of partial internal models will be described in the Appendix to this chapter.

MAJOR BUSINESS UNITS

Major business units can be defined as a segment of the firm:

- that operates independently from other parts of this firm;
- to which the firm dedicates governance resources and procedures; and
- that contains risks that are material in relation to the entire business of this firm.

Major business units are expected to reflect the economic reality of a firm or group. Taking into account the above criteria, the characteristic of its business and the environment in which it operates, the firm or group has to determine what constitutes a major business unit. The definition and justification of a major business unit are part of the firm's internal model governance and its internal model.

Changes to the firm's internal definition of major business units can impact on the scope of application of the internal model, triggering the need for supervisory approval, as in the case of an extension of the internal model coverage of risks. In other cases, the overall scope of the internal model may remain stable; however, as the definition of the business unit changes, this may require supervisory approval, as it constitutes a major change to the model.

What may be considered a major business unit by a firm or group varies. Some examples are:

- legal entities for groups (any legal entity belonging to the group is a major business unit or consists of several major business units);
- ring-fenced funds;
- branches;
- life and or non-life business for composite firms;
- liabilities arising from some specified lines of business;
- geographical regions;
- departments defined by type of customer (eg, partial internal model for retail business or corporate); and
- departments defined by the distribution channel (eg, brokerage or accepted reinsurance).

As groups can be very complex and their structure can vary greatly, the flexibility provided by the Solvency II framework with respect to the definition of business unit is important. For groups, the determination of what constitutes a major business unit may be done either at group or at solo level. This approach aims to mitigate issues arising when the size of the business unit is deemed appropriate at solo level (eg, because it adequately reflects the risk profile of the solo entity), but not at group level. When the size of the business unit is not deemed appropriate at group level, it is typically excluded from the scope of the group internal model as it does not fulfil the materiality threshold set out by the group.

For group internal models used for the calculation of the group SCR, legal entities are typically considered major business units. Different approaches may also be followed. For example, a group can define major business units taking into account the geographical location or type of lines of business (eg, car insurance, across several legal entities).

SPECIFIC SOLVENCY II PROVISIONS FOR PARTIAL INTERNAL MODELS

From a supervisor's perspective, the possibility of mixing and matching internal models for some risks and businesses with the standard formula for the rest raises potential concerns about cherry-picking. To help mitigate these concerns, the Solvency II framework sets out some additional requirement for firms using partial internal models.[3] These requirements apply in addition to the general provisions for the approval of full and partial internal models.

More specifically, for risks covered by a partial internal model, the firm needs to:

- justify the reason for the limited scope of the internal model;
- explain that the resulting SCR reflects more appropriately the firm's risk profile and, in particular, complies with the general principles for the SCR calculation; and
- ensure that the partial internal model's design is consistent with the general principles for the SCR calculation, so as to allow the partial internal model to be fully integrated with the standard formula's results.

With respect to internal models, Solvency II also requires the risk management function, among other tasks, to analyse and report on the performance of this internal model. For a partial internal model, this analysis and reporting should also include an assessment of the compliance with the specific partial internal model requirements.

Justification for the limited scope of the model

The firm's partial internal model application must include the rationale for the limited scope of application of the model. For instance, firms may justify the limited scope of their internal model by providing evidence that:

- the partial internal model represents a transitory step towards a full internal model;
- reliable information to model other risks or business lines is unavailable;
- taking into account the nature, scale and complexity of the risks borne by the firm, modelling all other risks or business lines would be disproportionate;
- the partial internal model covers only certain business areas with a view to encouraging innovation and specialisation in such areas; and
- there are other special circumstances (eg, mergers and/or acquisitions, where the individual entities employ different methods to each other).

Defining the scope of the internal model is not trivial, and is closely linked to the firm's policy for model changes.[4] Firms have to take into account their own specificities, risk profile and structure of their business. In doing so, they need to strive to ensure that the scope of the model is wide enough to include a sufficient number of uses so as to demonstrate compliance with the use test, but narrow enough to make it clear what falls inside the scope of the internal model and what falls outside it. Firms need to be clear with respect to what risks, major business units, assets or liabilities are included within the scope of the internal model and, most importantly, what risks are excluded.

To this end, it should be good practice to properly document the rationale for the use of the partial internal model, discussing it early with the supervisor and, where appropriate, developing a detailed transitional plan.

Defining the scope of a group internal model imposes additional challenges. Groups are often complex, covering a variety of lines of business and regions, and they are more likely to engage in mergers, acquisitions, spin-offs or restructuring. For example, a group using the standard formula may end up using a partial internal model when it acquires a new legal entity that is already using an internal model (either full or partial) to calculate its capital requirement. This situation cannot be considered cherry-picking.

Another instance would be a group using an already approved full internal model that has acquired an entity that was using the standard formula. In this case, integrating the acquired entity into the modelling framework within a short timeframe may be either impossible or disproportionate – eg, where it is possible to demonstrate that the standard formula adequately reflects the risk profile of the acquired firm.

Finally, a group may have other plausible reasons for excluding a particular legal entity from the scope of the internal model for the calculation of the group SCR. For instance:

- ❏ this entity is immaterial at group level;
- ❏ modelling the legal entity´s lines of business may be disproportionate – both taking into account the nature, scale and complexity of the risks inherent to the business of this entity and the business of the group as a whole;
- ❏ if the entity is included in the scope of the group, the number of parameters needed to run the group internal model may become unmanageable for the timely calculation of the SCR;
- ❏ reliable information to model the risks borne by the legal entity is unavailable; and
- ❏ the standard formula captures adequately the risk profile of the legal entity and, overall, the risk profile of the group is also adequately captured with the partial internal model.

The administrative, management or supervisory body (AMSB) of the firm is responsible for defining the most appropriate scope of application of the internal model. This responsibility also includes ensuring that the scope of the model is properly documented and well understood within the firm and/or the group. For this purpose, it is essential that, as part of the design of the internal model, the firm ensures on an ongoing basis that the design of the partial internal model reflects more appropriately its risk profile than the standard formula for those risks included within the scope of the model. To this end, the validation of the internal model should also cover the scope of the partial internal model and assess its appropriateness.

If a supervisory authority has concerns about the justifications of the limited scope of application of the partial internal model provided by the firm, it can ask for amendments, reject the internal model application or require the firm to submit a transitional plan to extend the scope of the model.

A clear definition of the scope of application and coverage of the internal model is also very important:

- for identification of the boundaries of what is subject to approval (ie, what can be used to calculate the SCR), and preventing any potential regulatory arbitrage through "cherry-picking";
- to establish the baseline for transitional plans and model scope extensions; and
- for public disclosure purposes.

In the particular case of groups, the supervisory authorities involved in the process[5] are interested in avoiding "cherry-picking" that arises from the exclusion of some legal entities from the scope of the internal model. It is therefore important that, during the group internal model approval process, the views of the supervisory authorities responsible for the supervision of legal entities or business units excluded from the scope of the group internal model are sought. These supervisory authorities should provide essential information to assess the appropriateness of the exclusions of these legal entities and/or business units.

Better reflection of the risk profile

To be able to use a partial internal model to calculate the SCR, a firm must demonstrate that the resulting SCR – taking into account both the part calculated with an internal model and the standard formula – reflects more appropriately the risk profile of the firm, and that it meets the principles set out in Solvency II for the calculation of the SCR with respect to calculation (risk coverage, calibration, impact of mitigation techniques, etc) and frequency of calculation of the SCR.[6]

In this context, coverage of risks means that the risks and business units covered by the partial internal model, in conjunction with the risks and business units covered by the standard formula, ensure the coverage of risks considered in the Solvency II framework.

Integration of the partial internal model with the standard formula's results

From a supervisory perspective, it is essential that the integration of the partial internal model and the standard formula results is being carried out in a prudent and consistent manner. To derive the overall

SCR, the third specific provision for partial internal models requires that firm's partial internal model results are fully integrated with the results from the standard formula. This represents a potentially significant challenge for firms, particularly for those firms where the internal model has been embedded in the business for some time and where the risks are not split along similar lines to the standard formula.

To perform this integration, firms need to apply specific methods or techniques. Although there is still uncertainty over the exact specification of these techniques,[7] the process that firms need to follow to integrate the partial internal model results with the standard formula is clear. The process is ideally split into three steps (see also Figure 2.1).

Step 1

Whenever the direct application of the standard formula correlation matrix coefficients is possible and there is not enough strong evidence to show it is inappropriate to integrate the partial internal model's results into standard formula's results, then the standard formula correlation matrix coefficients need to be used to integrate the partial internal model's results into the standard formula's results.

Step 2

If the firm demonstrates that the direct application of the standard formula correlation matrix coefficients is not possible and appropriate, it will need to apply one of the integration techniques set out in the Solvency II framework.[8]

Step 3

If, and only if, a firm is able to demonstrate that none of the techniques set out in the Solvency II framework are appropriate, it may, subject to supervisory authority approval, use an integration technique internally developed by the firm.

Appropriateness test

Taking into consideration the firm's risk profile and the design of its partial internal model, the technique or combination of techniques selected by the firm needs to ensure that the resulting SCR

Figure 2.1 Integration techniques flow chart

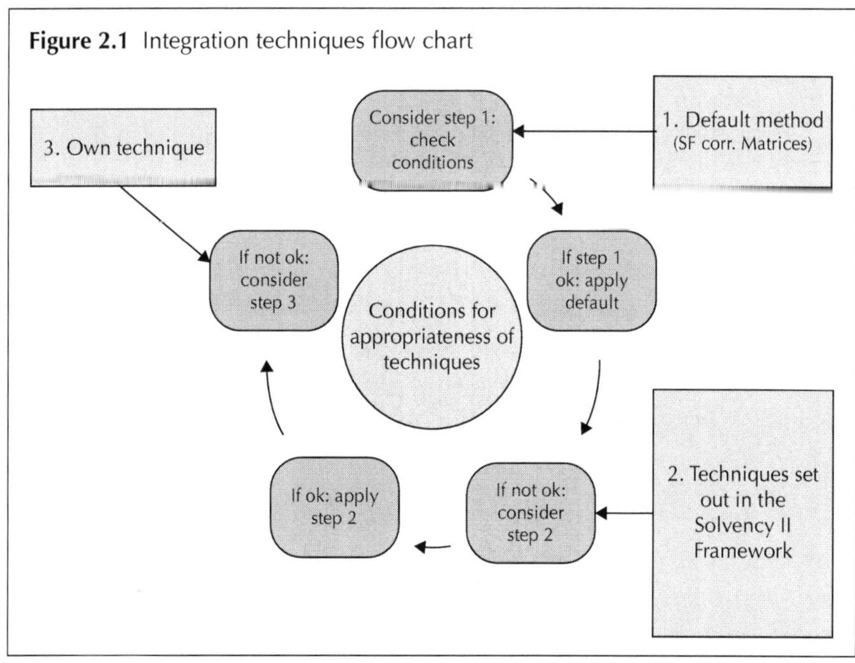

(integrating both the part calculated with an internal model and the standard formula) is both possible to be calculated and appropriate.

For instance, a direct application of the standard formula correlation factors may not always be possible and appropriate. Complications arise, for example, when a firm made up of two major business units limits the modelling to only one of them and decides to use the standard formula for the other one. In this case, a direct application of the standard formula correlation matrix is not possible, as correlation factors to reflect the dependency between the two major business units are not available.

The appropriateness of any integration technique is determined on the basis of the following criteria:

- the resulting SCR meets the general Solvency II requirements regarding its calculation;
- the resulting SCR reflects appropriately the risk profile of the firm or the group; or
- the structure of the partial internal model is consistent with the principles set out in Solvency II, and allows its full integration into the standard formula.

To demonstrate that an integration technique is not appropriate (eg, standard formula correlation factors), a firm can consider the following criteria.

- SCR equivalence: the resulting SCR resulting for applying this technique is not equivalent to VaR 99.5% over one year. This may include the use of stress and scenario testing to demonstrate that the resulting SCR is not equivalent to VaR at 99.5% over one year.
- Risk profile: the firm's risk profile makes the assumptions underlying the integration technique largely invalid. Deviations in the risk profile could be identified by either qualitative or quantitative methods. In addition, the firm may have sufficient information about the non-modelled risk and its relationship to the modelled risk to demonstrate that the integration technique is invalid.
- Data: the firm may have additional data or evidence that allows the analysis of the dependency structure, and shows a different relationship. This data may be either firm- or market-specific related to the dependencies between risks affecting that particular firm. In many cases, this data may also be linked to other elements used to show the strong evidence – specifically, the data may show that the risk profile varies from what is assumed by the standard formula.
- Use test: the fact that a firm can apply a different integration technique than the default one is not sufficient to reject the default technique.

Integration technique assessment

Taking into account the specificities of a firm, when selecting and assessing the most appropriate integration technique, both firms and supervisory authorities have to pay particular attention to the advantages or disadvantages of each technique. In particular, the elements to take into account are:

- whether the application of the technique is simple and straightforward;
- costs associated with the development and application of the technique, and whether the development of another technique would be disproportionate;

- ❏ the level of prudence that is obtained with the resulting SCR (in particular, the materiality of the diversification effects arising from the application of the technique and the level stability of the dependencies assumed can have a strong impact on the firm's SCR);
- ❏ whether the technique encourages the development of a full internal model;
- ❏ the level of knowledge and information available to apply the technique; and
- ❏ the level of expert judgement needed for the development and application of the technique.

Adaptations of test and standards for partial internal models

All tests and standards set out in the Solvency II framework for internal models apply equally to full and partial internal models. However, for partial internal models some adaptations to the approval process and tests and standards are necessary to reflect their potential limited scope.

The use test, as adapted for integration techniques, applies in a manner proportionate to the degree of modelling freedom allowed by the integration technique selected. First, it is important that the AMSB assesses the rationale for the partial internal model application. As part of the design, the AMSB needs to ensure that there exists a process to review the firm's risk profile. This needs to ensure that the design of the partial internal model allows for a better reflection of the firm's risk profile than the standard formula. Moreover, it is expected that firms take into account the results of the integration technique in their decision-making process. It is important that decision-makers at firms are aware of the difference of results arising from an integration technique prescribed by the supervisor and the one the undertaking may use for its steering purposes.

No specific adaptations are envisaged for the statistical quality, calibration and profit and loss attribution standards with respect to partial internal models' applications. The provisions set out in Solvency II framework apply equally to full and partial internal models, and are able to cope with the limited scope of a partial internal model. Moreover, the statistical quality standards apply to integration techniques developed by firms under step 3.

In respect of the validation standard, it is expected that the scope of the validation of the internal model by the firm include the integration technique used and its appropriateness. When testing the robustness of the partial internal model – for instance, through sensitivity testing – the firm can include in the analysis the integration technique selected. If, as a result of the validation process, a firm concludes that the integration technique selected and used is not appropriate, the firm needs to consider reverting to another technique. This would typically trigger the need for a major change to the internal model.

Finally, for documentation standards, it is expected that the firm documents the integration technique used, the process followed and the rationale behind its choice.

TRANSITIONAL PLAN TO EXTEND THE SCOPE OF THE MODEL

Solvency II allows supervisory authorities to require firms to submit a transitional plan to extend the scope of the partial internal model. For example, supervisory authorities may consider requesting a transitional plan when they believe that the limited scope of the partial internal model described in the firm's application is not properly justified. This can include situations where a firm has excluded some material risks but similar firms in the market are able to model them. This can also involve situations where supervisory authorities are aware that a firm has developed an internal model to quantify a specific risk for economic capital purposes, but has decided not to apply for the use of the model to cover such risk for regulatory purposes.

In some other cases, supervisory authorities may be concerned that the standard formula does not appropriately reflect some or all of the risks and/or business units that have been excluded from the scope of the partial internal model. A good example is when a firm excluded some lines of business that are unique (eg, niche business or other specialised classes of business). It is worth noting that, in these circumstances, a supervisor's request for a transitional plan is not automatic but is a supervisory option. After assessing compliance with the partial internal model requirements, supervisory authorities may come to the conclusion that a transitional plan is not necessary.

The supervisor's request should explain the reasons for the decision and set the minimum scope that the internal model should cover after implementation of the plan. This should include a description of risk sub-modules, modules and/or business units to be included in the scope. Supervisory authorities need to ensure that the revised scope covers a predominant part of the insurance operations for the risk modules included in the revised scope of the internal model.

When assessing the need for a transitional plan, supervisory authorities should consider the proportionality principle. This implies that under Solvency II, a partial internal model can be approved by the supervisory authorities as a permanent solution, if the:

- limited scope of application of the model is considered properly justified (see above), and there is no evidence of cherry-picking;
- resulting SCR reflects more appropriately the risk profile of the firm; and
- design of the partial model is consistent with the general principles so as to allow it to be fully integrated into the SCR standard formula.

In the particular case of groups, the supervisory authorities involved may consider requiring the group to develop a transitional plan to extend the scope of the model – for instance, when the supervisory authorities have concerns about cherry-picking when the group is not able to adequately justify the appropriateness of the exclusion of some legal entities from the scope of the internal model.

RISKS NOT EXPLICITLY INCLUDED IN THE STANDARD FORMULA

There are specific risks to which a firm may be exposed to, either at solo or group level, which are not explicitly considered by the Solvency II standard formula. Some examples of these risks are the underwriting cycle, commodity or contagion risks. When these risks are material and quantifiable, firms and groups using internal models need to take them into account in the calculation of the SCR.

Embedding risks not explicitly covered in the standard formula may have an impact on the application of integration technique used to derive the overall SCR. The biggest challenge is how to integrate them in the modelling framework. When a firm is using a full internal model, embedding these risks should not pose particular difficulties. However, in the case of partial internal models, decisions are not clear-cut. What should be done in those circumstances where a firm uses the standard formula (or a partial internal model) for the SCR calculation, but is exposed to material risks not explicitly covered by the standard formula (or the partial internal model) and therefore intends to develop (or extend) a partial internal model to capture them? Some of the options that firms can consider are to:

- assume that these additional risks are linked to existing risks of the standard formula;
- consider setting up a new risk module to take them into account; and
- assume that the risk is linked to a specific business unit and build a full internal model with respect to the risks covered by this business unit, taking into account these specific risks.

Improving risk management and reflecting adequately exposures to these particular risks are the main criteria a firm need to consider when choosing between the different options available. For the first option (ie, additional risks linked to existing standard formula risks), the least-complicated solution would be to integrate these risks with the other firm's risks and derive the overall SCR. Nevertheless, other options should be considered, as it may not be always possible to transfer these additional risks to existing standard formula modules.

A problem may emerge for the third option (ie, building a full internal model with respect to this business unit). The implementation of this option may be challenging when these additional risks are not linked to a business unit, as this may provide firms with the wrong incentives to build business units that do not reflect the economic reality of the firm.

CONCLUSION

This chapter has attempted to clarify some of the challenges that both firms and supervisors face when developing, reviewing and maintaining partial internal models. It provided examples of how such models are used to smooth an insurer's transition to full use of an internal model, or to deal with instances such as the merger of two insurers, one of which uses an internal model and the other a standard formula. It explained how, given the potential complexity of a full internal model, the use of a partial internal model is typically considered a satisfactory target provided its scope is properly defined (and approved by the supervisor).

The chapter also explained why, from a supervisor's perspective, the possibility of mixing and matching internal models for some risks and businesses with the standard formula raises potential concerns about cherry-picking. It therefore emphasised the need for supervisors to place the onus on the insurer to justify why they have chosen to only use internal models for certain business lines, and should, where appropriate, encourage the extension of the scope of the model or development of a full internal model.

Finally, it is worth concluding this chapter by stressing the need for firms to document effectively the rationale for the use of the partial internal model, and to discuss it early with the supervisor to ensure a more efficient approval process.

The views expressed in this chapter are those of the author and not necessarily those of EIOPA.

APPENDIX: PARTIAL INTERNAL MODELS EXAMPLES

As in the case of full internal models, firms intending to use a partial internal model may follow a different risk categorisation than the one prescribed for the Solvency II standard formula.

It is therefore useful to provide a few examples of what may constitute a partial internal model from a practical perspective. These examples are based on the EIOPA technical specifications for the Solvency II valuation and SCR calculations.[9] The list is not exhaustive and encompasses several dimensions, but tries to answer questions such as "are the risk categorisation and model calibration used by the partial internal model the same as set out in the standard formula?" and "are all business units within the scope of the partial internal model?".

Figure 2A.1 illustrates the simple replacement of a standard formula risk module (in this case, the "life" module) by the partial internal model. The results of the partial internal model are to be integrated with the modules of the standard formula to derive the SCR of the firm.

Figure 2A.2 depicts the replacement of a standard formula risk sub-module (in this case, the "interest rate" sub-module of the

Figure 2A.1 Modelling a single standard formula risk module

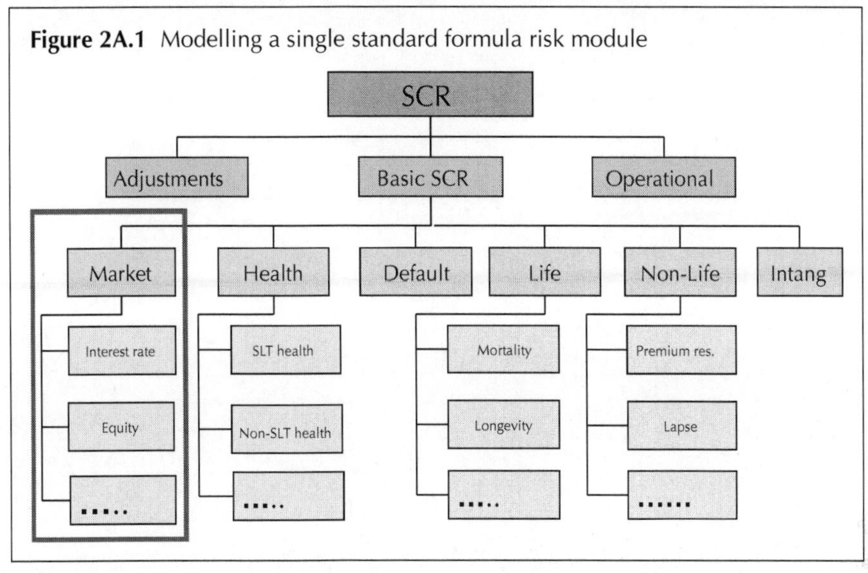

"market" module) by the partial internal model. The results of the partial internal model are to be integrated with the rest of the sub-modules of the same module under the standard formula, and with the results of the standard formula for the rest of the modules to derive the SCR of the firm.

Firms can also replace together two or more risk modules of the

Figure 2A.2 Modelling a single standard formula risk sub-module

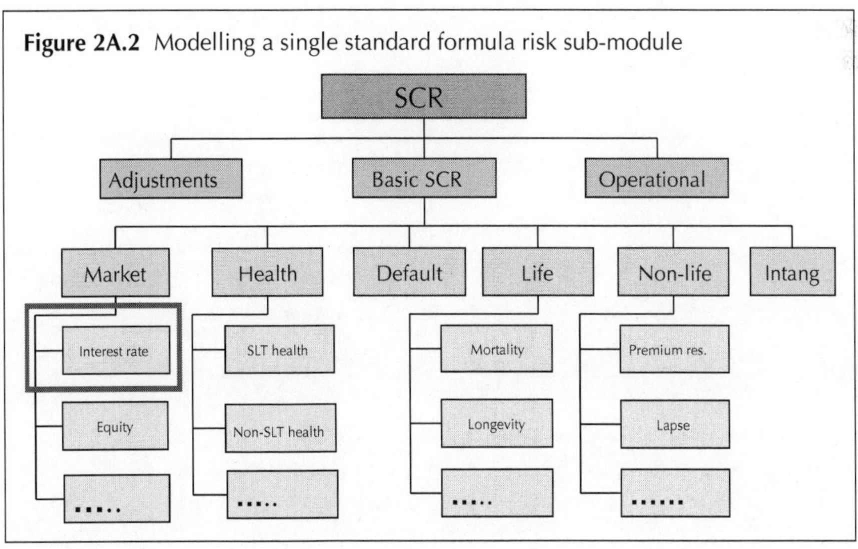

Figure 2A.3 Joint modelling of two or more standard formula risk modules

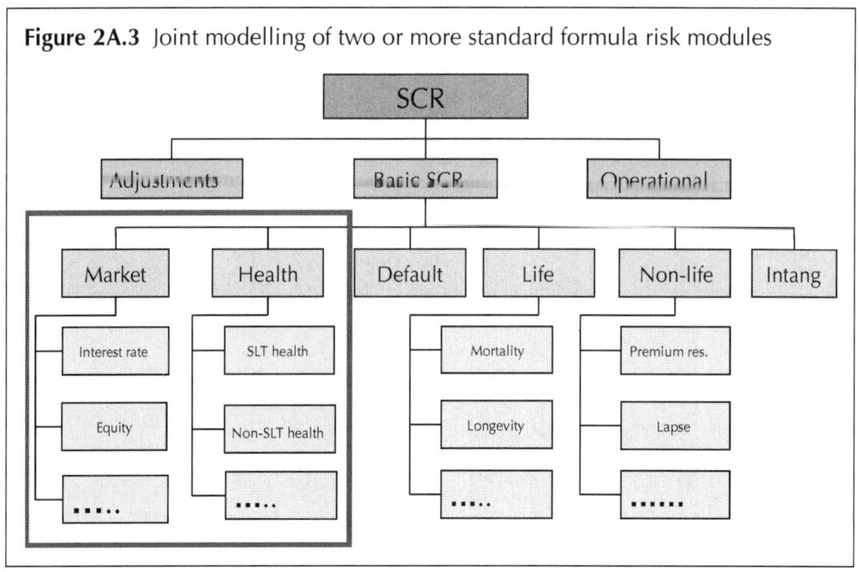

standard formula (in the case, of Figure 2A.3, three modules jointly: "market", "health" and "default"). The results of the partial internal model are then integrated with the results of the rest of the modules under the standard formula to obtain the overall SCR of the firm.

As for Figure 2A.3, firms can also model at the same time two risk

Figure 2A.4 Joint modelling of two (or more) standard formula risk sub-modules within the same risk module

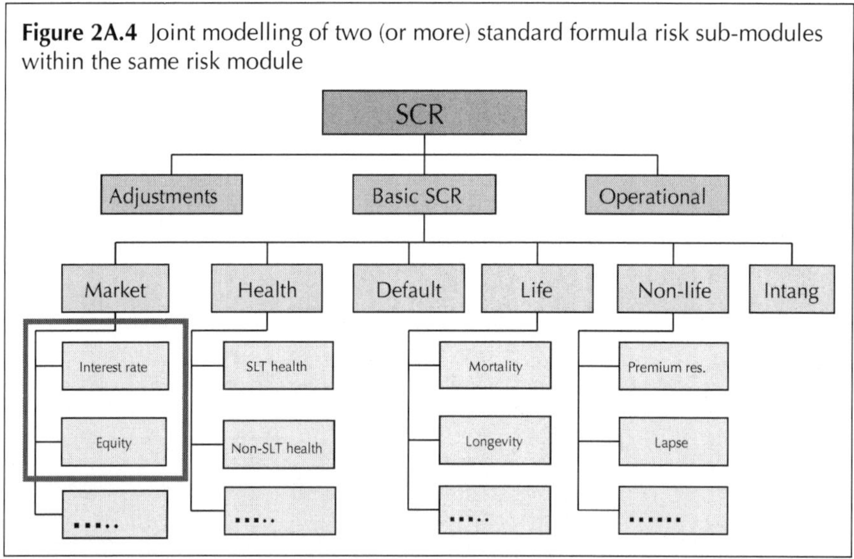

sub-modules of the same risk module, and then integrate the results with the standard formula results for the rest of the sub-modules of the same module and the rest of modules.

As has been explained, firms have a high degree of freedom in defining the scope of their partial internal model. As shown in Figure

Figure 2A.5(a) Joint modelling of two (or more) standard formula risk sub-modules that belong to different risk modules

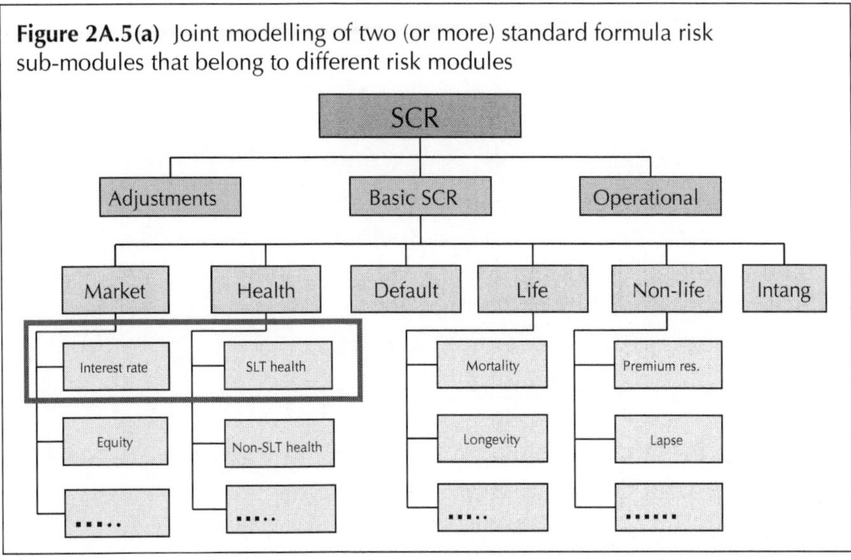

Figure 2A.5(b) Joint modelling of two (or more) standard formula risk sub-modules that belong to different risk modules

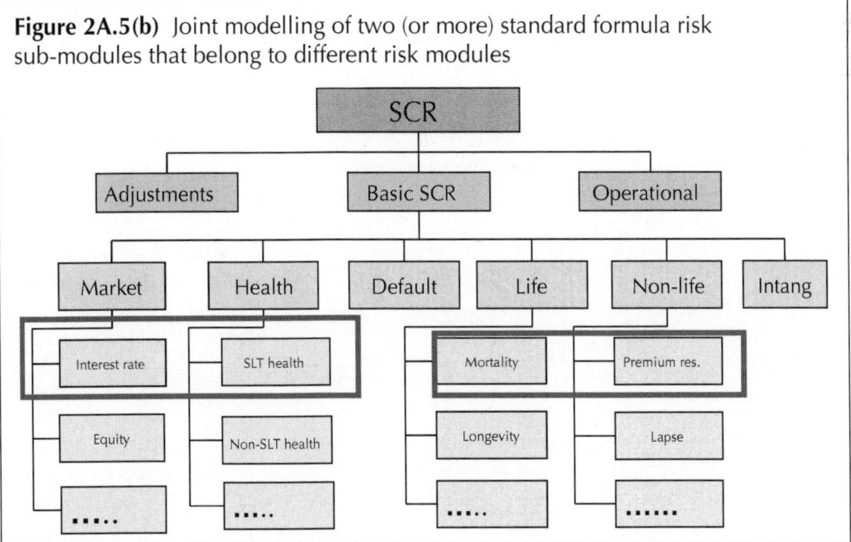

2A.5, firms can model two or more risk sub-modules that belong to different risk modules of the standard formula.

They can also model together two or more risk sub-modules that belong to different risk modules of the standard formula. This case is illustrated in Figure 2A.5(b).

Figure 2A.6 presents an example of a partial internal model for different lines of business of the firm. In the case of composites (firms carrying out life and non-life insurance business), the partial internal model may apply to the risks of only one of the business lines (in the case of the example the "life" line). The results of the partial internal model will be then integrated with the risks of the other lines to derive the final SCR of the firm.

Figure 2A.7 illustrates a partial internal model, under the major business dimension, for the calculation of the group SCR in respect of the coverage of legal entities (in the case of groups, a legal entity typically constitutes a major business unit). The group is composed by a holding company and three subsidiaries or legal entities: A, B and C. The illustration is based on the assumptions that:

- ❑ within the scope of the internal model, all material risks are covered;
- ❑ the accounting consolidation-based method is used for the group solvency calculation across the group;

Figure 2A.6 Modelling all risks for one or more lines of business (eg, composite: all risks for the life business are internally modelled)

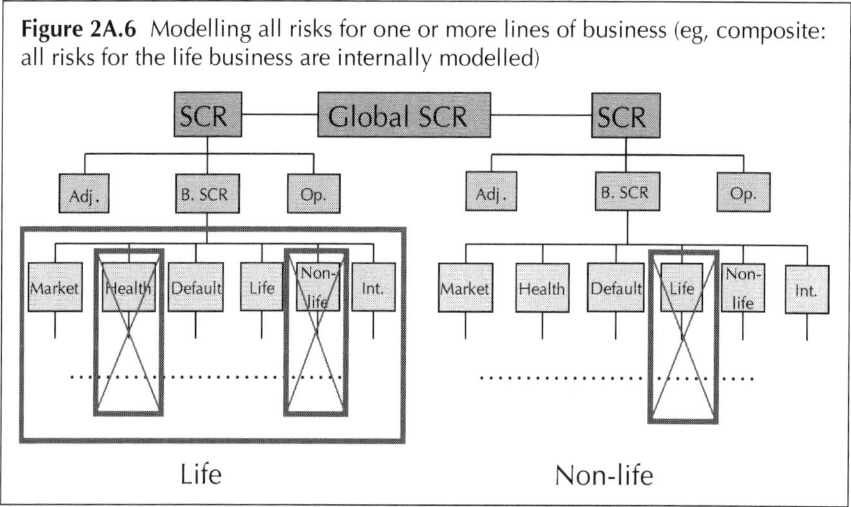

Figure 2A.7 Partial internal model (for legal entities) for the calculation of group SCR

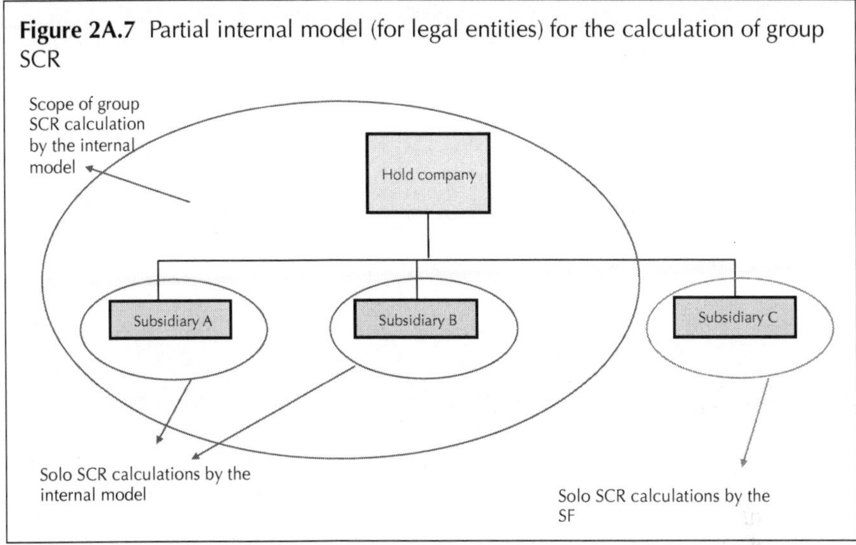

- the group structure is stable (eg, no mergers/acquisitions/spin-offs are foreseen);
- all subsidiaries considered are material to the group;
- the scope of the group SCR calculated by the group internal model covers subsidiaries A and B;
- the solo SCRs of subsidiaries A and B are calculated with the group partial internal model; and
- subsidiary C is excluded from the group internal model scope, and calculates its solo SCR with the standard formula.

Under this scenario, to derive the overall group SCR, the standard formula results of subsidiary C need to be integrated with the results of the group partial internal model using one of integration techniques referred to in this chapter.

1 Although the Solvency II framework does not provide an explicit definition of a full internal model, it may be inferred that a full internal model should cover all risks for all legal entities and major business units for all territories (including operational risk).

2 For instance, the IRB approach is calibrated to a 99.9% systematic stress over a year, the AMA is calibrated to a level comparable to a one-year holding period and a 99.9% confidence level, while market risk is calibrated to a VaR measure, with a 99% confidence level, over a 10-day period.

3 For more details, see Article 113 of Commission of the European Communities (2008).

4 Extensions to the scope of application of the model are per definition outside the model change policy scope.

5 The Solvency II framework defines "involved" supervisors as the national competent authorities of all the member states in which the head offices of related firms included in the scope of an internal model for a group are located. The "concerned" supervisor is defined as the national competent authorities of all the member states in which the head offices of each related (re)insurance firms included in the scope of a group internal model, and for which the SCR would be calculated by the group internal model, are located.

6 For more details, see Articles 101 and 102 of Commission of the European Communities (2008).

7 Details for these techniques will be set out in the Solvency II Delegated Acts.

8 This uncertainty is likely to be resolved with the publication of the Solvency II Delegated Acts.

9 For more details, see EIOPA (2013).

REFERENCES

CEIOPS, 2010, "Advice for Level 2 Implementing Measures on Solvency II: Partial Internal Models" (available at: https://eiopa.europa.eu/fileadmin/tx_dam/files/consultations/consultationpapers/CP65/CEIOPS-L2-Advice-Partial-Internal-Models.pdf)

Commission of the European Communities, 2008, "Directive of the European Parliament and of the Council, On the Taking-up and Pursuit of the Business of Insurance and Reinsurance (Solvency II)" (available at http://ec.europa.eu/internal_market/insurance/docs/solvency/proposal_en.pdf).

EIOPA, 2013, "Technical Specification on the Long Term Guarantee Assessment Part I" (available at https://eiopa.europa.eu/fileadmin/tx_dam/files/consultations/QIS/Preparatory_forthcoming_assessments/final/A/A_-_Technical_Specification_on_the_Long_Term_Guarantee_Assessment_Part_I_.pdf)

3

The Internal Model Approval Process

Stefano Pasqualini

The internal model approval process aims to assess if (re)insurance firms' internal modelling framework can be used to calculate the solvency capital requirement (SCR). This process requires firms to demonstrate compliance with several mandated tests and requirements. For example, among other things, (re)insurance firms need to provide evidence that:

- the internal model is able to calculate the SCR;
- the systems concerned for identifying, measuring, monitoring, managing and reporting risk are adequate;
- the use test, statistical quality, calibration and profit and loss (P&L) attribution, validation, documentation, external models and data standards have been met; and
- any potential interrelation between these requirements has been properly considered.

Moreover, if the application refers to a partial internal model, the (re)insurance firm also needs to:

- justify the limited scope of the model (ie, provide evidence that there is no cherry-picking);
- demonstrate that the resulting SCR reflects more appropriately the risk profile of the (re)insurance firm; and
- provide evidence that the partial internal model can be fully integrated into the SCR standard formula.

As firm's internal models may be extremely complex and varied (eg, with respect to the treatment of interactions and dependencies between risks embedded in the model), this would require supervisory authorities to spend a significant amount of time reviewing the internal modelling framework against the requirements before deciding on the application. However, the Solvency II framework imposes a tight timeframe of six months after receipt of a complete application, during which the supervisory authorities can reach a decision on the internal model's application. To facilitate this task and to ensure that the approval process for both the firm and its supervisory authority is conducted in an efficient, co-ordinated and effective manner, supervisory authorities have complemented the typical approval process with the introduction of a non-mandatory pre-application stage. Therefore, under Solvency II, the process that may lead to the approval of models for use in calculating the SCR has been structured as described in Figure 3.1.

This chapter will now provide an overview of the procedure to be followed for the approval of an internal model, describing the steps of this process. It will also provide an illustration of how this process has been implemented in the European Union, focusing on the most important aspects and experience gained so far.[1] Particular attention

Figure 3.1 The internal model review process

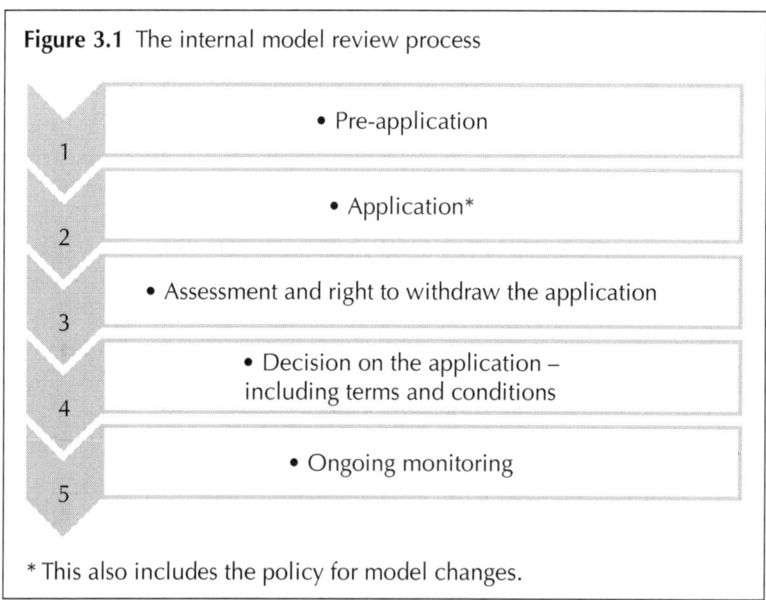

* This also includes the policy for model changes.

will be paid to internal models' application for groups, where co-operation between different national supervisory authorities is critical for the effective review of the application.

This chapter will also highlight the importance of firm's contingency plans if the internal model's application were to be unsuccessful (eg, the firm's ability to calculate the SCR by using the standard formula approach and the assessment of any potential impact on capital resources).

THE PRE-APPLICATION

To ensure that the procedure that is to be followed for the approval of an internal model for the firm and its supervisory authority is conducted in an efficient, co-ordinated and effective manner, supervisory authorities need to spend significant amounts of time reviewing the internal models against the requirements in the Solvency II framework. To facilitate this process, many firms have suggested that they would welcome a period of engagement with supervisory authorities prior to the submission of their formal application, to enable them to develop and refine their internal model practices in preparation for meeting Solvency II test and standards.

Taking into account these suggestions, the Committee of European Insurance and Occupational Pensions Supervisors (CEIOPS)[2] proposed in 2009[3] the introduction of a pre-application process for firms intending to apply for the use of internal models for the calculation of the SCR. In 2010, CEIOPS provided[4] further clarifications about this process describing its proposed structure and aim – ie, providing a view on the preparedness of a firm to submit a formal application.

Benefits

As described in Figure 3.1, the pre-application stage should precede the formal application; although insurance firms' participation is not mandatory, it was devised with the goal to deliver a wide range of benefits both to supervisory authorities and insurance firms. On the one hand, this would allow supervisory authorities to better plan resources for the assessment of an internal model's application, providing them with an opportunity to familiarise with the firm's internal models over a longer time period, and facilitating the assessment stage under the formal application.

On the other hand, the pre-application stage should present benefits to insurance firms as it gives them the opportunity to liaise with their supervisory authorities as they develop and embed their internal model and prepare their submission for the formal application. From a practical point of view, an insurance firm has the possibility to receive guidance and feedback from the supervisory authority at an early stage so that it can adapt the internal model over time, mitigating the risk of last minute surprises.

In principle, the pre-application stage is designed to facilitate the subsequent approval process and enable supervisory authorities to start from an informed position when reviewing the internal models for approval, and how prepared the insurance firms are to submit an application. Overall, the pre-application process is likely to involve similar activities to those carried out during the formal application and assessment stage. However, this does not mean that approval will definitely be granted, as the pre-application process is not a pre-approval. Therefore, an insurance firm needs to prepare for this eventuality and set up the necessary processes to enable it to calculate the SCR through the standard formula, as well as consider any potential impact on capital resources.

Essential elements of the pre-application are the commitment from the insurance firm and the need for the supervisory authority to maintain effective communication during the whole process. It is important for the supervisory authority to be aware and understand the internal model developments in order to form a view on the firm's progress. To this end, supervisory authorities should provide timely feedback to firms, so that they can promptly address any shortcomings that have been identified during the internal model review.

Continuing with the communication, some actions put in place by supervisory authorities (eg, organise regular industry fora with the purpose of identifying areas of good/bad practice with regard to internal models) are intended to help insurance firms meet the standards required under the Solvency II framework.

Benefits for groups

The benefits related to the pre-application stage are especially relevant for an insurance group that operates cross-border and intends to use a group internal model to calculate its group SCR. In this case, as the final decision requires the joint effort of several national supervisory authorities and insurance legal entities, a process that facilitates dialogue, co-ordination and co-operation between the different parties involved is critical.

In these instances, it is essential that at the beginning of the pre-application process, the group supervisor identifies the key features and issues of the group internal model. The group supervisor is typically better placed to access group information. After this preliminary monitoring phase, the other national supervisory authorities and the group supervisor need to co-operate and agree on a common approach to the pre-application process, mainly based on the preliminary findings and on the overall architecture of the group internal model. A similar approach should be followed by all insurance firms that are within the scope of the internal model. The co-operation with their relevant supervisory authority is necessary to ensure that local specificities are adequately taken into account. National specificities are more likely to emerge in the context of insurance underwriting risk (both life and non-life). An early identification and assessment of local specificities ensures that these are duly taken into consideration, mitigating the need of further actions (eg, the imposition of capital add-ons at solo level due to significant deviations from the assumptions underlying the group internal model of the risk profile of a solo insurance firm) and to avoid the circumstance under which a solo insurance firm may be required to calculate the SCR using the standard formula. These scenarios are quite common in practice, and it is therefore crucial that every insurance firm within the scope of the internal model engages early with its national supervisory authority.

From a supervisory perspective, sharing information helps to facilitate co-operation with the supervisory college[5] so that key issues can be discussed and resolved as soon as possible to ensure the efficiency of the process. Based on these findings, the college of supervisors would then start planning the framework to assess the internal model. The planning and organisation of the college of supervisors should reflect the overall structure of the group internal model. During the pre-application phase, it would be desirable that:

- the insurance firms explain to the supervisory authority the extent and nature of the intended use, scope of application and coverage of the internal model (eg, which risks, business units and exposures are to be covered, how internal model components are being rolled out across the insurance firms, governance and risk management arrangements, data collection and management, and testing);

- the insurance firms become familiar with the procedure to be followed for the approval of an internal model, and the test and standards concerning the information that it will need to submit; and
- there is early identification and communication of any specific concerns or issues that need to be factored into the process, with the aim of making it easier during the formal application phase.

Essential information

The supervisory authority may gather information from the insurance firms intending to participate in the pre-application process to facilitate planning. Some of this information is typically used to plan the allocation of resources within the supervisory authority. When an insurance firm intends to start the pre-application process, it is important that it takes into account the resource implications and plans effectively for the following milestones.

- When the insurance firm intends to submit the formal application.
- The scope of the internal model and coverage of the formal application. The scope should include the subsidiaries and the risk modules and/or business lines to be covered by the scope of application of the internal model.
- A detailed insurance firms' work plan, including a potential schedule for meetings with the supervisory authority and plans for demonstrating compliance with internal model requirements, such as an activity plan that involves a delivery schedule, dependencies and milestones, a resource plan, assumptions, constraints, risks, project organisation and governance, and a plan for reporting progress to the supervisory authorities. To accomplish this, it is important to set out checkpoints (eg, on quarterly basis) that define which priorities, plans, resources and budgets should be reviewed and validated. This aspect is important to ensure a continuous process to update and develop the plans.

- Insurance firms self-assessment on how the internal model meets the requirements for the approval for use. This self-assessment may be "co-ordinated" by the supervisory authority – for example, through the insurance firm's submission of an agreed self-assessment template.
- Internal model documentation, which should be clear and sufficient to allow supervisory authorities to understand the part of the internal model that will be reviewed during the process. The internal model documentation should follow a hierarchical approach to define the documentation to support its internal model and broader enterprise risk management. For example:
  - Level 1 documentation (eg, principles for the administrative, management or supervisory body, AMSB) – this documentation could be structured to enable the AMSB to describe the target environments that are required to ensure an effective governance of risk, capital and business performance;
  - Level 2 documentation (eg, chief risk officer, CRO, level) – this should set out the operation of the internal model in the context of function policies principles; and
  - Level 3 methodologies – these could provide guidance, methodologies and training materials for implementing and operating the requirements set out in the Level 2 policies.

Each supervisory authority can review the insurance firm's work plan and self-assessment with the aim to agree a schedule of work with the insurance firm, including areas suitable for early review and assessment. Nevertheless, during this stage, supervisory authorities usually need to review and assess the areas related to governance and risk management, how the firm uses the internal model, whether the internal model meets the required statistical and data quality standards, the calibration of the internal model, the processes used to validate the internal model, the use of external models and data, and the resultant SCR.

From a practical point of view, under the Solvency II regime, an example of what could be included in the documentation submitted in the pre-application process is reported in Table 3.1.

Table 3.1 Example of documentation to be submitted by firms during the pre-application process

1	Existing documentation related to the internal model's project, including supporting evidence about who has provided the internal sign-off
2	Results of the latest own risk and solvency assessment (ORSA), and details of the firm's business and risk strategies
3	Scope of application for full/partial internal models and model coverage (eg, in terms of business units and risks)
4	Risk management process and risk profile documentations (eg, how the firm developed a risk management system to ensure that the risks are adequately identified, measured, monitored and managed, and that the model is widely used in risk management and decision-making)
5	Documentation in relation to the level of compliance (eg, full compliance, partial compliance, not compliant) with the tests and standards for any risks/business units (eg, use test, statistical quality, calibration, P&L attribution, model validation, documentation and external models and data
6	Documentation relative to the technical characteristics of the internal model (eg, types of risk/business units, description of the key components/calculation steps within the model, aggregation of results and diversification effects, use and modelling of risk mitigation techniques), impact on the SCR, including links between components (eg, including a flow chart);
7	Documentation related to any external models and data used in the model
8	Model governance, systems and controls, including documentation and a copy of the organisation's charts
9	Up-to-date independent review/validation report and documentation on how the firm developed the validation process in order to monitor the performance of the internal model
10	Policy for changing the full/partial internal model and other policies for internal model governance
11	Plan for future model improvement, if any (eg, details of any aspects where the firm believes further planning is required, why this planning has not yet taken place and when the firm expect to undertake this)
12	Solvency capital requirement with the maximum level of granularity (eg, with the granularity of the standard formula)

Scheme of pre-application

It is quite common that the assessment phase starts with an evaluation of whether the insurance firm has met sufficiently some pre-application qualifying criteria (PAQC), as defined by the supervisory authority. These criteria are typically not stringent, and aim to ensure the necessary commitment from the firm to enter the pre-

Figure 3.2 The pre-application process

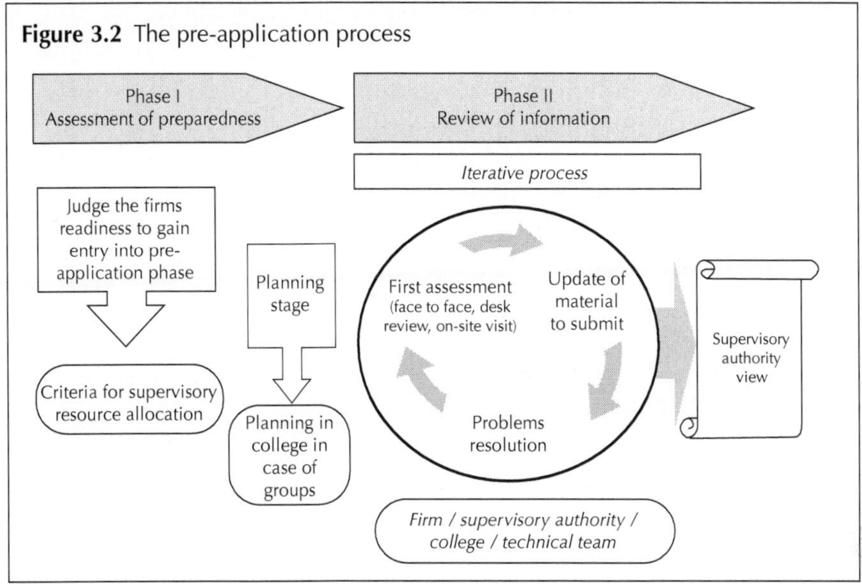

application phase. Once the supervisory authority has concluded that these criteria have been met, the pre-application process – as reported in the following scheme – is usually followed.

As described in Figure 3.2, the pre-application process is iterative – ie, the insurance firm should keep the supervisory authorities informed about the development progress during the pre-application phase via regular updates and agree on review points.

The pre-application process should include face-to-face meetings between the insurance firms and the supervisory authority, preferably during the start-up period of the pre-application phase. An initial face-to-face meeting is beneficial for both parties as it is an opportunity to clarify expectations and form the basis of close co-operation.

The pre-application review process may also involve on-site visits to support or supplement the information received by the firm, or to assess in greater detail a specific part of the formal application. The number of visits depends on the scope of application of the internal models and nature, scale and complexity of the risks covered by the model. These should be welcomed by the insurance firm as a means to facilitate the pre-application process.

In relation to group internal models, meetings and visits for the entities within the scope of the internal model should be decided and organised on a case-by-case basis, taking into account the needs and specificities of the group and the supervisory authorities. These tasks should be organised and performed in collaboration between the group supervisor and the national supervisory authorities. They should also be communicated to the college of supervisors with the aim to ensure a transparent and efficient process. From a supervisory perspective, to maximise the efficiency and effectiveness of the pre-application process, it is useful that the group supervisor, in agreement with the other concerned supervisors,[6] set out a clear process to provide feedback to the firm. This process could be structured as follows.

- Set out clear time limits – it is unrealistic to expect that a supervisor could review a significant part of the model in the absence of appropriate documentation. Therefore, it is important that firms submit the documentation necessary for the pre-application reviews to their supervisor a number of days ahead of the on-site visit.
- Before the meeting, the insurance group should gain appropriate feedback on the documentation submitted to the group supervisor (by letter or by e-mail). This should include ideally preliminary findings, etc.
- To achieve trust and co-operation, it is useful to put in place a good working relationship during the pre-application process. For instance, the insurance group should be informed that the group supervisor will not inform the other national supervisors before they feel that the documents are ready.
- Minutes from meetings between supervisors are prepared by group supervisor and distributed promptly, within a short timeframe (eg, 15 working days; for some type of meetings, such as technical meetings, it can be even faster).

An ongoing communication between all parties involved in the process (eg, insurance group, subsidiaries, group supervisor, national supervisory authorities), together with an agreed work plan, are the main aspects that an insurance firms/group should have in mind when deciding to enter the pre-application process.

THE APPLICATION

The formal procedure to be followed for the approval of an internal model begins with the insurance firm's submission of a cover letter requesting the approval of the internal model to calculate the SCR (ie, application phase) to the relevant supervisory authorities.

Attached to this cover letter the insurance firms should provide all the documents that constitute, as a minimum, the documentary evidence that the internal model meets the relevant requirements set out in the directive, including Articles 101, 112 and 120–126, and the specific provisions for partial internal models set out in Article 113, if applicable.

Cover letter and application package

The cover letter requesting the approval has to be approved and signed by AMSB, and should include at least:

- ❑ the application to start using the model from a specified date;
- ❑ a formal confirmation that the internal model has been used for a reasonable period prior to the application (eg, the firm needs to provide evidence that all the necessary measures and processes concerning the structure of the internal model have been implemented for a reasonable period prior to the application, and that the internal model has been used within the firm for the quantitative measurement and control of the insurance firm-specific risk for a reasonable period prior to the application);
- ❑ the necessary contact information to ensure that the communication between the supervisory authority and the insurance firms can be both effective and efficient (from a supervisory perspective, it is important to know the key people that have been involved in the modelling process, but not necessary to have to a complete, detailed list);
- ❑ a confirmation that material attached to the application is a true and fair summary; and
- ❑ a written declaration from the AMSB confirming the completeness of the application and that no relevant material fact has been knowingly concealed.

It is important to note that the internal model application should not contain any irrelevant information, to ensure that the application is focused appropriately and easily navigable. This aspect should be taken into account by the insurance firm, otherwise supervisory resources may not focus on the material parts of the model. From a practical point of view, all the documents provided by insurance firms should cover all the activities required to define and implement the insurance firm's internal model and achieve compliance with the Solvency II regulations.

When an insurance firm submits an application, it should explain the parts/areas of the internal model that are still being finalised, and therefore that the documentation provided reflects the status of development of the model and analysis carried out to date. Clearly, considering the tight timeframe foreseen in the directive for the application phase, the parts/areas where the internal model are still being finalised should be minimal.

The insurance firm should explain the work done to implement the key elements of the regulation, with specific reference to the governance structure in place, the eventual changes implemented across all of its businesses and the key technology elements of its solution for internal model purposes.

Essential information

The insurance firm should also provide the following information to enable the supervisor to understand the internal model (although this is not an exhaustive list).

- Details on how the internal model covers all the material and quantifiable risks of the insurance firms. In relation to a partial internal model, the explanation should be limited to the material and quantifiable risks within the scope. For the purpose of this requirement, the insurance firms should justify the limited scope of the model and, if applicable, the transitional plan to extend the scope of the internal model, as well as the reasons for including the risks modelled and for not modelling the risks outside of the scope of the internal model. Moreover, in relation to the partial internal model, it is valuable for the supervisory purposes to understand the reasons why the insurance firms considers that the SCR derived using a partial internal model better reflects the risk profile of the insurance firms than applying the standard formula.

- Information about the adequacy and effectiveness of the integration of the internal model into the risk management system, and how the internal model allows the insurance firms to identify, measure, monitor, manage and report risks. Using an adequate process of analysis, the insurance firm should be able to understand the nature of the risks it has identified, their source, their potential effects in terms of both losses and opportunities, and to which extent they can – or have to – be mitigated. In order to understand these features, a process of analysis, including a qualitative assessment and, for quantifiable risks, the adoption of methods to measure the exposure to risk, is needed.
- Considerations about the strengths, weaknesses, limitations or shortcomings of the internal model, including a self-assessment of the compliance with the relevant requirements. The insurance firm should also outline its plan for the future improvement of the internal model in order to address identified weaknesses, limitations or shortcomings or to develop or, where applicable, extend the internal model. In order to address identified weaknesses, limitations or shortcomings of the internal model, the insurance firm should outline its plan for future improvements of the internal model containing a description of the details of areas for improvement and, hopefully, an estimate of the plan within which these changes will be made.
- The technical characteristics of the internal model, including a detailed description of the structure of the internal model, together with a list and justification of the assumptions underlying the internal model where an adjustment to these assumptions would have a significant impact on the SCR.

The technical characteristics of the model are often the part of the assessment where most supervisors focus their attention. This is because choices about assumptions, methodology and data can significantly affect the calculation of the SCR. It is important that the insurance firm provide evidence about the overall methodology used to calculate the SCR, the key components of the relevant calculation steps within the internal model, the details of the embedded assumptions concerning management and policyholder actions assumed to occur and evidence that these assumptions are appropriate information about the methodology used for the aggregation and diversification effects.

In the case of a group internal model application, the group should indicate the extent to which the technical characteristics of the group internal model may differ when the internal model is used for both the group SCR calculation and the calculation of the SCR of different subsidiaries (eg, treatment of intra-group transactions, list of parameters within the internal model that may be set differently, group-specific risks only relevant in the group SCR calculation). This part is often the most complex due to the fact the development of the internal models often requires separate work on several different areas/departments of the firm/group. Therefore, the application needs to include the following.

- ❑ Details about the adequacy of the internal control system of the insurance firms, taking into account the structure and coverage of the model. The insurance firm should at least provide explanations about how an appropriate organisation and an adequate system of internal controls has been put in place (eg, proportionate to the size and operational characteristics of the insurance firms, and to the nature and complexity of its risks, taking into account the structure and coverage of the internal model).
- ❑ Information about the adequacy of the resources, skills and independence of the personnel responsible for the development and validation of the internal model. The insurance firm should provide information about staff involved in both the process of development and the process validation of the internal model. This information should go beyond the adequacy of the knowledge and experience of the people responsible for the development and validation of the internal model with respect to their particular responsibilities. The reporting structure in both the processes of development and the process of validation of the internal model should be useful for the supervisory purposes to understand the independence between two tasks, and how senior management have been involved in the process.
- ❑ The latest independent validation report of the internal model, and its results, should be provided. The insurance firms should provide details of this report, including what validation tasks

were performed, what recommendations were made and how they were acted on.

- Where an insurance firm uses external models and data (ie, obtained from a third party), the insurance firms should provide information on how the external models and data have been validated, how the results and performance of external models is regularly reviewed and re-assessed for its appropriateness to reflect the insurance firms' risk profile, as well as how the integrity of the external data has been verified. On this aspect, it is important, for example, to take into consideration EIOPA's opinion issued in 2012,[7] which tried to address some concerns expressed by insurance firms about the use of external models (eg, for the evaluation of catastrophic risks).

Group issues

During the application stage, some activities could be considered critical for the group internal model – eg, the completion of the internal model development iterations, testing and production of solo aggregations figures, embedding the validation process and the internal model governance, and documentation of the evidence to meet the requirements as required by the use test (both at group and solo level).

In the case of a group internal model application, all the above information should be provided in an official language of the member state, unless the supervisory authorities agrees that the information can be provided in another language. The insurance firm is therefore responsible for translating any documents related to the application.

To maximise efficiency and effectiveness during the application phase, it would be desirable if the language issue were to be resolved during the pre-application stage. For example, it is quite common that, during the pre-application stage, all the documents are provided to the supervisors in an agreed language.

Policy for changing the internal model

The development of a policy for changing the internal model is a requirement on all insurance firms applying for approval to use the internal model to calculate the SCR. The policy for changing the model forms part of the application from the firm, and shall be approved by the supervisory authorities. It is good practice for firms to update their internal models in order to keep the internal model and its parameters accurate and up to date (eg, to update methodologies as appropriate in order to reflect improved techniques).

The requirement for an approved policy for changing the internal model should not inhibit good modelling practice. The purpose of this policy is to describe the procedures the insurance firms have in place to ensure that the internal model is appropriate and meets the test and standards on an ongoing basis. The rationale behind an approved policy for changing the internal model is to facilitate the dialogue between supervisory authorities and insurance firms. Responsibility for creating such a policy remains with the insurance firm.

A good policy for model changes reflects the need for supervisory authorities to be aware of changes, and to be able to satisfy themselves that the internal model still complies with the requirement. In any case, having a policy for changing the internal model is a valuable discipline and should form part of the internal model governance of the firm.

When developing their policy for changing the internal model, insurance firms should specify when a change of the internal model will be considered as major or minor, and when a combination of minor changes shall be considered a major change. Major changes are subject to prior supervisory approval, whereas minor changes are only subject to a reporting requirement.[8]

Insurance firms should report minor changes to the internal model to the supervisory authorities quarterly, or more frequently where appropriate. Minor changes to the internal model shall be communicated in a summarised report that describes both the quantitative and qualitative impacts of each change, and the cumulative quantitative and qualitative effects of the changes on the approved internal model.

Through the policy for changing the internal model, the insurance firms have the opportunity to enhance its risk management – ie, the internal model provides a valuable tool for the insurance firm to develop and constantly adapt their analysis and knowledge of their risks. However, the policy for changing the internal model does not cover extension of the internal model scope, such as inclusion of additional risks or business units. Any such change to the internal model scope will automatically be subject to supervisory approval, following the same approval process as a major model change.

THE ASSESSMENT AND RIGHT TO WITHDRAW THE APPLICATION

Once the supervisory authority has received an internal model's application, it needs to assess whether the application is complete with respect to the signatory, content and minimum requirements, and with respect to all other essential features (including documentary evidence), and does not raise any significant doubt or concern about non-fulfilment in this regard. This task has to be completed in a timely manner from the date of the receipt of the application. It is expected that supervisory authorities should state whether the application is complete within 30 days from the date of the receipt of the application. The assessment of an application starts as soon as the relevant supervisory authorities are satisfied that they have received a complete application.

If the supervisory authority determines that an application is not complete, it needs to notify immediately that the approval period has not begun and specify the reasons why the application is not complete.

- ❏ Where the supervisory authorities determine that the application is complete, they shall notify the insurance firm that the application is complete and the date from which the foreseen period starts. That date shall be the date on which the complete application was received.
- ❏ The fact that the supervisory authorities have determined an application is complete does not prevent the supervisory authorities from requiring any further information from the insurance or reinsurance insurance firm that is necessary to assess the application to use the internal model. The insurance firm shall ensure that all documents necessary are made available, including in electronic form, to the supervisory authorities throughout assessment of the application.
- ❏ The assessment of the application shall involve ongoing communication with the insurance firm, and may include requests for adjustments to the internal model and for a transitional plan.
- ❏ If the supervisory authorities determine that it could be possible

to approve the internal model subject to adjustments to the internal model being made, they may notify this to the insurance firm.

- Whether the supervisory authorities request further information or adjustments to the internal model, the insurance firm may request a suspension of the foreseen approval period, and thus the approval period shall continue once the insurance firms has made the necessary adjustments and the supervisory authorities have received an amended application providing documentary evidence of the adjustments.
- The supervisory authorities shall then inform the insurance firms of the new expiry date of the approval period.

During the assessment, supervisory authorities shall analyse and assess the information submitted by the insurance firm as part of the application. The assessment should be mainly conducted through a desk-based assessment of the information submitted, and any additional information provided by the insurance firms or requested by the supervisory authorities.

Supplementary information provided by the insurance firms or requested by the supervisory authorities could be used in order to make a decision as to whether the insurance firm is allowed to use the internal model to determine its SCR.

This process shall not only assess how the internal model meets the requirements set out in the Solvency II directive in isolation, but also consider any potential interrelation between these requirements. The assessment stage should therefore include the necessary steps and tools to ensure supervisory authorities are able to satisfy themselves that these requirements are met or otherwise.

The documentation provided should demonstrate that the changes have been adequately tested and the impact of the changes has been assessed. This includes any implications for the design and operation of the model, as well as an assessment of the continued compliance with the other requirements foreseen in the Solvency II framework.

The assessment conducted by supervisors should comprise a technical review of the model (its scope, design, build, integrity and applications), its coverage and ability to calculate the SCR for the insurance firms, documentation, the risk management process, senior management role and their understanding of the model, and shall be partly carried out through a set of on-site examinations.

For the main risks area covered by the model, the depth of all independent review work should take into account the principle of proportionality. In this regard, experience indicates that, in the case of life firms that sell mainly traditional contracts (ie, with profits contracts), the main risks area are relative to the market risks (eg, interest rate risk, asset/liability management, ALM, spread risk, equity risk, real estate risk), while for the non-life firms the main risks area are relative to the underwriting risks (eg, premium and reserve risks). Where the internal model makes use of external models and data, the approval process shall also cover these components.

If the assessment of the insurance firm's application shows that the internal model has not met the requirements, then the supervisory authorities should not grant the insurance firms approval to calculate the SCR using an internal model. However, the insurance firms shall be given the possibility to withdraw the application.

Withdrawing the application

The insurance firm may withdraw the application to use the internal model to calculate the SCR at any time before the decision on the application is reached by written notification to the supervisory authorities.

The notification for withdrawal should be approved by the AMSB of the insurance firm, and the notification provided to the supervisory authorities immediately after it is approved. This is a further opportunity for the insurance firm to submit evidence for the ongoing update for AMSB in relation to the development and understanding of the internal model.

If the insurance firm does not withdraw the application when the supervisors are not satisfied on the basis of the documents provided, the supervisory authorities shall reject the application. In this case, if the insurance firm intends to use an internal model in the future, it will have to submit a new application for approval.

DECISION ON THE APPLICATION, INCLUDING TERMS AND CONDITIONS

Once the application has been submitted, it has to be assessed by the supervisors, a decision has to be taken on it (based on three steps:

application, assessment and decision, together with the compulsory pre-application, which constitutes the approval process). If the application is approved, the roll-out plan and any terms and conditions on which the approval was conditioned have to be monitored (ongoing monitoring).

The decision-making stage of the internal model approval process uses the outputs from the assessment of the internal model by the supervisory authorities to reach a decision on whether the model is appropriate to calculate the SCR, as described in Article 112(5) of the Solvency II directive. In particular, after the supervisory authorities have made their assessment, a decision has to be made whether or not to approve the use of the internal model for regulatory purposes.

An insurance firm cannot consider its application for an internal model approved until receipt of the decision from the supervisory authorities. Failure by the supervisory authorities to make a decision within the referred period does not result in the application being considered as approved.

When the supervisory authorities have examined the application and assessed the internal model of the insurance firm, and concluded that all requirements have been met or not, then the supervisory authorities shall approve/reject the use of the internal model for calculation of the SCR. This conclusion should be officially notified, without delay, in writing to the insurance firm. The decision should include some milestones, including:

- where the supervisory authorities approve the application, the starting date from which the model shall be used to calculate the SCR and the scope of the internal model; and
- where the supervisory authorities reject the application, the reasons on which the rejection is based.

When should the supervisory authorities reject the application?

The supervisory authorities should reject the application for the use of an internal model if they are not satisfied on the basis of the documents provided with the application or any further additional information received that the internal model fulfils the requirements foreseen in the Solvency II framework.

In the case of rejection, the supervisory authorities should not disclose that an insurance firm has applied to use an internal model to calculate the SCR, or that an application was rejected or withdrawn. In addition, where an insurance firm's application for approval to use an internal model to calculate the SCR has been rejected, the firm has to resort to the standard formula to calculate the SCR.

As set out in the Solvency II framework, any decision by the supervisory authorities to reject the application for the use of an internal model should be accompanied by the reasons for so doing. By stating the reasons, the supervisory authorities should indicate the areas in which an application has been considered deficient. This will help insurance firms if they wish to rectify the failings in their application and internal model and re-apply for approval.

However, it is likely that an insurance firm needs some time to rectify the deficiencies in its application and in its internal model. Thus, to mitigate the risk that insurance firms re-apply before they have appropriately addressed the shortcomings in their internal model application, it would be useful to recommend that supervisory authorities be allowed to enforce – on the basis of reasons communicated to the insurance firms – a "waiting period" before the insurance firms can submit a new application. Such a period could be also suggested when the insurance firms withdraws the application.

The waiting period should be agreed between insurance firm and supervisor, since it should be commensurate with the shortcomings that have been identified and proportionate to the deficiencies that have led to the rejection of the application.

When should the supervisory authorities approve the application?

When the supervisory authorities have examined the application and assessed the internal model of the insurance firms, and have concluded that all requirements foreseen in the directive have been met, then the supervisory authorities can approve the use of the internal model for calculation of the SCR.

In this case, the supervisory authorities have to disclose the fact that the use of an internal model has been approved, the start date from which the model should be used to calculate the SCR and the scope of the internal model.

An insurance firm can use the internal model to calculate the SCR as soon as it is approved by the supervisory authorities, or from a later date as set out in the decision document from the supervisory authorities.

The approval could be subject to terms and conditions. When determining these, the supervisory authorities should take into account:

- how realistic it is for the terms and conditions to be fulfilled by the insurance firms by a particular date (if any); and
- whether compliance by the insurance firms with those terms and conditions can be assessed in an objective and straightforward way (by the supervisory authorities).

When supervisory authorities have granted approval subject to terms and conditions, they may require the insurance firms to submit a plan indicating the necessary steps to meet the terms and conditions attached to the decision or permission document, and require reporting on progress.

CONCLUSION

This chapter has illustrated the procedure to be followed for the approval of an internal model. It explained how the approval process not only aims to assess how the internal model meets the test and standards foreseen in the Solvency II directive in isolation, but also the need to consider any potential inter-relation between these requirements.

When thinking about applying for internal model approval, insurance firms should pay attention to the test and standards, and seek to go beyond a simple regulatory box-ticking exercise. To increase the efficiency and effectiveness of this process, the communication between the supervisory authorities and the insurance firm is essential. To this end, it is best practice to begin the dialogue before the formal application is submitted to the supervisory authorities (ie, at the pre-application stage).

Communication between the supervisory authorities and the insurance firms should continue throughout the assessment of the application, and also after the internal model is approved through the supervisory review process. This last aspect underlines that the complying with the test and standards for internal models is not a one-off exercise, but that the requirements have to be met on an ongoing basis.

The views expressed in this chapter are those of the author and not necessarily those of IVASS

1 Most of the issues related to the procedure to be followed to approve the use of an internal model for the calculation of the SCR are addressed by the European Insurance and Occupational Pensions Authority, EIOPA (formerly CEIOPS) in its documents. EIOPA guidance does present an opportunity to increase convergence on outcomes and supervisory practices.
2 CEIOPS is the predecessor of EIOPA.
3 For further details, see CEIOPS (2009).
4 For further details, see CEIOPS (2010).
5 Colleges of supervisors refer to multilateral groups of relevant supervisors that are formed for the collective purpose of enhancing efficient, effective and consistent supervision of financial institutions operating across borders.
6 The Solvency II framework defines "concerned" supervisor as the national competent authorities of a member state in which the head offices of each related (re)insurance firms included in the scope of a group internal model, and for which the SCR would be calculated by the group internal model, are located. The Solvency II framework defines "involved" supervisor as the national competent authorities of a member state in which the head offices of related firms included in the scope of an internal model for a group are located.
7 For further details, see EIOPA (2012).
8 Further details about what may constitute a major and minor change are provided in Chapter 4.

REFERENCES

CEIOPS, 2009, "CEIOPS' Advice for L2 Implementing Measures on SII: Procedure to be Followed for the Approval of an Internal Model", formerly Consultation Paper 37.

CEIOPS, 2010, "CEIOPS Level 3 Guidance on Solvency II: Pre-application Process for Internal Models", formerly Consultation Paper 80.

EIOPA, 2012, "Opinion of the European Insurance and Occupational Pensions Authority of 2 May 2012 on External Models and Data".

European Parliament and the Council of The European Union, 2009, "Directive 2009/138/EC of the European Parliament and of the Council of 25 November 2009 on the Taking-up and Pursuit of the Business of Insurance and Reinsurance (Solvency II) (recast)".

4

Policy for Model Changes

Christian Kerfriden

Prudential Regulation Authority, Bank of England

The work of a firm or supervisor does not finish once the internal model application has been approved. After approval by the supervisor and the firm has started to use the internal model to calculate the solvency capital requirement (SCR), it is good practice for firms to update their model to reflect changes to the business and economic environment, and to keep the model and its parameters accurate and up to date.

The firm is responsible for ensuring that the model continues to operate properly on a continuous basis to adequately reflect its risk profile and comply with the requirements. The model change policy introduced by the Solvency II directive provides a framework for the governance of changes to the approved internal model, both internally and in relation to the supervisor.

The policy has to be approved by the supervisor as part of the internal model approval process. The model change policy is an essential component of the governance of the internal model. This chapter will therefore examine some important elements covered by the policy. A section on the changes, and the sources of changes, explores the reasons and triggers for changing the model, before we highlight how the appropriate governance of changes to the model can be set out. Some practical issues in setting and implementing the policy are also discussed, followed by an examination of the classification of changes between minor and major and how this attracts most or all of the attention given to the model change process. Finally, the chapter will explore the required supervisory approval of major changes to the model.

Figure 4.1 illustrates the different steps for changing the internal model that must be covered by the policy for model change. A broad set of sources is available for an organisation wanting to identify potential changes. The potential changes should be considered

Figure 4.1 Model changes from source to implementation

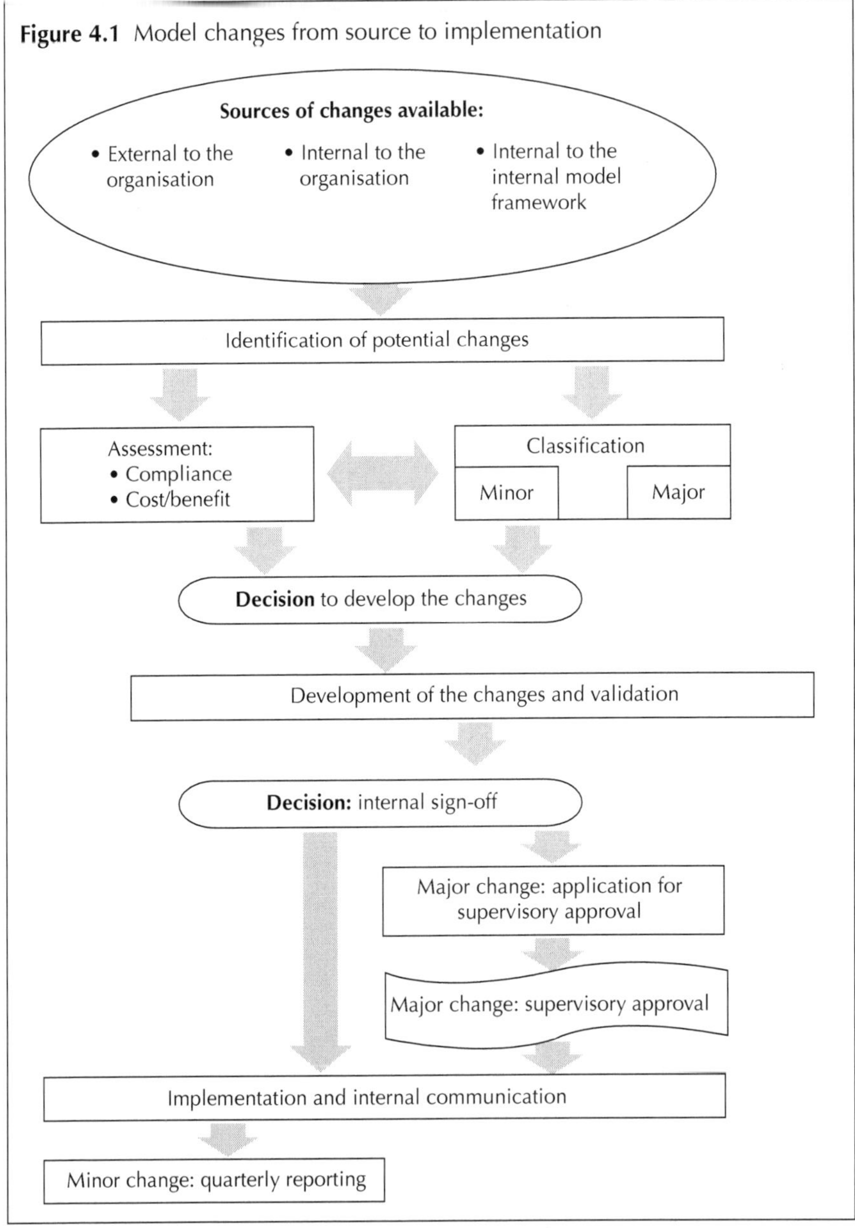

through appropriate governance, resulting in some being implemented within a controlled framework. The steps cover the classification of changes as minor or major, and the formal internal decision points, as well as the interaction with the supervisor through the reporting of minor changes and the submission for prior approval of major changes.

CHANGES AND SOURCES OF CHANGES

Why change the model?

The reasons and motivations for changing the internal model can be divided into two categories: changes made to react and adapt the model to changes that occurred outside the model (exogenous), such as changes to the business impacting the risk profile or changes in the economic environment of the organisation; or changes made to improve the model (endogenous). Exogenous changes are only initiated in a timely manner if the organisation is able to track and monitor the potential sources of changes that may trigger a change to the model. Below we will discuss changes to the risk profile, governance and environment as potential triggers for model changes.

Changes made to improve the model could, in some cases, be seen as less critical when – without those changes – the model could continue to be fit for purpose and comply with Solvency II standards. Nevertheless, such changes may be needed to ensure continuous compliance with the requirements, and also be symptoms and causes of an appropriate use of the internal model. For the model to be extensively used as a risk management tool and in other decision-making processes, it is expected that changes will need to be made regularly as new uses or ways to use the model arise and as experience and comfort in using the model develop. For example, this could lead to improvements in the granularity of the modelling or the model outputs. However, it could also lead to improvements in the modelling methodology to better reflect the characteristics of the risk, or to incorporate the latest developments in actuarial science.

Changes in the risk profile of the business

Changes in the risk profile of the business are likely to trigger regular changes to the model. This starts typically with the business strategy. The proper alignment of the internal model with the business model and its ability to support a forward-looking strategy is necessary for the model to be used in (at least some of) the internal discussions and debates that inform important decisions regarding future business developments.

The way the organisation embeds not only the use of the model, but also its development and changes to support its internal use, is likely to impact the benefit the organisation gains from developing, maintaining and using an internal model. It is a fair to say that developing and maintaining an internal model is expensive, but the opportunity to harness the potential benefits of this risk management tool should be a priority for the organisation. For instance, when considering changes to the model, if the choice is made to only reflect the model changes following a strategic planning process, the added value of the model is limited. Therefore, the model's ability to capture and reflect a forward-looking risk assessment also depends on how changes are made to the model after it has been approved.

Designing and adapting the internal model to harness the added value of risk modelling during the business and strategy planning is only one circumstance where changes to the model are triggered by changes – actual or foreseen – to the risk profile. More obvious, perhaps, is the need to consider changes to the model when the business, and its balance, changes. For instance, as a line of business growths – either in relative terms as a percentage of the total business or in absolute monetary terms – it might be appropriate to review if the methodology adopted to model the associated risks is still adequate. The change in scale and potentially in complexity associated may justify a change in the modelling to maintain compliance with the solvency standards, but also to provide useful information and input for internal uses.

A parallel can be drawn with the process for setting the risk appetite; as the business sets a risk appetite framework for the risks it undertakes, the risk management could consider "modelling appetite" in relation to the nature, scale and complexity of the risks covered by the model. For instance, this may lead to the classification of the modelling techniques available, and to derive objective criteria between the modelling techniques with regards to the nature, scale and complexity of the risks to be modelled. This approach may bring some benefit when considering and selecting changes to be made to the model.

Changes to the risk profile must also be considered in relation to the knowledge and information available to assess the risks that the organisation is facing. In particular, as more information becomes available – either through the internal collection of data, such as claims, or through an improvement in the understanding of the risk, such as academic research or broad data gathering – this should be considered as a potential trigger for a change to the model. A change in the perception or assessment of a risk might be treated the same way as a change in risk profile. For instance, a development in the knowledge of the natural catastrophe exposure of a particular country or region is likely – if material – to trigger a change in the assessment and modelling of this risk. An example is the 2011 flood in Thailand that led to a significant change in the assessment of that risk.

Impact of governance changes

Two types of governance changes are considered as sources for model changes: changes to the governance of the organisation and changes to the governance of the internal model. The consequences and implications of internal model changes can be distinguished between these two different governance changes.

A change in the governance of the organisation is a potential driver to changes to the model. A change in the legal structure – eg, the creation of a new subsidiary – is likely to require some changes to the model. Less severe are changes to responsibilities within the existing legal structure – eg, the creation of a new centre of responsibility. These changes are likely to require amending the model's ability to produce outputs at the relevant level of granularity.

Other functional changes in the governance of the organisation, and in particular – but not limited to – the risk management, also impact the model and are considered as potential sources of changes. For instance, the organisation and its risk management might decide that a particular risk needs to be monitored closely, requiring improvement to the modelling methods selected for this particular risk.

A second type of change is changes to the governance of the internal model itself. For instance, changes to the governance of the model, such as the seniority of the individuals or committees taking decisions on the model, or changes in the level of engagement of users, may impact the effectiveness of challenges to the model.

Similarly, changes in the validation process, validation policy or other policies that the organisation has decided to adopt need to be reflected in the organisation processes and related documentation. These changes might not impact the calculation engine, but alter the way the organisation complies with the Solvency II requirements, and might also trigger changes to some processes and the documentation for the internal model.

Changes in compliance with requirements to use an internal model

Once the internal model has been approved by the relevant supervisor or college of supervisors for calculating the SCR, the organisation is responsible for ensuring ongoing compliance with the Solvency II internal model requirements.

When the organisation identifies a breach of compliance with the requirements,[1] it should present a plan to restore compliance or demonstrate that the effect of the non-compliance is immaterial. Restoring compliance includes making changes to the model. Indication or evidence of non-compliance might arise from the application of some of the requirements – in particular the regular validation process – but might also arise from a source external to the model, such as the identification of a new emerging risk (currently not captured by the model) or any other risk management activities.

In addition, it should be considered that any approval to use an internal model to calculate the SCR is granted based on the application and supporting documentation. Post-approval, some information or documentation provided to support the supervisory assessment might become non-relevant to the current/actual status of the internal model. This can potentially invalidate the decision to approve the model. The organisation is responsible for ensuring that the supervisor is informed on changes that might impact on its original decision to approve the internal model.

Changes in the external environment

Changes in the external environment have frequent and significant impacts on the organisation, and can lead to changes in its business or the way it engages in that business. As with many of the tools and processes used by the organisation, the internal model is also likely to be impacted, and needs to be adapted to reflect some of these evolutions in the environment.

The question then arises of the best way to identify information or changes to the environment that should be considered as a potential source to change the model. As for other processes inside the organisation, a filter is needed for the organisation to respond or adapt to the change. For instance, a change in the market (eg, the entry of a new competitor likely to impact the whole market) could trigger changes in the profitability assumptions for future business for a specific line of business. The entry of a competitor assessed to be too small to impact the market might not trigger a similar change. To preserve the ability of the model to provide useful information for risk management and decision-making, a forward-looking approach is required. A backward-looking model (ie, that is only accurate for previous periods) is not deemed fit to calculate the SCR.

In addition to changes to the insurance market environment – such as the entry of a new competitor, as mentioned above – impacting directly on the business or its associated risks, some elements of the environment also have a direct impact on the organisation's performance or assessment and quantification of risks. For instance, changes in the law or tax code might have an effect on the performance of the organisation, and would need to be reflected in the internal model.

Arguably, financial markets rank as the top external factor impacting the asset side of the balance sheet. When designing and developing the model, a range of possible states of the financial markets is captured to reflect these risks. Nevertheless, the original modelling is highly imperfect due to the complexity and changing behaviour of the financial markets. Changes in those markets should then be monitored when their impact to the organisation is or can be material, and changes to the model should be made when relevant to capture new behaviour – eg, correlation patterns – or to reflect a better understanding of the dynamic of the markets.

A final external source of changes to the model is the change in the knowledge of risk. The organisation may allocate resources to develop a general or specialised understanding, as well as some tools and methods to assess the risks to which it is exposed. However, it is likely that other external sources, such as academics and professional bodies (eg, the actuarial profession), specialised providers (eg, catastrophe modellers), develop information useful to the organisation in its assessment and modelling of risks.

As discussed, some changes to the model will also be triggered by internal needs, the need to comply with the requirements for internal model, while other changes will be driven by response and adaption to changes in the environment. For some changes, failure to respond affects the model performances and ultimately results in non-compliance with the requirements.

GOVERNANCE AROUND CHANGES TO THE MODEL AND THE POLICY FOR MODEL CHANGE

To ensure that the management of model changes is performed in a manner that complies on an ongoing basis with the regulatory requirements and maximises the efficiency of internal resources, a formal governance process is necessary. This process, which should be designed with regard to the model scope, the model structure and the broader governance framework of the organisation, needs to cover the identification of likely potential changes, their assessment, selection and, ultimately, the internal sign-off process. Supervisory approval of major changes can be seen as an extension of the internal sign-off.

Identification of candidates for changes

The previous section introduced the sources of changes to the model. From these sources, the potential changes or candidates for changes need to be identified. An important process that should be harnessed to identify potential changes to the internal model is that of model validation. Material weaknesses identified during the validation are obvious candidates to trigger changes to the model. This highlights the importance of including, as part of the validation, an escalation process of the weaknesses, with the double objective of informing the users of the model outputs and addressing the material weaknesses. Nevertheless, considering only the most material issues (to contribute to the model improvement process) is likely to neglect an important source for the identification of potential changes. Organisations that use the result of the validation to capture not only material weaknesses, but a broader range of limitations as possible sources to improve the model – even if not all potential changes will be implemented – are likely to get most of the benefit from the validation.

This illustrates why the identification of limitations to the model during its validation should not be seen as a negative outcome of the validation but, if managed adequately, a strength of the internal modelling framework, and to create numerous opportunities to develop and maintain a high-quality model. This cannot be achieved without robust model governance, including a comprehensive validation process and the well-structured management of model changes.

The teams that develop and run the model (eg, capital modellers or actuaries) are likely to form views of changes that can improve the model, in particular with respect to the model outputs' accuracy, the robustness and reliability of the modelling process, and also the operating aspects of the model.

Other key contributors to the identification of potential changes are the users of the model and model outputs. Harnessing the specific expertise of model users and their knowledge of the business provides a valuable supply of change to the model. Governance of model changes, by setting the ways and means of engaging users in the identification of potential changes to the model, channel a diversity of needs and experience with the model. This should not be limited to technical aspects, but might also cover some governance aspects, such as validation of the model. For instance, this engagement of users and stakeholders can be achieved through user committees or forums where improvements to the model are considered, or through an established process for users to suggest changes to the model.

Assessment of changes to be developed

Starting from a list of potential changes to the internal model, the next step of governance is to assess those potential changes with the aim of selecting those changes that bring the most value to the organisation. The risk to compliance with the internal model requirements forms part of the assessment criteria. In addition to this risk, a standard analysis of cost and benefit for the organisation is also relevant.

The cost for the organisation in developing and implementing a potential change is likely to include resources such as the time of dedicated staff to develop, test, validate and document the change, but also the need for additional data and the associated cost of their collection, storage, analysis and maintenance, and update overtime. The opportunity cost needs to be considered when the development of the change implies the use of skilled resources that would otherwise be allocated to another activity, such as developing another change. The potential cost of changes will also include any increased run time, any increase in complexity of the process to run the model or the analysis and preparation of the model outputs resulting from, or required by, a specific change.

The benefit of a change for the organisation can be analysed in categories that, in particular, include the correction of errors, improving the accuracy of the results produced, developing the uses of the model and improving the operability of the model, leading to better information and ultimately better risk management.

For instance, improving the accuracy or reducing the uncertainty may lead to a better allocation of capital, resulting in a better alignment of the price of some insurance products with their true economic cost. In addition, it may also encourage the use of the model and its output by producing more reliable results for specific uses, such as improving the accuracy of the allocation of capital for different insurance products, allowing an extended use of the model to measure performances of these products.

Developing uses of the model through changing the outputs produced by the model (eg, their granularity) leverages on the modelling work already carried out. This could bring value to the organisation in exchange for a limited marginal cost. Developing the use of the model may also consist of taking into account the model outputs, or some analysis of the model outputs, in new risk management activities or decisions-making processes – for instance, by using the risk ranking produced by the internal model in some business development decisions.

Improving the ability to operate the model can include simplifying the operation of the model by reducing the risk of errors or reducing resources (eg, staff, IT hardware, run time needed).

Decision on changes to be developed

The decision on changes that needs to be developed is a separate step from the identification of potential changes and their assessments. The relevant decision-making body, depending on some predefined criteria, could be the holder of a specific position or a committee. The different predefined criteria applied to form a decision to proceed in developing the changes will, for instance, cover the foreseen impact on the risk management or on other types of decision, such as capital planning and capital allocation, pricing of insurance contracts or allocation of assets.

The decision-making body for the particular change under consideration is likely to involve committees or individuals able to inform the decision through an effective challenge of the proposed change based on their knowledge and specific area of expertise.

Internal sign-off of changes

When the changes have been developed, documented and validated, a formal sign-off of the changes provide another opportunity for the management and general governance of the organisation to engage in this process. The same, or different, decision-making bodies that approve the adoption of changes also have the opportunity to challenge the development and the impact of changes based on their experience, knowledge and the results of the validation. The validation of changes covering compliance with the internal model requirements provide the relevant information for the management to assess that the model continues to comply with the internal model requirements after implementation of the change.

This critical step in the process of changing the internal model provides senior management with an opportunity to engage with the changes developed before they start to impact the risk management, the decisions made by the organisation and, in some cases, the SCR. This step of the internal model governance also provides the opportunity to get buy-in from users of the model outputs and other internal, or even external, stakeholders. For instance, senior underwriters can be associated with the decision when the changes impact their area of responsibility, providing them with the opportunity to challenge and get familiar, if not comfortable, with the changes.

When dealing with a major change to the model, the approval process is made up of two distinct phases: (i) the internal approval by the board of the application to the relevant supervisor for a major change; and (ii) the assessment and decision by the supervisor/s on the application.

Implementation and internal communication of changes

The implementation is the last step of the transition to business as usual. This is also subject to validation to ensure that the changed model is performing in accordance with its new specifications, with the expectations being informed by the previous steps. To inform this process, the analysis of changes is typically used. This analysis links the changes observed in the outputs of the internal model to the different components of the change, and contribute to the validation, as well as being useful to support the communication and relevant reporting.

The internal communication of the changes is part of the governance of the changes and is essential to provide users of the model or model outputs with information that directly impacts their tasks and areas of responsibility. In the case of a minor change to the model, the communication should also include the external communication to the supervisor through the mandatory quarterly reporting of minor changes.

PRACTICAL ISSUES AROUND MODEL CHANGES

This section will consider some practical issues often raised by firms concerning the application of the model change requirement for internal models.

Definition of changes

A common issue when designing a policy for model changes or the broader governance process around the internal model is defining what a change is, or what constitutes a change to the model. This seems mainly relevant when considering the implications of regulatory requirements: what tools and processes within the organisation (or outside the organisation – eg, outsourcing activities or use of external models and data) should be subject to the internal model requirements and the model change policy in particular?

Without question, changes such as that to the method of modelling interest rate risk, constitute a change to the model and should be subject to the relevant governance. Addressing the question of whether that change should be classified as a minor or a major change might already have lead to different views. However, if changes are made to the tool used to calculate technical provisions, sometimes called the "heavy model" or "cashflow model", when this tool is not part of the internal model calculation engine, then some doubts may arise whether this constitutes a change to the model.

To address this, let us take a step back, and ask "what is an internal model?" In practical terms, it is a matter of what is in and what is out.

Looking at the Solvency II directive text, no definition of internal model is provided. Perhaps this is because an internal model is not a closed system. The internal model is a risk management tool designed to reflect risks to which an organisation is exposed. The quantification of risks covered by the model might require information produced outside of the organisation – for instance, to model market risk information produced by financial markets. Therefore, this means the internal model is an open system, and defining *a priori* in general terms or for a generic model what is in and what is out is not possible.

However, in practice, for a specific model, how does one identify what is in and what is out? Even in the case of a particular model, this question might be not specific enough to be answerable. A possible way forward is to look at the aim of the internal model, in terms of what it does rather than what it is. Arguably, a central role and function of the internal model is the quantification of risks, particularly with respect to the use of the model to calculate the SCR. Therefore, a practical answer regarding what is in the model could be sought in relation to what contributes directly to the quantification of the risks in the scope of the model, such as tools, processes or, more generally, information. For example, the information produced on a continuous basis by the financial markets does not impact directly on the quantification of risks or the probability distribution forecast produced by the model. Neither is the tool used to calculate the technical provisions (when it is not part of the calculation engine of the internal model).

Considering the internal model as a tool to quantify risks is a starting point, but the internal model is more than a calculation tool, it is also subject to specific governance to ensure accuracy and reliability. In particular, the validation requirement is an important aspect of the model. To perform appropriate validation, financial markets information as well as the technical provision tool might be necessary. In this respect at least, both are not entirely alien to the model. As a consequence, the requirements for internal models need to be considered in relation to the financial market data and the technical provision tool when they are used to validate, or for that matter calibrate, the model. It is noteworthy that the requirements for the internal model explicitly provide that the methods used in the internal model need to be consistent with the methods used to calculate technical provisions.

This does not mean that, in these examples, the internal model requirements apply to financial market data or the technical provisions calculation tool. For instance, the documentation requirements do not apply. The particular requirement discussed in this section – ie, the model change requirement – also does not directly apply. Nevertheless, the organisation needs to consider how a change to the technical provision tool, for instance, may impact on the internal model. More specifically, a change to the tool raises the question whether the change to the internal model is needed to reflect a change in views in the calculation of technical provisions or in the risk – eg, volatility – associated with the technical provisions. Therefore, a change to the technical provisions tools not included in the internal model is a potential source of change to the internal model, but not a direct change to the model. A similar reasoning should be applied to different tools, different internal model structures and particular situations – ie, type of change and its interaction with the internal model. In conclusion, a pragmatic approach needs to be developed that considers the specific risk profile of the organisation and the specifications of the internal model. One objective of the model change policy is to provide the organisation with a framework to build and maintain an effective internal model.

Changes to the model versus update of the inputs

Another practical issue is how to distinguish between a change to the model and an update of the inputs. Performing a new run of the model to reflect the new position of the organisation is not a change to the internal model. At the other end of the spectrum, changing the correlation coefficients between risks is a change to the model. Between these two, rest a series of modifications that raise some doubts whether they should be considered as changes to the model, such as updates to the financial markets dataset used to calculate the parameters for a statistical distribution.

To help clarify this issue, it might be worth distinguishing the different sets of data used by the internal model. "Exposure data" are related to the insurance policies and the composition of the asset portfolio of the organisation – eg, the number of insurance policies, the coverage of the policies, the premium associated with the policies, and the number and identification of the assets hold by the organisation. "Observational data" are used for the valuation or measurement of performance of the assets and insurance policies – eg, the market price of assets, as well as the claims data and mortality data.

One operational principle is to assume that the update and changes to the exposure data do not constitute a change to the model, unless it is a change in risk profile that triggers a change to the model. Changes to the observational data, on the other hand, do constitute a change to the model. The first proposition – a change to the exposure data does not constitute a change – will easily find a large consensus. The second proposition – a change to observational data is a change to the model – faces considerable practical challenges. In particular, given the high number of internal model parameters that are regularly calibrated and updated using observational data, classifying the update of those parameters as a change to the model raises significant and legitimate concerns. Nevertheless, practical challenges can be addressed through practical solutions, and do not necessary invalidate principles that are useful in providing a robust and simple framework.

At this point, it is worth remembering that not all changes to the model are major and, therefore, do not need supervisory approval.

It is worthwhile to reflect on the aim of identifying and reporting changes to the model, both within the organisation and to the supervisor. The objective is to ensure that the model is still fit for purpose and complies with the internal model requirements for the calculation of the SCR. Bearing this in mind, a single parameter change might be of very low interest as many parameters will be updated simultaneously, and it is their combined effect, including their interaction, that is of interest. In particular, considering observational data from financial markets used to estimate some parameters of the model, the combined effect of those updates and the process used to estimate the parameters using the observational data are of interest both to the organisation's governance and supervisor. For example, how the data are selected (source, type and list of index) and collected, their frequency and the length of the time series are of interest. In the example above, the process is of greater interest than the value of the data or, to some extent, the resulting parameters. Providing the process is robust, objective, transparent and forms part of the methodology of the internal model approved by the supervisor, the subject of change could then become the process for updating the internal model parameter itself. It is not good practice to apply the update process blindly, as unexpected changes in the observational data might make the estimation method inappropriate. Therefore, some safeguards and boundaries need to be put in place. Similarly unexpected changes to the resulting parameters might make the modelling methodology inappropriate, so some safeguard and boundaries need also to be in place there. When these safeguards are hit or the boundaries crossed, further analysis might be required and the reporting of the change, both internally and externally to the supervisor, should reflect this unexpected situation.

Reliance on the updating process should not form a single block for all the parameters included in the model. The updating processes will be diverse depending on the type and sources of observational data, and type and use of the resulting parameters. The organisation in its model change policy can define how it proposes to record the updates of different parameters and the reliance placed on the updating processes, subject to specified safeguards and boundaries. The safeguards could, for instance, be in relation to the observational data themselves – such as setting a range or movements outside of which a change is triggered – and the boundaries in relation with the resulting parameters or their impact on the result of the model.

By adopting a pragmatic approach as illustrated above, the organisation will be able to define an efficient process for managing the changes to the model while at the same time preserving the goal to build and maintain a robust internal modelling framework to the satisfaction of the supervisor.

It is worth noting that not only does the supervisor have an interest in the robustness of the process and the appropriateness of the internal model, but so does the management of the organisation. In addition, the risk management function is particularly expected and required to share this interest once they choose to use an internal model to calculate their SCR.

Frequency of changes and the maintenance cost of an internal model

When the model is approved and used by an organisation, numerous opportunities and needs to change and improve the model arise from the various sources discussed at the beginning of this chapter. The organisation may grow, change or acquire new business, which may need to be reflected in the model. The market and the knowledge about the risk, including actuarial methods, evolve and this also needs to be reflected in the model. As the uses of the model develop, users need more or different information from the model, which again may well lead to changes to the model. There is no ideal frequency for changing the model, although models with large scope for complex organisations are likely to require more regular changes and, in such cases, a regular cycle of changes – for instance every quarter – might be an efficient option. For models with smaller scope for less complex organisations, the frequency might be driven by specific needs for change as they occur.

From the changes considered and implemented, some can be classified as major and require prior supervisory approval. These changes are likely to require a longer time period from identification to implementation and use, as some are more likely to require longer internal development and validation time, but also because the supervisory approval required can take up to six months. Therefore, the time management of these major changes should also consider the supervisory approval period. Making the supervisor aware that an application for major change is likely to be submitted, and when, could be important for the allocation of supervisory resources in a timely manner. Engaging early with the supervisor on the area and characteristics of the change might also help to reduce the time necessary for the assessment of the application. There is no typical frequency for major changes, but models with large scope for complex organisations are likely to require fairly frequent major changes, and engaging with the supervisor through the model change policy, or as part of the application – or pre-application – can be helpful to align expectations.

The frequency of changes and the costs of maintenance and further developments of the model should not be underestimated. For an organisation using an internal model to calculate its SCR, these costs have to be met. The difference between two comparable organisations will not necessarily be in the costs associated with the model, but in the benefits that the model will bring to the risk management and other internal decision processes. The potential benefits are not only from the outputs of the models, but also in the processes and activities around the model, for instance the validation is an opportunity to learn about the uncertainties around the modelled risks, including some quantification of those uncertainties. It is also an opportunity to learn about the limitations of the risk assessment embedded in the model and to use this knowledge during the decision-making.

Before validation, the development of the model itself and the development of following changes are also an opportunity to learn, not only about the model, but also about the underlying risks being modelled. This knowledge can be set aside and kept largely unexploited, or can be communicated, discussed and used to support the business. This is largely up to the organisation. The cost is there, but the benefits are up for grabs.

MINOR VERSUS MAJOR CHANGES

The classification of changes between minor and major has an impact on interactions with the regulator. Minor changes to the internal model need to be reported quarterly, while major changes need to receive prior supervisory approval.

This classification between minor and major changes is not imposed on the organisation for its internal purposes, but is required for the interaction with the supervisor. An organisation might decide on a different classification and, in particular, a richer and more granular classification not only along the same scale – minor versus major – but also with additional criteria, as long as it is able to map or allocate its internal classification to the minor and major categories.

Criteria and granularity

The criteria used for an internal classification are up to the organisation to decide, but they can be set in relation to their consequences: different levels of governance might involve different committees or individuals for the approval and/or the sign-off of the changes. These committees might be interested in, or have an expertise and responsibility over, different areas of the business or of the risk. For instance, senior underwriters might be involved in the approval and sign-off of changes related to underwriting risks, but not for market risk. The internal classification might also consider the sources of changes in order to involve the appropriate individuals and governance bodies during the approval and sign-off processes. For instance, changes triggered by changes in the legislative framework might involve legal function. Other criteria for internal classification also include the need to involve different level of seniority depending on the importance or impact of the change. Importance and impact categories are for the organisation to define.

The previous paragraph touches on an internal classification of changes to illustrate that addressing internal needs first might go a long way to satisfy the requirement of classification in terms of minor or major. The same criteria that could be selected for internal use are also likely to be relevant for regulatory classification. In practice, building a regulatory classification in minor or major might prove more challenging than first building an internal classification for the organisation's own purpose.

In practical terms, the criteria for a classification – either internal or regulatory – will probably find their source in one of the following areas: the risk or type of risk that is affected by the change (eg, market risk versus underwriting, operation risk or other type); the aspect of the model that is changed (eg, the calculation engine, the validation framework, the use of the model); the methodological spectrum (eg, change to the statistical methods or a change to the way the methods are applied through parameterisation); and the impact on the output of the model (eg, quantification of the impact or changes to the type, such as granularity, of the outputs).

In addition, the organisation should consider when the accumulation of minor changes will result in a major change to the model, and an application for major change needs to be submitted to the supervisor.

However, before discussing the criteria in more detail, it is worth considering briefly another source of complexity: the use of an internal model in a group context. When an internal model is used to calculate a group SCR, a single model change policy will be approved. The framework set in that policy will apply for the calculation of the solvency capital at group level, but also, when approval was granted to do so, for the calculation of several individual ("solo") SCRs. In these cases, the criteria for the classification of changes are deemed to capture a larger diversity of changes, those that impact all entities capital requirement calculation, as well as changes for which the impact is limited to a single entity or individual capital requirement. A change classified as major requires supervisory approval, and therefore a major change for an individual SCR will mean a major change for the policy and be subject to supervisory approval.

Quantitative criteria

The impact on the SCR is the most used indicator to classify minor and major changes. It is useful as a "backstop" indicator, as the calculation of the SCR is of particular importance to the supervisor; therefore, changes that have a greater impact on the SCR will be of interest to the supervisor. Nevertheless, the impact on the SCR is a crude indicator and it will be very difficult to set a threshold that will satisfy both the organisation and the supervisor if the change of the SCR is the main or unique criteria to classify a major change.

The internal model cover a variety of risks, applying diverse modelling techniques based on specific assumptions, all of which are aggregated together to produce the probability distribution forecast from which the SCR is derived. The mixture of components and the range of risk or uncertainty associated with them calls for different thresholds. Where the modelling techniques are more established, a higher threshold might be more acceptable, while where the modelling techniques or the data available make the outcome of the modelling more uncertain or more sensitive to key assumptions, a lower threshold is appropriate. For example, for the modelling of the impact of natural catastrophes using catastrophe models based on the latest scientific and engineering knowledge, a threshold for classification as a major change can be higher than for the modelling of the impact of longevity risk on a life portfolio, or inflation risk on an insurance portfolio where the organisation needs to apply its expert judgement.

Therefore, to avoid an inconclusive discussion with the supervisor about which threshold for the change of the SCR is appropriate to classify a major change, additional criteria based on modelling modules or individual risks are useful. In practice, for a stochastic model, the additional criteria can include a percentile of the marginal distributions for individual risks (eg, the impact of longevity risk) or a percentile of the marginal distribution produced by the module (eg, the catastrophe module). For stochastic and non-stochastic models, the criteria can be based on certain points produced by the model or on some individual (stress) scenario. Those additional criteria will complement the change in the SCR.

More sophisticated quantitative criteria can also be designed and used. For example, indicators of the uncertainty of the results or of the parameters used in the model could be of interest, both for the supervisor but also for more senior individuals inside the organisation. Building on the example described earlier, where reliance is placed on the process to update some parameters of the model using data from the financial markets, criteria based on the measure of uncertainty resulting from the estimation of the parameters may provide reassurance that any material deviation from expected movements will be identified and reported internally and to the supervisor. When changes or increased volatility in the financial markets impact the uncertainty around the estimation of the parameters used in the model, this is picked up by the indicator and not only treated with more attention, but can also draw attention to a developing phenomenon (eg, the behaviour of the financial markets) that can impact the organisation.

The aggregation method within the internal model is an aspect of the modelling that deserves attention and a high degree of scrutiny. Therefore, it is very relevant to have some quantitative indicators to measure the changes in the diversification effect. Such criteria to classify a change as major need to be designed in such a way that they capture the effect of the diversification at a sufficiently granular level. The indicator does not have to be based on the technique used in the model itself, and the organisation should consider how this indicator captures the changes in the tail dependencies. For example, a possible criterion is the change in a simple measure of diversification, while another and more sophisticated example is for the organisation to build a reference matrix of pair-wise correlation between some standardised categories of outputs from the model – whether or not such an approach is similar to the one adopted in the modelling – and measure how the matrix departs from the reference after a change.

However, all quantitative criteria for the classification of changes as major do not need to be sophisticated. For example, very simple measures, such as the number and type of material expert judgements included in the change, the number and the type of uses that will be impacted by the change, can be used as indicators to set criteria to classify changes as major.

In conclusion, the SCR is an important quantitative indicator, but using only the SCR is probably not appropriate. Additional quantitative indicators can be simple or sophisticated, and do not need to be produced by the model itself.

Qualitative criteria

It is understood that based, on the Solvency II legislation, some modifications of the model – such as the extension of the scope of the model (eg, inclusion of new risks or new business units) and changes made to the model change policy – should follow the same process as the major changes. Those modifications are not formally major changes as they are outside the scope of the model change policy, but the governance around those modifications and, in particular, the need for supervisory approval are similar as for changes classified as major.

For changes within the scope of model change policy, in addition to quantitative criteria, qualitative criteria are necessary to capture aspects of changes that are not captured by the quantitative criteria. Two elements can illustrate this. The first is the methodology used in the modelling. A change in the methods applied in the internal model can encompass a change in the view of risk or a change in the way to assess risks in the internal model, and both are of interest for the supervisor and presumably for senior individuals or committees inside the organisation. This interest is legitimate, disregarding the immediate quantitative impact of the change on the outputs of the model, as such a change may have long-term implications and may impact significantly the outputs of the internal model, particularly the capital requirement in the future (if and when the business profile evolves or the financial and business environment changes). For instance, if the modelling of dependencies changes from a correlation matrix approach to the use of a copula, this change can be reasonably expected to be classified as major. Starting from the technical specification of its model, the organisation will identify which methods that, if changed, will trigger a classification as major, or how to use indicators to identify major changes triggered by changes in the modelling methods used.

The second element to illustrate the need for qualitative criteria is compliance with the internal model requirements. Before it is changed, the initial model will have been reviewed by the supervisor, and its compliance with the internal model requirements assessed prior to final approval. Some changes will not necessarily fail to comply with the requirements, but will make a material aspect of the previous assessment by the supervisor irrelevant due to the nature of the change. It is then necessary to submit to the supervisor the change as a major change for approval. For instance, this is the case for material changes in the use of the model with regard to the use test requirement, or in the validation process or validation policy with regard to the validation requirement. Other examples of such cases are the inclusion in the model of new types of mitigation technique, new management actions or the introduction of new elements to support the loss absorbency of deferred taxes.

Backtesting and dialogue with the supervisor

Setting criteria to classify changes to the internal model as minor or major is important for the future governance of the model, and deserves some attention. To define and select criteria for the classification, changes made in the past to the developing model or to a capital model can provide valuable insight. Backtesting the model change policy, by applying retrospectively the criteria being developed to changes made in the past to the capital model, can inform the development of the policy and the selection of the criteria, and is also useful in providing the supervisor with examples and reassurance that the policy is fit for purpose.

However, the model change policy is not only about setting criteria to classify changes. The internal governance around the changes – identification of need for change, internal challenges and validation, final decision and internal communication – should be covered by the policy to the satisfaction of the supervisor. It is important to remember that the policy is to be approved by the supervisor as part of the internal model approval. Setting robust governance around the changes to the internal model is critical, as weak governance fails to provide the assurance required that as an important component of the risk management, the model and particularly the capital requirement will satisfy the internal model requirements in the future. A weak governance of the changes to the model is likely to give rise to supervisory concerns about future downward drift of the capital requirement or other failure of compliance.

Engagement with the supervisor, during a pre-application process or in another context, is crucial in aligning the model change policy with supervisory expectations. It is the responsibility of the organisation to develop and embed its model change policy. A well-designed and used model change policy will facilitate the future interaction of the organisation with its supervisor on multiple aspects related to the internal model. A poorly designed model change policy, on the other hand, gives rise to uncertainties in the governance of the model and will require additional supervisory activities and engagements with the organisation in order to ensure that an appropriate oversight of the model is in place.

In particular, the organisation might include in its policy some indications and specifications about how the minor changes will be reported quarterly to the supervisors. Solvency II provisions do not require such a description to be included in the policy. Nevertheless, its inclusion will provide the supervisor with some comfort that relevant information on minor changes will be reported, which might be beneficial when assessing the criteria for the classification of changes. For the organisation, including in the policy some descriptions of the quarterly reporting bring the benefit of clarifying supervisory expectations, thereby reducing the need for unnecessary reporting and allowing for the collecting of information needed for the quarterly reporting.

APPROVAL OF MAJOR CHANGES

Major changes to the internal model are subject to supervisory approval. This provides a necessary supervisory oversight of the most significant changes to the approved model.

Early identification and planning

Major changes to the internal model need to be planned adequately to manage the time from initiation to implementation. Several steps in the development and implementation of a major change might require more time than for most of the minor changes. The development phase of most major changes – changing the modelling of the dependency structure, for example – might be longer than for most of the minor changes. In addition, some other phases – such as the validation and the internal approval process – might also require a longer timescale. The internal sign-off for the application of a major change should be carried out by the board, before the assessment and review by the supervisor, which can last up to six months.

The governance of changes set out in the model change policy supports the development and implementation of the changes that are tailored to the organisation. The early identification of potential candidates for changes, as discussed in the first section of this chapter, contributes to a timely selection and development of changes to be made to the model.

Managing the impact of changes as well as the approval is important. The development phase and internal decisions provide the opportunity to communicate with relevant internal stakeholders ahead of the final implementation. The management of changes and their impact on the model outputs, as well as any impact on the use, are essential, as poor management may jeopardise compliance with the use test and diminish the future engagements of some stakeholders.

Some changes are considered and rejected by the organisation as they are not appropriate – for instance, changes to the modelling of dependencies, as they do not capture tail dependency. It is important to consider that the application for approval by the supervisor might also be rejected if there is no clear evidence that the requirements are satisfied. Therefore, it is important that the organisation documents and collects evidence during the development and test process. This not only increases the likelihood of a successful application, but also reduces the time needed by the supervisor to come to a decision.

Time is a factor. When a change is planned to improve the model, the timing might be important but not critical. When a change is planned to the model to reflect a change in the risk profile that is not appropriately reflected in the model, or a change in the business environment not properly captured by the model, then time becomes critical. The early identification of a need for change to the model, and a clear identification and communication of the limitations of the model, will support the effective management of changes. Changes should be made under an adequately controlled framework.

Early engagement with supervisors

The decision by the supervisor on an application for a major change is made after the relevant assessment of the change. As for the internal model approval process, the time needed by the supervisor to take a decision on an application can be divided between the time taken to assess the compliance of the change with the internal model requirements and the time for the governance of the decision. An additional factor on the length of the assessment of the application is the availability of supervisory resources at the time of the application.

The time needed for the assessment of compliance will be reduced if the supervisor is informed early about the major change being developed, and an early dialogue – before the submission of the application – between the supervisor and the organisation allows the supervisor to understand the rationale for the change and to access information relevant for its assessment, particularly technical specification, justification of assumptions, evidence of compliance and result of the validation. Such early engagement – similar in some way to a pre-application process – might not be possible for all major changes, but should be considered when time is an important factor for the ongoing compliance of the model.

Similarly, the availability of supervisory resources for the assessment of the application will be facilitated by an early engagement of the organisation with the supervisor. The supervisory governance to take a decision on the application will depend on the context of the internal model. A group internal model requiring a joint decision by several supervisors or members of the supervisory college is subject to the same process – ie, a joint decision – for major change applications. Early planning by the organisation and the supervisors contributes to an efficient and effective decision process.

As shown above, the use of an internal model is likely to generate more interactions with the supervisors, through the submission of application for major changes, the quarterly reporting of the minor changes and as part of the supervisory process. Supervisors look for reassurance that the internal model and the SCR, in particular, are appropriate on an ongoing basis. A robust policy for changing the model, together with an effective validation process, provides essential contributions to that reassurance.

CONCLUSION

An internal model is a tool that contributes to the risk management of the organisation, first through the learning experience of developing the model itself, and then through the use and the maintenance of the developed model. When an application has been submitted to the supervisor and the internal model has been approved to calculate the capital requirement, the organisation must ensure the ongoing appropriateness of the model.

The policy for model changes sets the framework for changing the approved internal model and for the related interactions with the supervisors. As described, the organisation should actively monitor the sources for potential changes to the model inside and outside the organisation. The policy for model change should specify the governance around the change to be made to the internal model and, in particular, the internal approval of the changes.

The policy must also set the criteria to classify changes so that the minor changes are reported to the supervisor on a quarterly basis, while the major changes are submitted to the supervisors for prior approval.

The views expressed in the chapters are those of the author and not necessarily those of the PRA, Bank of England

1 In particular, in accordance with Article 118 of the Directive 2009/138/EC.

REFERENCES

CEIOPS, 2009, "Advice for Level 2 Implementing Measures on Solvency II on the Procedure to be Followed for the Approval of an Internal Model".

European Parliament and the Council of the European Union, 2009, "Directive 2009/138/EC of the European Parliament and of the Council of 25 November 2009 on the Taking-up and Pursuit of the Business of Insurance and Reinsurance (Solvency II) (recast)".

5

Internal Models to Calculate the Group Solvency Requirement: The Perspective of the Home and Host Supervisor

Agnieszka Groniowska; Perrine Kaltwasser and Regis Weisslinger

Polish Financial Supervision Authority; Banque de France and Milliman

An important aspect of the Solvency II directive is the development of requirements for the supervision of insurance groups. The strengthening of supervision at group level, which was only supplementary in the 1998 Insurance Group Directive, enhances the functioning of the European insurance market and facilitates the supervision of international insurance groups.

Group supervision under Solvency II is supported by the supervisory college[1] and the key role of the group supervisor. The supervision of insurance groups includes the requirement to calculate a group solvency capital requirement (SCR). As for the solo capital requirement, the consolidated group SCR can be calculated using an internal model as approved by the relevant supervisors.

This chapter will consider certain aspects of regulations relating to the internal models for insurance groups as provided in the Solvency II directive adopted in 2009. The chapter focuses on the practical challenges rather than on the many advantages that the appropriately implemented group internal models have on the group risk management systems and on collegial supervision. The emphasis taken here does in no way refute or disregard the role that Solvency II plays in strengthening group supervision by promoting risk management at group level. In addition, the development of a group model and the resolution of some of the challenges discussed in this chapter are also an opportunity to enrich the risk management system of the group.

The next section will examine the option provided by Solvency II to calculate the group solvency. The accounting consolidation or deduction and aggregation (D&A) methods raise implications and challenges, particularly where some group entities are excluded from the scope of the internal model. The treatment of entities located outside of the European Economic Area (EEA) is also considered. This is followed by a look at some modelling issues, specifically the challenges of modelling consistency both from the group and local perspectives (eg, the use test and the treatment of group risks). We will also consider the implications of two kinds of internal models dedicated to groups: an internal model application for the calculation of the group SCR only (application under Article 230 of the Solvency II directive) and an application to calculate both the group solvency requirement and the SCRs of the local entities, within the group. The next section then discusses the role of the supervisory college during the review and assessment of applications for the use of internal model for groups. It explains the powers of the group supervisor, the host supervisor and also the possible role of the European Insurance and Occupational Pensions Authority (EIOPA) in the joint decision. The chapter concludes by considering the application of the concept of materiality in a group context.

GROUP INTERNAL MODEL

Considerations on the group solvency calculation

For the purpose of calculating the group solvency requirement, the accounting consolidation method is the default method to be adopted by insurance groups. This should apply in the absence of an explicit decision by the group supervisor indicating that a D&A method or a combination of both methods should be applied instead. The choice of a consolidation method is not directly connected with whether a group uses or does not use an internal model; however, it does have some implications that deserve attention.

In a nutshell, with the default method (ie, accounting consolidation) groups are supposed to calculate their capital requirements as if the group were a unique entity, therefore consolidating the risks faced by each entity, with an appropriate elimination of intra-group transactions. On the other hand, using the D&A method compares the aggregated eligible own funds (ie, the capital resources) available at group level with the aggregated SCRs of the entities within the group. This approach gives no benefit for diversification between entities.

The group supervisor takes the decision about the application for the use of the D&A method or a combination of methods taking into account the criteria enumerated in the Solvency II delegated acts. The supervisor should consider whether the company is applying for the use of an internal model as well as the entities covered and excluded from the scope of the model. However, the exclusion from the scope of the group internal model does not automatically imply the use of the D&A method will be granted. The formulation of the criteria for allowing the use of the D&A method takes into account practical considerations that can make the application of the accounting consolidation method not appropriate. For instance, when reliable information is unavailable, as well as when the calculation is unduly burdensome and does not significantly impact on the SCR.

Specific considerations should be given to insurance entities within the group that are excluded from the scope of a group internal model. When the accounting consolidation method is applied, the group capital requirement should be calculated by integrating the component of the capital requirement determined using the internal model and the component calculated using the standard formula (for those entities excluded from the scope of the model). The choice of integration method for internal model which is partial with respect to risks may in many cases be challenging due to potential limitations in data availability and even more when the internal model is partial in respect to the entities. Further details on the method to integrate those two components are provided later in this section and in Chapter 2 on partial internal models.

Where the risks associated with the entities not covered by the internal model are not material in relation to the risk profile of the group, the group supervisors might consider that the D&A method is more appropriate for those entities.

How to produce consolidated accounts

The accounting consolidation method under Solvency II necessitates assessing consolidated exposures eliminating intra-group transactions. Although it follows the same principles as the financial accounting consolidation, there are various differences that need to be acknowledged and taken into account.

Indeed, some accounting standards are not adopted by the Solvency II balance-sheet valuation. For example, an intra-group loan may not have the same value in the borrower's and the lender's balance sheet within the Solvency II framework due to the asymmetry in taking into account the borrower's creditworthiness. On the contrary, both operations would perfectly offset each other in an accounting consolidation. This illustrates that, albeit the financial consolidation is already challenging for groups with many entities, the Solvency II consolidation needs even greater adjustment.

In addition to the consolidation of accounting figures to support the total balance-sheet approach, the Solvency II regime also requires the consolidation of non-accounting figures necessary to assess the group exposure to a specific risk. The consolidation of non-accounting items forms the basis for the calculation of the group capital requirement.

Finally, the way some subsidiaries are included in the consolidated balance sheet could be different between the Solvency II regime and accounting provisions – eg, the thresholds for the choice between the equity method and global integration are not always aligned between both frameworks.

Considering the choice of aggregation method in relation to the limited scope of the internal model

A limited scope (in respect of entities) of the internal model is a factor to consider in the choice by the group supervisor (after consultation with the firm) of the group solvency calculation method (ie, either accounting consolidation or D&A). It is expected that the firm's decision about the (limited) scope of the model should allow for a better reflection of its risk profile. In practice, the firm's choice of a limited model scope might have different motivations – for example, the intention to avoid or reduce the impact of capital requirements for one of the risks, or the inability of the group to build a full internal model. Therefore, the decision by the group supervisor on the calculation method should take into account how the activity of the entities excluded from the scope of the model is different from, or integrated with, the entities encompassed by the model and whether an extension of the scope of the model for these entities requires a different modelling approach or can be done appropriately within the current modelling approach.

Although the D&A method allows for a simple and comprehensive presentation of group results, when some entities are excluded from the scope of the model and where significant intra-group transactions are put in place, it might be difficult to implement. To be appropriate, the D&A method should, in particular, eliminate the intra-group creation of capital and any form of double gearing.

Third countries equivalent/non-equivalent related firms

From the beginning of the Solvency II project, the aim was to reinforce the group solvency assessment and, although the regime was designed by European regulators, group supervision should take into account all the risks to which European groups are exposed. These include risks arising from their activities in third country jurisdictions, namely countries outside the EEA.

The implementation of this requirement leads to some practical challenges, from both a supervisory and an industry perspective. To achieve a robust supervisory regime, EEA supervisors have to collaborate with third countries' jurisdictions, which are not necessarily assessing the solvency on the same or equivalent rules. The difficulties faced by supervisors vary depending on the way groups intend to include the risks located in third countries in their SCR calculation.

This section focuses on situations where the operations in the third countries are modelled either using a capital model subject to the approval of, or already approved by, the third country supervisor or using the group internal model approved under Solvency II rules.

For instance, let us assume that the results of the third country subsidiary are included through the D&A method. If the third country solvency regime is deemed equivalent[2] to the Solvency II regime, the SCR of the subsidiary can be calculated using the local capital requirement which, in some cases, may include the use of the capital model.[3] When a solvency regime is not deemed equivalent, the group needs to determine a capital requirement based on Solvency II rules. The insurance group can decide either to use the Solvency II standard formula or apply for the use of a Solvency II-compliant internal model to cover the risks associated with its activities outside of the EEA. The internal model does not necessarily need to be developed from scratch to the extent that it is appropriate for the group to leverage an existing local capital model. Such an approach can provide benefits with respect to the use test, as it can contribute to the alignment of the model used to calculate the regulatory capital requirement and some internal capital management activities.

When a related entity in a third country is covered by the group internal model, other issues need to be considered. By definition, the internal model tests and standards should be met by the internal model globally, and therefore also in relation with the coverage of third country risks within the scope of the model.

Besides, if the third country jurisdiction does not allow the use of internal models for the calculation of the solvency requirements, compliance with the use test in relation to the activities of the third country subsidiary could be a challenge, particularly if the local solvency regime leads to material differences between the Solvency II capital requirement derived by the internal model and the local capital requirement. In addition, the risk management implication of using an internal model could, in some circumstances, create some inconsistency with the local requirements. All those implications should be analysed by the group when making the choice on the method to calculate its Solvency II group capital requirement.

This third country is an example of specific cases where, although theoretically internal models provide the most appropriate way to assess the specific risks faced by a subsidiary, the challenges associated with their approval and use might sometimes provide groups with incentives to leave some subsidiaries outside the scope of the internal model. Nevertheless, when taking the decision to include or exclude a subsidiary based in a third country from the scope of the internal model, the group should also consider the implications (such as potential benefit) for the risk management of the group.

Calculation of the group SCR when some entities are excluded from the scope of the internal model

Where some subsidiaries are outside the scope of the model, it is necessary to integrate the SCR calculated by the model and the SCR calculated by the standard formula in order to assess the group SCR. The fact that some entities were left out of the scope will, by definition, lead the model to be partial, and the group will have to comply with the partial internal model requirements, This sub-section illustrates how the partial internal model described in Chapter 2 for solo entities will have to be adapted for groups.

For solo entities, even if the Solvency II framework allows for the use of partial internal models for the calculation of the SCRs in relation to major business units, it is expected that the use of internal models will be mainly partial in term of risk modules or sub-modules. On the other hand, in a group context, internal models are more likely to be partial in terms of legal entities (which form major business units).

As a preliminary remark, it is important to note that while a group internal model may include within its scope entities that are considered in the calculation via the D&A method, the issue of integration that is prescribed for partial internal models is not relevant in this case. Indeed, this method simply prescribes adding up capital requirements assessed at solo level.[4] Therefore, the focus is placed here on the default method, and it is supposed that some entities, although being considered within the consolidation scope, are not included in the internal model scope.

Theoretically, the same set of integration techniques that are available for a solo partial internal model could be used to assess the SCR for the consolidation scope, namely to integrate risks assessed through the standard formula and risks included in the partial group internal model. Nevertheless, at group level, the choice of the integration technique is likely to be different due to the following reasons. First, the correlation matrices from the standard formula are not appropriate for an internal model from which some entities have been excluded. Second, some default techniques rely on assumptions and have limitations that do not allow their use in some cases (eg, to integrate whole entities within the group). As a consequence, it can be expected that in most cases the choice is between simple, prudent methods and advanced techniques requiring thorough analysis of dependencies between risks.

In practice, it appears that the magnitude of the difference between capital requirements for the standard formula scope and for the internal model scope is the main factor leading to the choice between the simple sum (easy to apply) and the other integration techniques, allowing for some diversification benefit. Indeed, should the standard formula results be non-material compared to the model results (or vice versa, although it is not expected that a partial internal model will be developed in that case), then the expected diversification effects are also less significant and do not justify the use of a more sophisticated integration technique.

Where the expected diversification benefit between both the standard formula scope and the internal model scope is substantial, groups are incentivised to develop robust methodologies to derive the group capital requirement that reflect the diversification. A practical approach is to "sub-consolidate" two components of the capital requirements: one for the scope of the internal model and one for the risks covered by the standard formula. As a result of such approach, there is only one correlation to assess. However, this means creating a sub-consolidation level that might not be useful for any other purpose, such as accounting, and this might be not an easy task.

Additionally, it is very difficult to express a dependency between different entities, encompassing many risks, by a single number, especially when one would like to reflect possible stress scenarios. This would require the considerations to be based almost exclusively on expert judgement or to carry out detailed analysis of the dependencies between the risks covered in both components. In practice, justifying the appropriateness of the method might prove to be as challenging as using more sophisticated approaches. For additional considerations on the development and selection of integration techniques, please refer to the chapter on partial internal models.

GROUP INTERNAL MODEL: MODELLING ISSUES

Consistent approach for internal model for groups

The Solvency II directive provides for the possibility that a group internal model is used for the calculation of both the group and solo SCRs. However, anecdotal evidence from colleges of supervisors and groups highlights the challenges of putting in practice this uniqueness requirement. For example, assume there is a group with only two entities writing the same business in two different countries. One modelling option is to develop a risk module for each one of the risks covered by both entities (centralised model); another option is to develop two "sub-internal models", where the group internal model is merely the aggregation of the figures coming from the two sub-models (decentralised model). This very simple example illustrates the multiplicity of modelling options available and the associated challenges for supervisors to ensure a consistent treatment of internal model applications.

Arguments for the use of the same risk module of the internal model are the following. It ensures consistency across the group, and therefore is easier to implement from a group perspective (a unique methodological document, for example) and easier to supervise. Using the same risk module for different entities within the group also facilitates a better group-wide risk management and ensures consistent decisions (eg, measure of performance of business activities and capital allocation across those activities). From a more technical point of view, developing a unique modelling approach based on a bigger sample of data could reduce the model error and the uncertainty of the results produced.

The arguments in favour of a decentralised approach are usually based on the rationale that the insurance business is not strictly comparable from one entity to the other, and that each sub-model would reflect better the individual risks than a unique model covering all entities. This argument is especially relevant for life insurance, given the importance of the loss-absorbing capacity of technical provisions and the variety of products across Europe with different legal and contractual provisions (eg, profit sharing). In addition, it ensures that the solo capital requirements are explicitly in line with the contribution to the group SCR. In a centralised model, groups face more difficulties in assessing the solo SCR, as it is potentially challenging to demonstrate that the calibration of the model is relevant for both the group and the solo entities.

A possible way to reconcile a centralised and a decentralised approach is the adoption of a single modelling methodology that ensures consistency across the group but allows for specific calibrations of the methods for the group and the solo capital requirements. This approach should be considered during the validation of the internal model to ensure that the different calibrations reflect appropriately the risk profiles of the entities and, in particular, that the results at group level are consistent with the results at a solo level (for instance, the results do not overstate the diversification between entities).

Consistent assessment by supervisors

From a supervisory point of view, in order to achieve a level playing field, it is very important to ensure that the assessments of different groups' internal models are carried out in a consistent way. Supervisors need to co-operate closely within the supervisory colleges, as well as promoting common interpretations and a consistent implementation of the requirements. This is additionally supported by the development of guidelines by the EIOPA and other activities fostering a consistent implementation of Solvency II.

However the word "consistent" should not be understood as "similar". Every model has its own specificity. An approach that is right for one group is not necessarily appropriate for another. Similarly, the "right" model for one entity is not necessarily the "right" model for a different entity. These quite obvious statements have important consequences. First, supervisors are aware that they do not assess the model *per se*, but how the model reflects the risk profile of the company. Therefore, it is not sufficient to assess the technical aspects of the model but the assessment of the model must also consider whether, taking into account the whole activities of the entity or group, the SCR calculation is appropriate. Second, when a modelling approach is approved for use by an entity or a group, it does not imply that this approach is more suitable than a modelling approach submitted to the supervisory authority for the first time. Third, an approach that is accepted as current market practice may not be deemed appropriate by the supervisors. An accepted market practice is not necessarily compliant with the internal model requirements. In particular the implementation of the method, including the analysis and evidence supporting the justification, the validation, the documentation, the governance and the use of the model are important to achieve compliance with the requirements. Such universally used tools might generate a systemic risk, which is very difficult to identify and, even if identified, difficult to challenge and manage. In this context, supervisory colleges perform an important role by facilitating consistent model assessments.

Use test

The use test requires firms and groups to build and change their internal models, and so plays an important role in risk management and other decision-making processes.

For a group internal model that calculates both the group and solo SCRs, the use test has to be fulfilled both at group and solo levels. In these instances, particular attention should be given to the compliance of the group model with the use test at a solo level. Group models are often built and developed at group level, and present the group perspective, and some factors have different impact at solo and the group level. From the solo supervisor perspective, it is very important that the group point of view coincide with solo one in the sense that the model is embedded in the solo activity and not only used to calculate the capital requirement.

The solo entity using the model to calculate its SCR must demonstrate that it uses the model in its risk management and decision-making processes. An internal model for the group that is developed and operated without any involvement from the entities within its scope is unlikely to comply with the Solvency II requirements. This implies some active involvement by the solo entity in the development and operation of the model to be able to demonstrate the requirements – for example, to demonstrate the understanding of the model and to ensure that the model and its results reflect the solo risk profile. To this end, the solo entity may contribute to the documentation of the model, have the possibility to recalculate its capital requirement with the model if needed, and to propose and introduce changes to the model when the model does not reflect its specificity. Symmetrically, an internal model for the group that is developed and operated without taking into account the group perspective is unlikely to achieve compliance with the requirements at group level.

Group risks

In addition to the risks arising from the activities of the solo entities, some specific risks arise or become material at group level. When they are quantifiable and material they should be reflected in the SCR.

As the standard formula for groups applies *mutatis mutandis* the solo calculation methods, it does not reflect some characteristics that are specific to groups. For instance, the calibration of the standard formula (tailored to an average group) is less likely to be appropriate for a group due to the higher discrepancy of a risk profile at group level. Therefore, it could arise that even groups that intended to use the standard formula might have to build a partial internal model if the group-specific risks are material. As opposed to the standard formula, the internal model framework allows for an individual approach where the structure of the group, the capital links and the scope of activities can be appropriately captured. One could indicate that at the solo level the impact of group-specific risks can also arise. However, the group level is more appropriate because the consistency with the pure solo position is desirable and groups have more information on data for such risks.

Two types of group-specific risks can be distinguished. The first type are the risks that exist at a solo level as well at the group level (eg, concentration risk), which require a different approach to modelling or calibration at each level, particularly where they are material only at group level. The second type of risks materialises only through the existence of a group – for example, reputational risk, contagion risk or risks inherent to the activities performed at group level, such as asset management, when performed by the head of the group.

Some of the group risks could be managed or better addressed through risk management and by putting in place appropriate mitigation actions (eg, strategic risk) that are not covered by the Solvency II capital requirement. Nevertheless, other group risks need to be included in the calculation of the capital requirement. For instance, particular attention should be given to risks impacting the dependency between the entities component of the group, such as concentration or possible contagion.

A quantitative approach to group-specific risks creates a real challenge for both supervisors and groups. It may be implemented using specific scenarios, which would cover, for example, reputational risk materialising through a higher lapse rate (than in the basic case), higher acquisition costs, lower renewal rate or the earlier withdrawal of a counterparty from the contract. Lower participation values, a failure of an internal reinsurer (with its operational implications) or other member of the group to which the group is exposed may be used to build scenarios to reflect the contagion risk. The concentration risk might be analysed by another calibration of the solo cases or by a scenario lowering the value of specific concentrated assets. The tail dependency should also be considered between such risks.

The legal structure of an organisation is not neutral with regards to its legal obligations, especially in a crisis situation. Therefore, groups have to prove that their internal model appropriately reflects the various risks inherent to their structure via the calibration, specific risk modules or demonstrating that "group specific risks" are reduced via risk-mitigation techniques or adequate internal control processes.

Single entity approach, implication for internal models

The single entity approach is reflected in the Solvency II regime through the accounting consolidation as the default method to calculate the group solvency. This approach considers the group as if it were a single entity, and has some implications not only for the calculation of the capital requirement, but also for the calculation of eligible group own funds; however, the latter is not specific to groups using an internal model to calculate its SCR.

Supervisors should be aware that while the accounting consolidation may be useful for some purposes (for example, to form a view of the solvency position of the group as a whole), there could be many reasons why this concept might turn out to be purely theoretical. This can stem both from the company's management, who could be reluctant to provide capital injections into some subsidiaries, as well as from regulators who, in order to protect the policyholders in their jurisdiction, may prohibit the transfer of capital between entities in different jurisdictions. This is conceivable not only in relation with third country jurisdictions, but also within the EEA in the absence of a common insurance guarantee scheme.

In order to reflect the actual group situation, groups should demonstrate that the assessment of the restrictions of fungibility and transferability of the capital in the group are properly addressed in the group internal model overall via *inter alia* the assessment of the available own funds.

It is worth mentioning that theoretically the group has the possibility to restrict its responsibility towards the subsidiary to the level of its participation when they expect that some restrictions in capital injections may be introduced (eg, by shareholders in spite of reputational risk). Before adopting such a possibility to calculate the capital requirement of the group, it is important to consider that while the possibility may exist to limit the group responsibility *ex post* – when a particular stress situation occurs – its adoption *ex ante* – for the modelling of the group capital requirement – implies severe restriction to the diversification benefit that can be included in the calculation of the capital requirement. Indeed, the benefit of the diversification between the entities of the group arises from the ability to cover the deficit in one entity using the surplus in another one, creating some mutualisation that is restricted by a strict limitation of the group responsibility. The Solvency II regime assumes an *ex ante* approach as otherwise, in the case of intended limited liability, the single entity approach would introduce the inconsistency between the model and the practice.

GROUP INTERNAL MODEL VERSUS INTERNAL MODEL FOR THE GROUP SCR CALCULATION

Difference between internal models' applications under Articles 231 and 230

Within the Solvency II framework, there are two possibilities to apply for the use of an internal model that calculates the group SCR:

(i) an application for the calculation of both the group solvency capital requirement and some solo SCRs (hereafter called a group internal model); and
(ii) an application to calculate only the group solvency capital requirement (internal model for the group SCR).

The first approach refers to Article 231, the second to Article 230 of the Solvency II directive, respectively. When a group submits an application to use an internal model to calculate only the group SCR (ii) above, it should provide evidence to the supervisor that the choice has not been motivated by cherry-picking. Otherwise, the supervisors have to pay particular attention to whether the use of a group internal model to calculate the group capital requirement as well as the capital requirement for the solo entities within the scope of the model provides an application of the internal model consistent with the objectives of an internal model for groups (see below). The use of an internal model for the calculation of the group SCR alone may cause inconsistencies in the calculation of the SCR for entities within the group and may create other problems, which will be discussed further here.

Objectives of an internal model for groups

It is worth keeping in mind that the scope of a group internal model for the calculation of the group SCR – ie, the risks and entities covered by the model – can be different than the use of the model for the calculation of the SCR for the entities within the scope of the model. For instance, let us assume that a group is made of three insurance entities: A, B and C. The group internal model can be used to calculate the group capital requirement as well as the capital requirements for entities A and B, but not for entity C, which will calculate its capital requirement using the standard formula.

The advantages of a group internal model for calculating the group capital requirement as well as some solo capital requirements are many, both for groups as well as for supervisors. From an insurance group perspective, it provides a unique framework for the different steps of the lifecycle of the internal model – ie, design, calibration, implementation, operation and further changes – a unique process for the initial application, the reporting of minor changes and the application for major changes.

A group internal model also allows a better comparability and consistency of its use across the group, providing a powerful tool to assess, manage and report risks. For instance, some reports to the senior management or board of the group and the solo entities can be developed to provide similar and comparable information, the performance of the different businesses can be measured consistently and the capital allocation can be based on a very coherent approach.

The process of model development provides the framework for a consistent assessment of risks generated by the various parts of the group. The modelling choices can be informed by the similarities and differences in risk profile between the group and the local entities, allowing for benchmarking and backtesting between the group and solo SCR calibrations, as the group management needs to ensure that all risks are treated in a consistent manner.

In addition, the group internal model offers a unique integrated risk management tool to support consistent risk management processes and activities. For instance, some data collection processes can be streamlined and some consistent outputs produced. Finally, the group risk management has a better appreciation of the different risks of the group and also of their evolution over time. The group model also allows a more efficient challenge of the assessment of risks by the local entities and local risk managements.

From a supervisor perspective, an application for the use of a group internal model allows both the group and the solo supervisors to develop a comprehensive view of the model, and therefore provides the assurance that similar risks stemming from different entities are considered in a consistent way on an ongoing basis. It also allows the different supervisors involved in the process to receive comfort that some risks are not under- or overestimated at solo or group level, preventing concerns about the adequacy of the capital allocation within the group.

Moreover, an application for a group internal model through the collaboration of the supervisors promotes a consistent approach by the supervisors involved on the specific issues that might arise, largely by removing the burden for the group to face some divergent implementations of the solvency II rules. A group internal model application avoids the duplications of assessment by the supervisors that arise when several applications are submitted. This allows supervisors to share experience on modelling options used in a more efficient way. In particular, when assessing compliance with the use test and governance requirements, supervisors can ensure that the treatment of risks is adequate within the group through proper communication and challenges between the group and local risk management.

A group internal model reduces the incentive of creating regulatory arbitrage, either through the selection of inconsistent modelling techniques for different part of the group or the introduction of intragroup transactions to create possibilities of regulatory arbitrages.

Advantages and challenges for groups and supervisors for applications based on Article 230

When an application is submitted for the calculation of the group SCR alone, groups can focus on modelling from the group perspective and not have to reflect local specificities at the same level of granularity as when the model is also used to calculate the solo SCRs. This may lead to a less complex model that is easier to develop, maintain and review.

Additionally, if the application is assessed by only one supervisor, it can speed up and simplify the process. The limited scope of application could also reduce the administrative burden due to the need to translate the documents, and avoid potential delays in the supervisory assessment that might arise from the joint decision process on the application by the different supervisors that are part of the group internal model decision.

However, an internal model used to calculate the group SCR but not the solo capital requirements might overlook some local issues and risk specificities that are material at group level, due to an insufficient involvement of solo entities and solo supervisors that have an in-depth and detailed knowledge of the risks arising from those entities. For instance, the model for the group might address in a simplified way a risk which, in fact, taking into account its significance for a solo firm, would require a much more advanced approach. Therefore, for this type of model, due to the way they are formulated the fulfilment of the internal models standards is much more challenging than for group internal models. This is a consequence of the difference between models subject to Article 230 and group internal models subject to Article 231, as they are developed for different purposes and the former does not aim to calculate solo SCRs *ab initio*.

In the case of a group intending to extend the use of a model to calculate solo SCRs, the model developed might not fully reflect some solo specificities that are not material at group level, and which may make the model unsuitable at solo level. The question arises whether it would indeed be easier to expand the model that was built for the group solvency capital calculation purpose or to build a group internal model that also calculated some solo capital requirements and took into account a more comprehensive perspective.

An insurance group could consider developing the internal model in stages, first for its use at group level and later for a more intensive use for the local entities within its scope. In that context, the insurance group might submit an application to use the model only for the calculation of the group SCR in the first stage, and then extend the application for the calculation of some solo capital requirements as well at a later stage. Such an approach needs to be planned carefully, as a limited focus on the issues material at group level during the first stage might impair the ability to adequately reflect the local specificities at a later stage. It could be more efficient to take into account the local perspective at an earlier stage of the model development when key decisions are taken – for instance, decisions related to modelling techniques or the granularity that will significantly impact the dependency structure of the model.

Nonetheless, if planned carefully, the development of a model and the application for the calculation of the capital requirement in stages may in some cases be an appropriate option. There could be advantages for the group supervisor to deal initially with a simpler model that allows for concentrating the group and supervisory attention and efforts on the most material risks at group level. However, as mentioned earlier, the model might require fundamental changes in methodology to be used and approved by the supervisors for the calculation of some solo capital requirements at a later stage.

From a practical and legal point of view, if an application is submitted under Article 231 for a group model already approved under Article 230, it will be treated as a new application and the decision is likely to be made through a joint decision by the supervisors of the entities applying to use the model for the calculation of their capital requirements. The decision will be collegial unless all the entities applying to use the model are headquartered in the jurisdiction of the group supervisor. In most cases, solo supervisors participating in the joint decision are under time pressure, as at the time of the application they are less familiar with the internal model than the group supervisor, who gave previous approval for the calculation of the group SCR. Occasionally, this situation might create some additional difficulties due to the fact that a decision was made for the group calculation alone, while a decision on the same model now needs to be made for an extended use. If, for example, the modelling at solo level has some significant shortcomings and solo supervisors are not satisfied with it, they have to reject the model that has already been formally accepted. It is desirable to avoid situations that can create confusion. However, in this context, it is important to remember that an approval is given not for a model *per se*, but for the model to be used to calculate the capital requirement of the group (and solo firms, in this case).

Through the joint decision mechanism in Article 231, the legislator gives the solo supervisors the opportunity to take part fully in the analysis and assessment of the solvency calculation at the group level. This is an important decision as the financial condition of the group could influence the solo entities at the same time as it impacts the ability for the group to support its related entities. As discussed above, the participation of solo supervisors at an early stage may be beneficiary for the group and the group supervisor, to be aware of solo supervisors' expectation and reservations on the model based on their experience in solo supervision. Article 230 encompasses only the group capital requirement and not the solo ones, and is therefore not subject to the joint decision mechanism.

COLLEGES CO-OPERATION

Supervisors from all EEA member states are involved in group supervision through a college of supervisors. They share information within the college and co-operate to carry out their supervisory activities across the group. The assessment of an internal model application and the appropriate further reviews and assessments are only one area in which the supervisory college is deployed.

Role of the college in the assessment of an internal model application

The college of supervisors has an active role in the assessment of an internal model for the calculation of the group SCR. The group supervisor plays a key part in the assessment of the model, although other members or participants in the college also are involved. The responsibility of the solo supervisors depends on the scope of the internal model application. The supervisors of entities within the group that apply to use the model to calculate their capital requirement – referred to as supervisory authorities concerned in the Solvency II text – take part in the joint decision on the application. The supervisors of entities within the scope of the model that will not use the model to calculate their capital requirement –referred to as supervisory authorities involved in the Solvency II text – will be consulted on the application as their knowledge of the entities within the scope of the internal model is important for the assessment of the application. In addition, any supervisors of entities outside the scope of the internal model may be invited to participate in the review of the application in relation to the assessment of the limited scope of the model.

During assessment of the application, the supervisors within the college set out a work plan that includes the activities related to the assessment of the application, and co-ordinate and allocate the tasks between themselves and in consultation with the insurance group. This co-ordination is to ensure an effective assessment of the application in relation to the scope of the model. In particular, supervisors evaluate the appropriateness of a limited scope of the model for a partial model when either some risks or entities are not covered by the model or some solo capital requirements are not calculated using the internal model. A partial internal model is entirely consistent with the solvency II framework; however, supervisors pay special attention to the limited scope of the model that can result in an underestimation of the capital requirement.

This part of the assessment benefits from the contribution of the supervisors that are not part of the joint decision as appropriate, and in particular the supervisors of entities totally or partially within the scope of the model for the calculation of the group SCR. Their knowledge of the related entities, as well as their expertise in the risks involved in the insurance practices and insurance products offered in this market, is valuable for the assessment of the application. For this reason, their contribution to the assessment, through the college, aims at improving the effectiveness and also the depth of the assessment. For instance, the supervisor of an entity within the scope of the model can take on the task of reviewing technical aspects of the methodology for the modelling of insurance products or risks specific to that market. The solo supervisor can also be involved in the assessment of the use test and governance requirements related to the internal model applicable at the solo level.

The effective assessment of the application from the supervisors as well as from the insurance group perspective depends not only on the activities of the relevant supervisory authorities, but also on the preparatory work, the quality of the submission and the arrangements made during the assessment phase by the insurance group. Participation in the pre-application process provides the opportunity for the insurance group to be better prepared for the application, but its effectiveness also depends on the development plan and its implementation by the insurance group. As challenges arising from co-operation within the college are acknowledged by the supervisors, challenges faced by the insurance group and entities within the group to deliver a successful internal model application should not be underestimated. For example, planning activities involving a large set of functions, and skilled and delivered according to plan in a context of controlled resources and conflicting priorities, is an environment experienced by both insurance groups and supervisory authorities.

Overall, good co-operation between the insurance group and its entities and the supervisory colleges is key to achieving not only efficient pre-application and application processes, but also smooth ongoing interactions once the model is approved. Both supervisory authorities and insurance groups should consider and plan for the activities related to the internal model when approval is granted. The approval of major changes to the model may require the same or a similar level of interaction as the initial approval, but the quality of ongoing interaction may also reduce the workload related to model change approval.

Role of third countries supervisors

The supervisory authorities from jurisdictions outside of the EEA – ie, third country supervisors – in charge of the supervision of entities in an insurance group headquartered in the EEA may be invited to participate in the assessment of the application by the members of the college, subject to professional secrecy and confidentiality requirements. Where the third country regime has not been recognised as equivalent to Solvency II in terms of professional secrecy, the possibilities for exchange of information will be restricted.

The group supervisor, in conjunction with other EEA supervisors' members of the college, may engage with the third country supervisor during the assessment of the application for an internal model, particularly when related entities located in the third country are within the scope of the internal model for the calculation of the group capital requirement. As a priority, the co-operation might aim at ensuring that all risks are properly taken into account in the group capital requirements. In addition, the international co-operation between supervisors might also consider how the differences in the supervisory regimes could create the potential for regulatory arbitrage and the potential impact on the efficiency of the group supervision, especially for the SCR. In particular, the group supervisor and other supervisors concerned might consider how the treatment of intra-group transactions such as participation or internal reinsurance impacts the SCRs of the insurance entities within the group.

The level of co-operation with third country supervisors are constrained by the regime of professional secrecy, but also by the willingness and ability – for instance, in terms of resources and in relation to its experience in reviewing the capital model – of the third country supervisor to engage with the Solvency II college and to participate in some of its activities.

Role of host supervisors in the internal model approval process

The Solvency II directive sets some rights and duties to the group supervisor, particularly for the guiding of the college and also during the decision process related to the internal model application.

However, the role of host supervisors – ie, the supervisors of insurance entities within the group – is essential during and after the assessment of the application for an internal model. The first responsibility of the host supervisor is the supervision of the insurance entities headquartered in its jurisdiction, including the assessment of the SCR. When the capital requirement is calculated using the group internal model, the Solvency II regime grants the host supervisor joint decision in the approval of the group internal model. In that case, a close co-operation between supervisors that are part of the joint decision on the application is needed, not only to achieve an efficient use of supervisory resources, but also to ensure that the considerations related to the calculation of the solo capital requirements together with the considerations related to the calculation of the group capital requirement are taken into account in the decisions on the assessment activities, as well as during the final decision.

A practical challenge is the allocation of resources from both the group and the host supervisors to the supervisory activities related to the group internal model and, in particular, the assessment of the application. In order for the group and solo considerations to receive balanced attention, appropriate resources need to be dedicated by the group and host supervisors. Depending on the structure of the model and the business model of the insurance group, the review activities can be more efficiently performed by the group or the host supervisors. For instance, if the model is developed centrally within the insurance group, the group supervisor by its regular interaction with the group may have a better knowledge of the context and specifications of the model than the host supervisors. Nevertheless, it is important that the host supervisors participate in the assessment without any limitations and have detailed knowledge about the model to ensure that the risks are appropriately captured by the model, and that the capital requirements for the solo entities are appropriate as solo calculations are based on methodologies developed by the group.

The assessment carried out by the solo supervisor has a different aim than the one carried out by the group supervisor. The solo supervisor primarily assesses how suitable the group model is for the solo firm, while the group supervisor is interested in how the model appropriately reflects the group as a whole. Solo supervisors will not be able to take a decision within their responsibilities without knowledge about the model and whether the model is developed centrally or not.

Host supervisors are also expected to play a central role in assessing implementation within the local entity of centrally developed modelling techniques, processes and governance, including any specific calibration and validation in relation to the calculation of the local capital requirement. In cases where the internal model is built in a more decentralised way, due for instance to the structure and business model of the insurance group or to modelling choices, the assessment of the application might require an even greater role of the host supervisors.

Where applications are only for the calculation of the group capital requirement, host supervisors involved in the assessment may be unable to dedicate similar resources and a greater part of the review might have to be undertaken by the group supervisor. Nevertheless, an efficient assessment of the application may require an allocation of tasks not according to solo/group issues, but according to the topic and expertise of the supervisors, as well as from resource limitation.

During the review and assessment of the application, it is important that the supervisors involved exchange findings and views for the sake of efficiency, but also in order to identify as early as possible any difference in view, so as to prepare the decision process. The discussions in the college provide an opportunity for an early planning of review activities and the steps for the decision process.

Joint decision and mediation by EIOPA

As discussed, the decision on an application for an internal model to calculate the group capital requirement as well as the solo capital requirements for some of the group entities has to be made jointly by all the supervisors of the insurance entities applying to use the group internal model to calculate their capital requirement. The work of the college, as well as the specific activities related to the assessment of the application, form the basis for the decision. It is expected that the collaboration between supervisors will, for most of the application, lead to a shared supervisory decision. Nevertheless, each supervisory authority is expected to form its own view based on its own assessment and following its internal process. In some rare cases, it will not be possible to reach a joint decision within the timeframe set out in the directive.

One approach available to resolve situations where no joint decision can be reached is for a supervisor that is part of the joint decision process to refer to EIOPA, who may make a binding decision in according with its rules and regulation. In the absence of a joint decision, and as long as EIOPA has not been engaged in the mediation process referred to above, the group supervisor must make a decision on the application.

Where the solo supervisor considers the decision by the group supervisor or EIOPA to be unsatisfactory, it can impose a capital add-on to the solo capital requirement or require the solo entity to calculate its capital requirement by using the standard formula. In other words, where there are divergent views, the host supervisor can employ measures but only to be applied in exceptional circumstances. The asymmetry of power between the home and host supervisors is more visible when the group is granted permission to be subject to centralised risk management, as the power of solo supervisors to introduce even last-resort measures is also subject to binding decision of EIOPA.

It is worth mentioning here that the procedure of EIOPA making a binding decision provides an additional asymmetry between group and solo supervisors. According to the EIOPA regulation and Omnibus II directive, in cases where the group supervisor has the power of ultimate decision (eg, the group internal model application), the mediation panel proposal may be rejected more easily (through a blocking minority) than when the power of the ultimate decision is given to the solo supervisor (eg, capital add-ons under centralised risk management). The rejection of the recommendation means that the group supervisor decides about the application in spite of the fact that disagreements between supervisors should be resolved by the binding mediation procedure. Therefore, the mechanism of the blocking minority weakens the role of binding mediation.

MATERIALITY AND PROPORTIONALITY: HOW TO AVOID DISREGARDING IMPORTANT ISSUES FROM THE GROUP PERSPECTIVE

It is clear from the examples illustrated in this chapter that the use of internal models to calculate the group SCR raises numerous challenges, both from an insurance group and supervisory perspective. A particular issue is the application of materiality thresholds. At group level, this is more complex than in the context of an internal model for an individual (ie, solo) insurance entity.

For instance, when a quantitative threshold is set as a percentage of the capital requirement, the application of the threshold should be considered both in the group and solo contexts. In particular, it is inappropriate to treat a risk as non-material for the model based only on quantitative threshold at group level when the model is also used to calculate local capital requirements.

Another area that deserves attention is the impact of the application of material thresholds at solo level for the assessment of risks at group level. For example, some entities within the group might face individual exposures to a risk deemed non-material (at their level), while the accumulation of risks across several entities may result in the risk being material for the group. A practical example is the exposure to a natural catastrophe risk, where each entity is writing a small book of business in a given geographical area.

CONCLUSION

When groups are applying for the use of an internal model to calculate the SCR, as when supervisors are reviewing and assessing their applications, the group dimension brings some additional questions and requires additional considerations. From a supervisory perspective, the supervisory college provides the structure for the relevant supervisors – potentially including third country supervisors – to co-ordinate and allocate activities between supervisors, and ultimately to take a joint decision. Moreover, insurance groups play an important role in the stability of the insurance markets and, due to the complexity of their risk profile, some groups are expected to submit an application for the use of an internal model. Therefore, the proper implementation of the internal model regime for groups is of utmost importance to the supervisors. From an insurance group perspective, a consistent risk management system across the entities within the scope of the model is needed as a foundation for the development and operation of the internal model.

Another issue peculiar to group internal models is the need to strike the right balance between group and solo risks. In particular, the group internal model should reflect appropriately the risks that are material to the group, but should not ignore risks that are material at solo level. This is important, especially when the model is also used at solo level for the calculation of the SCR. The host supervisors who are responsible for the appropriateness of the group model for solo purposes need to have appropriate competences and allocate the necessary resources to perform the tasks required by the Solvency II framework and local requirements. In this context, the binding mediation procedure and possibility of an internal model calculating only group capital requirements should not be abused, resulting in neglecting of solo specificities.

The opinions expressed in this chapter are those of the authors and do not necessarily reflect those of their respective employers.

1 Colleges of supervisors refer to multilateral groups of relevant supervisors that are formed for the collective purpose of enhancing the efficient, effective and consistent supervision of financial institutions operating across borders.

2 The Solvency II regime differentiates between several equivalence concepts; the one mentioned here relates to the solo capital requirements as described in the Article 227 of the Solvency II directive. This equivalence can be either permanent or provisional in order to ease the phasing-in.

3 In some cases, third country jurisdictions will not allow firms to calculate the SCR through the application of an internal model.

4 Nevertheless, these capital requirements could be calculated via a group internal model.

REFERENCES

CEIOPS, 2009, "Advice for Level 2 Implementing Measures on Solvency II on the Procedure to be Followed for the Approval of an Internal Model", October.

European Commission, "Delegated Acts to Solvency II Directive", 2014.

European Parliament and the Council of the European Union, 2009, "Directive 2009/138/EC of the European Parliament and of the Council of 25 November 2009 on the Taking-up and Pursuit of the Business of Insurance and Reinsurance (Solvency II) (recast)", November.

European Union, 2010, "Regulation (EU) No 1094/2010 of the European Parliament and of the Council of 24 November 2010 establishing a European Supervisory Authority (European Insurance and Occupational Pensions Authority), amending Decision No 716/2009/EC and repealing Commission Decision 2009/79/EC".

6

Use Test: Challenges and Opportunities

Christopher Chappell, Elliot Varnell; and Coomaren Vencatasawmy

Pension Insurance Corporation; and Prudential Regulation Authority, Bank of England

The use test is arguably the most important yet most challenging of the requirements that European supervisors have developed for the Solvency II internal model. The 2007–08 financial crisis highlighted the fallibility of internal models, and much has been written about the way risks were wrongly assessed and how early warnings were ignored because of internal models. There has also been a lot of discussion about the use of Gaussian copulas, and how these might have contributed to the financial crisis (Salmon, 2009). It should be recognised, however, that all models are wrong. We are very far from internal models that can closely replicate all real-life conditions, especially emerging ones. Therefore, saying that models caused the crisis is a moot point. The crisis was caused just as much by decision-makers and by how outputs from the models were used. This is why the use test is so crucial.

Internal models' failings have been mostly about how the models have been used within the decision process of financial institutions. Most of the issues related to failures to understand the weaknesses of the models used to assess risks and how the models were used in decision-making. As models become increasingly mathematically sophisticated in the search for the precise answers, there is a risk of neglecting the need for increased expertise in decision-makers that this creates.

The importance of the use test derives from the "delegation" of authority from the supervisor to the regulated entity for the calculation of the supervisory capital buffer. This delegation of authority represents possibly the biggest step change in the supervisory landscape for a long time. This delegation of authority was proposed with the aim to promote better risk management by moving the management of risks to where they were supposed to be better understood. Such a move was considered to be within the firms themselves and hence the delegation of authority made a great deal of sense.

However, this approach raises the question of where within the company the risks are better understood, and whether models used by regulated entities to calculate their economic capital represented the house view. Untangling the web of different opinions as to the risks faced by a firm – let alone getting embroiled in the firm's internal politics – was going to be challenging for supervisors.

The solution was therefore to short-circuit all this with a simple test: ask firms to show that they used their supervisory capital models for decision-making within the firms. Little guidance was offered on how to carry this out. The test was, and remains, an open question to firms: "Show us how you use this model".

In effect, the use test is the evidence that should support the relationship of trust between the supervisor and the regulated entity. The trust is regarding whether the internal model used by the firm to calculate supervisory capital reflects the true view of its risks. It is the trust that the model is not designed and calibrated with a view to lower the supervisory capital as much as possible, while making decisions using different models or processes.

A poor execution of the use test undermines that trust, while a good execution helps to build that trust.

COMPARISON TO THE BASEL USE TEST

Although Basel II includes a use test requirement (Morris, 2008), significant effort has been spent on finding ways to ensure that the models fitted the data used for calibration or past events rather than focusing on how the model was going to be used. In areas where appropriate data were not available, expert judgement was used without recognising some of the biases introduced by setting parameters this way. The technical validation of such models was done with some rigour, but without paying the necessary attention or considering situations outside the data sample used. Furthermore, lack of understanding of internal models by senior managers and other non-technical staff was an issue.

There was complete faith in the capital numbers produced by internal models. Internal models were built, used and maintained by a small group of quantitative people, although most of them were from the risk management function (although, in the UK insurance sector, most of these people reside in the actuarial function). Therefore, the most important validation of such models – ie, the validation by the business – never took place. In most cases, the people who took decisions about the portfolio of risks and risk mitigation did not actually use the internal model, either because of they were not available to them, the models suggested counterintuitive actions or the personal incentives were out of line with decisions suggested by the model.

THE UK ICA EXPERIENCE

Some European firms, especially in the UK, have some experience of using economic capital in decision-making because of the supervisory approach to insurance supervision, ie, the Individual Capital Assessment (ICA) regime. Certain firms have routinely used economic capital models to calculate the impact of mergers and acquisitions (M&A) activities on their capital requirement. Others have used the impact on the required capital to assess their business strategies. However, Solvency II imposes more stringent requirements around the understanding the internal modelling approach used and the understanding of the weaknesses of the internal model methodology.

Therefore, the next section will list the Solvency II requirements of the use test, followed by a discussion of its challenges. The business case for the use test is also introduced and governance around the use test laid out. The chapter will also address the issue of evidencing the use test, and examine an approach that firms could use to implement the use test. Some practical implementation for supervisors is then discussed, before a case study is presented.

REQUIREMENTS OF THE SOLVENCY II USE TEST

In the advice by the Committee of European Insurance and Occupational Pensions Supervisors (CEIOPS) for Level 2 implementing measures on Solvency II (CEIOPS 2009), the experience of the Basel II's internal ratings-based (IRB) approach to the use test is discussed. The CEIOPS document explains that the use test is a fundamental requirement towards the approval of an internal model for the calculation of the solvency capital requirement (SCR). From a supervisory perspective, the use test amounts to a trust in the internal model by the business. As such, the results of the internal model should play a key role in ranking risk, setting risk tolerance limits, assessing risk appetite and monitoring risks.

Article 120 of the Solvency II directive[1] sets out that an internal model should play an important role in the risk management system, but also that risk management should provide a feedback loop to improve the internal model. Through their own risk and solvency assessment (ORSA), internal model's firms should use their model for capital management, albeit potentially using different parameters. It is also expected that the internal model will play a crucial role in decision-making.

From a supervisory perspective, the rationale for the use test is the comfort it provides in ensuring that the internal model is appropriate given the risk profile of the firms, and is in line with how the firm takes decisions about risk. As a consequence, the use test imposes a unique/single modelling framework for capital-related decisions. Some confusion has arisen, as firms have often referred to it as a supervisory model when used to calculate the SCR and an economic capital model when referring to business decisions. However, although it can be confusing having the same model with two different names, it does help to explain potential differences in parameterisation. The foundation principle of the use test lays the path for a robust and high-quality internal model: "The undertaking's use of the internal model shall be sufficiently material to result in pressure to improve the quality of the internal model".[2]

Therefore, although the various uses of the internal model are important, the process around use is also key, as this should lead to improvements to the model. As stated earlier, the use test principles are laid out in Article 120 of the Solvency II directive. The requirements are around the use of the internal model in the system of governance, in particular in the risk management system and the ORSA. Article 120 also states that the administrative, management or supervisory body (AMSB) should ensure that the internal model remains appropriate at all times and reflects the risk profile of the firm. This is further expanded by the Solvency II delegated acts.[3] These delegated acts set the tone regarding what is expected from firms, including their ability to explain the different model uses and ensure consistency between the various model outputs. An internal model can consist of a number of parts, which can potentially produce various outputs and can also be presented and used with different levels of granularity. Any of these outputs could be used as evidence that the use test is met, but because of adjustments that could be made at various parts of the model, the firm should ensure that the outputs are consistent and that the decision is not missing potentially key components of the outputs.

In addition, the Solvency II internal modelling framework introduces requirements around the alignment of the design of the internal to the business model in areas such as risks, reporting and the granularity required for decision-making. Furthermore, requirements are set out around the understanding of the internal model, including (and in particular) the AMSB's understanding of the model. Other requirements are set around the internal model as a support to decision-making and the role it plays in the risk management system (eg, frequency of calculations and use of simplifications).

Chapter 3 of the EIOPA guidelines on the pre-application for internal models[4] provides further information on the use test requirements. More specifically, what is meant by "fit to the business", "support to decision-making" and "frequency of calculation". Further, the guidelines deal with how the supervisory authorities should assess compliance with the use test and the implications of the use test for a group internal model.

USE TEST CHALLENGES

The challenging nature of the use test is such that it empowers the supervisor to closely examine the heart of a firm's decision-making while complicating the stakeholder dynamics within the firm. This is achieved as part of the internal model approval process, when a major change to the model is required, or when the supervisors are reviewing firms' compliance with the internal model's test and standards.

In the UK, many decisions are examined as part of a change control, which needs either supervisory approval or when firms informally notify the Prudential Regulation Authority (PRA) about a strategic decision. However, in these circumstances, the supervisor might only see a few of the alternatives and the final decision, rather than the end-to-end process, to reach a conclusion. On the other hand, with the introduction of the use test requirement, a supervisor could potentially require the firm to explain how the final decision was reached, rather than simply asking whether the conclusion has been validated by the internal model.

This can potentially complicate the supervisor/firm interaction, as the supervisory model cannot be free-formed to reflect the pure views of the firm. There are many (subjective) decisions to be taken in calculating the firm's reserves and capital. However, many of these views have been prescribed within regulation, which can result in different dynamics for the internal economic balance sheet and the regulatory Solvency II balance sheet. Examples include:

- asset admissibility;
- contract boundaries;
- own fund eligibility;
- transferability of capital;
- fungibility of capital; and
- liquidity premiums.

Where firms' views differ from the supervisor, the internal model will necessarily reflect the supervisory perspective and not the firm's one, as this would impose challenges with respect to the use test. The use test provisions require firms to assess the impact of a strategic decision on the SCR to avoid breaches to the capital requirement as a consequence of a firm's decision. However, firms are allowed, and even encouraged, to use their own view of the risks based on the examples listed above, as long as the same modelling framework is used. Many firms usually have an economic capital model that uses the same modelling framework as the supervisory model. However, there is an additional requirement to reconcile the economic capital view to the SCR. This requirement can be onerous to the firm if it has different views about the examples above. In any case, it might still be quite onerous to do this reconciliation for all the alternative views. Therefore, firms might be tempted to ignore the economic capital's view and base their decisions on the SCR. This may lead to some issues, as it would be difficult to convince the supervisors that the proposed course of action is in compliance with the use test.

Furthermore, there is always the risk that the supervisor might not be satisfied with the approach followed by a firm over the importance or severity of a risk factor. Where the firm adjusts its view to meet the supervisory request – or is forced to amend its view to be able to use its internal model for supervisory purposes – the model will increasingly reflect the view of the supervisor and not that of the firm. This is likely to impose further challenges to the ability of the firm to demonstrate compliance with the use test.

However, this could happen for good or bad reasons. A good example would be where the supervisor is able to evidence the inappropriateness of the firm's approach. For instance, based on additional information/insight gained during the internal model's review/monitoring process, the supervisor shows that the risk profile of the firm is not adequately captured by the internal model and provides feedback to help the firm improve its model. Sharing an understanding of the risk through a workshop is a good way of getting a common awareness of the risk, being clear where there are areas of disagreement and realising what steps needs to be taken to resolve the disagreement.

A bad example would be where a supervisor disagrees with the firm, but does not articulate the rationale for its views. This may generate confusion with the firm as to whether the additional reserves/capital required is due to a firm's failure to adequately capture a risk or to a supervisory benchmarking exercise whose results indicate the firm as an outlier. For example, is the firm discontinuing a specific line of business because it provides a poor return on capital, or does the return on capital look poor because the supervisor does not share the firm's views on the assumptions?

Another example is where the assumptions of the internal models are not widely shared across the firms, and are forced into the firm's decision-making process. This makes the relationship with, and messaging to, the owners of the business (who are typically the shareholders) more difficult. How shareholders will react to these potential scenarios is likely to emerge in the near future as product mixes change and investor perceptions of how the returns on capital in private sector insurance compare and correlate to those in other sectors.

A second difficulty is related to where the decisions are taken in the firm. According to Solvency II, the internal model should be owned by the risk function. However, many of the firm's decisions are taken outside the risk function. This poses a challenge. In some cases, decision needs to be taken quickly, but also some of the internal models are not easily portable to systems outside the risk function. Furthermore, the output of the internal model may need to be further processed before it can be used in decision-making. This requires an appropriate output format at the right level of granularity, and an internal model that is able to execute runs in a reasonably short time. Therefore, the challenge for the risk function is in developing a framework (for example, including risk limits) that works with the decision-making processes. Achieving this will help evidence the use of the model in decision-making.

However, risk-taking decisions do not originate in the risk function but in the front office of the business. For example:

- asset selection – in the investment function;
- funding structure – in the finance function;
- acquisitions – in the strategy function;
- customer communication strategy – in the sales function; and
- product design – in the marketing function.

Challenges will occur within the organisation, where the decision that would have been taken without recourse to the internal model would be different when the internal model is consulted. To some extent, this is precisely what Solvency II aims to achieve with its internal model regime – to increase the influence of (supervisor-approved) statistical models and the risk function in the decision-making within the regulated entities.

The first challenge in achieving this outcome is to ensure statistical models are a part of the decision-making process. Decisions are made according to one of the following mechanisms (Anand, 1993; Gigerenzer, 1999; and Kahneman, 2011):

- heuristics;
- logic/process; and
- statistical/uncertainty.

Of these, the most powerful technique is heuristics – shortcuts that people use to get quick decisions that are approximately right. This is the most fundamental decision-making process, as it is the type of decision-making that has driven evolutionary development. In business, it manifests as expert judgement/wise counsel/grey wisdom, etc.

Using logic is a more structured approach to decision-making, in that it is a process of deduction in which one event follows on from another. Typically, the logical sequence of events is based on a best guess of what will happen. While not having the evolutionary heritage of heuristic decision-making, the use of logic does date back over 2000 years to Aristotle (at least in western culture). In business, logic-based decision-making manifests itself as process engineering, project planning or just plain logical analysis.

By contrast, a probabilistic approach is a comparatively recent discipline, formalised only in the last 200 years or so. It is perhaps not surprising, therefore, if decision-making based on probability (or statistics) is somewhat rarer and less well accepted. The challenge for the risk function is to get probability and statistics a seat at the decision-making table, so that probability and statistics have a chance to compete with more well-established decision-making techniques such as heuristics and logic.

The chief risk officer (CRO) needs to ensure that the limitations of the internal model, as an accurate predictor of future uncertainty, are factored into the application of expert judgement of the other executives, which will naturally include heuristics and logical thinking.[5] When logic appears well thought through and is backed up by the expert judgement of well experienced executives, the defence of using a probabilistic statistical model to make the decision is no small task – and the model should expect to come under heavy scrutiny by the decision-makers. This leads us to the next challenge.

The second challenge for the risk function occurs where the decision-makers accept that probability/statistical models should have a say in the decision-making, but disagree with the model of the risk function. This can happen for a number of reasons:

- reality is too complex;
- model is developed in a silo;
- benchmark to other risk functions; and
- the model is complex to explain to a board.

The first of these, that reality is too complex, occurs when the risk function needs to develop a model than is not too complex and this model does not capture key dynamics of the real world – as seen by the risk-takers. An example would be where a credit model maps all its credit exposures using a credit rating and assumes a buy-and-hold strategy over one year, without accounting for the finer details of the credit portfolio assets or the ability to alter exposures in reaction to events.

The second reason refers to the situation where the model is built in a silo without recourse to the firms' decision-makers. An example of this would be a dedicated internal model team (perhaps using consultants or contractors) who build/design a model without recourse to the decision-makers in the organisation – for instance, a credit model built by an external consultant that was neither able to reflect important details in the credit portfolio nor the mitigating action that the firm could apply in the following 12 months.

In this scenario, the quants may effectively hijack the group decision-making process of the company. This happens by providing reasons that decision-makers can use to justify their decisions if things go wrong. It is easier to say that the model was followed than explain why it was right to deviate from the model.

The third reason refers to the situation where the risk function benchmarks their model to the results of other similar firms and seeks to generate a similar result. An example of this would be seeking a model calibration by recourse to consultant surveys that place the firm in the centre of range to avoid excessive supervisory scrutiny.

The fourth reason refers the challenge of explaining a complex mathematical model to a board that constitutes a number of members that provide a broader range than the technical skills needed to understand the model. As most decisions at board level require a majority, the model might be reasonable and justifiable but it does not follow that it will be supported. This challenge can result in the greatest influencer carrying the decision.

In each case, the result is the same. The risk function is open to the challenge that the decision implied by their model is incorrect and its decision should not be relied upon.

BUSINESS CASE FOR THE USE TEST

Businesses follow a regular cycle:

- developing a business plan and assessing the risks to delivering the plan;

- ❑ agreeing the one-year budget and the delegation of authority to the board's sub-committees as to the parameters within which this will be delivered;
- ❑ through the year, managing the delivery of the plan and taking actions as events deviate from the underlying assumptions made in the plan;
- ❑ board sub-committees reporting and evidencing what has happened and how it has been managed; and
- ❑ this feeding back into the start of the next strategic planning round and assessment of how effective management actions are, and whether the delegation of authority to the sub-committees remains appropriate or should be changed for the coming year.

Effectively, the use test is about evidencing to the board that the level of delegation of authority to make decisions within the business on a day-to-day basis remains appropriate and does not create undue risk for the business. This provides the framework for the business case for the use test. The output from an assessment of the use of the internal model should produce a feedback loop into enhancing the planning, management of risk and an improved ability for the board to delegate authority to management with confidence.

There has been a lot of discussion about the cost of Solvency II and whether there will be any benefits from this risk-based regulation. For internal model firms, a significant amount of money and actuarial time has been spent on building, validating and documenting the internal model. A lot of time has also been used by firms to discuss with supervisors about the appropriateness of data, assumptions and methodologies with a view to get their internal model approved for use to calculate the SCR. A way to benefit from this onerous investment is to use the internal model as a common and consistent framework for making decisions on capital strategy. To achieve this, the internal model should add value to existing processes on capital decisions. This can best be achieved by avoiding making the internal model a black box and embedding it in the decision process of the business, especially in the first line of defence. Some firms have successfully used their models to do "what if" experiments and resorted to using the model as a sounding board for some of the alternatives explored by the business. However, getting the internal model to be useful will take time and effort, although the use test helps firms to achieve this. It allows firms to build trust and buy-in of the internal model, and removes decision silos.

The use test has strong links with the other Solvency II internal models tests and standards,[6] but more particularly to both statistical quality standards and validation standards. The use test effectively acts as a conduit for imposing the statistical quality standards into the decision-making of the firms. The extent to which the requirements of the statistical quality test are aligned with the assumptions/views of decision-makers will determine the degree to which this causes an issue.

The resolution of a disagreement between decision-makers and model builders can either happen by the decision-makers accepting the model and allowing decisions to be heavily influenced by the model, thereby increasing the power of the risk function to veto decisions, or the decision-maker gets involved in the model build/calibration process to ensure that the nuances are included.

However, it has been argued that this underlines the importance of the validation standard as a link between the statistical quality tests and the use test. The validation test has two main components: technical validation; and fit to the business. Technical validation is concerned with checking that the implementation of the model works as intended, and involves undertaking some tests to check whether the calibration of the model is reasonable. This will not be discussed further here.[7]

Fit to the business is the second main component of the validation. The fit to the business requirement links the statistical quality standard and the use test. Ensuring that the model fits the business can be interpreted as ensuring that the model reflects the risk profile of the business. As suggested earlier, this task does not entail a simple comparison, as it needs to be clear whose view of the risk profile one is validating against.

If the view of the risk profile is that of the supervisor or a group within the firms that are not the decision-makers, then validation becomes a routine exercise in checking that the model reflects the risk profile that the model designers (or supervisors) envisaged. This should be enough to validate the statistical quality of the model, but does little to validate the model for the purposes of the use test.

In order to ensure the model fit to business that will support the use test, it is more appropriate to use the decision-makers to provide a validation of the model – or at least they should be involved in the process. In practice, this happens through reviews and challenge of the expert judgements in the model. The expert judgements are the choices that contribute to embedding the model into the business. This may seem a strong statement, but the examples of expert judgements presented below may help an understanding:

- choice of using a marginal distribution + Gaussian copula as the structure of the risk model;
- choice of risk drivers;
- choice of data to use for estimating marginal distributions/correlations; and
- inclusion of which management actions are allowed for.

What this underlines is that the capital requirement as calculated by the internal model is not an objective measurement of the capital – but an opinion as to the capital. If the opinion of the capital requirement is to influence the decisions being made within the firm, then it matters a great deal as to whether the opinion is that of the decision-maker or someone else.

Where the opinion has been developed without some input from the decision-makers, there is a risk that the business excludes the outputs of the model from the decision-making process. Where a validation process does include the decision-makers within the firm, this will expose these differences of opinion and increase the chances of the decision-makers seeing value in the internal model for decision-making purposes.

A concern – particularly for supervisors – might be that the decision-makers seek to steer the assumptions to be weaker and therefore weaken the capital requirement. This is not an unreasonable fear, as many risk managers have experienced this type of pressure. However, if a model is ever to be used to bring risk-centric decision-making into a firm, the challenge of the decision-makers to amend assumptions to a weaker capital basis needs to be met head on, the basis of disagreement needs to be identified and the additional data or analysis needed to bring the viewpoints closer together should be revealed.

The alternative seems to be to invite decision-makers to accept that an opinion on the risks that they do not agree about will be used instead of their opinion of the risks. The only successful outcome of this strategy would be that the decision-makers learn to accept the opinion of the risks handed to them. However, it seems unlikely that decision-makers with good domain knowledge for the decision they take will find this an acceptable outcome, or even professionally fulfilling.

If decision-makers are involved in the validation process, however, they have a conduit to share their domain knowledge and get the model to better reflect the risk profile as they see it. Meanwhile, supervisors and risk managers get more insight on the expert judgements being made, and are better able to help decision-makers improve their decision-making. The word "help" was carefully chosen in the last sentence. The word "challenge" could have been used, but this suggests a risk function whose role is only to critique the model. This is rarely a role that is welcomed by decision-makers, and does not serve to increase the influence of the risk function with the decision-makers within the firm.

By framing the role of the risk function as "helping", it can be repositioned as a force for good that is helping decision-makers to reflect on how decisions are made and seeking to provide additional information, analysis and perspective to help the decision-maker improve their decision-making capabilities.

USE TEST GOVERNANCE

In order to ensure that the internal model is used, there needs to be recognition that the risk function and the internal model are adding value to the decision-making of the enterprise. This effectively means that the senior decision-makers in the firm – ie, the executive team – need to share the recognition that the internal model adds value for decision-making in their areas of the business. To lead the executive team to this common shared understanding requires the involvement of the managing director or chief executive officer (CEO) of the business, as only they would have the authority to require the executive team to make efforts to engage with the internal model team.

Given the model will need to become accepted as valid by all decision-making areas of the business, the owner of the model – the CRO as head of the risk function – should have a voice at the board level to ensure that the input from the model is heard, and has authority and budget to propose initiatives that will improve the internal model and its ability to help decision-making. The importance of ensuring that the risk function has a voice at the board is critical to embedding risk in the decision-making within the firm. This role could be filled by a CEO who was convinced that risk should form part of the decision-making, and had the knowledge or influence to make the embedding work.

A more permanent step is to elevate the CRO to the board of the firms so that there is always a dedicated board member tasked with understanding the risk management and concerned with how it is helping to improve decision-making. This is a move that an increasing number of firms appear to be making.

One of the biggest challenges of the use test is its own success. If the use test is successfully embedded in the decision-making and several outputs are used, there is a risk that over time there will be confusion about what outputs were used and for what decision. There could be a risk that several "truths" coming from the internal model are floating around the firm, and which will eventually reduce the usefulness of the use test. Therefore, as well as making sure that the outputs of the model play an important role in decisions and have a governance framework that provides the "right" information at the right time, a firm should also ensure that there is an appropriate process for referencing and storing outputs that are used together with any specific decisions taken.

EVIDENCING THE USE TEST

In terms of evidencing the use test, it is suggested that the fundamental principle underpinning the use test is the best place to start looking for evidence. The fundamental principle is that there should be pressure to improve the model. If the firm can provide evidence that it is taking active steps to improve a model to enhance the quality of its decision-making, then this should provide strong evidence that the model is being considered seriously by the firm, since it sees it as a valuable part of the decision-making process. The shortcomings should be evidenced and taken into account when decisions are taken, and that there is a feedback loop to the internal model change log.

Involving the decision-makers in the validation process, and working in the feedback from these discussions with decision-makers into the model development cycle, could be considered as strong evidence that the pressure to improve the model was being actioned. This type of evidence also requires a flexible approach to model change by the supervisor. For example, a supervisor could impair the evolution of a model if they saw changing the model structure in a pejorative manner, such as by using frequent model change as evidence of poor model design or indecision.

In addition, this evidence documents how the internal model is taken into account in decision-making within the firm. This could be evidence from the board or committees where decisions are taken showing the papers where the feedback from the model was given and how it influenced the decision. For example, typically decisions might include:

- reinsurance purchase;
- hedging strategy;
- new product design;
- new distribution channel; and
- proposed acquisition/disposal.

The alignment of the expert judgement in the model with the expert judgement of the decision-makers is critical here. Should expert judgement (opinions) differ between the model designer (or supervisor) and the decision-makers, there is a material chance of disagreement on a decision.

If an alternative decision needs to be taken to that inferred by the internal model, the decision-maker then has a difficult decision to make. The minutes of the meeting could record that the decision-maker does not believe the model, although this would be a very crude action, and is highly unlikely to appear in the minutes of a meeting that the decision-maker thought the supervisor might be reviewing.

In practice, one might expect more subtle ways for decisions to be taken that were contradictory to the model, and of course there will be times when the decision is aligned with the model through chance rather than because the decision-maker necessarily believes the model. In such an environment, it would be very hard for a supervisor to identify clearly whether the decision-maker truly believed the model.

This is why the evidence of direct engagement in improving the model for better commercial decision-making is such strong evidence and why it is so important that decision-makers are involved in the validation of the models, as supervisors welcome model change in response to engagement between the model owners and the decision-makers in the firm.

IMPLEMENTING THE USE TEST

The reader might be wondering how they can get started on some of the themes advanced in this chapter. Our suggestion is to develop a proportionate approach that starts by tackling the most important drivers of risk and value first. Most importantly, do not wait until the internal model has been fully "completed". The value of the model is embedding it as soon as possible in the business, and using any feedback to improve and better adapt the model for business use. There have been a few cases where an internal model has been built, peer-reviewed, validated and approved by the board, and then a session held with business users to see how the model can be used. Following this discussion, it was soon realised that the list of uses which the business had in mind was very different and much broader than what the model was built for, and a result the model had to be re-designed at additional cost.

It is important to add value as a priority because many decisions that are undertaken in firms are not taken with a primary motive of reducing risk – rather, they are taken with the motive of adding value to the company. Therefore, firms are encouraged to do the following.

a) Understand how they add economic value to their firms and, in particular, how and by whom the decisions are taken in respect of the value-adding activity.
   - It is likely there will be several ways in which the firm seeks to generate value; therefore, the current generators of value should be listed in order of value added. Examples might be:
     - risk margin (eg, the premium for risk);
     - fees (eg, on unit-linked business);
     - investment spreads (eg, spread earned less spread paid to customers); and
     - profits from subsidiaries (eg, profits from agents, banks, investment managers).

- ❑ For a stable business, this should perhaps be based on a moving average over recent years to iron out random fluctuations in well-developed business. However, where a business line is growing quickly, this should be the most recent value generation.

b) Understand the main risks the firm is exposed to and, in particular, what decisions are taken in respect of these risks.

- ❑ This is more subtle than just looking at the net risk profile. The net risk profile will typically be net of:
  - ❍ reinsurance;
  - ❍ hedging (dynamic and static);
  - ❍ management actions; and
  - ❍ operational processes.
- ❑ When a decision is taken to mitigate a risk, the gross risk must first be understood and the degree of the beneficial effect of risk mitigant also needs to be understood to be sure that it is cost-effective.
- ❑ Therefore, it is important that the gross risks and the effect of the risk mitigant to the firms are understood, so that it is clear how and by whom decisions are taken to mitigate risks or to leave the capital base exposed.

The focus should first be on the most important value drivers and risk drivers.

Take, for example, where a firm makes most of its income through the generation of an investment margin over and above what it pays to its policyholders. It is expected the decision-making regarding asset selection and policyholder crediting rates will be the main focus. Questions should be asked regarding how these decisions are taken and to what extent risk (and the internal model) is used in making these decisions.

Another example is a firm that is most exposed to credit risk and holds most of the capital against this risk factor. It is expected the decision-making regarding the overall credit exposure and the constituents of the exposure will be the main focus. The emphasis should be on the risk mitigation and to what extent this is reducing the risk versus the cost of the reduction. One would expect that risk be a key consideration in such decision-taking, but the extent to which the internal model is used to make these decisions will be a good focus for the use test.

Ultimately, the success of the use test will depend on how well the model is understood beyond the internal model builders and validators, especially by senior managers, including the administrative, management or supervisory body, who will use the model for decision-making. Developing a training schedule to ensure that senior managers are apprised of the development of the internal model is relatively important. Having training schedules that last one year or more is sometimes not sufficient, especially if senior management do not see or use the internal model regularly. It might help to have a brief summary of key technical and development aspects of the internal model as part of committee or board papers to keep the knowledge of the senior managers up to date. It might also be helpful to use some examples of the outputs of the internal model together with training about technical aspects of the model and relevant uses to bring some of these technical aspects to life. Having an easy reference guide to the internal model can also be of assistance. An understanding of the internal model is a key requirement of the use test and, based on what the authors have seen, it takes a long time to get non-executive directors up to speed on some of the key technical aspects of the internal model. Developing a training programme early and at regular intervals will help to achieve this.

It is also important to identify the key stakeholders of the internal model. The obvious ones are the board members, the CEO and the chief financial officer (CFO), but there will be other staff whose work may be affected by the introduction of the use test. Identifying these stakeholders would allow a better understanding of the expectations regarding timescale around the use of the model although, most importantly, the structural challenges of getting a decision made can create a bottleneck in using the internal model in decision-making. Achieving the buy-in of these stakeholders would also help to ensure that embedding the model in the business is successful. For a group internal model, this may mean senior managers of subsidiaries, whether they are included in the scope of the internal model or not.

The group internal model will require good quality data to produce information that is useful for decision-making and getting the buy-in of the subsidiaries that are using the standard formula for calculating their SCR. In some uses, as explained above, one may want to use the economic view in business decisions, and so more information could be required than the SCR numbers. Furthermore, the use may require a change in existing processes and these changes can sometimes be tricky. Making sure that enough time has been left prior to submission of evidence for the approval of the internal model is very important. Supervisors will look for evidence of past use, as well as whether the firm has the right process in place to satisfy the use test as proposed by firms.

The biggest hurdle could be aligning the outputs of the internal model to other metrics that are being used or will be used by the firm in decision-making. Firms use a number of metrics for decisions, some of which are purely accounting, others are accounting but risk-based and some are based on economic value using some outputs of the internal model. In some cases, the indicators can provide conflicting messages, and it is quite important that it is understood why to ensure that use of the models do not compete with other, more familiar, metrics, reducing the relevance of the outputs taken from the internal model. As part of the profit and loss attribution,[8] firms should be able to relate changes to their profit and loss to the outputs of the internal model, and this understating should be part of the development of the use test by bridging the gap between the model output and the other metrics used routinely by the business, especially if the other metrics drive remuneration and bonuses.

PRACTICAL FIRST STEPS FOR SUPERVISORS

Supervisors play an important role to ensure the use test works properly. The way supervisors interact with firms can determine the way in which the internal model is used. Different supervisory styles and culture provide incentives/disincentives to a correct application of the use test. Below are some suggestions for how this can be achieved.

Being open to model change

If a model is used for decision-making – or is becoming increasingly important for decision-making – there will be pressure to improve it over time to reflect and incorporate new information, methodologies, data, etc. Supervisors need to be open to changes, and even encourage them.

Being open to validation by decision-makers

If a model is to be used by decision-makers, then it is important that they are key stakeholders in the design and calibration of the model. This is not to say they will have *carte blanche* over the design and calibration of the model, but they do need to have a voice in the design process – and that voice needs to be listened to as well as being open to challenge and education. The most effective way is to involve the decision-makers in the validation process, so that they have a chance to regularly challenge the structure, assumptions and judgements of the model, and better align the model with the information set that decisions are made on.

Being open to sharing understanding of risks

Where a supervisor disagrees with the firm's assessment of the risk factor or risk interaction, the remedial action could include a capital add-on to restore compliance with the 99.5% confidence level. A firm that takes the use test seriously, and is seeking to do the right thing, will be keen to understand the rationale for this supervisory choice so that the understanding of the firm can be improved and better decisions can be taken.

If supervisors are not open to providing constructive and open feedback with respect to the areas of disagreement, they will reduce the connection between the supervisory capital held and the understanding of the firm in question of their risks. This will make it harder for firms to appropriately implement the use test.

Not placing reliance on benchmarks

There is a significant risk that the supervisory approach places a great reliance on simplistic industry benchmarks, which could give rise to unintended consequences, including systemic risk. Benchmarking can easily result in anchoring to the industry average, which works against the development of models that reflect the decision-making within individual firms. Therefore, if it is accepted – and indeed welcomed for the purposes of financial stability – that there is a plurality of decision-making processes within the insurance sector, then it follows that plurality of models should also be welcomed, and benchmarks should not be used to justify the viewpoint of a supervisor.

CASE STUDY

This case study illustrates the concepts explained in the chapter. It is based on an event that occurred in the UK during the early months of 2014, specifically the flooding of the Thames Valley near London, UK, which impacted several thousand homes.

A general insurance (GI) company with a strong presence/exposure to the household insurance market was considered. They have a lot of policyholders in the well-off Thames Valley area and, as a result of the floods, had a large number of claims arising. In the wake of the event, there was a great deal of press focus on the reaction of insurers. This led the Prime Minister to summon the CEOs of the leading insurers (including the CEO of the firm) to discuss how the insurers were going to support policyholders.

The board of the firm conducted a series of emergency board meetings to discuss the impact of the flooding crisis on the finances and the reputation of the insurer. The non-executive directors (NEDs) highlighted that a great deal of money and time had been spent on an internal model in preparation for Solvency II, and wanted to understand what insight the model can provide about the state of the firm and how the firm should react to this crisis.

In particular, they were keen to understand:

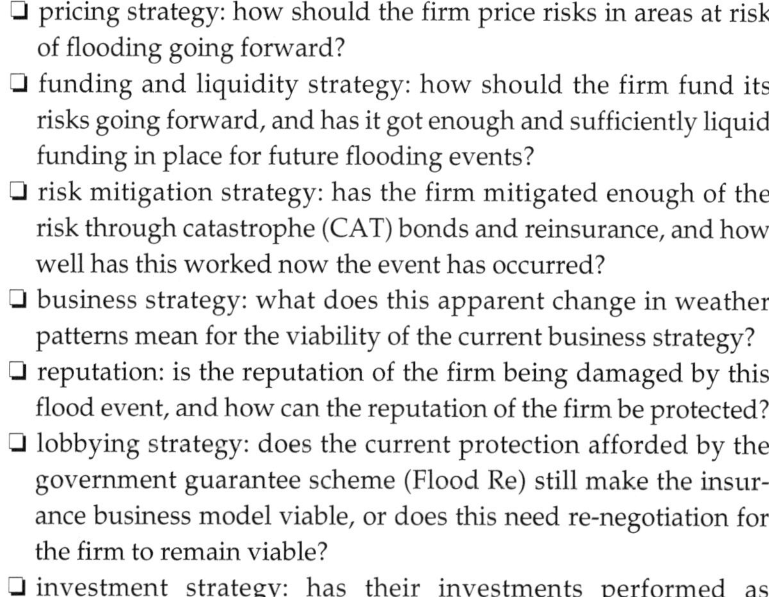

- pricing strategy: how should the firm price risks in areas at risk of flooding going forward?
- funding and liquidity strategy: how should the firm fund its risks going forward, and has it got enough and sufficiently liquid funding in place for future flooding events?
- risk mitigation strategy: has the firm mitigated enough of the risk through catastrophe (CAT) bonds and reinsurance, and how well has this worked now the event has occurred?
- business strategy: what does this apparent change in weather patterns mean for the viability of the current business strategy?
- reputation: is the reputation of the firm being damaged by this flood event, and how can the reputation of the firm be protected?
- lobbying strategy: does the current protection afforded by the government guarantee scheme (Flood Re) still make the insurance business model viable, or does this need re-negotiation for the firm to remain viable?
- investment strategy: has their investments performed as

expected during the flood event, and have they been able to liquidate enough assets at good prices to cover the cash outflow?

The CRO was asked to provide the board with a paper to explain how the internal model can be used to answer these questions.

The model followed a typical GI approach using off-the-shelf CAT model outputs to assess the projected gross claims amount due to the floods. The marginal distribution from the CAT model was then fed into the internal model along with marginal distribution from expenses and investment returns (produced using in-house models). These marginal distributions were combined using a copula. The internal model also included the risk mitigation strategy; in the case of this firm, there were excess of loss (XOL) policies to cover extreme flood events, which were modelled precisely in the internal model. The investment and expense models were broad brush using aggregated historical data.

Table 6.1 considers how the CRO could have assessed the ability of the internal model to answer the board's questions.

What can be concluded is that, for a typical firm (in 2014), the internal model has limited use for the questions that the board needs answering in order to take key decisions. On the face of it, this is not a good advertisement for the use of internal models in decision-making.

However, it is expected that the outcome of this analysis would be a model improvement plan that increases the ability of the internal model to support decision-making. A conclusion might also be that an extension of the internal model for the ORSA is needed to deal with the "non-quantifiable risks", which are very prevalent in the questions the board have asked and which, despite a lack of data, have a very real impact on the financial health of the firm.

CONCLUSION

In this chapter, the rationale and requirements for the Solvency II use test were explored and the perspective of other regulatory regimes to the use test were highlighted. The implementation challenges of the use test were also explored. In particular, it was discussed how the use test induces change in the firm/supervisor dynamics, and the influence that it tries to exert on the autonomy of private enterprise firms.

Table 6.1 Summary of the analysis performed and of the key findings and actions

Pricing strategy – how should the firm price risks in areas at risk of flood going forward?	The pricing team uses a pricing matrix based on its own historical claims data. The model accounts for the reinsurance in place, and models the net distribution of the flood risk. Only 20% of its household risk is reinsured and the same CAT model used for the internal model is used to decide the reinsurance cost – which, in turn, affects the premium. However, the CRO concludes that the firm's own historical data is effectively setting the premium level.
	The CRO notes that the distributions for expense risk and investment risk are consistent with the premium setting process in that pricing team use the mean of the distribution. However, the downside tail of the expense and investment models has no effect on the premium.
	They make a note that the downside risk calculated by internal model is therefore not having much influence on the premium setting.
	The CRO recommends an entry on internal model change log in order to more tightly integrate the internal model with the approach to pricing.
	As an emergency measure, the risk function and the business proposes to the board an approximate adjustment to premiums.
Funding and liquidity strategy – how should the firm fund its risks going forward, has it got enough capital and has it sufficiently liquid funding in place for future flood events?	The own funds of the firm are partly equity, but around 50% are subordinated debt. However, the CRO notes that the internal model does not make any allowance for the own fund limits imposed by Solvency II – all capital is assumed to qualify. The model does not match up the payment schedule on issued debt, reinsurance and the expected payments to policyholders.
	The CRO concludes that the model is not able to help determine the funding strategy, but should help with the quantum of own funds required.
	The CRO recommends enhancement to the management information framework to better manage liquidity requirements. They also add better integration of liquidity assessment and capital modelling in their ORSA process.
	More immediately, the CRO assesses the ability to liquidate assets in response to a range of scenarios that could occur and require rapid cash outflow.
Risk mitigation strategy – has the firm mitigated enough of the risk through CAT bonds and reinsurance, and how well has this worked now the event has happened?	The internal model relies heavily on the CAT model that is used for reinsurance decision-making.
	The CRO concludes that the internal model is well placed to help with setting the reinsurance strategy.
	The CRO makes no additional recommendations in respect of the reinsurance programme.

Business strategy – what does this apparent change in weather patterns mean for the viability of the current business strategy?	The CAT model does not update frequently, so the firm is reliant on the CAT model provider to take account of the flooding in its model.
	The internal model does account for liquidity risk, alternative assumptions about future climate, reputational damage or political decisions. Also, as noted above, there is only a loose connection between the model and pricing.
	The CRO concludes that the internal model will struggle to help the board make decisions on business strategy in the near term.
	The CRO proposes a new (higher) capital risk appetite in the light of the shortcomings identified in the internal model.
	The CRO concludes that this event should trigger a business plan review, and makes this recommendation to the board.
Reputation – is the reputation of the firm being damaged by this flood event, and how can the reputation of the firm be protected?	The model does not take account of reputation, as it was deemed to be a non-quantifiable risk and therefore was excluded from the scope of the model.
	The CRO recommends that brand and reputation should be included as a future dimension of the risk appetite.
	The CRO recommends that the communications team develop draft responses to a number of scenarios (such as bad publicity from using high-tariff call lines for flood victims).
Lobbying strategy – does the current protection afforded by the government guarantee scheme (eg, Flood Re from the UK government) still make the insurance business model viable, or does this need re-negotiation for the firm to remain viable?	The internal model has a detailed description of Flood Re and therefore the degree to which the reinsurance policy works can be assessed.
	However, the impact on the wider business strategy was not reflected by the internal model, so the lobbying situation is unclear.
	The CRO recommends engagement with peer group companies (perhaps through the trade bodies) to understand the impact on the viability of the sector and prepare a white paper to share with the government.
Investment strategy – have our investments performed as expected during the flood event, and have we been able to liquidate enough assets at good prices to cover the cash outflow?	The investment model is broad brush as it does not include enough granular information on the range of investment strategies available to the firm or the current prices of the modelled investment. It also does not model the bid/offer spread, so the model does not allow for a lack of liquidity in the invested assets.
	This will require changes to the model to be answer this question.
	The CRO recommends that the issues surrounding asset granularity are added to the model change log.

A business case for the use test was presented. In particular, it was argued that there is value in bringing frontline decision-makers into the model validation process to better align the model with the way decisions are made in practice, and to increase engagement between risk-takers and risk managers.

The governance of the use test was discussed, and especially the need for endorsement of the use test and the internal model at the highest levels in the firm. A case for the CRO to permanently embed a risk perspective at board level was also made

In addition, how firms might implement the use test was discussed. In particular, the chapter explored how important it is for firms to understand how decisions are made to add economic value, as well as in mitigating risk. A case for identifying the most material value and risk drivers was made, and it was acknowledged that firms should start by focusing attention on the decisions made in respect of these.

Some suggestions for the way that supervisors should act in order to facilitate an appropriate implementation of the use test were made. Specifically, the need for open communication was highlighted, and the avoidance of the overuse of the benchmarking of internal model, which can anchor the perspective of the regulator.

Finally, a case study showing how a catastrophe event can lead to a board questioning how the internal model could help with decision-making was worked through. Using knowledge of common market practice, it was shown how a CRO might evaluate the ability of their internal model to help the board make decisions.

1 For further details, see European Parliament and the Council of the European Union (2009).
2 See CEIOPS (2009).
3 For further details, see European Commission (2014).
4 For further details, see EIOPA (2013).
5 The authors are aware that in some sectors internal models only use historic data for their calibration, and are therefore backward-looking in their assessment of uncertainty. Some sectors have started to investigate more forward-looking modelling approaches.
6 For further details about the Solvency II internal model tests and standards, see Chapter 3.
7 For further details about validation, see Chapters 11 and 12.
8 For further details about profit and loss attribution, see Chapter 10.

REFERENCES

Anand, Paul, 1993, *Foundations of Rational Choice Under Risk.* Oxford: Oxford University Press.

CEIOPS, 2009, "Draft CEIOPS advice for Level 2 Implementing Measures on Solvency II: Supervisory Reporting and Public Disclosure Requirements", Consultation Paper 58.

EIOPA, 2013, "EIOPA Final Report on Public Consultations No. 13/011 on the Proposal for Guidelines on the Pre-application for Internal Models", September.

European Commission, 2014, "Delegated Acts to the Solvency II Directive".

European Parliament and the Council of the European Union, 2009, "Directive 2009/138/EC of the European Parliament and of the Council of 25 November 2009 on the Taking-up and Pursuit of the Business of Insurance and Reinsurance (Solvency II) (recast)".

Gigerenzer, G., Todd, P.M., and the ABC Research Group, 1999, *Simple Heuristics That Make Us Smart.* Oxford: Oxford University Press.

Kahneman, Daniel, 2011, *Thinking, Fast and Slow.* London: Penguin UK.

Morris, D. S., 2008, "The Basel II 'Use Test' – A Retail Credit Approach: Developing and Implementing Effective Retail Credit Risk Strategies Using Basel II".

Salmon, F., 2009, "Recipe for Disaster: The Formula that Killed Wall Street", *Wired,* February 23 (available at http://www.wired.com/print/techbiz/it/magazine/17-03/wp_quant).

7

Statistical Quality Standards: Challenges in Internal Model Implementation

Markus Bellion, Christopher Lotz and Peter Müller
Bundesanstalt für Finanzdienstleistungsaufsicht – BaFin

Statistical quality standards stand out among the internal model test and standards as they address the core of the matter, the internal model in the narrow sense.[1] They do not primarily take on the perspective of model purpose or model use (in contrast, for example, to the use test and the calibration standards).[2] The regulatory requirements refer to a generally comprehensive methodology used by firms to calculate the probability distribution forecast (PDF). The internal model is thus not reduced to an instrument of arbitrary nature that already meets the requirements if all it does is, providing as output, a distribution of profits or losses with high forecast quality. Instead, besides the resulting PDF, the individual elements of the calculation methodology are subject to quality standards; these are mainly the underlying assumptions, the actuarial and statistical techniques used, and the data and information used as basis for model specification and parameterisation. This corresponds to the view that an internal model is more than a collection of mathematical/statistical relationships, but rather reveals fundamental and hopefully persistent connections between its inputs and outputs. This accounts for the fact that an internal model, due to its complexity, only in rare cases can solely be judged on the basis of its output alone. A good past performance of the model can be purely coincidental; just by considering the model results, one cannot get sufficient comfort that model performance will hold in future, possibly in a changed environment.

The statistical quality standards set out in the Solvency II directive[3] generally allow considerable modelling freedom to firms. Article 121(4) of the Solvency II directive states that "no particular method for the calculation of the probability distribution forecast shall be prescribed." Accordingly, the quality standards are strongly principles-based, and abstract enough to be of sustainable use to the various risk categories and a wide variety of different model approaches (eg, geophysical natural catastrophe (natcat) models in contrast to scenario-based operational risk models). It should therefore not be a surprise that the statistical quality standards for a large part comprise universal standards of good practice in modelling as applied to other fields. At the same time, aspects of particular importance to risk modelling in insurance and reinsurance firms are covered (eg, financial options and guarantees, diversification benefits and risk mitigation techniques).

The statistical quality standards set the boundaries within which firms have to take responsibility to specify their own approach to assess and aggregate risks; hence, methods and implementations that would meet the standards in each and every imaginable case cannot exist. In conjunction with the validation standards,[4] they promote a well-structured, documented and controlled process of model development and refinement that should be consistently applied across the firm and to the different modelling areas. In this sense, the label "statistical quality" is probably a bit too restrictive. Practical experience shows that the dialogue between firms and the supervisory authorities regarding model quality is not dominated by the debate of statistical quality in a narrow sense, or the application of some statistical tests.

Solvency II challenged firms with the internal model tests and standards, and thus certainly contributed to substantial technical progress in risk modelling. For example, significant improvements have been observed in the application of the replicating portfolio technique in market risk measurement. Another example is the introduction of the one-year view to underwriting risks, compared to the ultimate view alone. Some of the changes are more fundamental: operational risk modelling is finding its way into insurance firms, and vendor models – especially those for natcat – have started to become more transparent and accessible for review and adaptation. During the first years of internal model pre-application, these developments have been observed to promote variety rather than convergence in internal risk modelling. While the replicating portfolio technique, for instance, has become increasingly popular, the actual methodologies implemented by firms are still diverse. The Solvency II approach of strongly principle-based requirements not only admits such a bouquet of methodologies, but even fosters the constant exploration of new methodologies because of its tough requirements for model quality. In this way, the statistical quality standards support Guideline 10 of the use test requirements from the European Insurance and Occupational Pensions Authority (EIOPA) Guidelines on Pre-Application of Internal Models, which requires firms to use the model in such a way that there is pressure to improve the quality of the internal model itself. In such a dynamic environment, it is a perpetual challenge for supervisors to apply the abstract and principle-based requirements to the concrete implementation at hand (and derive adequate assessments).

This chapter does not aim to compile the regulatory requirements in the area of the statistical quality standards, and in particular it does not set new ones. There are already a number of publications that provide an overview of contents, and describe how the corresponding forthcoming Level 2 delegated acts follow the structure of Article 121 of the Solvency II directive, and which topics are detailed in the EIOPA Level 3 guidelines. Instead, we will discuss the statistical quality standards in light of the implementation efforts on the part of both firms and supervisors within the internal model pre-application phase. By means of representative examples, the chapter will present the main challenges and issues relating to statistical quality standards, which are subject to discussion ahead of the anticipated entry-into-force of the new solvency regime and the date of first-day model approval at the beginning of 2016.

The examples are specific to a particular risk category or model component, although the views expressed should be general enough to be transferred to other areas as well. In that way, the examples can provide assistance to modellers or reviewers facing similar issues. The selection of examples is based on the experience gained by the authors during their internal model reviews since the start of pre-application in 2009. The intention is not to compile a comprehensive survey of the most important do's and don'ts by supervisors for firms, which, if followed in the minutest detail, gives a virtual guarantee of compliance with the statistical quality standards. Such an interpretation would contradict the individuality of each firm and its risk profile, which requires firms to implement specifically tailored risk models, and supervisors to take case-by-case decisions based on principles.

The questions that risk modellers ask themselves when developing and running the model, and that supervisors raise when assessing compliance to the statistical quality standards, are the result of iterative processes and do not follow a particular sequential order. However, to facilitate the understanding, the general structure of this chapter follows roughly the sequence of the themes in Article 121 of the Solvency II directive. It starts with a review of the requirements on methods and assumptions, with a special focus on the required and desired properties of the output of any internal model, the PDF. The technique of replicating portfolios is used as an example to outline some of the main challenges and trade-offs model developers face when constructing internal models that satisfy regulatory requirements. Two further methodological topics concern the consistency between the risk model and the valuation model, and the internal model's ability to rank risks. After the discussion of methodological standards, the chapter covers data and its close relationship with expert judgement. Through various risk categories, practical implications of the regulatory standards on data are described, and some general principles on the control of expert judgement are reviewed. The chapter continues with a discussion of the requirement that all material risks need to be covered by the internal model, and some typical examples for incomplete risk coverage are provided. The next topic, diversification, while forming the basis of all insurance activity, is hotly debated among regulators at the time of writing because of its potentially huge impact on solvency capital requirements (SCRs). Emphasis is put on the connection between the structure of the risk model and how this influences diversification, as well as on how diversification effects can be challenged. Subsequently, some risk mitigation techniques are explored in conjunction with the corresponding regulatory requirements. Future management actions, as well as financial guarantees and contractual options, are also briefly discussed.

METHODS AND ASSUMPTIONS

According to Article 121 (2) of the Solvency II directive, the methods used to calculate the PDF must be based on adequate actuarial and statistical techniques, and be consistent with the methods used to calculate technical provisions. Furthermore, firms must be able to justify the assumptions underlying their internal model to the supervisory authorities. This section on methods and assumptions initially discusses the concept of PDF and the richness of the forecast as a guiding principle for risk modelling within Solvency II. Then, methodological issues are presented. The example of market risk measurement for a life insurance firm using the replicating portfolio technique is used to illustrate these issues. Next, the requirement of methodological consistency in the context of non-life underwriting risk is analysed. Finally, model adequateness in terms of the internal model's ability to rank risks is explored.

Richness of the PDF as guiding principle

One ultimate goal in risk modelling is to provide transparency about all of the risks that a firm faces. In this view, between two models of comparable quality, the model that is often preferred is the one that provides higher transparency of risks. Higher transparency translates into better risk management, and can also help to improve the relationship with regulators, facilitating better communication and understanding of a firm's risks. The level of transparency that is achieved depends significantly on the methods chosen for risk quantification and their ability to reflect all material features of the firm's risk profile.

For the calculation of the PDF underlying the internal model, according to Article 121(4) of the Solvency II directive, any relevant methods available come into consideration in the first place. The Solvency II internal modelling framework, likewise, requires firms to be aware of the generally accepted market practice, provided one has been established, and of the current progress in actuarial science.

However, when choosing methods, the actual intention is too often disregarded. Internal models within Solvency II by definition provide a PDF. According to Article 13(38) of the Solvency II directive, the PDF is defined as a mathematical function that assigns a probability of occurrence to an exhaustive set of mutually exclusive events. This means that the PDF is intended to generate a distribution of outcomes. Instead, during the pre-application process it has been observed that many firms developed a risk model that in some parts corresponds to a point estimation of a single quantile of the distribution function related to the (ideal) PDF. Among these, there are often shock factor models that sometimes resemble (or are even equal to) the standard formula.

Consider a market risk modelling example. A capital markets model (ie, an economic scenario generator (ESG) complemented by an approximation technique for revaluation, where necessary) enables generating profits or losses in a multitude of capital market scenarios. A stress scenario approach, in contrast, informs about the loss in selected shock scenarios only – for example, a one-in-200-years drop in interest rates (implemented by a parallel shift of the interest rate term structure). It is self-evident that the results from the capital markets model in general represent a much richer source of information. This level of richness represents the bar that firms facing material market risks should strive to surpass.

There are many reasons to favour methods that provide a rich PDF capturing all relevant characteristics of the risk profile. Richer PDFs generally provide a stronger basis for the firm's risk management and provide better support for its decision-making processes. Manifold options for in-depth analyses of the risk profile arise. The impact of possible risk management tools can be tested more easily. Furthermore, rich PDFs facilitate the application of validation tools (eg, when testing model results against experience) and allow for sophisticated methods for aggregation and capital allocation.

A rather low richness of the PDF (eg, when the distribution is known or deemed reliable in some parts only) can have several negative impacts. An entire range of possible outcomes may be overlooked. The effect of some risk mitigation techniques might not show in model results, and therefore be disincentivised. The aggregation with other marginal distributions can be difficult. Likewise, there is the danger of misallocation of risk capital.

Compared to the standard formula, the internal model is simply expected to be superior: Article 113(2)(a) of the Solvency II directive states that the SCR for the modelled scope more appropriately reflects the risk profile of the undertaking.

While there are other quality criteria and a balance must be struck (eg, with competing criteria such as intelligibility and understanding of stakeholders), for the reasons mentioned above the richness of the PDF is an important criterion in the assessment of model adequateness by supervisors. So far, only a few firms take richness explicitly into account in model development and improvement.

A prerequisite for a rich PDF is a comprehensive knowledge of the risk profile and the availability of powerful calculation techniques. The practice, however, is plagued by limitations. Mainly, relevant information or data such as loss experience may be scarcely available, or existing calculation techniques are not capable of processing the information. Such challenges tend to be bigger in some risk categories or business segments than in others.

Given a model that provides a PDF of comparatively low richness, supervisors may form either a negative or positive view on whether the forecast is sufficiently rich. An example of a borderline case is a model for mass lapse risk of a life insurance firm, assuming that this risk is both not immaterial, but also does not belong to the top underwriting risks. The model basis is typically a shock scenario with the associated difficulty of setting a value for the stressed lapse rate. This is mainly because the drivers of mass lapse may be diverse or hardly known, and the insurance markets fortunately have known only a few such events, which may not be representative for the current risk profile of a particular firm. Nevertheless, a careful analysis of external data for historic events may facilitate the firm's assessment of its own exposure to mass lapse, and help to justify the specification of the shock scenario, especially the expert judgement used in relation to the stress parameter. By analysing the dynamics of past events, one might get a notion of the time evolution of the lapse rate. The lapse level may also be elevated in years subsequent to the mass lapse event occurrence. The firm may choose to enrich the resulting PDF, which by then is known in a single quantile only. When this is done just for the sake of convenience without a strong motivation, firms often struggle to demonstrate that the enrichment is founded. Of course, a clear idea of the spectrum of possible mass lapse events is needed to this end. The evaluation of a number of individual lapse events with differing severity is likely to be more transparent than fitting an overall loss distribution.

The requirement of a rich PDF is not intended to generally exclude these risk categories or business segments from internal modelling. Supervisors (as well as risk modellers) judge on a case-by-case basis, and consider the nature, complexity and scale of the risks to be covered. For this assessment, the following questions might be relevant.

- ❑ Which methodological limitations are responsible for the comparatively low richness of the PDF? Are there any methods available that make better use of the knowledge of the risk profile?
- ❑ Is the risk profile nevertheless sufficiently well captured?
- ❑ Where necessary, is it possible to enrich the PDF with additional information? What is the basis for this?
- ❑ What are the implications of the low degree of richness when using the model for the purpose of risk management and decision-taking? Has the firm put in place any mitigating measures? What is the impact on other model components or risks within the scope of the internal model?

A PDF of comparatively low richness still provides more transparency than no PDF at all. Still, it should be a top priority for any serious modelling department to constantly strive to increase the richness of the PDF by improving the underlying methodology or data of the risk model. There is a continuous stream of modelling innovations in the field, which good modelling departments will constantly monitor for opportunities to improve their modelling, the richness of their PDF and transparency over risks in general.

Methodological issues of replicating portfolios

Risk models often need to bring together the evolution of risk factors, on the one hand, with their impact on the firm's portfolio, the so-called exposure, on the other hand. In particular, in the area of market risk, developers can base their risk models on an abundance of data for the underlying risk factors. It is much more demanding to model the complicated exposure of insurance companies, especially in the life sector, where many options and guarantees are embedded in the insurance liabilities. Therefore, this section focuses on the methodological issues of modelling the market risk exposure of life insurance firms.

A large part of the market risk profile of a typical life insurance firm is determined by the special nature of its liabilities, and in particular by the financial guarantees and contractual options that policyholders have received, or by the allocation of its surplus funds and other management actions. The complicated contingent claims embedded in the liability structure make it hard and time-consuming to determine a PDF as required by the Solvency II directive. Closed-form solutions do not exist and, in a typical Monte Carlo set-up where the underlying market risk factors are simulated, a large number of cumbersome revaluations would be needed.

There are a number of potential solutions for this problem, all of which present advantages and disadvantages. In the following, for ease of presentation only, the focus is on replicating portfolios. Replicating portfolios are an advanced and challenging technique for calculating the market risk of the liabilities or the own funds of a life insurance firm. Replicating portfolios are widely used by life insurance firms. Methodological issues arise at a number of steps in their construction process.

As a first step, the constituting elements of replicating portfolios need to be selected from a large universe of simple instruments, such as bonds or swaptions that can be valued through closed-form formulas. At this point, the parsimony of the model needs to be weighed against the precision of the representation of the market risk – a larger replicating portfolio may seem to give more detail about the market risk of the firm, but it is also more sensitive to small changes in the calibration process, may become unstable and is prone to overfitting. Balancing these two competing goals is still more of an art than a science, and involves a certain amount of trial and error.

The actual calibration of the replicating portfolio has to be appropriate in the sense that it has to satisfy a large number of competing modelling goals. It is supposed to represent the firm's current position by matching the current value of its target (liabilities or own funds). At the same time, it has to adequately represent this value as well as its sensitivities to market moves, also under stressed conditions. Obviously, matching a larger number of targets (ie, liability revaluations under stressed conditions) can improve the representation. The stresses are typically applied to risk factors such as interest rates, volatilities or credit spreads, and can include complicated movements of the term structure such as curve twists.

In this context, special consideration has to be given to joint stresses in several risk factors, because here a sufficiently similar behaviour of a replicating portfolio and its target are often most difficult to attain. When using many such targets, care must be taken so that an overfitting of the replicating portfolio is avoided. Requiring an exact fit of the replicating portfolio to all the targets may result in a superficially well-calibrated portfolio, but such a portfolio may suffer from, for example, large offsetting long and short positions in neighbouring maturity buckets, as well as certain instability issues, where the portfolio composition changes completely for any small change in risk factors or exposure at future dates.

It is important to assess whether the replicating portfolio is in the end fit to be used for the firm's risk management and for regulatory purposes. This requires a measurement of the replication quality and a firm control of the inherent approximation errors through statistical or exploratory data analysis. Often the calibration residuals are used to gain further insight into potential calibration issues. The most powerful validation method, brute force recalculation of the target value in stress scenarios or those generated by the risk model, and analysing the differences to the replicating portfolio prediction, is also the most time-consuming, and therefore must be used judiciously. In addition, comparisons between the replicating portfolio and revaluations of own funds or liabilities in scenarios not used for calibration (out-of-sample), as well as revaluing the replicating portfolio and comparing it to its target at later dates, have become standard procedures of validation in this area. Also, the cashflow profiles of the replicating portfolio and the original valuation, put side by side, can provide important information about possible discrepancies and highlight potential issues. Although continuous improvement in techniques for replicating portfolios has increasingly been observed, there are still a variety of approaches and not all of them achieve the required quality.

To decide whether to replicate only the liabilities on their own or the total firm's own funds, a number of issues need to be taken into consideration. On the one hand, a replication of the liabilities only can improve the granularity and precision of the individual risk representation of both the asset and the liability side. In such a set up, policyholder cashflows are potentially replicated with greater precision, using zero-coupon bonds for guaranteed policyholder payments and options for policyholder participations. In addition, the market risks on the asset side are not subject to any approximation from replication at all. On the other hand, the required degree of precision for a liabilities-only replicating portfolio is much higher than for one that targets the own funds directly. After all, for a typical life insurance the liabilities are much larger than the own funds, so that even a relatively small residual error from the liabilities replication can cause a large relative error in the own funds calculation. On top of this, assets and liabilities are usually highly correlated, which can make it even harder to calculate the difference with sufficient precision. The goal of an accurate representation of the individual risks for assets and liabilities needs to be weighed against a sound view of the change of own funds of the firm, both for internal risk management as well as for regulatory purposes.

In a similar way, the replicating portfolio is usually used for market risk measurement only. Other risk factors that are relevant for life insurance firms, such as mortality, longevity or lapse rates, often have to be treated outside of the replicating portfolio. When combining all these different classes of risk into a holistic picture of the risk profile of the firm, care should be taken to provide transparency on the interplay of the different risks so that end-users can understand the model behaviour on an intuitive level. This is especially true when issues such as the loss-absorbing effects of policyholder participation are concerned, or when certain buffers are used as risk mitigants and it has to be ensured that no double-counting of the risk mitigating effects occurs for individual buffers.

While this section has used the example of replicating portfolios to illustrate the methodological requirements of the statistical quality standards, there are a number of other methodologies that aim to capture the market risk profile of life insurance firms. This is a fast-evolving field. The best available methodology is likely to change, and firms need to keep up-to-date with developments in this area, which is also emphasised in Guideline 10 of the use test requirements from the EIOPA guidelines that requires firms to use the model in such a way that there is pressure to improve the quality of the internal model itself.

Consistency

The final determination of the solvency of a firm is on own funds versus SCR. SCR refers to the risk of a decrease in own funds. Clearly, own funds and their change are influenced significantly by technical provisions and their change. It is therefore self-evident that methods used to calculate the PDF (risk model: change of own funds or technical provisions) and the methods used to calculate the technical provisions must be consistent – this is an explicit requirement set out in the Solvency II directive (Article 121(2)). However, the requirement of consistency cannot be restricted to technical provisions alone, but also applies to the valuation of all assets and liabilities, as EIOPA pointed out in its guidelines (cf. Guideline 23 and explanatory text). While this section focuses on consistency with technical provisions, other more general important consistency issues (without elaborating the details) include:

- different (re-)valuations at different calculation steps in the model;
- simulation based versus analytic approaches; and
- data/assets/liabilities before and after data processing or model point building (cf. EIOPA Guideline 23).

In this section, a number of (quite obvious) non-life examples are named in which deviations between methods used in the risk model and methods used for calculating technical provisions can be sensible and necessary. Further, a way in which the consistency requirements can be sensibly applied in reserve risk modelling is shown. Guideline 24 of the EIOPA guidelines makes clear that the consistency requirements are not restricted to the "methods" in a narrow sense, but apply to data, parameters and assumptions as well. Each aspect is touched on in the following.

The firm's usual incurred but not reported (IBNR) claims reserving methods and processes are regularly used to also determine technical provisions under Solvency II.[5] The methods include a variety of reserving techniques, starting with the chain ladder method up to incremental loss ratio, Bornhuetter–Ferguson and many other, even exotic, methods. Reinsurers and industrial insurers, in particular, use numerous complex methods. The processes include actuarial judgement (eg, on data included or excluded) based on business knowledge, underwriting or portfolio changes and claims experience.

The risk model, on the other hand, is frequently based on one or two methods, such as Merz–Wüthrich (one-year Mack model based on chain ladder), a one-year version of an incremental loss ratio model or resampling methods (plus an "actuary in the box" for the one-year view) that again are based on the Mack or cross-classified methods. Furthermore, it is not even possible to define a statistically sound risk model for each and every reserving method. Data adjustments might differ from reserving for good reasons (eg, the exclusion of a large claim and its separate reserving is hardly possible, or at least connected to severe difficulties in the risk model). The answers to even more basic data questions, such as using paid or incurred data, might differ for good reason.

Good reasons for deviation are also obvious when considering the fundamental aims of reserving and risk modelling. While reserving is clearly focused on the best estimate, the objective of risk modelling is the whole distribution. When estimating a mean, a far more granular segmentation in lines of business leading to more homogeneous segments (with scarcer data) might be sensible. This might be completely inappropriate if estimating a whole distribution is the aim.

As has been shown, it is important to realise that differences between reserving and risk modelling can be sensible and necessary. Only in exceptional cases where perfect equality between reserving and risk modelling reigns, do consistency issues not need to be addressed explicitly. However, consistency cannot be interpreted as a degree of similarity or even equality. There is a trade-off between equality on the one hand and a statistically sound model on the other hand.

Nonetheless, for the reasons given earlier, the quantity modelled in the internal model must reflect the change of the own funds (or the technical provisions), and the results of the internal model must reflect the variability of the best estimate technical provisions of the solvency balance sheet.[6] The firm has to demonstrate this. The basis of such a demonstration must clearly be a detailed analysis of the differences between methods, data used and results in reserving and reserve risk modelling. Comparing best estimates obtained from reserving, with means calculated out of the reserve risk distribution or reserve ranges obtained from reserving with the reserve risk distribution, can be a good starting point. An evident reasoning, preferably quantitatively, but at least qualitatively, explaining why deviations in numbers and methods are acceptable in the light of "reflecting the variability of the own funds" is necessary. This includes an assessment of the impact of deviations in isolation and in combination, and a justification that they do not lead to inconsistencies (cf. Guideline 25 of the EIOPA guidelines). Often, if risk modellers and reserving actuaries are not identical, the latter have much more information on the claims, the business, the structure of the portfolios, etc. It is difficult to understand why risk modellers deliberately refrain from this valuable information. In some firms, increased exchange between reserving actuaries and risk modellers has been observed, with positive effects on the work of both.

Ability to rank risks

At first glance, the result of an internal risk model may appear to be a risk number for the total risk of a firm. Solvency II distinguishes two important steps on the way to this risk quantification. Indeed, as an end-result, a number for the total risk is required. However, beforehand, the statistical quality standards require a ranking of the risks, which – from an individual risk manager's perspective – may be even more important than the total risk. Success in one step does not imply success in the other. Firms that have properly ranked all their risks might still over- or underestimate their total risk, while even a very precise calibration of the total risk figure does not ensure that individual risks are properly ranked. The latter may happen in highly integrated models where the aggregation of risks is determined by the granular dependency structure of all underlying risk factors rather than an explicit aggregation algorithm for different risk or business classes, and therefore extra care must be taken to get not only the total risk figure right, but also the figures for the individual risks (discussed later in this chapter).

The requirement on risk ranking emphasises that the purpose of the internal model is not only to determine regulatory capital, but that it should also be useful for internal risk management by distinguishing different risks by their relative importance and use this information for management purposes.

This is not as straightforward as it seems at first sight. Typically, different risks evolve over different time horizons, exhibit different distributional characteristics and consequently might be managed to different quantiles in their distributions. If we look at the risk regulation in the banking sector, we see a wide variety of time horizons and quantiles for different risks. Similarly, in the insurance sector, the traditional property/casualty (P/C) actuary might prefer a view of the ultimate premium and reserving risk, while on the other extreme their colleague from the asset management department monitors risks with a weekly, or sometimes even daily, horizon. The tricky question therefore is: "How is it possible to compare the risks from a long-tail property or casualty line of business, where losses can develop over a period of 10 years and longer, to the risks from financial markets which change and take effect on a daily basis?"

A useful framework was given by the Committee of European Insurance and Occupational Pensions Supervisors (CEIOPS) (now EIOPA) in its "Advice for Level 2 Implementing Measures" (paragraph 5.221), under which the risk ranking could be interpreted by setting out the following four dimensions.

- Coverage: the risk-ranking ability should exist for all material risks covered by the internal model.
- Resolution: the differentiation between the various risks and risk drivers has to be sufficiently precise to allow management to take appropriate decisions.
- Congruence: the structure of different kinds of risk ranking reflects the structure of risks or risk categories, and the risk management system.
- Consistency: risks of a similar nature are ranked consistently throughout the undertaking and over time. The overall risk ranking is in line with the capital allocation.

An internal model capable of ranking risks ensures that all the different risks covered are comparable. This could be achieved in a variety of ways. However, in practice, firms typically decide to implement a common risk measure throughout the firm to measure, report and control risks.

The advantage that this common risk measure brings, namely having a common currency and basis for comparison for all the risks covered, are offset by disadvantages that have to be accepted. Not all the particular characteristics and the temporal emergence of individual risks can be reflected in the common risk measure. A risk horizon of one year disregards all events that happen afterwards, and using a 99.5% VaR is blind to the one-in-1,000-years events.

Consequently, the fact that all risks need to be made comparable does certainly not imply that special characteristics of individual risks should not be taken into account in risk management: the opposite should be aimed for. This consideration shows again that a one-dimensional view is not the best way to look at risks, but that a multitude of measures may be useful for proper risk management.

Also, the requirements for risk ranking should be seen in conjunction with the requirements on profit and loss (P&L) attribution in Article 123 of the Solvency II directive. One evident question would be to ask whether highly ranked risks also explain the bulk of the P&L change over a given period.

DATA AND EXPERT JUDGEMENT

Any model, however sophisticated, can produce forecasts only on the basis of data and other inputs provided to it – a model is not a crystal ball for the future. Therefore, the data used to build the model are one of the main drivers for the model's performance. While in Solvency II methods and data are covered in separate paragraphs of Article 121, in practice the underlying data strongly interacts with the methods used in the model. Therefore, the focus in this section is not on data alone, but on its interaction with the assumptions and methods used.

A model and the data used to develop and test it influence each other and impose mutual demands. A strong foundation of data often allows for detailed modelling, while data of lesser granularity usually requires a more resilient modelling approach. Setting up a very detailed model on a very coarse foundation of data may introduce artificial precision, lead to overfitting and, in this way, introduce hidden model risk. If a model and its foundation of data do not match each other in this way, one of them has to be adjusted – whether it is the modelling approach or the foundation of data will depend on the precise circumstances, such as the availability of more or alternative data sources or alternative modelling approaches. In cases where little data is available, it may sometimes be better to use a simple, sparsely parameterised model with transparent assumptions in a controlled environment, based on expert judgement, rather than to get caught in the trap of artificial precision, overfitting and hidden model risk, or to have no model at all.

In any case, model characteristics and limitations that originate from the quality of the underlying data should always be transparent to users of the model results (cf. Guideline 20 of the EIOPA guidelines).

There is a fluent transition between the area of methods from the previous section and the area of data covered in this section, with the notion of "expert judgement" taking some middle ground. For example, in the context of aggregating different risks, the methodology choice between a normal copula versus a t-copula can be reframed as a parameter estimation for the degrees of freedom of the t-copula, based on observed data. Since there is rarely enough data to confidently estimate such parameters, there is usually some expert judgement involved in their choice.

Expert judgement also influences areas where sufficient data is available, since data inputs are rarely useable as they are. There is always a certain amount of expert judgement involved when selecting data for the model. The impact of expert judgement occurs on a sliding scale. In this section, some examples are given, along with considerations involved when making those judgements. At one end of the scale market risk is concerned, although it is usually considered as a data-rich modelling category. At the other end of the scale there is operational risk, where forward-looking scenarios, created by experts, play a strong role next to the historically observed cases of operational losses. Between these two extremes lies non-life underwriting risk modelling.

Market risk

Market risk models, whether they are based on a complex ESG or other simpler approaches, are supposed to project realistic scenarios of financial markets' risk factors into the future. For this purpose, they make certain assumptions about the dynamics of those risk factors, or their marginal and joint distributions. However, regardless of the exact methodology chosen, the parameters of these models all need to be estimated based on historical data in order to consistently reflect the existing and observed market characteristics.

Ideally, any model should be both robust and sensitive (cf. CEIOPS, "Advice for L2 Implementing Measures for Solvency II:

Tests and Standards for Internal Model Approval", 5.62). While it should not exhibit undue and spurious fluctuations, it should at the same time react to changing market conditions. This characteristic is not only determined by the model's methodology, but also by the foundation of data it uses. Modellers have to make a decision about the extent of use of historic data. Any choice has certain advantages and drawbacks. A longer time series makes the model more stable, and might ensure that previous crises in financial markets are reflected in the model dynamics. This is particularly relevant for certain types of parameters that need a lot of data to be estimated reliably, such as correlation parameters. However, lowering the estimation error by using a longer time series also means that the model responds more slowly to changes in the market environment, such as regime changes from high to low interest rates or a sudden crisis. This choice has to be made even if using more sophisticated weighting schemes for historic market data, such as the well-known exponentially decaying weights for older data, instead of the simpler equal weighting of a given time horizon.

The actual choice depends on the intended use of the model. Therefore, when making the choice, modellers should discuss the intended applications with the ultimate users of the model, including the supervisors. They interpret the resulting risk numbers and use them for management and supervisory decisions, respectively, and need to be aware of the market situations reflected in the model (see, also, Guideline 20 of the EIOPA guidelines).

As shown, even when measuring market risk where plenty of data is available compared to other risk categories, at the very first stage of modelling, choices can play a major role and significantly impact model output. In order to assess the impact, firms might use different calibrations based on varying historic time periods. A prerequisite for this exercise is obviously that firms can actually obtain the required calibrations of the model, either because they themselves can carry out such calibrations or because the ESG provider is flexible enough to supply them.

This would enable them to assess their capital needs and, even in benign periods, be prepared for sudden market turmoil. However, so far a separate "stress value-at-risk (VaR)" calculation, as it exists for the market risk of banks and which uses a specially selected period of historic market stress as the basis for the calibration, is not required under Solvency II. In any case, the model needs to be forward-looking and choices such as the historic time period to use are required to be subject to regular internal validation in order to ensure their ongoing appropriateness (cf. Article 124 of the Solvency II directive).

Non-life underwriting risk

In non-life, non-cat underwriting risk modelling there are well-established and wide spread methods available and used in internal models. In premium risk modelling, among those used in internal models, frequency/severity models are still the ones that use most data (the usual alternatives, yearly total loss, frequency/average severity or "derivatives" of triangulation techniques, use less data). In claims frequency, modellers usually have to rely on only one observation per year, while data for claims severity is richer, but still not as comprehensive as, for example, capital markets data. In reserve risk modelling – usually based on triangulation techniques – there is one observation per calendar year for each accident year, which forms a solid basis but does not free modellers from cogitating about appropriateness (accuracy) and completeness of the data.

Along with these well-established methods are the data: it is quite clear what data must be considered for modelling. There are numerous reasons why data might be sparse or of poor quality, such as new lines of business, numerous claims databases, changes of claims databases, mergers and acquisitions or simply a poor data collection and administration process. In these cases – besides working hard on improvements – it is very obvious that expert judgement is needed.

However, also in cases when historical data is accurate and complete, it might be appropriate to not use it or to enrich it with further information. Examples of such cases are representativeness (for premium risk modelling, portfolio changes; for reserve risk modelling, changes in claims handling/processing; for both risks, legal or underwriting policy changes) or freedom in parameterisation (for premium risk, choosing large loss thresholds or data for trend modelling; for reserve risk, choosing the extrapolation method and data used for tail factors and their volatility).

Choice of data (and of methods and assumptions), including anything that is called "actuarial judgement", must be justified and documented in an appropriate way. According to experience, firms usually have well-established processes for this in reserving, but need to develop similar activities in risk modelling.

Beyond this, a typical discussion with firms is about the exclusion of claims "that cannot appear again", such as asbestos claims, which meanwhile may be excluded from the risk insured. The latter is not an entirely satisfying justification for exclusion. The risk profile might still be such that asbestos-like claims may appear ("what is the next asbestos?"). Another example is the discussion about very large claims that hit a competitor but could have hit the firm in the same manner. Usually, it is necessary for firms to consider using data or information additional to their own historical data. Pure data-driven modelling without exposure analysis will only be sufficient in exceptional cases.

In addition to the methods discussed so far, there are special risks that require special modelling. There are numerous examples of latent claims, liability accumulation or further "realistic disasters" whose modelling require even more expert judgement than those of the common risks.

Operational risk

Operational risk is one of the risk categories that make the largest use of expert judgement. It is explicitly recognised that during a period where structured collection of loss data on operational events is only just about to begin, the existing set of historic data is not sufficient for the modelling of operational risk, and many firms make heavy use of scenarios when building their operational risk models. In the absence of data, the use of expert judgement is a way to compensate for this lack of objective information, and using expert judgement is better than not taking a view at all. At the very least, it allows a structured and deliberate examination of the underlying information basis and the associated risks. However, using probably subjective views as the basis of a model carries its own risks. Therefore, the use of expert judgement needs a strong control environment (cf. Guideline 19 of the EIOPA guidelines).

Even when a little data is available, it is sometimes a better choice for modellers to rely on expert judgement for parameter setting than use the little available data directly. Worse than the resulting artificial precision, overfitting and hidden model risk, when new data points arrive, model results can become unstable and jump. A case in point is the occurrence of new and large operational risk events in the tail of the existing loss distribution. These can impact and change the distribution heavily. Such a potential impact can be reduced if similar operational risk scenarios already exist. In this way, expert judgement can by its forward-looking nature ensure the required stability of the model. However, existing data should not be disregarded, but form the basis of the expert judgement and should be used to regularly question, validate and update the expert judgement (cf. Guideline 22 of the EIOPA guidelines).

In the case of operational risk, new data on operational losses may lead to new views on the adequacy of the scenario parameters determined through expert judgement, which will then be reviewed and updated accordingly.

General points

As has been illustrated, expert judgement is involved both in cases where a lot of data is available and where very little data is available. However, expert judgement by its nature is subjective, which makes it hard to check the quality of the judgement by itself. To compensate for this, the process of arriving at the judgement and using it has to be controlled rather than the judgement. The EIOPA preparatory guidelines offer three dimensions along which such controls can be implemented. After some general comments on materiality, we will examine these three dimensions in more detail.

Overall, the guidelines stress a proportionality-oriented view in emphasising that all those controls should be applied in line with the materiality of the judgement in question. Since ensuring a high standard of data quality and tight controls around the expert judgement processes can be cost-intensive, firms usually take into account the materiality of the impact of data or expert judgement on model results in order to focus their efforts. A prerequisite for this is that firms have an overview of their instances of expert judgement, together with the respective impacts on model results (cf. Guideline 18 of the EIOPA guidelines and CEIOPS' "Advice for L2 Implementing Measures for Solvency II: Tests and Standards for Internal Model Approval", 5.129ff). In order to handle all such model inputs consistently, some firms develop a general framework for expert judgement. The framework also distinguishes between expert judgements that are subject to the framework and expert judgements that are out of bounds due to materiality or other considerations.

Governance

As has been illustrated, some model assumptions are taken for granted and modellers will not always be aware of their impact or the limitations they place on the model. Such hidden assumptions can be a dangerous source of model risk when external circumstances change and those hidden assumptions do not hold any longer. Designing processes around such hidden assumptions and thus making them transparent is an important step towards reducing model risk.

Establishing a sound and well-documented process with clear responsibilities is also important because it provides the associated process controls, and also facilitates the regular production of expert judgement and its review. In order to set up such processes, firms have to identify all sources of data and expert judgement, determine quality criteria depending on their use and materiality, and find possibilities for cross-checking these model inputs. It is also useful to break down the actual production of expert judgement into smaller steps, such as those presented in the explanatory text of the preparatory guidelines (cf. the explanatory text for Guideline 19 of the EIOPA guidelines).

In the case of scenarios for operational risk, for example, it may be important to link the estimates of frequency and severity of operational risk loss scenarios to observable indicators, so that any change in these indicators can lead to a reassessment of the scenario.

It is good practice to communicate more important expert judgements with a large impact on model results to senior management, and require sign-off at sufficient levels of seniority. Here, it can be a challenge to adequately explain the way in which particular expert judgements impact model results. However, overcoming these challenges will lead to a well-controlled framework for expert judgement and also improve senior management knowledge about the internal risk model.

Communication and uncertainty

Sources of expert judgement can be spread far around an insurance firm. In particular, they can be distant from the actual users of model results. A correct interpretation and use of model results relies on the knowledge of model assumptions, the characteristics of the underlying data and, in particular, on any expert judgement used in modelling. This is why Guideline 20 of the EIOPA guidelines looks at the communication between suppliers and users of expert judgement, as well as how the uncertainty around model results is made transparent.

Often, it is only when a change in model results is difficult to explain that assumptions are reviewed in the search for an explanation. For example, a sudden drop in market risk figures may raise questions since the underlying positions have not significantly changed, and this may draw attention to the fact that a certain stress period has moved outside of the calibration window of the market risk model. The model and its results will be more useful if such effects are known in advance.

Documentation and validation

Generally, expert judgement – much more than other external data sources – faces the risk of being forgotten or irreproducible once it has been delivered, which increases model risk when judgements become out of date. Appropriate documentation and regular monitoring of such assumptions are therefore key, and also provide the basis for internal validation processes that ensure the ongoing appropriateness of data sources and expert judgement.

COVERAGE OF ALL MATERIAL RISKS

A typical insurance firm faces a large number of risks with very different characteristics. One purpose of the internal model is to provide a common basis for the measurement of all these risks. Risks that are not captured by the internal model may make it difficult to implement an integrated risk management framework. While firms therefore aim for a complete representation of their risk profile, some risks may be excluded from the internal model. It is of utmost importance that any exclusion of risks from the model does not happen by accident, but is a deliberate choice, well justified, documented and made transparent to all relevant parties.

Throughout the pre-application phase, firms have been able to clarify the intended scope of their internal model and, in particular, if they intend to apply for a partial or full internal model.[7] The Level 2 delegated acts define "internal model scope" as the risks that the internal model is approved to cover. Also, risks are said to be "covered" by the internal model if they are reflected in the PDF underlying the internal model. Article 121(4) of the Solvency II directive requires the internal model to cover all of the material (quantifiable) risks to which the firm is exposed. The baseline against which the coverage of the internal model is measured is, of course, the scope of the internal model.

These requirements mean that firms do not need to model risks within the internal model scope if they are immaterial. However, the internal model scope may also include risks that are not reflected in the standard formula for the SCR, but which are material and which, therefore, have to be modelled. One example is implied volatility as a risk driver for derivative financial instruments or options and guarantees embedded in insurance liabilities.

In practice, the firm has to specify the internal model scope and demonstrate that all material risks within its scope are covered. With a modular structure of the internal model, this is typically done module-by-module. Then, the interaction between modules must not be ignored as a potential source of risks not covered. Demonstrating completeness is not easy. Firms approach this problem by trying to convince supervisors that there is no evidence that the risk coverage is incomplete. This leads to the question of the materiality or immateriality, respectively, of risks that are not covered by the internal model, or at least, not accurately covered. There is no single answer to this question. It depends on how these risks compare to the risks covered by the internal model, as well as the methodology used to assess materiality. Regardless of the type of risk measure used, a connection to the Solvency II risk measure must be established anyhow. In the context of a group internal model, it is worth noticing that risks that are immaterial from a group's perspective may be material at solo level or, vice versa, a concentration of risks may appear at group level.

It is good practice to compile the risks that were assessed to be immaterial at inception and monitor them regularly, making sure that these risks do not accumulate such that if considered in aggregate they would significantly contribute to the SCR. Evidently, the internal model itself does not come into consideration as an indicator for the materiality of the risks not covered. It is sometimes necessary to resort to separate models or analyses designed only to estimate materiality. The complexity of such models or analyses is typically lower as compared to the actual internal model. In other cases, the use of simple exposure measures as proxy risk measures may be sufficient to come to a conclusion.

A quantitative assessment is not mandatory in every case. Although quantitative indicators are deemed to be very likely more objective, the Level 2 delegated acts allow for qualitative indicators for the materiality of risks, too. Firms choose this option when a quantitative assessment is either hardly possible or very resource-intensive.

Different reasons for incomplete risk coverage have been observed.

- *Some exposure is disregarded from risk measurement*
  In market risk and credit risk, for example, full model coverage may be compromised if no thorough analysis of the exposure is carried out. If the model is built to cover the exposures to market and credit risk that are supposed to be material, some balance-sheet items may simply be disregarded. This often concerns assets and liabilities that are managed in organisational units very distant from risk management, and can often happen when the construction of the Solvency II balance sheet is still in a conceptual stage at the time of model development.

  Often, balance-sheet items apart from capital market investments and technical provisions are too easily disregarded. Examples of these are other receivables, deposits on retained and assumed reinsurance business, pension liabilities, mortgage loans and cash. On closer inspection, the risk from some of these exposures or the risk in total may turn out to be non-negligible.
- *Parts of the business are deliberately not included into the model*
  Newly introduced insurance products are not included in risk measurement from the start. This is in most cases because the internal model as it stands is not fit to capture the different features of that business. For example, consider a life insurer that recently started writing a new product. As long as the portfolio of the new product is negligibly small in comparison to the overall portfolio, it may not need to be covered by the internal model. However, if an increase in volume is foreseeable, measures need

to be taken to extend model coverage to this type of business. A similar situation holds after the acquisition of an insurance firm or some insurance portfolios. Before the business acquired can be captured by the internal model, different infrastructure and data systems often must be aligned.

- *Some risk drivers are neglected*
  An example of a risk driver that is neglected is inflation. Internal models sometimes do not have inflation as a driver of market or underwriting risk. In non-life reserve risk, some firms argue that claims inflation, although not explicitly modelled, is taken into account implicitly as being included in historical claims (when triangles are not adjusted for inflation). It is clear, however, that calendar year effects such as inflation cannot be properly reflected in standard triangulation techniques.
  Another area is risks arising from the use of risk mitigation techniques. Firms need to take care that these "other risks", if material, are taken into full account. Examples are counterparty default risk of over-the-counter (OTC) derivatives or the basis risk of alternative risk transfer (ART) instruments – for example, if sponsoring a cat bond with a trigger that is not indemnity-based.
  A popular assumption in natcat risk modelling is that claims are largely settled after one year – ie, there is no material reserve risk. This assumption is under debate as claims development for big catastrophe events suggest the contrary to be true. Sometimes it is loss experience that reveals the actual relevance of risk drivers. For instance, the severe Thailand Flood event in 2011 showed that a whole market was surprised by the high losses due to liability for contingent business interruption. High complexity of supply chains and lack of corresponding data make detailed modelling prohibitively challenging.
- *Possible changes to valuation assumptions are not considered as risk drivers*
  Adverse events during the one-year time horizon do not regularly influence own funds merely by payments and provisions directly related to the events. They rather lead to a revaluation of the whole portfolio based on new assumptions triggered by these events.
- *Definition of risk and boundaries to other risk categories are not sufficiently clear*
  The most prominent example of this is operational risk. The loss potential due to inadequate or failed internal processes, personnel

or systems, or from external events might to some extent already be reflected in market, credit or underwriting risk. Firms must make the effort of clearly drawing a line in order to avoid double counting and ensure adequate risk coverage.

In filling a gap in risk coverage, firms rely frequently on simplified techniques that provide a rough estimate rather than a precise quantification of risk. For instance, with the aim to include some missing parts of the business, the loss distribution obtained for the explicitly modelled part is scaled. A prerequisite for this is that the risk profiles of both parts share important characteristics – ie, the risks "behave" similarly. Of course, depending on the materiality, the adequateness of such approximate approaches must be demonstrated thoroughly.

This section concludes with an example applicable to an internationally operating insurer with a global natcat exposure. To ensure that there are no material gaps in the natcat risk coverage, the insurer would establish a regular assessment that comprises at least the following main steps:

- identification of the own peril landscape by materiality assessment of the currently existing exposures, taking into account expected future exposure changes;
- reconciliation of this peril landscape with the current model landscape and identification of any gaps;
- for each peril, assessment of completeness, particularly in terms of:
  - coverage of exposures or features of exposures that are not explicitly modelled;
  - coverage of secondary perils (eg, storm surge or tsunami risk);
  - implications of approximations (eg, regarding financial structures); and
  - reflection of hardly quantifiable risks (eg, contingent business interruption).
- planning to fill any material gaps identified.

DIVERSIFICATION EFFECTS

The aggregation of risks, together with the inherent modelling of diversification effects, has a huge impact on model results and at the same time is a very challenging task. This is due to the fact that, in many cases, both model choice and parameterisation cannot be carried out in a quantitative manner. On top of that, regulatory requirements are very demanding, as will be discussed.

A comprehensive treatment of this topic would deserve its own book, one that would be about the same size as the present one. As there are already several publications on the topic, this section is restricted to aspects that – according to experience – are sometimes disregarded.

The ubiquity of diversification

This section starts rather unusually, with a statement that seems both trivial and is nonetheless sometimes forgotten: the concept of balance within a portfolio (ie, diversification) is one of the fundamental principles of insurance.

There is diversification everywhere – between insurance policies of the same products or lines of business, between products, between lines of business, between German and US bonds, between Italian and Brazilian equities, between bonds and equities, between real estate and deliverables, between assets and liabilities, between internal fraud and North Atlantic hurricanes. Therefore, when discussing aggregation and diversification, it is of the utmost importance not only to focus on aggregation between the overall risk categories market, credit, underwriting and operational risk (sometimes called inter-risk aggregation) or between legal entities, but also on the diversification on the levels below (sometimes called intra-risk aggregation), which may have an effect as big or even bigger than the inter-risk aggregation.

Clearly, these manifold links between risks cannot all be reflected explicitly in an internal model. Regardless of whether the firm employs a building block approach (where risks are modelled separately in categories and then aggregated, not unlike the procedure in the standard formula), a full stochastic model (sometimes called dynamic financial analysis model, where all "risk drivers" are simulated at once) or a blend of the two approaches, in no case are all dependencies between each and every risk specified explicitly. This implies that not every diversification effect is controllable or even visible – usually, it is impossible to specify the explicit diversification effect between a policy in the annuity portfolio and a US bond in an internal model. This applies not only on this granular level: if the firm opts for an integrated capital market risk model, it might be impossible to measure a diversification effect between market and credit risk.

The role of the structure of the risk model

Another important example of the influence of the internal model's structure on diversification effects is the number of steps used to aggregate risks or, equivalently, the number of risks to be aggregated within one aggregation step. The inter-risk diversification effect seen is certainly lower when aggregating capital market, underwriting and operational risks than when aggregating market, credit, life underwriting, non-life underwriting, health underwriting and operational risks. (Obviously, this does not mean that an overall lower diversification effect is indeed realised, it is just realised elsewhere.) There are numerous examples of this – eg, in terms of assets, risk factors, (group) lines of business or scenarios on lower levels.

Further, the diversification effect is influenced by the size of the risks to be aggregated. A risk that dominates the others will certainly lead to a lower diversification effect than aggregating a number of rather equally sized risks. Therefore, besides the evident factors influencing diversification effects, such as the risk measure including time horizon and quantile to be considered, and the model choice and parameterisation, the structure of the risk model and resultant effects, including individual shares of risks, need to be carefully considered when assessing aggregation and diversification. Accordingly, it is important to note that diversification visible in an internal model depends on the model structure, and Solvency II allows far-reaching freedom in the structuring of internal models.

It is therefore clear that one must be very careful when comparing diversification effects. As soon as there are slight differences in the structure of two models or in the risk profile of the firms, this might be the reason for very different diversification effects. This implies that the intensively discussed limitation of modelled diversification effects by stakeholders without due consideration of the model at hand lacks a sound theoretical underpinning (although such a limitation might be considered for individual aggregation steps in an internal model).

Understanding and challenging diversification

In general, modelling aggregation and diversification requires a large degree of expertise and experience. There are many pitfalls in multivariate (normal) frameworks and correlations, asymptotics versus properties of the joint distribution tails (tail areas), bivariate versus multivariate dependencies, copula concepts in general, their interplay with marginal distributions particularly in determining the joint distribution and the distribution of the sum of the risks, etc.

The area of conflict between highly sophisticated models and the understanding of all stakeholders, operational effectiveness, transparency, robustness (especially in a framework that is rolled out in a large insurance group) particularly applies to aggregation and diversification.

Texts on aggregation and diversification often focus on model choice and parameterisation, as they are the critical steps in modelling. As mentioned, the burning desire to base aggregation and diversification on quantitative methods turned out to be wishful thinking in many cases. The simple reason is that there is not sufficient data; while it is already difficult in many instances to model based on one observation per year, this is hardly possible when modelling dependency. Firms and supervisors have to accept that the choice of aggregation methods and their parameterisation are predominantly expert-driven. This implies, in many instances (see "Data and Expert Judgement" earlier in this chapter), the necessity to look beyond data and quantitative methods for justification of the expert judgement.

It is therefore key to implement good processes around the expert judgement involved, including clear criteria for the change of the model and its parameterisation. More generally, good model governance and the pertaining management attention at levels of sufficient seniority are very important – management should be aware that aggregation is a modelling step that has a very special nature and involves many sources of uncertainty.

This does not mean, however, that quantitative exercises are completely useless. Given the above-mentioned facts on the model structure, analysing implied dependencies (or conditions on them) as a result of parameterising a dependency model is a valuable challenge. Usually, it is possible to try alternative risk model structures (ie, aggregation steps), parameterise them and compare the results with the results of the original dependency model. Further, even simple comparisons of results in the fully dependent and the independent case can deliver useful insights. Moreover, rather obvious exercises, such as sensitivity and stability analysis, benchmarking and external data, are clearly good procedures to justify, challenge and validate the model and its parameterisation. Often such exercises are easily carried out; sometimes they are rather laborious. However, the above-mentioned significance of aggregation and diversification justifies an increased effort compared to other, less important model parts.

Regulatory requirements

Finally, the Level 2 delegated acts make some demanding requirements. Firms are required to take into account any non-linear dependency and any lack of diversification under extreme scenarios. The supervisors' motivation is obvious: an area with such a huge impact on model results on the one hand, and so many degrees of freedom on the other, should be addressed with high demands. However, recalling that diversification is everywhere and that links between risks are so manifold, a practicable application of this requirement is to oblige firms to make considerable effort to analyse non-linear dependency and the lack of diversification under a selection of extreme scenarios.

Further, it is required that insurance and reinsurance undertakings should be able to justify the assumptions underlying the system used for measuring diversification effects on an empirical basis. An immediate interpretation might be that "empirical basis" must be related to data. Recalling the scarcity of data, this leads to similar problems as with above-mentioned non-linear dependency and lack of diversification under extreme scenarios. "Empirical", however, may also be interpreted as "originating in or based on observation or experience" (Merriam Webster's Dictionary), from which a clear link to expert judgement may be derived (see our earlier discussion).

RISK MITIGATION TECHNIQUES

The requirements on risk mitigation techniques follow the general spirit of the Solvency II directive – ie, no particular method for modelling risk mitigation is prescribed, but all risks originating from the risk mitigation itself must be covered by the model. A large number of effective risk mitigation techniques exist. In this section, reinsurance, as one of the most common, is illustrated.

Obligatory reinsurance

Reinsurance (or retrocession, respectively)[8] is the classical liability risk mitigation technique, particularly for non-life firms. For premium risk, firms are fairly advanced in modelling obligatory reinsurance based on single claim simulation (necessary for most non-proportional reinsurance). Such simulation models are widespread and able to adequately reflect non-proportional reinsurance in premium risk.

Reserve risk, on the other hand, gives rise to more complications when modelling reinsurance. Usually, firms do not use reserve risk models on the basis of single claims, but based on triangulation techniques. This means that non-proportional reinsurance cannot be directly modelled on single claims, so that the reinsurance payouts observed in reality are not represented identically in the model. The demonstration of the appropriateness of any such approximation is often laborious, and typically includes considerations of the reinsurance programme for relevant accident years, the effect on different parts of the distribution or case studies on the effect of large claims on the portion ceded (per accident year).

Facultative reinsurance

Many firms, in particular those with a large portion of industrial business in their portfolio, make extensive use of facultative reinsurance. This type of reinsurance is often characterised by ceding very special risks, increased responsibility of the underwriter, no central department responsible and no (separate and overall) facultative reinsurance strategy. It is common that an insurer has thousands of facultative reinsurance contracts in place. In some cases, firms even struggle to attain a view over the whole existing facultative reinsurance programme as the relevant data is not collected centrally. Even in cases where data is available, it is often impossible to model this facultative reinsurance case by case. The single claim simulation would need much more information about the specifics of the individual facultative reinsurance contract (eg, exposure of the policy versus coverage of the facultative reinsurance (basis risk), also with respect to the cause of potential claims) and similarly detailed information for the (simulated) claim itself. In addition, obligatory reinsurance is normally set up for a whole line of business (or several lines of business), and so the structure of reinsurance contracts fits the model structure – whereas facultative reinsurance regularly applies for single policies only.

It is therefore necessary to make an appropriate approximation – eg, applying such reinsurance only for the highest facultative deductible in place in the respective line of business. To demonstrate the appropriateness of such an approximation, it is essential to assess the facultative reinsurance programme addressing the above-mentioned specifics of the facultative reinsurance contracts. Due to the tremendous effort this exercise would take in return for – in many cases – a relatively modest SCR relief, some firms refrain from modelling facultative reinsurance. However, even in this case, a firm still has to demonstrate that the model reflects its risk profile appropriately.

There are several difficulties with the appropriate modelling of other risk mitigation techniques apart from reinsurance discussed so far, and not only related to liabilities. Without going into their details, some of these are:

- modelling of co-insurance, (participations in) syndicates or other forms of joint account business;
- modelling of deposits (as mentioned earlier);
- modelling of hedging (eg, related to variable annuities);
- strong conditions on recognition of risk mitigation techniques (eg, with respect to techniques that are in force for a period shorter than 12 months);
- special-purpose vehicles (eg, finite re); and
- collateral arrangements, including segregation of assets.[9]

Generally, problems with the modelling of such risk mitigation techniques are similar to the ones mentioned above, and revolve around the availability of data on the effect of the risk mitigation, its representation in the respective IT systems, its compatibility with simulated claims, the ability of the risk model to handle such detailed information and the centralised collection and cataloguing of the necessary details.

FUTURE MANAGEMENT ACTIONS

The area of future management actions is a highly insurance market- and model category-specific one. In some markets (eg, in Germany), they play a key role in the cashflow models in life and health insurance. The German life and health insurance business models are based heavily on financial guarantees and contractual options, and allow management to determine policyholder participation to a certain extent. A key feature is the strong dependence of the value of the liabilities from the performance of the assets (the allocation of which, in turn, depends on the value and cashflows of liabilities). In addition, there are many product features that result from national contractual and regulatory decrees. These specificities make it necessary to run long-term cashflow models simulating these mechanisms and, in particular, the pertaining management actions even for valuation. In other markets with less complex business models, future management actions might be negligible.

Further, in many risk model categories, future management actions play a minor role. Typical examples are models that follow the instantaneous shock approach, rather than explicitly model the course of the one-year time horizon in detail. For instance, typical market risk models revalue the unchanged portfolio under a number of scenarios without explicitly modelling the possible impact of a specific asset allocation during the one year under each and every scenario (and firms refrain from this kind of modelling for good reason). There are some exceptions, such as "actuary in the box" techniques for modelling the one-year time horizon in reserving risk or slight adjustments in planning data for the new underwriting year (premium risk). As mentioned, the most important exceptions from this rule are the cashflow models in life and health insurance. This means future management actions are predominantly a life and health insurance cashflow model topic.

Against this background, only one aspect is named here that might be relevant for a number of insurance markets across Europe – an additional challenge on modelling management actions generated by the risk model. Many cashflow models were developed for, and consequently focus on, valuation. However, modelled future management actions such as profit participation or asset allocation also have to be appropriate under stressed market conditions, where the challenging task of implementation and justification of appropriate real-world management actions in a risk-neutral valuation environment gets increasingly difficult.

For supervisors, it is hard to challenge modelled future management actions against history, as it is not possible to find a catalogue of historical decisions from which rules for each future situation can be derived. Many factors influencing real management decisions cannot even be modelled – such as the behaviour of the competitors or information about conditions in the whole insurance market. According to the Level 2 delegated acts, firms shall develop an extensive rule and justification framework, and let their senior management sign off the management actions implemented in the model. Again, the concrete measures to be taken are very market- and model category-specific.

FINANCIAL GUARANTEES AND CONTRACTUAL OPTIONS

Similar to future management actions, both financial guarantees and contractual options are predominantly a life and health topic, as well as being insurance market- and model category-specific. Therefore, as with the previous section on future management actions, only a few aspects will be discussed in a general context.

The Solvency II directive requires material financial guarantees and contractual options to be accurately assessed in the internal model. In this light, the whole area of policyholder behaviour is sometimes not treated sufficiently. Examples are lapse modelling (in particular, the different types of this: depending on the business model/insurance market, surrender lapse, paid-up lapse, premium increase lapse, etc), premium reduction or premium increase options by the policyholder, lump-sum option in life or tariff conversion in health. Moreover, in many cases, firms lack consideration of the interplay of all these options and guarantees with (financial) market conditions.

Further, some firms underrate the significance of certain options and guarantees of the policyholder under stressed market conditions. For example, the sensitivity of the own funds with respect to lump-sum options might be completely different under stressed conditions than in a normal environment.

Finally, it has been observed that the options of a firm are sometimes mis-valued in one or the other direction. For example, the (conditions to be allowed to use) possibilities of premium adjustments are modelled too roughly – if at all.

CONCLUSION

The statistical quality standards provide extensive modelling freedom to firms. They offer the opportunity to implement tailor-made risk models and make the most use of them. The standards require a minimum level of model quality and encourage ongoing model improvement and innovation. Firms adhering to this are likely to gain superior risk management capabilities as well as competitive advantages based on their internal model. However, the use of this modelling flexibility is not for free, but is counterbalanced by regulatory demands on transparency that can put considerable burden on firms. Regulators have attached great importance to the documented justification and internal testing of the assumptions underlying the internal model and other modelling decisions. They require firms to put in place regular internal controls, such as internal model validation, acting as a line of defence against model risk. However, the burden weighs not only on firms but also on the supervisors who review the model prior to approval and judge on its ongoing adequateness afterwards.

Although the calculation kernel[10] of the internal model, its foundation and its input and output are central to the statistical quality standards, the impact of these standards goes far beyond the calculation methodology, and is noticeable throughout the firm. Typically, the risk management function, the owner of the internal model, involves a number of organisational units and relies on their information and expertise in model development and maintenance. Users of the model and its output are likewise spread across the organisation. As the model results are meant to inform decision-taking, a modelling decision can have far-reaching consequences and directly affect business performance. It is a gross underestimation of the significance of the statistical quality standards to think that they only affect some figures on unimportant risk reports. For example, internal model output also have an impact on business opportunities and strategic alignment.

According to this interconnectedness of the calculation kernel of the internal model, the statistical quality standards are rather broad and widely linked to the other tests and standards (especially use test and validation standards), and the system of governance. Given this, it is obvious that the statistical quality standards are clearly not targeted at the development of the "best" or most sophisticated model, and do not take a purely technical perspective. As has been shown by the examples, there are always numerous competing dimensions of model quality.

The national supervisory authorities (NSAs) and EIOPA face a big challenge to establish a level playing field among European internal model firms, and ensure harmonised supervisory decisions on model approval and ongoing appropriateness. The highly principles-based nature of the statistical quality standards, necessary because of the wide variety of risk categories it has to cover and the great speed of technical innovation, is an important driving factor of this challenge. In light of this, in 2013 the EIOPA Internal Models Committee in close collaboration with NSAs strengthened efforts to facilitate the exchange of experience gained by supervisors during the pre-application phase. In particular, NSA modelling experts share their views on common modelling issues with the aim to foster a consistent application of the statistical quality standards. Clearly, efforts to harmonise the supervisory application of regulatory standards must gain momentum, but one should not forget that this is an ongoing task. This is not only because both risk models, on the one hand, and regulatory standards and their interpretation and application on the other, do evolve over time.

Ahead of the envisaged point in time of first-day model approval, supervisors are giving increasing thought to the future day-to-day supervision when they will have access to that highly risk-sensitive and powerful tool: the tailored internal model, and the results that it produces. For firms that have made significant headway along the pre-application process, NSAs and colleges of supervisors may want to use the remaining time to practice their regular internal models communication approach with firms in the way they envisage carrying it out after model approval.

In the future, one would expect that a large number of model changes[11] will relate to the internal model calculation methodology and hence affect compliance with the statistical quality standards. Taking notice of model changes, and taking a decision on the application for approval in the case of major changes, however, will not create sufficient checkpoints for supervisors to keep track of the internal model and its appropriateness for use in risk management. Supervisors should not risk losing the detailed knowledge and comprehensive understanding that will be gained until the completion of the pre-application phase. Therefore, a large part of the ongoing interaction between firms and supervisors after initial model approval will likely be based on up-to-date internal model results and related information about the firm's current risk profile.

It is in the interest of a firm to establish a regular internal model report that supplies its supervisors with rich information. In this way, a firm can contribute to a common understanding and support this special relationship with supervisors that is entered into with an internal model once approved. The experience with the regular internal models communication will likely shape the information package that a firm is expected to regularly submit to its supervisors.

Statements made here are the authors' personal and private views. They should not be construed to reflect BaFin's opinion, and do not represent official BaFin statements.

1 For a definition of an internal model in the narrow sense, see Chapter 1.
2 For further details about the use test and calibration standards, see Chapters 6 and 9.
3 For further details, see Directive 2009/138/EC.
4 For further details about the validation standards see Chapter 12.
5 Adjustments due to requirements under different accounting principles are made, if applicable.
6 The EIOPA guidelines on pre-application of internal models provide guidance on the consistency assessment to be performed by firms. Guideline 23 lists a number of consistency checkpoints relevant for a model part under consideration.
7 The SCR can be calculated by either an internal model, the standard formula or a combination of both, resulting in a partial internal model. The risks that the SCR shall cover at least are set out in Article 101(4) of the Solvency II directive.
8 In this section, reinsurance always means passive reinsurance, including the (passive) retrocession for reinsurance undertakings.
9 Specifications of the requirements on the recognition of risk mitigation techniques for the last three of these bullets for standard formula users are to be found in the respective articles of Level 2 delegated acts.
10 For a definition of calculation kernel, see Chapter 1.
11 For further details about model changes see Chapter 4.

REFERENCES

CEIOPS, 2009, "Advice for L2 Implementing Measures on SII: Tests and Standards for Internal Model Approval", November.

EIOPA, 2013, "EIOPA Final Report on Public Consultations No. 13/011 on the Proposal for Guidelines on the Pre-application for Internal Models", September.

European Parliament and the Council of the European Union, 2009, "Directive 2009/138/EC of the European Parliament and of the Council of 25 November 2009 on the Taking-up and Pursuit of the Business of Insurance and Reinsurance (Solvency II) (recast)".

8

Representation, Reality and the Solvency II Data Challenge

Dean Buckner

Prudential Regulation Authority, Bank of England

The European Solvency II directive[1] for insurance and reinsurance was one of the first regulatory regimes to introduce explicit requirements for data quality. Article 121 of the directive stated that data used for an internal capital model should be "accurate, complete and appropriate". Later, the European Insurance and Occupational Pensions Authority (EIOPA) guidelines provided high-level principles for data governance, such as implementing and maintaining a data policy and compiling a data directory, specifying the "source, characteristics and usage" of the data.[2]

Since the original directive was published in 2009, the insurance industry has grappled with the problem of imposing systems of data governance. This has been partly due to the generic and high-level nature of the directive requirements and the associated guidelines, and the subsequent need to interpret these in different ways. However, it has also been partly due to confusion surrounding the idea of data governance itself. This chapter will explore some of the common confusions surrounding data governance, as well as some of the common traps and pitfalls to avoid. These include the difficulties of distinguishing data governance from the science of information technology, the problem of measuring and controlling data quality, and understanding the purpose of a data directory. The traps and pitfalls are many, but this chapter identifies two serious obstacles to successful data governance, namely the fragmentation of systems caused by the growth of end-user computing in the late 20th century and the failure to recognise common principles of data governance, leading to failure to develop it as a discipline in its own right.

The examples relate to asset risk management (general insurance and life insurance), longevity risk management (life insurance) and catastrophe risk management (general insurance).

THE NEED FOR DATA GOVERNANCE

In the early days of computing, there was no need for data governance. Early computers were physically large "mainframe" systems that required such careful maintenance that they were carefully guarded by an elite corps of specialists.

> The IBM 704 cost several million dollars, took up an entire room, needed constant attention from a cadre of professional machine operators, and required special air-conditioning so that the glowing vacuum tubes inside it would not heat up to data-destroying temperatures. When the air-conditioning broke down – a fairly common occurrence – a loud gong would sound, and three engineers would spring from a nearby office to frantically take covers off the machine so its innards wouldn't melt. All these people in charge of punching cards, feeding them into readers, and pressing buttons and switches on the machine were what was commonly called a Priesthood, and those privileged enough to submit data to those most holy priests were the official acolytes. It was an almost ritualistic exchange.
>
> > ACOLYTE: Oh machine, would you accept my offer of information so you may run my program and perhaps give me a computation?
> >
> > PRIEST (on behalf of the machine): We will try. We promise nothing.[3]

There was no need for IT security for these leviathans. The computer occupied an entire room, so you could prevent access to it simply by locking the door. "It was assumed that anyone allowed near this expensive, arcane hardware would be a fully qualified professional expert".[4]

Data quality was guaranteed by controls on the way that the computer "programs" worked. So-called "data integrity rules" were (and still are) performed on the syntax, rather on the semantics of the data. Characters were checked to ensure they came from a specific set: telephone and house numbers must contain digits only, street names and proper names must be alphabetic. "Strings", or sequences, of characters were checked to ensure they came from a valid set, such as a determinate list of company names or client names. There were sometimes more sophisticated checks, such as inspecting the expected range for values (no negative ages or heights), consistency between fields (if Title = "Mr", then Gender = "M"; if building = wooden, then max number of floors = 17).

Output data quality was controlled by extensive testing and validation of the "programs" that performed mechanical functions on the input data. Designing the programs, originally written on punched cards,[5] was a highly skilled operation.

For a long time, the mainframe was the public perception of a computer, supported by the portrayal of the computer HAL in the movie *2001: A Space Odyssey* (as well as the computer in Ridley Scott's *Alien*). Such depictions also contributed to the perception of computers as supernaturally intelligent. Although the imagery lingers, the reality of computing has changed dramatically in the early 21st century. Computers have become more powerful, as well as cheaper. Computing as a practice has become widespread. The use of hardware-independent operating systems such as UNIX, universal languages such as C and the development of relational databases in the late 1970s partly freed computer users from dependence on a professional priesthood. The 1980s saw a proliferation of applications in banking and insurance. Thousands of separate systems were implemented for specific purposes: general ledger systems, payment systems, loan systems, claims systems, etc. In the 1980s and 1990s, cheap desktop computing became available, first to hobbyists and then to the general public.

By the 2000s, practically all office workers were using a computer. Increasing numbers used programmable applications such as Excel, or even database applications such as dBase and Access. Computer use has grown from the tiny priesthood of the 1950s to practically everyone who works in an office, and the computing power at their disposal is huge in comparison to that available to those early pioneers.

Fragmentation

Although the widespread use of computing brought many benefits, the resulting fragmentation of business processes had a hidden cost. A modern firm may have hundreds, even thousands, of systems that must exchange data in a meaningful way with one another – for example:

- reserving actuaries take data from a central claims system;
- an annuity valuation model combines exposure data sourced from policy systems with mortality data sourced from actuarial tables;
- a value-at-risk (VaR) model takes data from bond portfolio systems and joins it to credit spread data sourced from external market data providers; and
- catastrophe models combine exposure data from policy systems with vulnerability data and event tables sourced from the model vendor.

This fragmentation has caused a dramatic yet almost unremarked change in the way that data is used. The original computers were designed for interaction with humans only, and it was probably never envisaged that computers would one day have to communicate with other computers. For a long time, systems were designed in a way that forced users to print reports from a source system and then type them in by hand to the destination system. UNIX systems were accessible only to the skilled members of an IT department, and could not communicate effectively with users' desktop machines.

Gradually, methods were developed for allowing different systems to transfer data. Mainframe computers were modified to drop "flat files"[6] or spreadsheets onto Unix directories or the popular user-orientated Windows system. These files were then reconfigured either automatically or by users to match the format of the destination system. Most modern systems are designed to interact directly with spreadsheets, instead of print-outs or flat files. For the first time in the history of computing, different computer systems are now interacting with one another on a massive scale.

The Babel problem

> And the whole earth was of one language, and of one speech. And they said, Go to, let us build us a city and a tower, whose top may reach unto heaven; and let us make us a name, lest we be scattered abroad upon the face of the whole earth. And the Lord said, Behold, the people is one, and they have all one language; and this they begin to do; and now nothing will be restrained from them, which they have imagined to do. "Go to, let us go down, and there confound their language, that they may not understand one another's speech". Therefore is the name of it called Babel; because the Lord did there confound the language of all the earth.[7]

The parable of the Tower of Babel claims people once understood one another because they all originally spoke one language, but now cannot because of the fragmentation of one language into many. Fragmented computer systems must now communicate with one another in a way that is unparalleled in the history of computing. However, the unremarked and largely unaddressed problem – the "Babel" problem – is that computers also find communication quite difficult, because they also speak different languages.

The problem is not widely understood outside computing. It is not really understood inside computing. Proposals for mechanical translators of languages pre-date the invention of the digital computer. The first recognisable application was a dictionary look-up system developed at Birkbeck College, London, in 1948. Following the breakthrough in code-breaking during the Second World War, computer scientists such as Warren Weaver suggested that a document in one language could be viewed as having been written in code. Once this code was broken, it would be possible to output the document in another language. From this point of view, Chinese was English in code. As Weaver wrote in 1947: ". . . one naturally wonders if the problem of translation could conceivably be treated as a problem in cryptography. When I look at an article in Russian, I say: 'This is really written in English, but it has been coded in some strange symbols. I will now proceed to decode.'"[8]

Such proposals failed. US funding of machine translation research had cost US$20 million by the mid-1960s. The Automatic Language Processing Advisory Committee (ALPAC) produced a report on the results of the funding, concluding that "there had been no machine translation of general scientific text, and none is in immediate prospect". There was renewed interest in the 1980s with the emergence of "artificial intelligence", but there has been no significant breakthrough in the problem of designing computers that can learn to communicate meaningfully with one another without significant human intervention.

Deceptively difficult

In the era of the big mainframe and mini-computers, the Babel problem did not cause any serious difficulties. When a computer communicates with itself, it passes the output of one function to the input of another. These outputs and inputs typically consist of "pointers" to the same address in memory that, if incorrect, will usually be picked up through the software development process.

To make a computer communicate with another computer in the same way is much more difficult, because the systems are physically different and cannot "point" to each other's memory, and because software development projects are typically conducted independently of one another. Resolving this became a necessity in the era of fragmentation, when computing systems (including user-built computing systems) attempted to communicate meaningfully with one another.

The difficulty of getting computers to communicate with each other has never been properly recognised. It is an example of a "deceptively difficult problem": one whose solution seems easy, particularly by the application of technology – but which is not easy at all. As we have seen, communication between systems is incredibly difficult. It is not like "code breaking" at all, although it once seemed easy to experts.

The problem also seems easy to non-specialists, because of the superstitious reverence for "technology", and because of the rapid and seemingly unstoppable progress of communications networks. The Internet became embedded in popular consciousness in the 1990s and 2000s, and the development of wireless technology in the late 2000s meant that signals could be sent from almost any device to any other device. The problem of sending data from one place to another seemed to be solved. However, these merely technological developments did not solve the communication problem. Using modern technology, I can access a Chinese website thousands of miles away, in the middle of nowhere on a train, using a mobile phone – but I cannot understand what it says.

The problem is difficult to solve for a number of reasons. As noted above, a single computer system has a compiler that ensures its components can communicate easily with one another, but there is no corresponding compiler for a set of fragmented systems. A single computer system does not worry about the meaning of the symbols it manipulates. It keeps the "meaning" of every symbol in just one place, and everything else inside the system points to it directly (a pointer is simply a mechanical means of moving from one address to another). Information entered into the system by users is via a menu system that forces an acceptable set of values. A well-designed database system will also enforce "referential integrity" to ensure that, for example, the name of every child corresponds to a parent, or that every stock transaction has a recognised stock ticker. Thus, wherever the string "Vodafone Group Plc" is held in the system, it is understood as representing the same company. However, no one has yet invented a universal compiler, a system of imposing referential integrity that ensures that the data held across different systems is consistent in the same way. There is no automatic way of ensuring that "Vodafone Group Plc" held in system A is recognised as the same as "Vodafone Group Public Limited Company" in system B.

The deceptively difficult problem is exacerbated by the proliferation of apparently simple solutions. Data warehouses are a frequently marketed solution to the problem of aggregating data. The idea is to send all the data from disparate source systems into one place (the "warehouse"). Then you have it all in one place. However, of course, the problem remains – you have all the different languages in one room, but with no way of translating them. Even worse, when the translation was done on spreadsheets, at least the users understood what was going on. Now nobody knows what is going on.

Another apparently simple solution is the "front-to-back" system. System vendors and consultants persuade firms to replace all their different systems with a single system, *à la* 1960s, which will serve all their needs. This is extremely difficult, if not impossible, to achieve. Computer systems are different because they are optimised to deal with different problems (profit and loss (P&L), client lists, historical data, etc). They are expensive to build for a reason, and they evolve in a quasi-Darwinian process over the years as bugs are found and fixed and user-suggested improvements are incorporated, often by a maze of spaghetti code. The end-result can be millions of lines of code. It is difficult to replace any of these. Replicating the complex wiring between them is equally difficult for the same reason. If any firm tells us they are planning to do this, the Prudential Regulation Authority (PRA) moves them to a high-risk category immediately.

Another solution is to build a universal "data dictionary", a central database containing all the terms used in each individual system. An analogy is how Latin was a universal language in the Middle Ages (or French in the 18th century, or English today). Such systems are complex and difficult to build. They are difficult to maintain because each time a system is changed upstream, the dictionary has to be told. A similar, and slightly more workable, approach is to build individual *ad hoc* translators between any systems that communicate with one another. The analogy is the translators used in the UN or the Eurovision song contest ("douze points"). This can be a practical alternative to the first method, and it avoids Stalinist central planning type issues.

However, these strategic solutions typically fail, leaving tactical solutions often built by data end-users, usually involving spreadsheets or user-built databases or code hacks. Chambers and Hamill (2008) mention a reconciliation spreadsheet that compared the trade records within the main trade processing system with those in the general ledger system.

> The spreadsheet had to load reports from the two systems, parse them, and construct pivot tables to make the comparison. This was automated to some degree, with a 400-line (recorded!) VB macro. But once the macro had run, heavy manual editing was needed to make good the deficiencies in the original reports. To put a set of controls around the process as it existed would have made no sense: in effect, the only way to test the process would have been to produce a duplicate report independently.[9]

It is common to see audit reports or project plans that recommend replacing spreadsheets and manual processes with some end-to-end solution. This is unlikely to happen. It is impractical to replace two or more fragmented systems with a single system. Replacing the spreadsheet operations with "IT designed" ones only compounds the problem and removes any ability of users to address problems. Probably the best solution is to eliminate the worst processes, and to apply appropriate controls to the ones that remain.

The first problem of data governance is that the main problem facing it, namely the communication problem caused by the proliferation of fragmented systems, is still not widely recognised or understood.

PRINCIPLES OF DATA GOVERNANCE

The second problem of data governance, and a serious obstacle to its development into a science, is that many people do not believe in the possibility of its existence. People who use data or do things to it are often specialists of some kind (market risk managers, insurance reserving actuaries, capital managers, reinsurance credit managers).

It may seem to them that what they are doing is specific to their discipline and to no other. If they were right, it would mean there could be no such generic (ie, non-specialist) function of data governance. Such governance would amount to no more than "do your job well" or "hire specialists". If that were true – if there really were no common, generic principles of using and manipulating data – we would not need data governance, and there could be no science of it, nor any guiding principles.

However, this is far from the truth. There are many things that people do with data, and there are many kinds of data that are common to many different disciplines in life insurance, general insurance, banking and asset management. It is probably difficult for specialists to see this precisely because they are specialists. They are typically unable to identify which aspects of their work are common to other specialisms, and so may imagine that everything they do is specific to them. The reality is that, across life insurance, general insurance and asset management, people make the same judgements about data, they perform the same kind of operations on data and they need to apply the same kind of controls.

Data standards

The Solvency II directive[10] requires that data used for the internal model shall be accurate, complete and appropriate. The Level 2 delegated acts[11] will contain further details of these three requirements, both for technical provisions (data used in the calculation of technical provisions) and internal models (data used in the internal model). For example, firms should be able to articulate how they define and assess the quality of data, and should have specific qualitative and quantitative standards for different datasets based on these three requirements.

It is impossible to establish such standards without understanding the represenational nature of data. Representation is a relation between two things: the representation and the thing represented. It is not a property of one thing: it is obviously circular to define accuracy as being "freedom from error" and error as "inaccuracy". Accuracy is the closeness of agreement between the data and what it represents.[12] Completeness is agreement between the data received, and the data that it is intended or expected to represent. Note, "intended or expected": completeness is always relative to an intention or expectation about what the data should be. The set of records of policyholders over 50 is not complete if the records of all policyholders were expected. However, if only policyholders over 50 were expected, it is complete.

Because data is representational, the notions of completeness and accuracy apply to all types of data: not only to upstream "terms and conditions" data such as policy data, and transaction data or valuation data such as market data or ratings, but also to transformed or abstract data such as sensitivities, principal components, correlation matrices, distributions, and so on. At all stages of data transformation, users of data should be able to identify what their data represents, and how they would test its agreement with the reality it is representing. The same qualitative judgements apply even when data has been transformed. For example, a set of sensitivity records is complete in that it represents all the original policies or securities that created them. It is accurate in that it is an accurate representation of how the original security would behave as the risk factor changes, in that the change in value imputed by the sensitivity closely agrees (or reasonably closely agrees) with the way the represented exposure would behave, under the same change in the risk or valuation factor.

Appropriateness is essentially a relationship between different types of data, as discussed below.

Generic types of data[13]

All firms try to classify their data, but classification is generally only useful if it corresponds to a common risk, impact, control method or other characteristic relevant to data governance.[14] Most firms struggle with this. Frequently, classifications bear little or no relation to the control or risk characteristics of the data – for example, separating data by country or business entity, even when the risk drivers were of a fundamentally similar type.

The distinction between exposure data and valuation data is fundamental. Exposure data represents contracts between a firm and other parties. It may be the legal contract itself, or a "master agreement" or template that captures common forms of agreement. It could be the terms and conditions of a bond issuance. In life and general insurance, it is likely to be a policy of some kind. Valuation data, by contrast, is data about facts in external reality that have an impact on the financial value of the contract, such as market interest rates, mortality expectations, expected hurricane strength and location.

Controls over data quality will be different depending on whether they control exposure data or valuation data. Contractual exposures by their very nature should be fixed and static, even when subject to periodic payments (eg, a bond coupon is a contractual obligation to pay a coupon at fixed intervals over the life of the bond; the fact that some of the obligated payments have already occurred does not impact the nature of the obligation itself). It is therefore essential that the contractual details are correct. This means: (i) confirming that the other party agreed to the terms of the contract; (ii) identifying the correct version of the contract that the other party agreed to and labelling it as a master version; (iii) ensuring that all other records represent the master version and no other, and ensuring that the details match; and (iv) in the case of records that are an approximate representation of the exposure, ensuring that they are materially correct. Many frauds have involved the misrepresentation of exposure records, and for this reason best practice is to ensure that transaction records cannot be modified by anyone (traders, underwriters, etc) with an interest in manipulating its value.

Valuation data by its very nature represents aspects of reality that are typically beyond the control of agents of the firm. This makes it easier to independently verify the accuracy and completeness of such data, and many firms in the financial sector have "product control" departments to check valuation data against external sources. It is less material in proportion to the rate it changes. Frequently changing data is relevant for no longer than the frequency it represents.

Other types of data include "static" data or "metadata", which set, for example, units for prices, codes and allowed values. The Solvency II internal modelling framework alludes to static data in the Level 2 delegated act when specifying "the use and setting of assumptions made in the collection, processing and application of data". Static data also includes widely used market values such as foreign exchange rates. Changes in static data have a large impact because they potentially have a large impact across a firm, and can also have unforeseen consequences, so they should be carefully controlled against malicious or accidental change.

Risk data is a type of valuation data representing the probability of a specified change in the data (or risk factor) to a certain degree of confidence over a specified time horizon. It may consist of historical data, market-implied data (typically, options volatility) or simply expert judgement.

Generic operations on data

There are also common types of operation on data. The simplest operation is to move or copy data from one storage point to another in the same form. Herein lies another hidden trap in data governance, namely the illusion that data is rarely transformed as it "moves" from one place to another. Of course, there are many cases where the data remains in the same form (eg, when data is sent across a network, when spreadsheets, text files or documents are sent by email, or when tables are copied from one database to another). Typically, however, data is transformed as it moves around. There are many types of transformation common to asset management, life and general insurance, and there are common causes of error, and hence common quality control requirements.

Aggregation is when records are grouped into sets according to some common property, and the values combined, typically by addition. For example, records of costs are grouped and combined by department, or VaR numbers are combined (non-additively) across trading divisions by a "VaR engine". Aggregation always results in a loss of detail because of the loss of individual records, including unique record identifiers. If these are lost completely, it is difficult to reconcile for completeness of data, as completeness is defined with reference to the unique identifiers.

Bucketing, or gridding, is a form of aggregation where the values used to group the records are approximations, usually to values at regular intervals. For example, a motor insurance firm groups the age of drivers so that they can be priced assuming the same risk profile (eg, 17–19 year old males are modelled as 18), or to price an annuity, annuitants aged between 49.5 and 50.5 years old are treated as all being aged 50. In asset management, cashflows are "gridded" to regular intervals, so that all cashflows with maturity between 9 and 11 years are assumed to be at maturity 10 years. Bucketing is often performed on spreadsheets. The granular values are held in one column, from which the approximated values are derived in another column then grouped together, often by means of the "sumif" function.

Subtle completeness errors can be caused by inappropriate bucketing methods. In actuarial calculations, it is common to bucket policy terms and conditions into "model points", representative of a large set of policyholders. For example, two policies, one with a sum assured of 10,000 written to a 42 year old male and the other of 15,000 to a 44 year old male, may be combined into a single imaginary sum assured of 15,000 to an imaginary person aged 43. In the early days of realistic balance sheets, people used this technique too enthusiastically and found that results could be significantly understated when option-like policies with widely varying "moneyness" were averaged. This is because of "Jensen's inequality" – the average level of a convex function over a range of values is typically higher than the level of the same function on the average of that range.[15]

"Joining" is when data is enriched, or "joined", to other data with which it shares a common property. For example, property details are joined to a simulated wind force by means of a common geocode, the details of an annuity policy are joined to a Qx factor by means of a common age, security terms and conditions are joined to security prices by means of a common ISIN or stock ticker code. It is an important but risky operation, because the joined datasets are typically from different sources and must be transformed in various ways. Typically, the "key" or common property is encoded in different ways. For example, the code for the security price may use a data vendor's reference, whereas the code for the bond may use an ISIN. This means that a "mapping table" must be constructed to map the key used from the one source to the key used in the other.

The common property may be gridded in different ways. For example, interest rate data may be gridded at five-year intervals, but swap exposure data gridded at one-year intervals. This means that either the exposure data has to be reduced in granularity by further bucketing, or the valuation data has to be interpolated to increase the granularity, with the inevitable errors that are introduced. When one or the other dataset is incomplete, it is common for records to be "dropped" or lost, causing further incompleteness. If the join is performed using obsolete data, or the data is incorrect, the destination process will succeed but with incorrect values. This will impact the accuracy of the data. There is also a risk of joining datasets that match one another poorly. For example, earthquake data from one country is joined to property exposure data in another country, or stock exposures from the Eurozone are joined to risk data for the UK derived from US indexes.

Joining is one of the most important operations on data. However, it is rarely identified as such by the data governance function, and is often performed on spreadsheets, using the error-prone "vlookup" function.

Functional transformations occur when the structure or order of data is completely transformed in order to better represent one of its key properties. For example, a set of historical scenarios is ordered not by date, but by its impact, to create a "distribution"; the historical changes at the many maturity points in a yield curve are summarised into a smaller set of "principal components"; the vulnerability of a building to a hazard is expressed as a damage relating the hazard intensity (wind force, ground speed) to the damage caused as a fraction of the property value.

For example, a sensitivity is a transformation of the terms and conditions of a policy or a security into a representation of how its value changes according to a specific change in valuation data. It could be produced by valuing the policy or security at current valuation levels, then "perturbing" or "bumping" the valuation by a determined amount and then revaluing the portfolio. Thus, actuaries use a standard set of Qx factors (mortality per year) in an expectation-of-life calculator to compute the base value of an annuity portfolio, then plug in a new set of values factors to compute a perturbed value and subtract one from the other to compute a sensitivity. Sometimes, there is a closed-form solution to the sensitivity, such as with the "duration" of a bond, or the "delta" of an option. For catastrophe modelling, this is done by empirical methods – for example, by using past observations of building damage and peak ground velocity during an earthquake to compute "damage ratio".[16]

It is common to think of such transformed data as not really being "data" at all. However, such sensitivities still represent key characteristics of the original data, in a way that reflects the concerns of the user or convenience of computation. Data cleaning is an important operation, and will be discussed below.

Generic controls

If data has been classified correctly, then it should be clear where controls are necessary. Reasonableness tests will typically show which individual exposures or groups of exposures have a significant impact on valuation or risk. Resources should be focused on exposures that are material, or that collectively taken might have a material impact. Resources should be divided according to the potential complexity of the control. Checking electronic policy records against paper originals or copies is a relatively mechanical task that does not require specialist resources.

If data is classified so that common methods are evident, it should be obvious where a firm can benefit from economies of scale. Many firms struggle with this. The PRA often finds highly skilled and highly paid staff trying to reinvent solutions to problems that are well known, simple, and cheap to operate, or we find different staff solving the same kind of problems in isolation from one another when a single team could have resolved the problems more economically.

Good practice (and the principle of proportionality) suggests focusing controls where they matter most. Does the firm know that information is comprehensively captured for the exposure attributes that have a marked impact on reserves and capital requirement? In catastrophe modelling, this may be done by assessing the level of geocoding resolution to determine its impact on the variability in modelled losses, or by determining the impact of omitting core vulnerability attributes, such as occupancy, construction class, year built and number of storeys. For securities, this may be done by looking at concentrated positions or ratings and determining the impact of rating change, spread widening, errors in security characteristics, and so on. Where complex terms and conditions (such as callability and step-up) have been represented by simple data models, it is essential that management information captures this fact in case the positions become material. The key principle – perhaps it should be called the "Rumsfeld principle" – is to quantify possible unknowns. It is not just whether exposure data is incomplete, but whether a firm knows it is incomplete, whether it knows how incomplete it is and whether this can be easily captured as part of an overall reporting system.

Tests for model exposure sensitivity are a useful control: model a policy and compute a price for it using one model and a given set of information about the exposure. How would the price change if we had more information about the building, or the lives insured or securities under management? A firm should be able to model the impact of approximation for any current or expected exposure, and assess this against its data risk appetite. Where data has been infilled or corrected, is there a metric and a report that tells a manager the extent of infilling and the current and future expected impact? (See below on data cleaning.)

Many controls can be automated. The simplest check on completeness is a "byte count", when data from one location is moved or copied to another without transforming it in any way. These checks can easily be automated – such as by computing a checksum or hash total algorithm on the source data and repeating it on the destination data. A good algorithm will give a different result with high probability that the data is accidentally corrupted, and the same result with a high probability that the data is free from accidental errors. However, as pointed out, data is rarely moved without transforming it in some way.

It is not absolutely essential to perform quality controls at every single point of the data flow. For example, if data passes from A through B to C, and there is a control to check C against A, then there is no need to check the quality at B (unless B is feeding another point elsewhere). Intermediate checks may be more practical, however.

When data is reconciled to check completeness, the nature of the reconciliation should be clearly defined and identified. For example, what values (nominal amounts, unique ID checksum, aggregate sensitivities, etc) are being reconciled? The nature of the expected data should be clearly defined (ie, what exactly is the data you are reconciling to?).

When data is lost through aggregation, whatever data is necessary to perform downstream reconciliations should be retained. Record count may suffice, or checksums on key fields (currency amounts, IDs, etc). The best practice would be to maintain an array of unique IDs as a vector and pass it downstream.

Joining is a high-risk operation and requires appropriate controls. All join points should normally be identified. Static data used in joins should be maintained at an appropriate frequency and with regard to the materiality of the process. Use of joined data where it would materially affect the value of the end process should be regularly reviewed. It is preferable (although difficult) to use a firm-wide "master static" system in order to control the use of static data centrally. Use of the Excel vlookup function (which is symptomatic of joining operations, often badly or crudely performed) should be monitored in some way, and reviewed where risk is likely to be material. There should be close checks on the key used to join the two datasets to ensure referential integrity (the key should either be identical, or there should be one-to-one mapping and a regularly maintained mapping table).

Joining nearly always involves joining different types of data, and so joins require appropriateness checks. If it involves joining valuation or risk data to exposure data, is the valuation data up to date? The Solvency II internal modelling framework requires firms to identify the process for carrying out data updates, including the frequency of regular updates. If bond terms and conditions are joined to ratings, are the ratings appropriate to the bonds? Solvency II requires that data should be consistent with the purposes for which it will be used. What management information needs to be produced to monitor this? If cashflows are bucketing at one-year intervals but rates data is bucketed at five-year or irregular intervals, how appropriate is the interpolation method? Other controls might be required where risk or valuation data for one geolocation is applied to exposure data from a different, possibly inappropriate, location.

Data cleaning

If data quality controls find material errors, data should be cleaned. The basic principles of data cleaning are not always clearly understood, although it is probably the only function that specialists would recognise as having characteristics in common with other disciplines. Many practitioners do not understand the distinction between coherence and correspondence checks, for example, and it is important to identify which method is being used in order to understand the traps and flaws in each.

Correspondence checks involve comparing the data to the original material it represents – for example, by comparing the published terms and conditions of a security, or a paper copy of a policy, to an electronic representation. This can be laborious and difficult, particularly where there are many thousands of records. Many firms have old contracts for which they hold very limited paperwork, and even no paperwork at all, other than the fact that the contract exists and a name, and count on the fact that the person with whom they have the contract will come and demand what they are actually owed, not realising they could demand absolutely anything and they would most likely get it paid out. Policy records often underspecify the data required to value the exposure correctly. In catastrophe insurance, data on primary vulnerability attributes, such as occupancy, construction class, year built and number of storey, is critical to model the likely damage from a peril. In 2005, in order to understand why some companies' modelled losses for hurricane Katrina differed from actual losses, catastrophe model vendor AIR conducted an analysis of exposure data from companies representing more than half of the total US property market. The study, which focused on four data types – property replacement value, construction, occupancy and location – found "significant problems" with data completeness, particularly replacement values, which were of "questionable accuracy" for approximately 90% of the companies analysed.[17]

The Rumsfeld principle is important. Even if a firm does not know the exact amount of the exposure, it needs to demonstrate which records are potentially missing or inexact, and to be able to quantify the possible impact of error. Vendor models may not cater for all lines of business – for example, personal accident policies with UK territorial scope may not be represented by a specific vulnerability curve in the catastrophe model, which in turn could lead to material underestimation of potential loss from windstorm. This risk can usually be addressed by reasonableness checks to ensure the exposure is not material. If these are not sufficient or not available, it may be necessary for a firm to assume it does have a risk to a whole exposure class. For example, a policy located in Melbourne, Australia, will have little exposure to cyclones, but a policy identified only as "Australia" should be assumed to be significantly at risk from that peril.[18] No firm should be in the position of not knowing what it does not know.

For correspondence checks, it is essential to specify the source of the correspondence data in order to avoid the trap of "false correspondence". If data source A and data source B are both derived from some true source Q, checking A against B or B against A is merely a form of consistency check, and can be deeply misleading when the query or filter used for B contains the same error as in A. Suppose that a SQL query has been badly written so as to omit people aged over 60. Data is downloaded into A using the query. To check the completeness of A, another source B is used, which also downloads from the database using the same faulty query. The two sources will appear to match: false correspondence. A rigorous check requires an independent view of the true source, usually only possible by loading all records onto a separate system, perhaps a spreadsheet, and checking it manually.

Reliance on broker quotes also creates the risk of false correspondence. Trader A submits a price of X, and suggests broker B as a source for an "independent price check". The valuation manager checks with B, unaware that A is colluding with B. B submits X as the price, which appears to agree with the trader's submitted price, but is a false correspondence. The notorious Libor manipulation of the mid-2000s was another similar case. Correspondence checks, as far as possible, must be from a source that is as close as possible to the origin of the data.

Consistency, or coherence,[19] checks are where the data is tested against known properties. It is sometimes known as data profiling. Coherence checks include identifying improbable attributes, verifying high-impact attributes and checking the distribution of data for known expected properties that can be used to detect individual or systematic errors. There are obvious lower bounds of zero for age, interest rate, number of storeys, probability etc, and likely or expected upper bounds such as age (110), probability (1), credit spread (100%) and number of storeys of a wooden building (17). As noted above, most "correspondence" checks are really coherence checks in disguise. It is generally difficult to access the true source Q, so most correspondence checks really involve comparing different sets of data A and B, both derived from Q. As noted, this gives rise to the risk of false correspondence.

Data cleaning is probably the most common operation on data, yet few users really understand the process for what it is, namely the joining or combining of two types of data: the data to be cleaned, and the data used (either implicitly or explicitly) to clean. For example, a missing record is found in data source A. The user checks data source B and finds the missing data, which is in effect a form of correspondence check. Best practice is to record this join by identifying its date and time, the name of the user who performed it and the data used for the correction. If the missing record cannot be located, the best practice is to identify it (on the Rumsfeld principle) as missing data, using a null value. Copying values from other records (for example, by copying Monday's data to Tuesday's, if missing) or interpolating missing points is common practice, but leads to the risk of statistical inaccuracies, such as confusing the interpolation with a "trend" in the data.

DATA DIRECTORY AND CONTROLS

A "data directory" is a useful and important way of representing or pictorialising controls. The underlying purpose of the "data directory" requirement in Solvency II is to ensure that there is good governance over data quality, and that firms think carefully about their approach to governance. The data directory is meant to be a documented repository where different users can go to understand which data is being used in the model, where it comes from ("source"), how it is used ("use") and what its specific "characteristics" are.

As the Financial Services Authority (FSA) noted in its 2012 survey of data governance,[20] if a data directory is too simplistic for future use or too complex to maintain, this will defeat its intended purpose. When documenting the data items, firms should apply the principle of proportionality that runs through the Solvency II directive. Documenting all data items at every level of granularity may involve unnecessary detail. Therefore, firms should consider all data and document the data items relevant to the internal model at a level of granularity that is appropriate for ongoing maintenance and use. A "data directory" in this sense should not be confused with a "data dictionary".[21]

There is no reason why a data directory need be any more complex than a data flow diagram. The purpose of the latter is to represent the flow of data in a way that users, rather than technology specialists, can understand. There is no need to identify the platform or transmission medium unless it is relevant to controls over data quality. Thus, it is useful to indicate the existence of spreadsheets or manual processes as they can create the risk of error. It is useful to indicate a system name for reference purposes only. Hosting or infrastructure information is usually not relevant, unless it contains information relevant to quality controls.

The directory or diagram should identify the types of data coming in, and the operation that is performed to produce the type of data going out. For example, exposure data consisting of bond IDs is combined with valuation data consisting of prices to produce a list of bond values. This is simple to do, and yet is almost never done. If a data governance manager does not have the management information to provide an understanding of the types of data flowing through a system, the kinds of operation performed upon it and the impact these are likely to have, it will be impossible to make a judgement about whether controls are required, and of what type. Their job will be an impossible one.

Given the relatively small number of data types and data operations, identifying them on a diagram (or directory) should not be difficult. Data types include security identifiers, exposure terms and conditions, rates, event types, prices, risk factor sensitivities (loss functions, P&L functions replicating formulas, etc), aggregated or bucketed terms and conditions ("model points"), distributions or time series of the above. Operations include aggregation, joining and filtering. Given the prevalence and limited number of these types, it would be easy to introduce icons for them, and so represent an apparently complex fragmented data system in a relatively simple way.

All firms struggle with this, and typically the descriptions they use lack any informational value at all. "Perform model runs" tells us absolutely nothing. Is it a model, or a feed to the model? What is the data type that this operation receives as input? What is it doing to it? What is the output type? It is the same for "model set up suite". By contrast, "create model point files for asset model" identifies the type of operation (aggregation), although even then you would have to be a specialist to understand this ("model point" is jargon only used in insurance).

CONCLUSION

In summary, there are two serious obstacles to the development of data governance as a discipline in its own right, namely the fragmentation of systems caused by the growth of end-user computing in the late 20th century and the failure to recognise common principles of data governance. The first problem is deceptively difficult, one whose solution seems as if it ought to be easy, particularly by the application of technology – but which is not. The only way to apply technology to the problem of fragmented systems is to replace them with a single system, but this is in principle extremely difficult to do. The only solution is to recognise that technology on its own is not a solution.

The second problem is in understanding how data governance can be a science. Specialists are the main end-users of data, and specialists by definition have a specific type of discipline. They often fail to recognise that many things they do are not specific to their work. However, in many cases, the judgements, classifications, operations and controls that specialists in one discipline apply to data are common to other disciplines. I have given examples of these from life insurance, general insurance, banking and asset management. Where there are techniques and principles common to many different disciplines, there is a science, but we also need to recognise there is a science.

The financial services industry has been plagued for years by the problem of bad data. A solution is possible, but people have been looking in the wrong place. Solvency II, for all its flaws, has been a significant step forward in locating the right place.

The views expressed in this chapter are those of the author and not necessarily those of the Bank of England.

1 For further details, see European Parliament and the Council of the European Union (2009).
2 For further details, see EIOPA (2013).
3 Levy (1984); see also . . . "Only a select few programmers were allowed in the computer lab. The rest of us were barred from that temple to technology" (Fisk, 2005).
4 Sterling (1992).
5 Fisk (2005).
6 Data tables with columns separated by a delimiters such as a commas, pipes, etc.
7 *Genesis* 11, 1, 4–9.
8 http://www.mt-archive.info/Weaver-1949.pdf.
9 Chambers and Hamill (2008).
10 For further details, see Article 121 (statistical quality standards), paragraph 3, of the European Parliament and the Council of the European Union (2009).
11 Adoption of the Solvency II Level 2 delegated acts is expected in late summer, 2014.
12 "Truth is the agreement between reality and understanding" (*Veritas est adequatio rei et intellectus*), Aquinas (*Summa Theologica*): I^{a} q. 16 a. 2 arg. 2.
13 Part of this section is based on FSA (2012).
14 See FSA (2012): 4.27.
15 The same error may have even found its way into the Solvency II world. Many industry estimates of credit risk were informed by the Merton model – an option model using equity price, asset volatility and company leverage ratio to compute a "realistic" credit spread of risky securities. Such models typically used average leverage ratio, although the value of a Merton option is highly convex with respect to leverage ratio. This led in some cases to significant underestimates of credit risk.

16 Miyakoshi, *et al.* (1997).

17 Lalonde (2005); see also Lavakare (2008), where it was claimed that 20–45% of the gap between modelled and actual losses after hurricanes Katrina and Rita in 2005 was due to poor data quality at the time of underwriting.

18 See ABI (2014).

19 The distinction between the coherence and correspondence theories of truth was first made in Joachim (1906), Chapter 2.

20 FSA (2012).

21 As per McDaniel (1994), a data dictionary is "a centralized repository of information about data such as meaning, relationships to other data, origin, usage, and format".

REFERENCES

Aquinas, Thomas, *Summa Theologica.*

Association of British Insurers, 2014, "Non-modelled Risks: A Guide to More Complete Catastrophe Risk Assessment for (Re)insurers".

Chambers J. and J. Hamill, 2008, "Controlling End User Computing Applications" (available at http://arxiv.org/ftp/arxiv/papers/0809/0809.3595.pdf).

EIOPA, 2013, "Guidelines on Pre-application of Internal Models".

European Parliament and the Council of the European Union, 2009, "Directive 2009/138/EC of the European Parliament and of the Council of 25 November 2009 on the Taking-up and Pursuit of the Business of Insurance and Reinsurance (Solvency II) (recast)".

Fisk, D., 2005,"Programming with Punched Cards", 2005.

FSA, 2012, "Solvency II: Internal Model Approval Process – Data Review Findings, September (available at http://www.fsa.gov.uk/static/pubs/international/sii-imap-data-review-09–12.pdf).

Joachim, H., 1906, *The Nature of Truth* (Oxford: Clarendon).

Lalonde, D. A., 2005, "Catastrophe Modelling – Challenges and Best Practices", Casualty Actuarial Society.

Lavakare, A., 2008, "Exposure Data Quality is a Key Indicator of Operating Risk", *Best's Review.*

Levy, S., 1984, *Hackers, Heroes of the Computer Revolution* (Garden City, NY: Anchor Press/Doubleday).

McDaniel, G. (Ed.), 1994, *IBM Dictionary of Computing (10e)* (New York: McGraw-Hill).

Miyakoshi, J. Y. Hayashi, K. Tamura and N. Fukuwa, 1997, "Damage Ratio Functions of Buildings Using Damage Data of the 1995 Hyogo-Ken Nanbu Earthquake", 7th International Conference on Structural Safety and Reliability, 1, Kyoto, Japan, November 24–28, pp 349–54.

Sterling, B., 1992, *The Hacker Crackdown: Law and Disorder on the Electronic Frontier* (New York: Bantam Books).

Weaver, W., 1949, "Translation", memorandum, Rockefeller Foundation Archives (available at http://www.mt-archive.info/Weaver-1949.pdf).

9

The Calibration Standards

Ishtiaq Faiz and Paolo Cadoni

Prudential Regulation Authority, Bank of England

Under Solvency II, firms using an internal model to calculate the solvency capital requirement (SCR) may derive the SCR using a different time period or risk measure from that set out in Article 101 of the directive,[1] as long as they demonstrate to the supervisory authorities that policyholders and beneficiaries are provided with an equivalent level of protection.[2] These requirements are known as the calibration standards.

The Solvency II definition of calibration is different from the general definition of calibration used in statistics and actuarial science. For example, model calibration is often defined in statistics as the process of adjustment of the model parameters to obtain a model representation of the processes of interest that satisfies pre-agreed criteria (eg, goodness of fit).

The Solvency II definition of calibration, on the other hand, specifically refers to:

- conditions under which other tests and standards are applied to; the calibration standard is set out in Article 101 of the directive; or
- additional conditions that need to be met if an internal model targets different conditions than those referred in Article 101 (Article 122).

As most internal models developed by firms use a value-at-risk (VaR) measure (targeting a 99.5% confidence level, or higher), many practitioners pay little consideration to the Solvency II calibration standard. In these instances, the VaR can usually be read directly from the probability distribution forecast (PDF).[3] As a consequence, these Solvency II requirements are not as "famous" as other standards such as validation, statistical quality or the use test. However, as will be illustrated in this chapter, the calibration standard is a fundamental building block of Solvency II and is intimately interlinked with the other well-known standards.

This chapter provides an explanation of the calibration requirements set out in Solvency II, and presents a few examples of common practice observed during the internal models pre-application process that point out particular issues needing to be considered during the development, monitoring and review of internal models. However, the chapter does not deal with how the balance sheet is constructed over the time horizon (see Chapter 1).

THE REQUIREMENTS

Article 101(3) of the Solvency II directive requires insurers to hold capital that corresponds to the VaR of the basic own funds subject to a confidence level of 99.5% over a one-year period. In addition, Article 122(2) requires insurers to be able to derive the SCR directly from the PDF of the basic own funds. The VaR risk measure, one-year period and 99.5% confidence level are therefore the Solvency II "reference risk measure(s)".

Many practitioners consider the calibration standard an easy requirement to comply with compared to other Solvency II internal modelling standards, such as the statistical quality standards (SQS), validation standards and the use test. It is certainly true that if the SQS, validation and use test can be met, then the calibration standard does not represent a major issue. However, if these requirements are not met (eg, if the SQS cannot be easily met by the "one-year" methodology or the model is not used by applying the same risk measure or time horizon) or the SCR cannot be directly read off the PDF, then the alternative requirements around the calibration may need to be considered, as they may help to overcome these challenges.

Article 122(1) allows insurers to model using an alternative risk measure and/or time horizon as long as they ensure that policyholder protection is equivalent to the level set out Article 101(3). Alternatively, if the SCR cannot be directly calculated from the PDF of the basic own funds, Article 122(3) allows insurers to use approximations or alternative variables other than basic own funds.

The use of a different time period, confidence level or risk measure does not exempt a firm from complying with any of the internal model requirements set out in the Solvency II framework. The choice of the time period or risk measure used for internal modelling purposes has to be both appropriate and justified. In particular, if the time period used is different from one-year, the firm has to:

- ❏ demonstrate that all significant risks to which it is exposed over a one-year period are properly managed;
- ❏ pay particular attention to the data used; and
- ❏ justify the choice of the time horizon (if different from one year) in view of the average duration of the liabilities of the firm, of the business model and the uncertainties associated with a longer time horizon.

Where some reconciliation is needed between the outcomes of the internal model and the SCR, the SCR calculation has to be consistent with the methods used for internal purposes. The firm has to demonstrate to the supervisory authority the equivalence set out in Article 122 of the Solvency II directive at least annually, but also when there are significant events or changes to the firm's risk profile. On the one hand, if the reconciliation process shows that the capital held by the firm is lower than the SCR calculated using a VaR at 99.5% over a one-year period, the firm has to hold additional regulatory capital to make up this difference. On the other hand, if the capital held by the firm is greater than the SCR calculated using a VaR at 99.5% over a one-year period, the excess is considered free capital.

If the SCR cannot be derived directly from the PDF, the firm has to:

- ❏ explain how it rescales risks and justify why the bias introduced when doing so is immaterial; and
- ❏ explain the shortcuts used to reconcile the outputs of its internal model with the distribution of basic own funds, if any.

Moreover, if the firm is using for economic capital calculations a time horizon longer than one year, it has to:

- show that any probable situation or negative asset value occurrence earlier than the time horizon has been properly taken into account; and
- justify the particular assumptions made to adequately take into account any temporal dependency effects.

All the other internal model requirements apply *mutatis mutandis* to the approximations used for the purposes of calibration. Firms have to compensate for the approximations made by additional provisions. In particular, the assumptions underlying those approximations have to be thoroughly tested against alternative assumptions in line with the validation standards.

Supervisors may require firms to run their internal model on relevant benchmark portfolios or use external assumptions whenever they have concerns about the calibration of the internal model and the adequacy of its specification. This may occur during the approval process or as part of the ongoing supervisory review process. In particular circumstances, this request may apply to the whole market (or segment of it).

Should the test's results raise questions about the appropriateness of the calibration of the internal model and of its specifications, its consequences may encompass the rejection of the model or one of the actions set out in Article 118 of the Solvency II directive.

Additional regulation and guidance around alternative risk and time horizon is laid out in the forthcoming Level 2 delegated acts[4] and the Level 3 EIOPA guidelines.[5] A version of the interim Level 3 has been published by EIOPA as preparatory guidelines for internal models. A summary of the draft regulations is provided below.

- When insurers are not using the "reference risk measure", they need to ensure the appropriateness of the alternative risk measure not only at the level of the overall SCR, but also in lower risk categories and major business unit levels. This is to ensure that the other internal modelling standards such as the SQS and profit and loss (P&L) attribution are appropriately captured.
- Insurers need to ensure material error is not introduced by using an alternative to the "reference risk measure", and ensure that estimation of the SCR is not materially lower and the stability of the result is maintained even under extreme scenarios.

- If insurers are using rescaling methods in approximating the SCR under Article 122(3), they need to ensure that the rescaling methods do not impair the outcome of the approximations.
- If the time horizon is different from the one-year time horizon, then insurers need to ensure timing of the events are adequately captured and risks over the one-year are managed properly.
- If the time horizon used is longer than one year, then insurers should give consideration to the solvency position during the one-year time horizon. Also, insurers need to take into consideration any uncertainties, management actions and dependencies associated with modelling a longer time horizon.
- In approximating the SCR, if insurers are using another underlying variable other than the basic own funds, then they need to ensure the difference between that variable and basic own funds is not material at any time, or that the difference does not change even under extreme scenarios.

While some of the above requirements may look burdensome at first glance and difficult to meet without actually calculating the SCR as defined in Article 101(3), they are designed mainly to ensure that equivalent protection is provided to policyholders. They can be considered analogous to the requirements under Article 101(3).

MARKET PRACTICE AND ISSUES TO CONSIDER

The majority of market practitioners are modelling the SCR as required by Article 101(3) and Article 122(2) of the Solvency II directive. Evidence from the internal model pre-application process shows it is uncommon for firms to use an alternative to the "reference risk measure". However, it has been observed that some insurers are struggling to meet the SQS, particularly with methodologies to calculate risk over the one-year risk horizon. It has also been noticed that some insurers are using an alternative time horizon or risk measure for internal use even if they are able to derive the SCR directly from the PDF of the basic own funds.

One-year time horizon

Ultimate to one year

Before Solvency II enters into force, insurers calculate non-life underwriting risk in their economic models based on an "ultimate" view of the risk. The ultimate view can be considered as the value of the liabilities when claims are paid off. The methodologies to calculate the one-year view of the risk are all usually based on scaling or replication of valuation methodologies to calculate a one-year view from the ultimate view. While this is particularly true for firms operating in the UK, similar methodologies are also being used across Europe.

The scaling methods used by non-life insurers are based on three generic methods: i) simple percentage reduction; ii) selecting another percentile of the distribution based on cashflow profile; and iii) mathematical methods based on ultimate methods (eg, the Merz–Wüthrich method used to calibrate the standard formula which is based on the Mack method). These methods are generally new to non-life insurance. It is therefore often difficult for insurers to justify and validate the appropriateness of these methods.

The other main method used by non-life insurers to rescale results is called the re-reserving method. The model tries to replicate the valuation process at the end of the one-year period. A drawback of this method is related to the difficulty of replicating the actuarial judgments applied to valuation, especially following 99.5th VaR scenario.

Instantaneous shocks

Insurers sometimes model market risk as an instantaneous shock to the market values of their asset holdings. Insurers often assert that modelling the market values of an asset during the one-year period is immaterial to their SCR. Although this may be true in most instances, insurers need to consider if some of their liabilities are path-dependent or have optionality (eg, variable annuities). In this instance, insurers need to consider modelling their SCR over the one-year period.

Use of the internal model

Insurers sometimes use different time horizons to manage their business than the one-year horizon mentioned in Article 101(3). For example, insurers can manage their business over the insurance or economic cycle, or for historical reasons. For instance, non-life insurers are used to estimating the ultimate values of their liabilities rather than their view of the ultimate risk at the end of one year. Also, the pricing of insurance and reinsurance contracts is usually based on an ultimate view of the claims. If insurers do use a different time horizon, thanks to the calibration standard they can still do so and at the same time derive their SCR from the same model.

CONCLUSION

This chapter has provided an illustration of the calibration standards requirements set out in the Solvency II directive, and provided a few examples of the challenges faced by firms in meeting these requirements. Although insurers usually derive their SCR in line with Article 101(3), ie, using the VaR of basic own funds at 99.5% over a one-year period, evidence collected during the internal model pre-application process indicates that they are struggling to meet the statistical quality and validation standards, and the use test, adequately. In such situations, insurers should explore if alternatives to the "reference risk measure" – ie, resorting to the alternatives suggested by the calibration standard – may help to overcome these challenges, and allow them to be in a better position to meet the other tests and standards.

The views expressed in this chapter are those of the authors and not necessarily of the PRA, Bank of England

1 For further details, see European Parliament and the Council of the European Union (2009).
2 Namely, it shall correspond to the value-at-risk of the basic own funds of an insurance or reinsurance firm subject to a confidence level of 99.5 % over a one-year period.
3 For further details about the Solvency II statistical quality standards and probability distribution forecast, see Chapter 7.
4 For further details, see European Commission (2014).
5 For further details, see EIOPA (2013).

REFERENCES

EIOPA, 2013, "Guidelines on Pre-application of Internal Models".

European Commission, 2014, "Delegated Acts to Solvency II Directive".

European Parliament and the Council of the European Union, 2009, "Directive 2009/138/EC of the European Parliament and of the Council of 25 November 2009 on the Taking-up and Pursuit of the Business of Insurance and Reinsurance (Solvency II) (recast)".

10

Profit and Loss Attribution

Andrew Candland and Christopher Lotz

EIOPA and Bundesanstalt für Finanzdienstleistungsaufsicht – BaFin

Profit and loss (P&L) attribution is an important tool of model risk management that has a long history. It is very well known in banking circles, especially in the area of traded markets, and the concept of analysis of movement is widely used in insurance. Much can be learnt about the risks of an undertaking by closely studying its P&L, because this incorporates all the effects that have materialised over a given horizon from all the risks that the undertaking faces.

With the advent of Solvency II, especially Article 123 of the directive, regulators have required firms that use an internal model to carry out a P&L attribution at least annually.[1] This formalises the link between P&L and risks and means it has a permanent position in the armoury of techniques of any insurance undertaking seeking approval for an internal model under Solvency II.

P&L attribution is the process of analysing the change between two valuations, linking this to the developments of their causes and sources (risk drivers) between the two valuation dates. The two valuations in question can be two balance sheets at the top level of the firm, but they can also be the valuations of an asset portfolio or the insurance reserves on a property/casualty (P/C) book. The Solvency II internal modelling framework requires the specification of profit and loss to be consistent with the increase and decrease of the monetary amount underlying the probability distribution forecast. A successful P&L attribution allows its reader, starting at the top of the firm (the balance sheet), to drill down to the depths of individual risk drivers.

P&L attribution requires the close co-operation of two departments that, in a typical insurance firm, usually work side by side but rarely interact with each other: the accounting department and the risk department. Each has its own data sources, methodologies and IT systems and often very different organisational cultures. It is therefore clear that a prerequisite for a successful P&L attribution is a strong link between the systems and people working in those two departments, combined with a deep knowledge of the model, its data and methodologies, and the simplifications used.

The aims of any P&L attribution exercise are twofold:

- to understand how events and decisions over the past period have contributed to a change in the solvency position of the undertaking, and draw conclusions for management decisions, and
- by running the internal model with the actual outcomes for each risk driver, the performance of the internal model, its coverage and precision can be assessed and then improved.

P&L attribution is one of the six tests and standards for internal model approval. The first aim above is relevant to both standard formula and internal model undertakings, although it is only required explicitly for the latter.

The concept of P&L attribution is not new. It has been common and good practice to analyse the movement of insurance reserves and solvency, both as an aid to understanding the development of the financial position and as a checking tool. The European Insurance CFO Forum's European embedded value (EEV) and market-consistent embedded value (MCEV) principles included a requirement to disclose an analysis of the movement in the embedded value. However, due to its requirement to link P&L with underlying risk drivers, the concept of P&L attribution is much easier to interpret for firms in the life sector than the non-life sector. After all, in a collective loss model that is often used by property/casualty (P/C) insurance firms, it is not easy to identify risk drivers as these models are built on the collective loss experience. However, even in the non-life sector, it is useful for risk management to understand the loss development. It is an ongoing challenge to identify suitable loss drivers for their use in P&L attribution.

Because P&L attribution touches most aspects of both the risk model and the balance sheet, and its supporting valuation method-

ology, it is a huge topic; however, this chapter will only be able to touch on a small number of its aspects. In the following sections, we will first present some examples of the results of P&L attribution exercises, before describing the prerequisites needed for a successful P&L attribution. We then outline its use in model validation and risk management, and conclude by mentioning some special issues and challenges around P&L attribution, as well as presenting a view on future developments.

PRESENTATION OF THE P&L ATTRIBUTION

In an artificial world where the assumptions made in valuing the assets and technical provisions (TPs)[2] are borne out in the period following the initial valuation, and there is no random or stochastic influence, the claims and expenses paid out will exactly match those assumed in the opening balance sheet. The relationship between the opening and closing market-consistent balance sheets will be straightforward: the own funds (the excess of the value of the assets over the TPs) will have increased at the risk-free rate.

In practice, the assumptions in the opening balance sheet will not be borne out as assumed in the opening valuations – assets might grow at a different rate, the claims paid out might be different and views about future assumptions might also change.

Each of these deviations from what was assumed in the opening balance sheet will give rise to a change in the level of the own funds. An example of how this is presented in a P&L attribution is shown in Table 10.1.

The following provides an explanation of each of the lines in Table 10.1.

(1) Net assets are defined here as the assets backing the insurance liabilities, adjusted for the (usually small) current assets less current liabilities. This approach might differ from the presentation of the balance sheet for accounting purposes. An accounting balance sheet would also contain items (eg, deferred acquisition-cost assets or goodwill) that would not be applicable for the Solvency II balance sheet. TPs are the best estimate liabilities plus the risk margin. Own funds are taken as net assets less TPs.

(2) During the year, the model used to calculate the TPs was

Table 10.1 Sample P&L attribution report

		(A)	(B)	(C)
		Net assets	**Technical provisions**	**Own funds**
(1)	Opening balance sheet (December 31, 2014)	5,000	4,000	1,000
	Opening adjustments			
(2)	– model changes		16	(16)
(3)	– other restatements	(7)		(7)
(4)	New business	493	382	111
(5)	Expected return	208	166	42
(6)	Experience variances			
	– interest rate risk	3	2	1
	– mortality risk		28	(28)
(7)	Assumption changes			
	– interest rate risk	(47)	(36)	(11)
	– mortality risk		61	(61)
(8)	Dividend	(27)		(27)
(9)	Changes to current assets and liabilities	1		1
(10)	Currency adjustments	3	2	1
(11)	Unexplained amount	2	9	(7)
(1)	Closing balance sheet (December 31, 2015)	5,629	4,630	999

refined. The opening balance sheet was recalculated using the new model, which increased the TPs by 16.

(3) The approach to valuing some asset classes was reviewed and found to slightly overstate the value. The assets on the opening balance sheet would have been seven lower if the improved approach had been used A more significant example of a restatement would be acquisition or disposal of a part of the business.

(4) Profitable new business written over the year increases the own funds.

(5) The expected return is the investment return on the assets accumulated at discount rate used to derive the TPs in the

opening balance sheet. For the TPs, this item is also sometimes called the unwind of the discount rate.

(6) Experience variations show the impact of the outcome for each risk factor over the year (2015) being different from that assumed in the opening balance sheet. In the example, the return on investments was not equal to the risk-free rate and mortality experience was less favourable than assumed.
(7) Assumption changes show the impact for each risk factor of changed assumptions about experience from January 1, 2016, onwards. In the example, the closing balance sheet makes less optimistic assumptions about future interest rates and mortality than the opening balance sheet did.
(8) A dividend of 27 was paid out from the firm over the year.
(9) Since current assets and liabilities are included in the opening and closing balance sheets, any movement in them over the year will contribute to a movement in own funds.
(10) Where there are subsidiaries operating under a different currency, any movement in the subsidiary currency relative to the parent's currency will contribute to a movement in own funds.
(11) This line is the balancing item: the difference between the change between the opening and closing balance sheets less each of the items in (2) to (10) If the P&L attribution identifies and quantifies every source of difference between the actual and assumed movements over the year, the unexplained item should be zero. In practice, this is unlikely to be the case.

This example shows one possible approach to the presentation of a P&L attribution. The design of the P&L attribution and its presentation should be driven by the use to which it is being put. A firm might carry out several P&L attributions at different levels of granularity and different frequencies. Granularity can apply in different ways, for example: group → business unit → product group → individual product or risk group → risk → risk driver (eg, market risks → credit risk → rating migration).

Table 10.2 shows an example of a more focused P&L attribution, highlighting how the movement in the asset values for three bond funds over a week has been analysed into its components.

For each fund, the movement is analysed in two ways. First, it

Table 10.2 Sample P&L attribution report for investment manager

Attribution for bond funds			
	Fund A	**Fund B**	**Fund C**
Asset value at 12/1/15	256.90	518.70	39.40
Asset value at 19/1/15	259.13	524.34	39.82
Change over week	**2.23**	**5.64**	**0.42**
Analysis of change #1			
Performance of benchmark	1.99	5.83	0.41
Impact of bond selection	0.25	(0.19)	0.01
Unexplained	(0.01)	0.00	0.00
Total	**2.23**	**5.64**	**0.42**
Analysis of change #2			
Yield curve movements	(0.87)	(0.51)	(0.06)
Spread movements	3.08	6.52	0.48
Rating changes	0.00	(0.34)	0.00
Defaults	0.00	0.00	0.00
Unexplained	0.02	(0.03)	0.00
Total	**2.23**	**5.64**	**0.42**

depicts how much of the change in value was down to movement of the underlying benchmark for the fund and how much was due to the fund manager's choice of stocks that are different from the benchmark. Over the week, stock selection has added value for Fund A and lost value for Fund B. This information over longer periods can show the performance of fund managers relative to the fund's benchmark. Second, the analysis shows a split by components of the bond price.

A presentation to the board or shareholders might show only the movement in own funds over the past year, perhaps as a waterfall graph with smaller items grouped together, so that the significant drivers can be clearly seen. A P&L attribution for the asset manager might focus only on the deviations caused by one or more market risks, split by sub risk factors and showing the movements over a week or month.

The order in which items of the P&L are analysed or presented is not specified in Solvency II. The order is likely to be determined, firstly, by the approach used by a firm for similar analyses (eg, for MCEV) and, secondly, by practical considerations, such as the ease of running a new version of the model on the previous period's data.

This example assumes that the movement in own funds is being used as the measure of profit or loss. It is possible that other measures of profitability are used, for example International Financial Reporting Standards (IFRS) profits, if the management of the firm uses those measures in decision-making or running the business, or even to calculate the solvency capital requirement (SCR). A reconciliation to Solvency II own funds will be needed.

The example in Table 10.1 separates the impact of deviations on the net assets and TPs. This can be helpful when a risk can impact both assets and liabilities. For a high-level presentation, a single column showing own funds would be appropriate. The question of whether to also show the movements in the SCR will be considered later in this chapter. A further possibility is to have movements split by type of cashflow – for example, a split of deviations by claims and expenses might provide insight to pricing managers.

Solvency II requires the P&L attribution to be split by major business unit and risk. The granularity of the P&L attribution has to be sufficient for its application in model validation and risk management. In practice, this is will involve attributions being carried out at several levels within a firm and with varying degrees of granularity.

A further requirement of Solvency II is that the attribution should be consistent over time, which is important to facilitate analysis of trends. For example, if the experience variation for a particular risk is negative over several successive periods, it suggests the risk is not being adequately quantified.

PREREQUISITES FOR P&L ATTRIBUTION

This section will cover some of the foundations that are required as a basis for generating a P&L attribution. P&L attribution connects the actual P&L, which is based on "actual" valuations, to the observed development of the risk drivers underlying the internal model, or other causes and sources.

Figure 10.1 Overview of P&L attribution

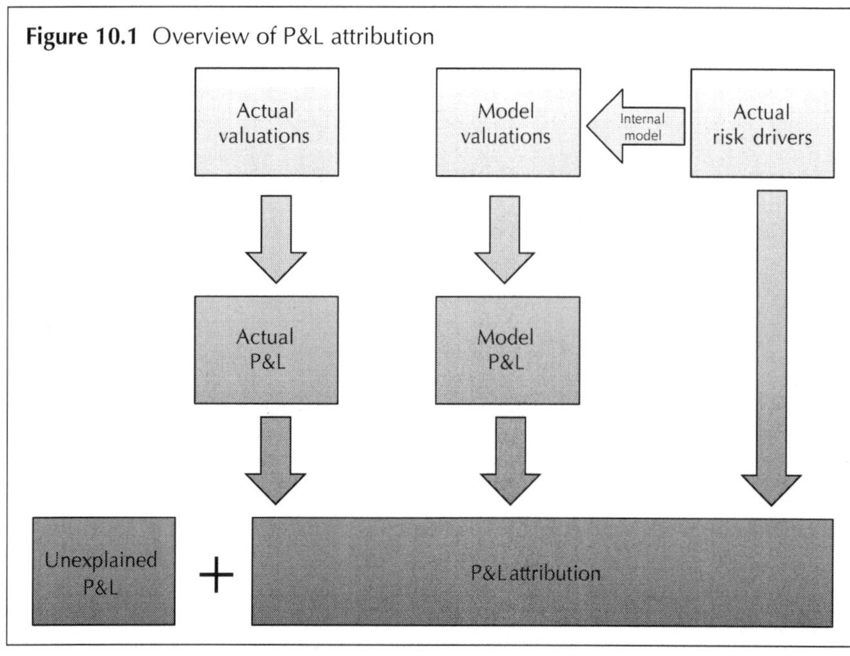

A proper P&L attribution requires appropriate data, methodologies and particularly an appropriate organisational foundation. Prerequisites concerning the quality of the input data of the individual elements are covered in more detail below. However, an important and unique aspect of P&L attribution is often overlooked: it connects two often very different views of an insurance company, namely the financial/accounting view reflected in the balance sheet and the P&L and the risk management view underlying the internal model.

This can be a challenge on many different levels. On the organisational side, in a typical insurance firm a successful P&L attribution requires the close interaction between two departments that often speak different languages. These departments may also use very different IT systems that need to be brought together to create the P&L attribution. They may also use different structures and granularities in the way they record valuations and risk figures, respectively, and these need to be made equivalent so that one can be linked to the other.

It is therefore clear that a prerequisite for a successful P&L attribution is a strong link between the IT systems, data and methodologies used in those two departments, as well as good communication and mutual understanding.

Valuations

P&L attribution connects the "synthetic" world of the internal model, based on many approximations and simplifications, to the "actual" world of the valuations on the balance sheet. The internal model delivers a forecast of the economic balance sheet and the own funds distribution over the one-year horizon at the top level of the undertaking, or the distribution of asset values or technical reserves at a lower level. Therefore, at the end of a forecasting period, a natural question to ask is how the "actual" world behaved over this period and how this compares to the equivalent development in the synthetic world.

For that purpose, the actual valuations that enter into a P&L attribution should be as real as possible and free from all simplifications, approximations or modelling assumptions. If characteristics of assets or policies are not recorded correctly, or options are not priced properly, then P&L attribution cannot be relied upon to identify modelling issues in these areas. Market prices will not be available in all areas as a basis for the actual valuations. However, it has to be clear that all impurities that contaminate the "real" valuations may reduce the reliability of P&L attribution later on. Therefore, extra care has to be taken, and potentially additional validation loops have to be included for those valuations that are based on valuation models ("mark-to-model").

P&L

Originally, the term P&L was used for a change of value based on valuations at the start and end of a period. In the context of Solvency II, the term P&L has to be interpreted much more widely to cover not only changes of values, but also changes of own funds or alternative monetary amounts, as explained in the preceding section.

Causes and sources of P&L comprise changes in risk factors, assumptions and also changes in the risk exposure – for example, through changes in the portfolio composition or new business. P&L numbers that are free from the changes in portfolio composition are called "clean" P&L, and there are a number of possibilities to generate them.

One possibility is to "freeze" the portfolio at the beginning of the period, and to revalue exactly the same portfolio at the end of the period under the new market environment. Even with a frozen portfolio, other effects, such as premium increases or top-ups, have to be taken into account. Alternatively, the "dirty" P&L that results from comparing valuations based on different portfolios can be "cleaned" by accounting for the changes in portfolio composition between the start and end of the period. Similarly, future new business is not usually included in the balance sheet, but will be seen in the actual P&L and has to be isolated.

Other events that may impact the P&L are model or parameter changes. Their impact on P&L also has to be quantified appropriately so that it can be separated from other effects.

Development of risk factors

A major part of any P&L attribution exercise is the identification of the impact of individual risk factors from the internal model on the P&L. These risk factors are usually based on market data already, so the problem of non-available market data that was mentioned above in the case of valuations is less pronounced here. However, even some risk factors can change over the observation period – for example, stocks may be split or merged, and indexes used as risk factors can change their composition. Such events have to be taken into account when using these risk factors as explanatory variables.

In some cases, overall P&L may be impacted by the P&L of individual events that are not easily related to risk factors (examples are individual credit events such as defaults, catastrophe events or losses from operational risk). It is very important to separate the P&L impact of these events, to assign them to the correct model component and to make use of this new information for validation and risk management purposes, even if the standard methods explained below cannot be easily applied in such cases. For example, in scenario-based models of operational risk, actual losses may trigger a review of the assumptions of the corresponding scenario.

GENERATING THE P&L ATTRIBUTION

The process of actually generating the P&L attribution, after all the necessary data are in place, follows a number of distinct steps. First, the impact of particular events such as portfolio, assumption or model changes on the P&L figures have to be identified so that the remaining P&L can be meaningfully related to the developments of risk factors over the observation horizon.

The second step consists of relating the P&L figures to developments in risk factors. For this purpose, the actual and realised P&L is compared to predictions of the P&L that are based on the actual and realised developments of the underlying risk factors. There are a number of methodologies of how to do this, each with their advantages and drawbacks, which will be explained below.

Finally, P&L attribution is a top-down exercise. While any portfolio, contracts book or business unit can serve as a starting point, the process will usually try to break this down into its constituting elements, in order to see where large unexplained P&L comes from, or to gain a better understanding of the importance of individual risk drivers. Therefore, in the last step, P&L figures will be broken down into sub-portfolios or model components, and the second step will be reiterated on a more granular level.

Step 1: Identification of P&L not related to risk factors

The goal of this step is to prepare P&L figures in such a way that they can be meaningfully compared to the development of risk factors. Originally, P&L figures that have been calculated as the difference of two valuations contain a large number of causes and sources that are not related to changes in risk factors. These include new business, changes in portfolio or asset composition or the business mix, and even reorganisations. To the extent that valuations are based on models rather than market data, changes in the methodology or parameters of these valuation models will also impact P&L.

To account for all of these changes is useful in its own right, and can give important hints for business or risk management. However, this is only a preliminary step.

Step 2: Attribution to risk factors

Linking the carefully prepared and remaining actual P&L with the developments of the risk factors underlying the internal model is the core of the P&L attribution exercise. The goal is a decomposition of the actual P&L according to the movements of the selected risk factors. For this purpose, a model or predicted P&L is prepared based on the movements of the risk factors. This can be viewed as an equation that has, on the left side, the actual P&L, and on the right side, the sum of the predicted P&L slices:

$$\text{Actual P\&L} = \sum \text{P\&L slices} + \varepsilon$$

To achieve equality between the two sides, an error term ε was included, which is called the "unexplained" P&L.

The main issue now is about how to come up with the P&L slices so that they correspond to the movements in the selected risk factors. This question actually contains two separate questions: "For a given change in a risk factor, how do we calculate the associated P&L slice?" and "How do we define and order the movements of risk factors?"

To improve the clarity of our further elaborations, we will make the following assumptions. Let us assume that we have a portfolio that depends only on two risk factors, interest rates (*IR*) and mortality (*mort*). We observe these risk factors at time 0 (IR_0, $mort_0$) and at time 1 (IR_1,$mort_1$).

Recalculation of P&L

For a given change in a single risk factor, we have two options on how to calculate the resulting change in P&L: full recalculation or making use of sensitivities. As an alternative to the classic calculation of sensitivities, in Monte Carlo settings regressions of changes in valuations to changes in risk factors are sometimes used for faster computation.

P&L attributions based on first-order sensitivities rather than full recalculations will not take into account non-linearities in the valuation function. Therefore, additional work may be needed to quantify the impact of non-linearities in order to minimise the unexplained P&L term.

Movement in risk factors

The movement in risk factors between time 0 and time 1 can be decomposed in two main ways: "bump and reset" and "waterfall".

Bump and reset

The procedure for bump and reset differs from the waterfall in that changes to risk factors are always based at their original values:

$$(IR_0, mort_0) \quad \text{->} \quad \begin{matrix} (IR_1, mort_0) \\ \\ (IR_0, mort_1) \end{matrix} \quad \text{->} \quad (IR_1, mort_1)$$

Consequently, the P&L attribution based on a bump and reset decomposition, and using full recalculation, could look like this:

$$\text{Actual P\&L} = \{f(IR_1, mort_0) - f(IR_0, mort_0)\} + \{f(IR_0, mort_1) - f(IR_0, mort_0)\} + \varepsilon$$

where f( ) denotes the value given the indicated realisations of risk factors IR and mort.

In this procedure, the resulting P&L slices will not depend on the sequence of calculation, because all calculations are based on the origin at time 0. However, no consideration is given to joint movements of the risk factors.

As an alternative to full recalculation, sensitivities in the individual risk factors can be used. This may be a practical approach if sensitivities are already available or easy to calculate. However, using first-order sensitivities instead of a full revaluation also does not take into account potential non-linearities in the change of valuation, and therefore these effects will end up in the "unexplained" term ε at the end. As a consequence, the analysis of the unexplained term will be more complicated.

Waterfall

For the waterfall, the decomposition will change consecutively one risk factor at a time without going back to the origin. In our case, a waterfall decomposition might look like the following:

$$(IR_0, mort_0) \text{ -> } (IR_1, mort_0) \text{ -> } (IR_1, mort_1),$$

where the movement in the first step is associated with the P&L attributed to the risk factor *IR*, while the second step corresponds to the P&L attributed to the risk factor *mort*. Consequently, the P&L attribution based on a waterfall decomposition could look like this:

$$\text{Actual P\&L} = \{f(IR_1, mort_0) - f(IR_0, mort_0)\} + \{f(IR_1, mort_1) - f(IR_1, mort_0)\} + \varepsilon$$

In the waterfall decomposition, the attribution of P&L to individual risk factors will depend on the ordering and the sequence of the decomposition, and therefore, if the sequence of the decomposition is changed:

$$(IR_0, mort_0) \text{ -> } (IR_0, mort_1) \text{ -> } (IR_1, mort_1)$$

Attributed P&Ls will also change, although the unexplained P&L will stay the same.

Another characteristic of the waterfall decomposition is that the effects of joint movements of risk factors are incorporated into the attributed P&Ls.

The waterfall decomposition is usually combined with a full revaluation of the portfolio under consideration at the intermediate points, because sensitivities are usually not available there.

As we can see from the above, the different methodologies all have their pros and cons. An appropriate combination of the different methods allows the separation of the various effects from non-linearities and joint movements, and can improve the insights gained from P&L attribution.

Step 3: Decomposition into sub-portfolios or model components

Having attributed the actual P&L to the selected risk factors, we are left with a portion of "unexplained P&L". This warrants further analysis. In the search for the root cause of the unexplained P&L, and in order to see where the unexplained P&L comes from, the next step is to break down the P&L attribution into sub-portfolios and model components.

Assessing unexplained P&L

In order to determine where such a breakdown should be carried out, an assessment of the materiality of unexplained P&L is required. This can be based on several different indicators, such as:

- ❑ absolute size;
- ❑ size relative to the total value or total P&L of the portfolio; and
- ❑ size relative to the probability distribution forecast of the P&L for the portfolio, expressed as a quantile or percentage of standard deviation.

Using this top-down procedure will ensure that further analysis is only carried out where certain indications exist, and will aid the overall efficiency of the exercise. Sometimes, judgement, skill and experience are needed to determine areas for further analysis that seem fine at first sight. In any case, a minimum granularity of the P&L attribution is necessary because errors can cancel out in the aggregation of P&L over large portfolios.

As the different approaches to breaking down unexplained P&L into sub-portfolios or model components differ, we will explain each in turn.

Sub-portfolios

Breaking down P&L into sub-portfolios is simple as long as data of sufficient granularity is available. However, while P&L is additive, and the sum of the P&L of the sub-portfolios will add up to the P&L of the total portfolio:

$$\text{Actual P\&L} = \text{Actual P\&L}_1 + \text{Actual P\&L}_2$$

This is not necessarily true for the unexplained P&L due to non-linearities or other effects:

$$\varepsilon \neq \varepsilon_1 + \varepsilon_2$$

Narrowing down the sub-portfolio that gives rise to unexplained P&L is a necessary step to finding the root cause of the unexplained P&L, and starting other validation measures or model improvements.

Model components

While (within one undertaking) the P&L from different sub-portfolios simply adds up to the total P&L, this is not true for the impact of consecutive model components. As an example, we will use the natural catastrophe premium risk model of a P/C insurer. In a simplified view, this can be seen as consisting of two modules:

- The "loss module", which simulates potential losses (gross losses) based on risk drivers; and
- The "reinsurance module", which applies existing reinsurance treaties to the simulated gross losses and results in net losses.

In order to find the root cause of unexplained P&L, it is not enough to compare the actual net loss to the risk models' predicted net losses. Total unexplained P&L will be a compound of unexplained P&L from the first and the second module. It can originate from either the first component or the second, and therefore both modules need to be checked individually.

For this purpose, a three-step procedure is necessary.

1) Actual net losses are broken up into gross losses and the impact of reinsurance.
2) P&L attribution for the loss module: The loss module is re-run based on the observed realisation of loss drivers, and the observed result (the predicted gross loss) is compared against the actual gross loss. Unexplained losses are clearly due to the loss model, and may be attributed to the loss drivers as described earlier and may trigger further validation efforts.
3) P&L attribution of the reinsurance module: The reinsurance module is re-run on the actual gross losses, and the resulting predicted impact of reinsurance is compared against the actual impact of reinsurance. Differences between the two can be analysed, and may point to issues in the reinsurance module and can be addressed accordingly. Using the actual gross losses as the basis for this exercise ensures that all differences in the impact of reinsurance are due to the reinsurance module and are not contaminated by unexplained P&L from previous model stages.

For non-catastrophe models, only the last step in this procedure may be relevant because loss drivers for a collective model may not have been identified.

USING P&L ATTRIBUTION FOR MODEL VALIDATION

One of the main areas of application for a P&L attribution is the validation of the internal model as required by Article 124 of the Solvency II directive. There are a number of potential issues in the internal risk model that can show up as suspiciously large unexplained P&L. In particular, P&L attribution is one of the very few validation tools that has the potential to identify unmodelled risks. It can also show if something else is amiss, and can be used to narrow down the area where the problem might lie by drilling down into sub-portfolios or model components, as explained above. However, the attribution exercise itself will usually not identify the precise problem. Rather, it can serve as an indicator or trigger for further validation efforts, which can then be focused on a particular area of the risk model.

Also, a word of warning is in order: a small, unexplained P&L does not necessarily mean that everything is fine. Unexplained P&L

figures can cancel out or diversify between sub-portfolios or model components. To avoid a false sense of security, the P&L attribution exercise must reach a minimum granularity. That is, starting from the top level of the total balance sheet, the P&L attribution exercise must drill down into consecutively smaller policy groups or assets, as well as refine the types of risk factors used for the purpose. Even a highly granular approach is not a guarantee that significant, but offsetting, elements of the P&L will be identified.

In the following, we present a number of examples that explain how certain modelling simplifications, approximations or missing risk factors will show up in the unexplained P&L. In order to properly take into account such simplifications or approximations, the firm should make use of the list of modelling assumptions compiled during model development. As mentioned, a sound knowledge of these is a prerequisite of a successful P&L attribution.

Common examples of simplifications and approximations in risk models include:

- the use of a market index or other proxy, such as:
  - a basket of equities modelled using a stock market index;
  - a single interest rate used to represent the whole yield curve; and
  - an average lapse or mortality rate used for a whole group of policies.
- simplified model assumptions, such as:
  - assumptions on management actions that deviate from actual decisions;
  - non-modelled details of reinsurance contracts or other mitigants; and
  - simplified assumptions about the timing of cashflows in the model (eg, everything happens at the start or end of a calendar year).

We will now elaborate on the examples above to make the procedure more transparent.

Equity portfolio

For a given equity portfolio with i stocks, initial prices $p_i(0)$ and weights w_i, its initial value will be:

$$\text{Value }(0) = \Sigma\, w_i * p_i(0)$$

and the actual P&L of the portfolio between times 0 and 1 will be:

$$\text{Actual P\&L} = \text{Value }(1) - \text{Value }(0) = \Sigma\, w_i * (p_i(1) - p_i(0))$$

Let us assume that, in the risk model, this portfolio is mapped to an index with initial value I (0) with a multiplier m so that:

$$m \times I\,(0) = \text{Value }(0)$$

and the predicted P&L from the model will be:

$$\text{Predicted P\&L} = m * (I(1) - I(0))$$

Comparing:

$$\text{Actual P\&L} = \text{Predicted P\&L} + \varepsilon,$$

we see that the actual performance of the equity portfolio will be very different from the index if the portfolio weights w_i differ significantly from the index weights, and correspondingly the unexplained P&L ε will be large, signalling that the modelling of the equity exposure needs to be improved.

Replicating portfolio

In the construction and use of replicating portfolios (and other so-called proxy modelling approaches), a number of approximations occur simultaneously, and it is important to separate their effects for the purposes of an adequate P&L attribution and be able to pinpoint potential issues. A first approximation occurs when the actual cash-flow profile of the undertaking is translated into a static portfolio of simple securities, such as bonds and swaptions. A second approximation occurs in the risk model when these simple securities are revalued at the risk horizon, because not all risk factors from the real word will be represented in the risk model.

The overall P&L attribution for a replicating portfolio will compare its predicted P&L against the actual P&L from a revaluation using a full stochastic undertaking model (such as an MCEV model). This can be broken down into several distinct steps, according to the approximations applied. In a first step, the predicted P&L of the simple securities is compared against their actual P&L based on market values. The further breakdown into risk factors will reveal the materiality of approximations, such as the simplified modelling of risk factors – eg, the evolution of implied volatility or basis spreads. In a second step, the actual P&L from the replicating portfolio is then compared against the actual P&L from the stochastic undertaking model, with the difference being due to the approximation of dynamic cashflows and an evolving balance sheet with a static portfolio of securities.

P&L attribution and backtesting

P&L attribution can also be used in conjunction with backtesting in order to generate model validation results on more granular levels than only on the top level of the model. Backtesting can be carried out at the top level of the model by comparing actual P&L against the probability distribution forecast generated by the model. An alternative is to apply backtesting on the lowest level of modelling, by comparing the realisations of risk factors against their model distributions. This comparison can shed light on whether the risk model assumptions capture the behaviour of the underlying risk factors. However, backtesting can also be carried out at all levels in between by making use of the attributed P&L.

For this purpose, actual P&L is broken down into sub-portfolios or model components, as described above. The resulting actual P&L numbers are then compared against the probability distribution forecast at the same level of granularity for this particular sub-portfolio or model component. A prerequisite for this exercise is that the corresponding probability distribution forecasts are easily available. This is often the case in P/C areas, where individual lines of business are modelled separately and the resulting distributions are aggregated. This can also shed some light on the plausibility of correlation assumptions, in particular when data is collected over a number of historic time periods. Because of the higher granularity, even over only one time step a large number of such backtests can be carried out, and can together yield statistically meaningful results on risk model performance.

Both backtesting and P&L attribution can be carried out for artificially designed portfolios rather than the real ones. This is sometimes called "hypothetical backtesting" or "hypothetical P&L attribution", and can shed light on particular model characteristics, provided that the artificial portfolios are constructed accordingly.

USING P&L ATTRIBUTION FOR RISK MANAGEMENT AND USE TEST

This section considers how the output from a P&L attribution can help a firm in the areas of risk management and the use test.

Gaining benefit from the attribution relies on being able to produce the analysis when required, and is likely to require an automated solution. The attribution should not be thought of as solely backward-looking (analysing the movement between two past balance sheets), but also forward-looking. For example, when projecting the balance sheet (and solvency position) under future scenarios, it can be helpful also to show a P&L attribution under these scenarios.

- Allocating the P&L movement to risk categories shows which risks have caused the profit or loss over the period. Management can compare the actual losses by risk and by business unit with the risk ranking and the risk appetite.
- P&L attribution can be used to shed light on the impact of past decisions – eg, allocating P&L to particular tranches of business might show the adequacy of pricing assumptions. Another example is to split investment performance into strategic (market performance in each sector) and tactical (performance of fund manager against the market). Definitions can be important here, such as the failure to implement correctly a hedging programme shown as an operational loss experience loss or hidden within investment losses.
- By showing P&L movements gross of hedging and other risk mitigants, with the impact of the hedge or mitigant as a separate line, light is shed onto the effectiveness of the hedge. Similarly, large losses might point to ineffective controls in the business or governance issues – eg, if unexplained movements in the profit and loss comes from new or emerging risks, why were the risks not previously identified?
- Comparing the relative sizes of different drivers of the P&L can inform decisions based on materiality – eg, where do risk drivers/calculations need further analysis by internal model (IM) team (or internal audit)?

CHALLENGES

Including the SCR

An extension of a P&L attribution showing the movement in own funds is to also show the movement in the SCR. This allows a firm to explain the movement in its solvency position, either expressed as the absolute difference in own funds and SCR, or a coverage proportion of own funds divided by the SCR.

Including the SCR introduces additional challenges, such as the following.

- Needing to allocate the diversified SCR across major business units, etc. A firm might already have developed an approach to allocating capital across units and products.
- Longer run times, as an SCR needs to be recalculated for each row of the attribution. Approximations can be used to avoid a full recalculation each time, but care must be taken to ensure that these do not undermine the usefulness of the attribution.
- Needing to decide the assumptions on which to calculate the SCR for each row of the attribution. If the assumptions for the opening and closing SCRs are different, the changes have to be allocated to lines of the P&L attribution. One option is to have an additional line for SCR assumption changes in the analysis. In some cases – eg, where a large experience variation has led to a re-assessment of the relevant SCR assumptions – the movement in the SCR could be assigned to that experienced variation line. However, too much sophistication here is unlikely to yield greater insights.

Solvency II does not require the inclusion of the SCR in the P&L attribution. However, SCR attribution (called the "analysis of change" of model results) is one of the additional validation tools mentioned in the preparatory guidelines for internal models from the European Insurance and Occupational Pensions Authority (EIOPA).

A related challenge is calculating the movements in the risk margin, which will be an element of the movement in own funds. Strictly speaking, the risk margin should be recalculated for each row based on the SCR. In practice, many firms use approximations even to calculate the risk margin in the opening or closing balance sheet. This is an area where a proportionate approach should be used.

Partial internal models

Where an undertaking uses a partial internal model, a possible question is whether the P&L attribution is carried out for the full undertaking or just for the business in the scope of the partial internal model. The answer is both!

The group-level movement in own funds will be more naturally analysed for the whole undertaking. P&L attribution in greater detail might be carried out just by using the business in the scope of the partial internal model – or a subset of it – as part of the model validation process.

New business

To provide useful analysis, it is necessary to have accurate data about when new policies started and consider how the timing of new business interacts with the timing of experience variations. An ideal presentation would be to allocate profit or loss at the point of sale to the new business line of the P&L attribution, and any subsequent movements to the relevant experience variation or assumption change line. This will give a true picture of the profitability of new business.

A further complication involving new business comes when the P&L attribution includes movements in the SCR. Since the SCR includes 12 months of new business following the calculation date, the movement in the SCR over (say) a year will involve an element arising from the difference in the new business assumed in the opening SCR and the actual new business written.

CONCLUSION

The P&L attribution is never a static process. Every time the model is changed, the P&L attribution will need to be reconsidered and possibly changed. Changes outside the model (eg, if the tiering limits for own funds suddenly restrict the eligibility of own funds, or an undertaking makes use of ancillary own funds)[2] might also require a new line in the high-level P&L attribution output.

The biggest challenges for a successful P&L attribution exercise are mostly not of a mathematical or methodological nature, but rather lie in linking together a wide variety of systems, information sources and organisational units. In practice, a key requirement is to achieve a high degree of efficiency in this link. P&L attribution is most useful when it is run on as granular a basis as possible. However, to manage the huge amounts of data generated by a granular P&L attribution, a high degree of automation is necessary. This will enable human experts to direct their attention only to those few areas where large unexplained P&L hints at potential problems in the risk model or the P&L itself, and where more analysis can produce the biggest improvements in risk modelling or risk management.

We have described a systematic approach to minimise the risk of missing causes and sources of profits and losses. However, a lot of judgement, skill and experience are needed when carrying out the P&L attribution: a good P&L attribution relies on a mixture of art and science.

The most important insights from any P&L attribution exercise do not arise from the finalised report, but appear while carrying out the exercise. In this sense, in P&L attribution as in many other things, the journey is the reward.

Statements made here are the authors' personal and private views. They should not be construed to reflect EIOPA's or BaFin's opinion, and do not represent official EIOPA or BaFin statements.

1 For further details, see European Parliament and the Council of the European Union (2009).
2 Technical provisions under Solvency II comprise a market-consistent best estimate of the insurance liability and a risk margin.
3 Ancillary own funds are commitments that an undertaking can call upon in order to increase their financial resources, such as members' calls, guarantees or letters of credit. They can be recognised under Solvency II, subject to supervisory approval and limits.

REFERENCES

CEIOPS, 2009, "Advice for L2 Implementing Measures on SII: Tests and Standards for Internal Model Approval", November.

EIOPA, 2013, "EIOPA Final Report on Public Consultations No. 13/011 on the Proposal for Guidelines on the Pre-application for Internal Models", September.

European Parliament and the Council of the European Union, 2009, "Directive 2009/138/EC of the European Parliament and of the Council of 25 November 2009 on the Taking-up and Pursuit of the Business of Insurance and Reinsurance (Solvency II) (recast)".

Morini, M., 2011, *Understanding and Managing Model Risk: A Practical Guide for Quants, Traders and Validators* (Hoboken, NJ: Wiley).

11

Internal Model Validation: The Regulatory Perspective

Ravi Bharos, Christian Kerfriden and Vesa Ronkainen

De Nederlandsche Bank, Prudential Regulation Authority, Bank of England, and Finanssivalvonta

Validation is a fundamental requirement for institutions wishing to qualify for an internal model to determine regulatory capital requirements. It requires institutions to demonstrate that they have in place a rigorous process[1] by which to establish whether their internal model framework is sound or if improvements are necessary. Different and distinct, this should not be confused with the process that supervisors undertake when approving a model for use.

This chapter aims to provide insight into the validation standards for internal models. It will show that a correct application of the validation process contributes to reducing the misalignment of the interests of the insurance industry and the regulator.

Internal model validation is possibly the most important step in the model building sequence. Even in the absence of regulatory requirements, it should be good practice for firms to review and validate their internal models to ensure that appropriate risk and capital management processes are in place. As part of the internal model design, supervisory authorities would also expect them to include a regular cycle of validation and necessary updates of the internal model. However, it is perceived that validation practices quite often tend to be weak, particularly when the total capital adequacy of the firm and the overall calibration of the model is an important consideration. Once approved, the improvement of internal models is viewed by firms as a cost of doing business and a compliance hurdle, rather than a source of potential business benefit. It is recognised that validation is a demanding exercise when it requires evaluation at high quantiles of loss distributions combined with data scarcity and complex dependencies between multiple variables. Nevertheless, from a regulatory perspective, weaknesses in validation practices might result in firms operating with inappropriately calibrated models. Similarly, inadequately implemented validation should be of some concern to investors and the rating agencies.

Validation is important as it provides evidence that an internal model works as planned – ie, it meets its intended requirements in terms of methods employed and results produced, addresses the right problems and provides better information about the system being modelled. Validation is concerned with the predictive properties of internal models. These models embody forward-looking estimates of risk, and their validation is intimately bound up with assessing those estimates. For an internal model to be accepted and used by management to inform its decision-making, it must first be understood to be a robust representation of prospective risk, not just at firm level but at component and sub-component level. To this end, validation should enable the firm to understand better the internal model's capabilities and limitations, and confirm that the internal model and the processes supporting it are adequate and appropriate for the purpose.

It must be emphasised that validation should be viewed as an iterative process, not a one-off event, by which a firm using an internal model periodically refines validation tools in response to changing market and operating conditions. Similarly, it is important to recognise that there is no universal validation method, and the structure of the validation approach naturally depends on the technical specifications of the internal model, its purpose and its intended use. Typically, an effective validation process develops a series of attempts to invalidate the internal model. The end-result of this process is not a validated model, but rather an internal model that has passed all the validation tests.

Appropriate validation should allow firms to quickly identify problems in their models and help them to adapt their internal models for optimal performance. For example, an internal model may embody assumptions about relationships between variables or about their behaviour under stress. Validation strives to assess with a

certain degree of confidence that the assumptions are appropriate. Securing this outcome is likely to involve a range of people within a firm, including making use of some skills not traditionally involved in capital management and modelling activities.

Validation should encompass both quantitative and qualitative elements. While it might be possible to think of validation as a purely technical/mathematical exercise in which outcomes are compared to estimates using statistical techniques, it will likely be insufficient to focus solely on comparing predictions to outcomes. In assessing the overall performance of an internal model, it is also important to assess its components, as well as the structures, governance, data and processes around these parts.

Finally, to achieve an effective validation, objective challenge is essential. Independent model validation helps financial institutions to evaluate and verify the overall performance of their internal models. Proper independence of the validation function is therefore important, whether the validation is done internally or externally. Individuals performing the validation must possess the necessary skills, knowledge, expertise and experience. For some firms, the use of external validation may be an acceptable and suitable approach, at least in part. In this case, firms should demand that these external validators help their staff build validation expertise so that the firm can run the validation process itself in the future. Nevertheless, as will be discussed, firms should maintain ownership of the model validation process. Regardless of the firm's control structure, internal audit should have an oversight responsibility to ensure that validation processes are implemented as designed and are effective.

Given the role that model validation plays during the model building sequence and in the monitoring of its ongoing appropriateness, it is not only necessary that this process is appropriately sourced by the organisation, but also that its governance is appropriately thought through. Therefore, this chapter will begin discussing the governance around the model validation process before discussing the planning and execution of the model validation activities. It then looks at some of the tools that can be used in the model validation process, and concludes by dealing with the reporting of the outcome of the model validation activities.

This chapter does not deal explicitly with the model validation policy (MVP), partially because the Solvency II framework already contains explicit requirements for it. Where items that are not specifically mentioned by the Solvency II framework as part of the MVP are discussed in this chapter (such as model validation reporting), it should be understood that their inclusion in the MVP would be good practice.

GOVERNANCE AROUND MODEL VALIDATION

The Solvency II regulations require that the model validation process is independent from the development and operation of the internal model. However, the same regulations introduce a certain level of ambiguity by stating that the model validation process is part of the risk management function,[2] which is also responsible for model development. The choice that is made here is that for the model validation process to be effective, it should be carried out by people with the necessary skills, knowledge, expertise and experience, and that the best place to accommodate these experts is within the risk management function. The combination of these potentially conflicting tasks within the risk management function (eg, model validation should continue to be able to objectively and freely challenge the model, which has probably been developed by other experts sitting in the room next door) underpins the need for provisions that ensure an appropriately independent model validation process. This is to avoid situations where model validators are not sufficiently impartial towards their colleagues from the model development unit, or where short-term interests and/or tunnel vision are prevailing over a more thorough and independent assessment of the internal model.

The following provisions can/should be present to safeguard the thoroughness and independence of the model validation process:

- ❑ an appropriate segregation of duties and a clear path for escalating within the organisation for issues arising from the model validation process;
- ❑ strong reporting lines to enable model validation to communicate freely and effectively their thoughts and opinions;
- ❑ a recognition and awareness that independence in mind is also needed;
- ❑ good co-ordination of the model validation process activities where these are not combined within a single department;

- ❑ understanding the need for independent testing; and
- ❑ clear responsibilities for the involvement of external personnel.

Appropriate segregation of duties and clear escalation paths

To resolve potential conflicts of interest that might compromise the independence of model validation, an appropriate segregation of duties within the organisation is essential. To prevent model validation being outranked by hierarchy within the risk management function, model validation should report directly to the manager with overall responsibility for risk management, preferably the chief risk officer (CRO) or a manager that sits no more than one level below the management board. This practice is commonly used by most (re)insurance firms.

When a different structure is chosen, model validation should have at least a clear and direct escalation line to the management board. However, having only this escalation line is considered suboptimal as it may prove to be an insurmountable hurdle in many cases. In fact, bypassing the direct line manager to escalate issues might exacerbate potential conflict of interest. For example, would validators take steps to escalate issues to the management board when this is likely to affect negatively their careers?

Reporting lines

To strengthen model validation independence, it is important that validators are able to communicate freely within the organisation, raise questions, express doubts and criticism without the risk that critical issues are being swept under the carpet. To this end, the distribution of validation reports should not be limited to the small circle of people that are directly involved in the model activities, but to all relevant stakeholders (at least model developers, model users, management that uses the output of the models for decision-making and internal audit). This will mitigate the risk that validators' opinions are being ignored or downplayed.

Model validation should also have the possibility to explain its findings and ratings at committee's meetings where they are discussed. This would ensure that findings are properly understood and that appropriate remediation actions taken. In order not to compromise their independence, it should be good practice that model validators have a standing invitation as a non-voting member to these meetings.

Although desirable, senior management at firms are not likely to review all validation reports and detailed findings. To overcome this potential problem and ensure that senior management is made aware of the issues and limitations of the internal model, it is essential that the management board and/or the firm's highest risk committee are informed directly and with a certain frequency (eg, quarterly) about the major validation findings and their status, together with more general information on model validation (validation progress, staffing issues, etc).

Independence in mind

Organisational structure, escalation possibilities and reporting lines can only partially achieve independence. An essential component is the "independence in mind"[3] of the model validator. This requires a professional sceptical attitude towards validation topics, not taking the adequacy of any relevant item for granted until proven. Organisations should appreciate this independence in mind and seek to hire professionals with this attitude for model validation.

Co-ordination of model validation activities

It is good practice for model validation to combine its activities into a single validation department within the risk management function that has no responsibility for the development and operation of the internal model. This department can develop the specific expertise needed for an effective validation, and ensure that validation is performed in a consistent manner and that an appropriate amount of resources are available and deployed to perform validation tasks when needed.

However, it important to point out that, in line with the proportionality principle, the Solvency II framework requires a model validation process, but does not prescribe how this should be accomplished. Therefore, this process does not necessarily need to be performed by a separate model validation department.

In a few cases, firms have distributed the validation tasks among several parties (and/or departments) involved in the development and/or operation of a part of the internal model. The rationale used by these firms is that these parties/departments have a more detailed knowledge of the model than a remote model validation department, and that there is always a trade-off between independence and knowledge. In such instances, an appropriate segregation of duties with respect to validation is achieved by a specific allocation of the validation tasks – such as when validation activities for a specific part of the internal model are performed by a different department from the one originally involved in the development/operation, thus effectively shifting the validation tasks between departments.

In other cases, especially with respect to some large groups, it has been observed that validation activities are allocated to different validation teams across the group – for example, to a central or group validation team supplemented by local or regional validation teams. In these instances, effective co-ordination, safeguarding of independence, applying of uniform standards and consistent execution are based on appropriate:

- independence of the validators;
- development of an MVP and model validation tools;
- validation and resource planning;
- level of expertise tailored to each specific case;
- hiring of external resources;
- performance of validation activities that ensure consistency and meet the minimum quality standards;
- reporting of the model validation findings;
- communication channels that inform the management board of major findings and progress of the model validation activities; and
- follow-up of model validation findings.

Therefore, if firms decide not to have a dedicated model validation department, they should provide for appropriate co-ordination to take care of the above-mentioned issues, ensuring independence and quality.

A different situation that can arise is when model validation activities are performed by another internal party. The model validation process has a broad scope, comprising various disciplines. Most model validators tend to have a quantitative background; therefore, they are less likely to be equipped to validate topics such as governance, data accuracy and completeness, or IT. There may be other valid reasons (efficiency, shortage of validation staff) to perform validation activities elsewhere within the organisation, as long as they meet the requirements in terms of independence and expertise. What is important in these instances is that there should always be a clear rationale for such internal "outsourcing" – eg, reallocation of the quantitative core activities or even the entire validation function – otherwise this will be hard to justify.

Reliance on others (eg, the internal audit department)[4] to perform certain validation activities requires a clear demarcation to prevent gaps and/or overlaps. This also applies to the situation when testing is performed by model developers on behalf, and under the direction, of model validation. In cases where the model validation process is partially outsourced, it is important to document the allocation of tasks, clarifying scope and deliverables. This documentation should facilitate communication between the different parties involved, articulating what is expected from them. In some cases, organisations have laid down this demarcation in the MVP, in some others a separate demarcation letter was used.

Testing

Solvency II requires certain validation tests (sensitivity testing and testing against experience, ie, backtesting, among others) to be conducted. In practice, most model developers, and sometimes model users, already perform (several) tests as part of the model development process, and validators tend to rely on those for part of their tasks. From a supervisory perspective, the key question in these situations is whether model validation relies on the tests and activities already performed by model developers. What should model validators look at to have the necessary comfort that these tests have been adequately conducted, and that the outcome of this process is fairly presented?

A four-step approach could provide a higher degree of comfort:

1) model validation independently draws a test plan to determine which tests have to be performed;
2) model validation checks the tests already performed by model developers and/or users;
3) based on the output of the tests and its assessment of their quality, model validation forms its opinion; and
4) random sampling or risk-based re-performance of some of the

tests already performed by the developers and/or users by model validation.

First, before starting the independent model validation, model validation defines the test plan, which identifies the full set of validation tests that have to be performed on the model. Building this independent test plan aims to mitigate the risk that model validation is steered too easily in the direction chosen by model development (or model users), and therefore can provide an independent challenge to the model. This plan does not need to be very detailed (eg, up to two pages), and should describe at a high level the set of tests to be performed (completeness) and the most important aspects to be considered (ensuring appropriateness) for a particular model component. Furthermore, the test plan should also indicate the appropriate dataset to be used to perform these tests. It is also possible that test plans are already incorporated in the MVP, although this is likely to leave less room for a customised validation approach. Moreover, it is possible to acquire new insights during the execution of the model validation and adjust the test plans accordingly.

Second, model validation checks whether:

- the model developer has duly conducted all the tests set out in the test plan (eg, appropriate parameters and other inputs);
- the test results can be reproduced; and
- the model developer can appropriately justify deviations from the test plan.

Based on the outcome of these checks, model validation will decide whether the outputs of the tests are reliable. If model developers did not perform all the required tests (according to the test plan) or if there is doubt about the quality of the testing, model validation is expected to fill these gaps and perform these (or some of these) tests or direct the rerun.

Third, the output of the tests will provide evidence to draw conclusions. Model validation should always review and assess the output of the tests, and decide whether appropriate conclusions have been drawn by the developers and/or users.

Finally, taking the internal model as a whole, model validation performs some of the tests itself (or directs the execution by the model developer) based on a random sampling of tests or a risk-based approach. Where model validation decides not to conduct any tests, the model validation report should clearly state the reasons for this decision and provide evidence that this was the most appropriate course of action.

External personnel

There can be many valid reasons for hiring external personnel to perform some of the validation activities – eg, scarcity of, or a limited need for, a certain expertise. However, Solvency II's model validation requirements for independence and expertise apply also to external personnel. In these circumstances, it important that the organisation retains ownerships of the model validation activities performed so that it can manage appropriately the external personnel, understand the outcome of the validation, follow up issues and understand the limitations of the internal model.

To ensure independence and expertise, the following is needed:

- the engagement with the external party is the responsibility of an independent function such as model validation; this independent function is in close contact with the external party and takes ownership and responsibility for any follow-up;
- the terms of the engagement are free from restrictions or limitations (eg, restrictions in working methods and tests to be applied) that might influence the outcome; a realistic budget and timeframe are available to perform the services;
- the external party and the people that will perform these validation activities on its behalf do not have undue conflicts of interest (either in its general meaning or with respect to the internal model development in particular); and
- the persons who will perform the validation activities on behalf of the external party possess the necessary skills and experience; simply stating, "it is a very famous consulting practice" is obviously not sufficient.

To achieve ownership, it is necessary that:

- the organisation has sufficient internal knowledge/expertise available to direct the content of the validation activities of the external parties;
- the model validation policy of the organisation is complied with;

- model validation is involved in the high-level execution of the validation (assessing the test plan and contributing to the knowledge about the specifics of the organisation); and
- model validation is involved in the reporting (to form the opinion, monitoring the follow-up) of the findings of the external validator.

MODEL VALIDATION APPROACH

The solvency capital requirement (SCR) is defined to correspond to the value-at-risk (VaR) of the basic own funds of an insurance firm subject to a confidence level of 99.5% over a one-year period.[5] Under Solvency II, an internal model should be able to produce a probability distribution forecast (PDF) of the basic own funds (assets over liabilities), and to select the corresponding quantile of that distribution.

Stochastic modelling and simulation provide tools for this risk modelling task. Realistic modelling techniques for insurance, market, credit and operational risk and their dependencies are often rather complex, and their proper application and validation requires considerable expertise and effort. In that work, the insights from good practice in modelling and forecasting, and from the more specific requirements provided by the internal model framework, should both play a key part. Chronological modelling steps are helpful in two respects: i) they provide a general framework to analyse and validate several types of models that model validation may be required to assess; and ii) they provide another point of view on the regulations. These aspects of model validation will now be discussed.

Modelling process

There are a few general steps in a typical forecasting and statistical modelling project, as summarised in Figure 11.1.[6]

Each one of these steps is important and should not be omitted. This also holds true in the case where an internal model or part of it is developed by an external third party (eg, an external vendor model). A few examples in support of our argument will be provided in this section. These examples are relevant when reviewing an internal model. However, it is important to point out that they by no means constitute an exhaustive list.

Figure 11.1 Summary of a forecasting and statistical modelling project

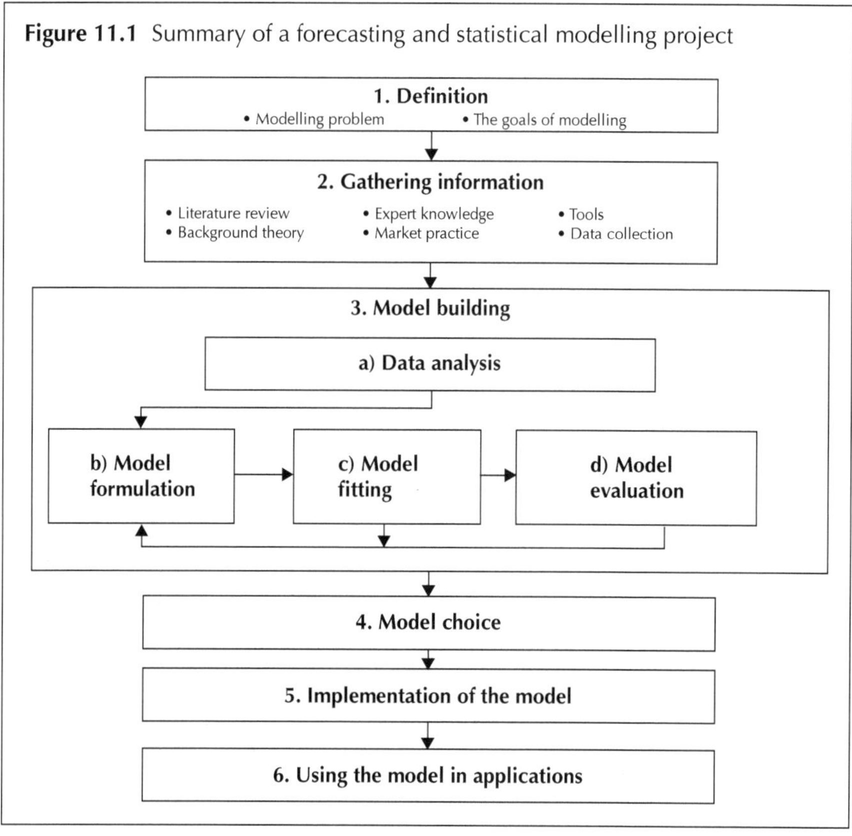
1. Definition
• Modelling problem
• The goals of modelling
2. Gathering information
• Literature review
• Background theory
• Expert knowledge
• Market practice
• Tools
• Data collection
3. Model building
a) Data analysis
b) Model formulation
c) Model fitting
d) Model evaluation
4. Model choice
5. Implementation of the model
6. Using the model in applications

Examples of applying modelling steps to internal model validation

Step 1 above raises the question of how to define exactly the VaR in the internal model. Mathematically, the aim is to consider a joint PDF of a vector of random variables, which often have features that are not well captured by the multi-normal (or, more generally, the multi-elliptical) distributions for which the necessary theoretical and computational tools are readily available. Simulation provides flexibility for modelling the marginal risk distributions, and there are techniques such as copulas that provide flexibility to model the dependency structure. However, these more complex methods are not without restrictions either. Large number of parameters may have to be estimated from a limited amount of data, and the uncertainty of estimates may be high. There may also be time variation in the underlying stochastic processes themselves, in the sense that key parameters such as mean, volatility and correlation may be time-dependent. Moreover, for some risks, volatility and correlation tend to increase during a time of stress, an important aspect to consider for the calculation of the SCR. For market risk modelling, there are a large number of models and alternative fundamental approaches available. For instance, model parameters might be estimated statistically from historical data or calibrated to market prices.[7] Instead of a one-year forecast, an instant shock might be applied.[8] Even for the basic definitions of VaR[9] and SCR,[10] there are several alternatives available in the literature.

In practice, it is possible to conclude that many substantial decisions are subject to expert judgement and approximations before arriving at the SCR. Therefore, the computation process and the underlying distributions and factors must be accurately specified and justified, which calls for careful documentation and validation.

It is also important to appreciate the potential differences between economic capital modelling and SCR modelling. The latter is far more restricted and regulated. However, many internal models have originated as economic capital models that were used solely for the firm's own purposes. For SCR purposes, it is especially the tail of the joint PDF that is of interest, rather than the average observations around the mean of the distribution. Therefore, the assumptions about marginal distributions and their dependence structure and tail validation should play a key role when model validation assesses the appropriateness of calibration against Solvency II criteria.

As an example of step 2, a review of the literature is necessary to be able to choose the most appropriate model for a specific use and to understand the assumptions and limitations underlying the chosen model. The availability and quality of data often limits the potential modelling options and increases the use of expert judgement. Moreover, the data chosen should be appropriate for the application, ie, modelling a one-in-200-hundred-year event means that appropriate data – when processed through the chosen method – would produce a probability distribution of the possible future events. The data period chosen and sampling frequency may have a major impact on results. Therefore, these aspects should be part of the model validation process.

Step 3 – the model building step – is fundamental. The initial data analysis gives ideas of suitable candidate models that might fit the data. Data, literature and expert knowledge may reveal stylised facts about the data-generating process that should be reflected in the model formulas. The model formulation should be accurately reflected in the model documentation, and relevant simulation algorithms should also be provided. Model fitting should be based on statistically sound methods. Point estimates should be supported by the assessment of parameter uncertainty. Parameters may be correlated, which may complicate the analysis. However, the analysis of key parameters is a necessary part of the model validation process (see next section). The (re)insurance firm is responsible for these steps, even when an external vendor model is used.

The choice of the model can be made after reviewing practical testing and/or theoretical studies of some alternative potential models, and choosing the most appropriate on the basis of some predetermined criteria. Goodness of fit and parsimony, as well as the ease of practical implementation, are likely to influence the decision. There are also theoretical tools that can provide useful input for the model choice, which are based on statistical information criteria. Vendor models may readily include several alternative models from which to choose. The process and justification behind the choice of an internal model is important, and should be adequately documented so that it can be reviewed.

Modelling loops may have been run many times during the model development phase, in some cases well before the content of Solvency II was fully known. Validation tools may differ at different stages of modelling (development, implementation and use). This aspect also relates to the design and the application of the policy for model changes (PMC). Model development history may act as a guide to the classification (minor/major) and the timing of potential model changes in the future, which is to be reported or submitted for approval.

Attention to detail at each modelling step is the best way to control model risk. Model risk is an important concept in financial valuation, risk management and capital adequacy applications. It arises as a consequence of incorrect modelling, which includes model identification or specification errors, inadequate estimation procedures and erroneous implementation. Model risk is unavoidable but must be managed to the extent possible, and validation has a key role to play in this.

As illustrated in step 1 above, expert judgement is, to some degree, inherent in each of the modelling steps. There are certain good practices and limitations of judgemental forecasts that have been generally recognised. In Hyndman and Athanasopoulos (2012), the following list of key principles is provided: set the forecasting task clearly and concisely; implement a systematic approach; document and justify; systematically evaluate forecasts; and segregate forecasters and users. Validation of expert judgement should consider both the good practices and limitations discussed in the literature and the specific requirements for expert judgement in the Solvency II framework.

Regulators are working together with the insurance industry such that all decisions on applications for Solvency II internal models are of the required quality, so that models approved for use are appropriately calibrated (see Chapter 10 for more detail). Internal models should first of all be based on good modelling and forecasting practice. Tests and standards in the regulations provide specific requirements for achieving the goal of an appropriate internal model framework.

Validation process

The model validation process should cover all tests and standards in the regulations, and also all modelling steps as described above. Model validation thus ranges from governance issues to advanced modelling topics. Therefore, realistic and detailed resource planning is essential. When deciding on the scope and depth of the annual model validation work plan, a risk-based approach and materiality considerations are likely to be necessary, as it may not be possible to cover all areas in one year. External resources may also be used to assist model validation. However, the responsibility for validating the internal model and complying with the requirements rests with the firm.

A comprehensive validation processes includes several steps that cover all phases of the model's life cycle and all parts of the internal model. A proper validation set-up must cover at least the following:

- methodology (theoretical basis and conceptual soundness – do we have the right model?);
- calibration of parameters and statistical testing;
- suitability of the model for the different business lines, portfolios, etc (is the model fit for the business?);

- implementation of the model (is the model that is now operational the same model that was validated initially?); and
- qualitative aspects of modelling (eg, model governance, use, data, IT, documentation).

Sometimes, all these steps are combined into a single process. However, in some others, they could also be split into one or more different steps. Although all the mentioned steps are important, implementation validation is sometimes forgotten or not deemed necessary. What can be seen in practice is that knowledge gained after the initial development and validation might be "efficiently" processed during the translation into computer coding. This may result in significant deviations from the model originally approved for use, and therefore also produce different outcomes. Implementation validation addresses this issue.

The model validation process is a continuous process from model building to implementation and use, and is part of the model cycle. An example of such a cycle is shown in Figure 11.2.

After the internal model has been approved for use, the regular cycles of validation together with the model governance framework, including actions taken on the basis of the model change policy, provide the tools to monitor and control the quality of the internal model and ensure that is kept up to date to respond to the changing risk and business environment. When designing the validation process, the regular frequency of the different activities will be

Figure 11.2 Validation in the model cycle

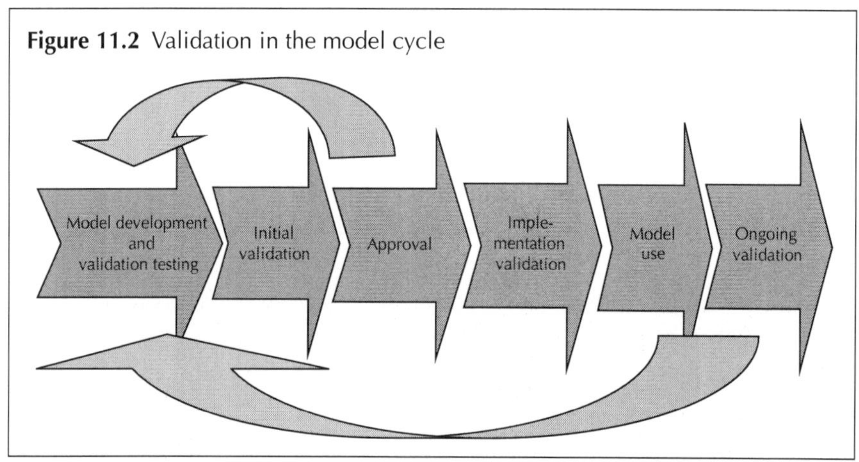

defined. On one hand, not every single part of the internal model will be subject to an annual cycle of validation. However, at least a regular pre-determined frequency is expected for all parts of the model. On the other hand, there may also be good reasons to increase the frequency of validation for some material or high-risk parts of the internal model. In addition, triggers or thresholds to bring forward the next validation round may be specified *ex ante*. Examples of such triggers are specific model changes, changes in the risk profile, outcomes of certain tests, such as profit and loss attribution, or changes to the external environment.

Therefore, in addition to the general MVP document and the more detailed annual validation plans and reports, it is important to be ready to perform *ad hoc* validation tests and analyses whenever new information provides evidence that the internal model framework needs to be improved.

There are generally a large number of competing models available from which to choose. Therefore, literature review and analysis of key modelling assumptions should be part of the regular validation cycle, and should not be restricted only to the model development phase. The own risk and solvency assessment (ORSA) also addresses this question.

MODEL VALIDATION TOOLS

Internal models can be more or less complex depending on the underlying risks and the modelling choices. The tools applied to validate the models should be selected considering the specifics of the model and the risks covered by this model. This section describes some of the tools available for the validation of internal models, providing examples on how these tools can be applied and how they can contribute to an effective validation framework.

The application of validation tools is not exclusively a highly technical exercise to be left to the responsibility of actuaries or other technically skilled people. Although the technical aspects of the validation are critically important, the broader scope of validation (eg, adequacy of the performance of the model through a sense check of its output) on which the senior management and the risk management function of the organisation should play an active role is sometime overlooked.

This section is neither intended to provide a complete and

comprehensive list of tools applicable nor a full description of the tools and techniques considered. It aims to provide the reader with some examples of good practice.

Purpose of the validation tests and pass/fail criteria

The tools used, the techniques applied and the tests performed are likely to bring little value to a robust validation if the purpose for using these tools, techniques and tests is not clearly established. The absence of purpose leads at best to the unnecessary use of scarce resources and the overcrowding of the activities around the internal model, and is likely to lead to an incomplete validation, leaving part of the expected scope of the validation untouched or part of the model untested. While the validation process is a comprehensive framework, individual tests and validation tools are limited in their scope and effect. Therefore, to design, operate and maintain an effective validation, not only the added value of some specific tests is important, but also the scope and coverage of the set of tests and tools. For instance, testing the goodness of fit of a statistical distribution might be achieved using different tools (eg, out-of-sample testing) than validating the selection of the specific distribution (eg, sensitivity testing).

Setting an explicit purpose for using the different validation tools assists achieving a comprehensive scope of the validation with an effective use of resources. An explicit purpose also helps setting objective thresholds for pass and fail criteria. Indeed, running tests without identified criteria for assessing what results will be positive (pass) and what results will be negative (fail) might result in a collection of test outputs without any useful conclusion, bringing limited value to the organisation.

Risks and risk drivers

Arguably the first step of a validation is to ensure that the model actually covers the risks that the business is exposed to. Although not all the risks might be considered with the same level of detail based on their materiality and, more generally, their relevance to the business, a clear (supported by an unambiguous definition), comprehensive and sufficiently detailed (to capture relevant characteristics) list of risks is usually seen as an appropriate start for risk modelling. Such a list can also form the starting point for the validation, and is relevant for both approaches to the validation: a "top-down" challenge that puts great emphasis on the key, more material or more relevant risks, as well as a "bottom-up" approach that builds up from the most detailed characteristics of the risks being modelled. Both approaches are complementary.

A top-down approach to validation might be more suitable for senior management and the relevant committees. It supports a holistic view of the model and is implemented with a large focus on ensuring that the model is the right one for the organisation. A bottom-up approach scrutinises the technical foundation and building blocks of the model, with a large focus on ensuring that the model does what it is intended to do. Both approaches should not be seen as mutually exclusive, with a good validation needing to cover both perspectives.

As part of the identification and, if relevant, selection of risks to be covered by the model, great attention should be given to the drivers of risk. Risk drivers, such as interest rates or inflation, can impact several risks simultaneously. During the validation, the way those common drivers are captured, their effect on the modelled risks and the correlation of the modelled risks should be addressed.

Backtesting against experience and testing against other data

Testing the performance of the model against experience is a necessary step of the validation. However, before performing actuarial and statistical tests, it is often useful to question and identify the historical experience relevant for this. The final model is used to support decisions and risk management activities oriented toward the future, so not all past experience is relevant for the validation of a forward-looking internal model. A selection of the past experience and the historical data to be used during the validation should form part of the validation process.

Different purposes shed light on different features and characteristics of the past experience and data used. For instance, some tests are designed to validate the ability of the model to capture trends in the cost of claims. For those tests, historical data might need to be adjusted: when a trend of claims inflation is identified, it is not good validation to test against average or observed values of 10 or 20 years of historical data. Other tests are designed to test the goodness of fit of some statistical distributions. Those tests are more effective when using out-of-sample data, as relying on the same data as used during the development of the model might seriously compromise the effectiveness of the validation.

When testing a model against experience, not only the experience of the firm is relevant. To the extent that it complements the firm's experience, that it is relevant to the firm and is easily available, experience and data from external sources – such as industry data or market data – can enrich the pool of experience available for the validation.

Testing against the experience is carried out at different levels of the model. For instance, the impact of specific risks drivers is tested along with modelled results for specific lines of business or insurance products. In addition, a good validation also tests the results of the model at aggregate level, as this captures particularly the interaction between different risks. The profit and loss attribution (see Chapter 11) is a useful tool, as it may help not only to validate the quantum of losses originating from a specific risk or combination of risks, but also to identify missing risk not captured or risk inappropriately captured by the internal model.

Sensitivity to key underlying assumptions

Testing the sensitivity of the model results to key assumptions is an important step to validate that the model can be used to inform future business decisions. The purpose here is to identify how the model results change in relation to changes in assumptions embedded – explicitly or implicitly – in the model. A high sensitivity of the results to small changes in the assumptions is not desirable, as ultimately it will lead to chaotic movement that will limit the reliable use of the model (an obvious example is the challenges faced by weather modellers that limit the horizon of a credible weather forecast).

When a high degree of sensitivity is identified, a good practice is to look for actions to reduce the sensitivity. When such reduction is not achievable, due to limitation in available knowledge and data for instance, additional validation of the assumption to which the model is highly sensitive is recommended.

The first step to test the sensitivity to key underlying assumptions is to identify those assumptions. This step should not be overlooked, particularly when changes in the business or market and external conditions may result in changes in the impact of some modelling assumptions. For instance, assume that a model originally includes a line of business whose impact on the overall risk profile of the firm is deemed immaterial. As the size of this line of business grows over time, assumptions made in respect of this line that were deemed immaterial in the past may become significant.

The assumptions subject to validation should not be limited to the obvious statistical parameters. For the purposes of identifying the key assumptions, the broad range of assumptions made during the design and the development of the model should be considered. In particular, the structure of the model that impacts on how risk drivers interact and are correlated, and the mathematical and statistical methods chosen, including the statistical distributions, should all be considered as assumptions underlying the model.

To identify the sensitivity of the model results to the key assumptions, it is important to consider the plausible ranges of variation of the key assumptions. Certainly, it is not a good use of validation resources to focus on changes to the underlying assumptions that are deemed impossible. However, symmetrically testing the sensitivity with respect to a too narrow range of changes could be misleading and result in an ineffective validation. In practice, different assumptions are subject to different plausible ranges and even similar parameters (for instance, loss ratio) applicable to different lines of business (eg, motor and professional liability) are subject to different ranges of variability. Readers will not be surprised if it is suggested that, as the degree of uncertainty increases, an appropriate degree of prudence in the range to be tested is recommended.

The use of expert judgements in the design and development of internal models is likely to contribute to some key assumptions. Those key expert judgements to which the results of the model are highly sensitive require a validation proportionate to their importance. The validation should cover both the process in building the expert judgement and its outcome. The process includes, for instance, the selection of the experts, the definition of the issue or questions to be assessed through expert judgement, and the communication of this judgement back to the modelling team. The validation of the outcome of the expert judgement covers, for instance, any parameter or quantitative value, as well as the uncertainty around the judgement.

Use of stress testing and scenario analysis

Stress testing and scenario analysis are powerful tools. Stress testing is the analysis of the impact of a single adverse event, while scenario analysis is the analysis of a combination of adverse events. Those tools are used typically as risk management tools to test the ability of an organisation to sustain some severe adverse conditions. This important aspect will not be discussed in this section, as the objective is limited to the use of stress testing and scenario analysis for the validation of internal models. In this context, the goal of using stress testing and scenario analysis is not about ensuring that the capital requirement is sufficient to cover stresses and scenario, but rather that the model produces reliable outputs.

It is possible to use a set of stress tests and scenario analysis of different severities to test different segments or percentiles of the PDF produced by the model. For example, the impact of the selected stress tests and scenario analysis on the financial resources of the organisation are calculated outside of the model and compared with the results computed by the model when the specifications of the stress tests and scenario analysis are used as inputs to the model. When stress testing or scenario analysis is associated with a probability of occurrence, they can also be used to validate the related percentiles of the relevant distributions produced by the model.

A key step in using stress testing and scenario analysis is the selection of the stresses and scenarios. Existing stresses and scenarios aimed at testing the financial strength of the organisation can also be used for the validation of the model. However, different stress tests and scenario analysis tailored to the business of the organisation and the specificities of the model can be built with the main purpose of validating the model.

In addition, to validate different modules or components of the model, tailored stress testing can be designed. Scenario analysis, on the other hand, is particularly useful to test the interaction (eg, correlation) or dependency of different risks or risk drivers under stressed conditions.

Stress testing and scenario analysis can be useful tools to engage with senior management and users of the model outputs for decision-making and risk management. Indeed, stress tests and scenario analysis are usually well understood. Their use as validation tools might create confidence in the outputs of the model or, even more positively, allow stakeholders such as users of the outputs of the model to provide a challenge to the model, while at the same time building their understanding of the model. For example, an experienced underwriter can easily understand the severity of the stress tests affecting their area of responsibility, and likely to be able to develop an informed view on the results of the model for those stress tests.

A symmetrical approach here is the use of reverse stress tests to validate the model. In such an exercise, starting from a given severe amount of loss, the aim is to validate that the events captured by the model as generating this amount of loss cover the set of events identified by the risk management as likely to generate the given amount of loss. In particular, reverse stress testing can be used to identify risks that are not, or are improperly, captured by the model.

Stability of the results

Validating the stability of the results of the model aims primarily at ensuring that the internal model produces the same results when run using the same inputs. This ensures, for instance, that the computational tool (eg, IT platform or software) produces stable results.

When using a stochastic model it is also important to validate the stability of the outputs that are to be used for decision-making or risk management, and particularly the SCR. Greater stability in the results can be achieved by running a higher number of iterations. To test this stability, several sets of simulations can be performed and the results of targeted percentiles from several sets are compared. Another approach is to look at the stability of the results between a targeted percentile and a collar of simulations around the targeted percentile. For instance, when testing the 99.5 percentile, a test could assess how the results change between the 99.45 percentile and the 99.55 percentile. The bigger the change around the targeted percentile, the greater the uncertainty and the less stable the result is likely to be.

Stochastic models should also be tested for their stability when using different random seeds. Different initial values can be tested to see if they have an influence on the estimation, forecasting or other numerical method applied.

Distinct from the validation of the stability is the analysis of changes. Analysing the changes in the results generated by changes in the inputs is useful to validate the performances of the model. Small changes to the inputs are expected to generate reasonably small changes to the outputs. Any divergence from expectation should trigger additional validation, as this may be an indication of a high sensitivity of the model to some underlying assumptions.

Limitations of the model

Internal models, as with all other models, are a simplification of reality and will never provide a perfect match for reality. Some limitations in the representation of the risks being modelled are identified and actively chosen during the design and implementation of the models. Some of the limitations and weaknesses are addressed and corrected over time, while others are recorded and accepted. Similarly, the validation process also identifies over time some limitations and weaknesses. No stakeholder expects a perfect model. An effective validation process is not only a static assessment of the model at a given point in time, but also provides information on the performance of the model to drive improvements to the model.

It is important that the results of the validation tests are also analysed with the objective of learning from the tests on the model limitations, and on potential improvements to the model. Following the governance process developed in previous sections, not all the weaknesses need to be addressed as soon as they have been identified. For instance, a limitation that is not material, given the risk profile might not be addressed immediately, but recorded and communicated. Such that, when the risk profile of the firm changes following the development and growth of the business, the limitations previously identified might become material and need to be addressed.

Learning from the validation

More broadly than the aspects discussed, the validation also provides opportunities to learn more about the risks that the organisation is facing. Although the chapter discussed the benefit of the validation as a model-centric exercise, the validation is also a learning activity for risk management and the management of the organisation generally.

Through analysis of the tests, but also by challenging the model, lessons can be learnt and the risk management can progress. Testing

and challenging the interaction between different risks under stress provides opportunities to improve the understanding of those interactions. Generating simulated and forecasted data by the model, and using graphical and statistical tools to illustrate and analyse them, offer valuable insights both for the validation of the model and for learning about the risks being modelled.

In order for this learning exercise to be effective and bring some value to the organisation, the validation work and the result of those activities have to be communicated internally, reported to the senior management and the governance bodies, and discussed, as appropriate. This topic will be developed in the next section.

REPORTING PROCEDURE, SCORING AND OVERALL OPINION[11]

Once model validation has been properly organised and the validation assessment performed, the outcome of the assessments has to be reported. When dealing with reporting, several aspects have to be considered: the scope of the activities should be clear (what was included and excluded); the activities and tests performed to achieve these results; the level of severity of the findings; and the overall outcome of the assessment.

These reporting issues can therefore be divided by: i) level of comfort; ii) scoring of findings; and iii) overall opinion. In the context of this chapter, reporting means a written text by which model validation accounts for the validation activities performed, including a clearly defined scope, details of the results of these activities, the findings and their scoring, and, potentially, the follow-up on findings and the validator's overall opinion. Scoring means the weights assigned to individual findings. An overall opinion is the outcome of a validation, not a mere aggregation of weighted findings.

Level of comfort

In principle, every validation assessment should lead to a validation report. A validation report is the result of several activities and may cover several topics (eg, methodology, assumptions and data quality). Therefore, it may be a challenge to determine the value (the level of comfort) of a validation report and the corresponding overall opinion. In order to achieve this, it is necessary to include in the model validation report enough information about the extent of the activities. To be useful for management, a summary with the outcome expressed in an overall opinion is needed. Other parties that have been more involved in the modelling activities will appreciate a more complete set of findings. Combined, this leads to the following minimum requirements for a validation report:

- a management summary with the overall opinion for that validation, the key messages and important limitations;
- the topics that are covered and not covered in the particular validation (ie, the scope);
- the nature (eg, interviews, desk research, tests) and extent of the activities performed during the validation;
- limitations of the validation activities performed;
- circumstances where additional activities are deemed necessary; and
- the full set of findings and their scoring as set out below.

Any deviations from the model validation policy should be stated in the validation report. If any topics were out of scope, the organisation should take measures to ensure that these items are validated at a later stage.

The above-mentioned requirements might seem obvious, but model validation is still a very young discipline and model validators tend to be concise in their reporting. Sometimes this can result in just some graphs and written text about the outcome of tests being reported, and what the conclusion is, which topics were not covered, etc, is left to the interpretation (and imagination) of the reader.

Scoring of findings

The weight assigned to a validation finding can be important. The wrong weight can lead to false priorities, or worse, to false degree of comfort from accepting an unsatisfactory model. Also, the situation can occur where the findings of the model validation are debated by the model developer and pressure exerted to soften wordings and findings. Therefore, a robust scoring methodology, facilitating consistent weighting of findings and preventing arbitrary decisions is required. Although every scoring methodology will involve a degree of subjectivity, a best effort in making it as objective as possible can be achieved by substantiating the reasons underlying the subjective assessment. Organisations should therefore develop their own scoring methodology, consistent with their risk appetite and as objective as possible. This methodology should be consistently applied in the reporting.

Overall opinion

An overall opinion presents the final result of a validation and summarises the underlying findings. Much of what has been said about the need for scoring findings also applies to overall opinions. However, the overall opinion should not be merely a mathematical exercise presenting the average score of the findings. Although in some instances the mathematical exercise might give a valid result, in other cases a single finding might be crucial on its own account, or several high-risk findings may together be decisive. A good methodology takes this into account by, for example, allowing for the possibility of substantiated "overrule".

A good methodology also sets limits on the number of qualified findings for a certain overall opinion – for example, not allowing more than one high-risk finding, or four medium-risk findings being for a "satisfactory".

To ensure the overall opinion is well understood by all stakeholders, model validation should use a limited number of possible outcomes. Usually, the overall opinion takes the form of a number (usually three or four types of overall opinions) of clearly defined outcomes, in terms of requirements to be met and of consequences. Preferably, a methodology states whether the internal model meets the Solvency II requirements and whether it is fit for use. This will support internal models that are conceptually sound and fit to the business for the identification, measurement and management of risks, and to meet the applicable Solvency II requirements. In other words, the overall opinion should make clear whether it is the right model for the particular organisation, and that it operates as it should.

Sometimes, the materiality of the particular model component being validated within the whole internal model is taken into account when determining the overall opinion for a specific validation. This is not appropriate for the following reasons.

- Model validation is responsible to assess whether the internal model is conceptually sound and fit to the business. Model validation is not responsible for setting priorities by taking the materiality of the particular component as a factor in the methodology. The first line should weight all the factors and decide which risks to accept (temporarily).

- A satisfactory rating based on the immateriality of certain model components, although there may be significant underlying findings, can give the wrong signal and false comfort.
- An immaterial component today could become material over time.

Components or modules of the internal model should therefore meet the criteria on their own. Materiality of a certain component or module only becomes relevant in the view of the total internal model. The consideration whether a component or module is material or not is a management decision and should not be included in model validation.

The views expressed in this chapter are those of the authors and not necessarily those of De Nederlandsche Bank, Bank of England or Finanssivalvonta.

1 For further details, see Article 44 of the European Parliament and the Council of the European Union (2009).

2 For further details, see Article 44 of the European Parliament and the Council of the European Union (2009).

3 Independence in mind is typically defined as the state of mind that permits the performance of an attest service without being affected by influences that compromise professional judgement, thereby allowing an individual to act with integrity, and exercise objectivity and professional scepticism.

4 Overreliance on the internal audit department to perform model validation may change the perception of what validation is meant to do within the firm. It would be undesirable if firms were to think about validation as a cost of doing business or a compliance hurdle, rather than a source of potential business benefits.

5 For further details, see Article 101 of the European Parliament and the Council of the European Union (2009).

6 For a more detailed discussion, see, for example, Hyndman and Athanasopoulos (2012), Chatfield (1995) and Law (2000); for illustrative examples, see Ronkainen (2012).

7 For further details, see Fitton and McNatt (2002).

8 For further details, see Morrison (2013).

9 For further discussion and literature references, see McNeil, Frey and Embrechts (2005).

10 See Christiansen and Niemeyer (2012).

11 By overall opinion it is meant the overall conclusion of a particular validation report, taking all underlying findings separate and in connection with each other into account. Overall opinion in this chapter does not refer to an opinion over the whole internal model.

REFERENCES

Chatfield, Chris, 1995, *Problem Solving: A Statisticians Guide (2e)* (London: Chapman & Hall).

Christiansen, M. and A. Niemeyer, 2012, "The Fundamental Definition of the Solvency Capital Requirement in Solvency II", University of ULM Preprint Series, 02.

European Parliament and the Council of the European Union, 2009, "Directive 2009/138/EC of the European Parliament and of the Council of 25 November 2009 on the Taking-up and Pursuit of the Business of Insurance and Reinsurance (Solvency II) (recast)".

Fitton, B. and J. F. McNatt, 2002, "The Four Faces of an Interest Rate Model", in Frank J. Fabozzi (Ed), *Interest Rate, Term Structure, and Valuation Modeling* (Hoboken, NJ: Wiley).

Hyndman, Rob J. and George Athanasopoulos, 2012, *Forecasting: Principles and Practice* (available at http://otexts.com/fpp/).

Law, Averill M., 2000, *Simulation Modelling and Analysis (3e)* (Boston: McGraw-Hill).

McNeil, Alexander J., R. Frey and P. Embrechts, 2005, *Quantitative Risk Management: Concepts, Techniques and Tools* (Princeton, NJ: Princeton University Press).

Morrison, Steven, 2013, "1-year VaR Economic Capital Assessment: Adjusting 1-year Risk Factor Scenarios When Using Instantaneous Stresses", Barrie & Hibbert Research Report 2013/2 (available at www.barrhibb.com).

Ronkainen, Vesa, 2012, "Stochastic Modelling of Financing Longevity Risk in Pension Insurance", PhD dissertation, University of Eastern Finland (available online as scientific monograph E44:2012 at www.bof.fi).

12

Model Validation: An Industry Perspective

Ben Carr

Aviva Plc

Insurance companies use models in pricing, underwriting, reserving, claims management, asset/liability management, marketing and distribution, as well as in risk management and economic capital modelling. The use of models will continue to grow over the coming years as a result of the increase in computing power available, the growing importance of online marketing and distribution channels, and the burgeoning use of – and interest in – predictive analytics.

Wherever models are used, it is important that they are validated to ensure that:

- the models are fit for the purposes for which they are being used;
- the controls surrounding the operation of the models are adequate;
- changes to the models are subject to appropriate governance and testing; and
- the users of the models understand their weaknesses and limitations.

If models are not validated to ensure that these requirements are met, insurance companies will be exposed to undue model risk. If this risk crystallises it could not only have an adverse impact on an insurance company's short-term financial performance but, in extreme cases, could undermine aspects of the business model and the long-term future and financial standing of the company. As a result, insurance companies have already invested heavily in the development and maintenance of models, and the controls surrounding their use, in order to ensure that they remain competitive and to minimise the model risk they are exposed to.

One of the key areas in which insurance companies have invested is the development and maintenance of economic capital models. These models are designed to help them identify, measure, manage, monitor and report the risks they are exposed to, and to support their risk management framework, processes and controls. These economic capital models tend to be more sophisticated than those used by external parties, such as insurance supervisors and rating agencies, to determine how well protected policyholders or bondholders are from unexpected losses, although they are all based on an assessment of the risk profile of the insurance company compared to how much capital it has available to absorb unexpected losses.

This chapter will next describe briefly the European regulatory requirements due to enter into force on January 1, 2016, which are resulting in insurance supervisors having an increasing focus on the model validation processes and procedures that have been put in place by insurance companies. We will then set out one way in which the regular cycle of model validation could be organised by an insurance company in practice in order to ensure the model validation process is implemented pragmatically and adds real value from an insurance company perspective, while still adhering to these requirements.

SOLVENCY II

The European Union (EU) is in the process of reforming the prudential regulatory framework for insurers.[1] These Solvency II reforms aim to:

- ❑ develop a harmonised prudential regulatory framework across the EU, as the existing patchwork of different regulatory regimes impedes the development of a single market in insurance services; and
- ❑ introduce a more risk-sensitive approach that ensures risks are properly captured and insurers are incentivised to properly identify, measure, manage, monitor and report their risks.

An essential element of the design of Solvency II is that it allows insurance companies to use their own internal economic capital models to calculate their regulatory solvency capital requirement (SCR), as long as they can demonstrate to their insurance supervisor that it meets a number of tests and standards.

ARTICLE 124 – MODEL VALIDATION STANDARDS

One of these tests and standards – Article 124 of Solvency II – explicitly relates to model validation. It requires insurance companies to "have a regular cycle of model validation which includes monitoring the performance of the internal model, reviewing the ongoing appropriateness of its specification, and testing its results against experience." This regular cycle of model validation must also "include an analysis of the stability of the internal model and in particular the testing of the sensitivity of the results of the internal model to changes in key underlying assumptions" as well as "an assessment of the accuracy, completeness and appropriateness of the data used by the internal model".

In addition, insurance companies' regular cycle of model validation must include an effective statistical process that enables them to demonstrate to their insurance supervisor that the SCR produced by the model is appropriate. Consequently, insurance supervisors are increasingly focusing on the model validation processes and procedures that have been put in place by insurance companies to minimise the model risk arising from the use of their internal models.

EIOPA GUIDELINES ON INTERNAL MODELS

In order to ensure that insurance supervisors across Europe adopt a consistent approach to approval of the use of internal models by insurance companies to calculate their SCR under Solvency II, the European Insurance and Occupational Pensions Authority (EIOPA) issued guidelines on internal models.[2] These guidelines cover all areas that need to be considered by insurance supervisors when considering an internal model application, including: use, methodology and assumptions; expert judgement; data quality; profit and loss attribution; and model governance and documentation, as well as external models and data. In particular, they include 12 guidelines specifically regarding insurance companies' regular cycle of model validation (see Table 12.1).

Table 12.1 EIOPA validation guidelines

Guideline	Title
39	The validation policy and report
40	The scope and purpose of the validation process
41	Materiality
42	Quality of the validation process
43	Governance of validation process
44	Roles in validation process
45	Independence of the validation process
46	Specificities for group internal models
47	Universe of tools
48	Stress tests and scenario analysis
49	Application of the tools
50	Validation datasets

MODEL VALIDATION FROM AN INSURANCE COMPANY PERSPECTIVE

This top-down perspective and focus on controls makes sense from the point of view of an external third party looking to review the adequacy of an insurance company's model validation processes and procedures. However, from an insurance company's perspective, in order for the model validation process to add real value, it needs to be focused on the users of the model. It should give them confidence that the outputs of the model are fit for the purposes for which they are being used, while at the same time ensuring that the users of the model are aware of its weaknesses and limitations, as well as the circumstances in which it would not be appropriate to rely on the outputs of the model.

In addition, the model validation process should be a key input into the future development plan of the model through the identification of ways in which the model could be improved to either make the outputs more appropriate for the decision-making processes they are already used for, or to enable them to be used more widely in decision-making.

One of the key challenges in ensuring that the model validation process does help to drive future developments is to ensure that, where potential improvements are identified, the costs and benefits of implementing these improvements are understood and effectively communicated to relevant stakeholders (eg, budget holders, model developers and users).

In addition, for model validation to add real value, it needs to effectively make use of other controls and processes that are already in operation in the company, not to duplicate them. Avoidance of duplication is also crucial with respect to model validation documentation and reporting. As far as possible, existing documentation and reporting should be used to make sure that the model validation process is as efficient and effective as possible. Making sure changes to models are subject to appropriate governance and testing is also important in this regard, as it enables model validation to focus on changes made to the model and reviewing whether changes in the risk profile of the insurance company, or in the external environment, could impact the model's ongoing appropriateness.

In the rest of this chapter, we will set out one way in which the regular cycle of model validation could be organised in practice in order to ensure the model validation process is implemented pragmatically and adds real value from an insurance company perspective, while also adhering to the regulatory requirements.

The process is presented in a way that should make it generally applicable to all insurance companies, although to embed it fully into an insurance company's systems and controls it would clearly require tailoring to ensure as efficient and effective implementation as possible, and align it with the nature, scale and complexity of the insurance company's business.

MODEL VALIDATION POLICY AND THE ROLE OF THE BOARD

To ensure that the model validation process is efficiently and effectively conducted across all aspects of the economic capital model and all business covered by the model, insurance companies should have an economic capital model validation policy (the policy). This policy should be approved by the board (or sub-committee) in order to confirm they are satisfied that, if the policy is implemented effectively, then:

- ❑ the model will remain fit for the purposes for which it is being used, subject to identified weaknesses and limitations;

- the controls surrounding the operation of the model will be adequate subject to identified weaknesses and limitations; and
- the board (or sub-committee) will receive timely and appropriately detailed information on the performance of the model, including the identification of new weaknesses and limitations and the status of efforts to remediate previously identified weaknesses and limitations.

SPLIT OF MODEL VALIDATION ACTIVITIES

The policy should split validation activity into two aspects. The first is the production and collation of evidence demonstrating that a clearly defined set of common requirements has been met, while the second aspect is the independent review of that evidence and reporting of the results of that review to the board (or sub-committee). The policy should clearly identify different individuals who are responsible for these two aspects of model validation to ensure clear accountability and maintain independence.

The person(s) responsible for the production and collation of evidence should be the person(s) responsible for the development and maintenance of the economic capital model, including its methodology and assumptions. The persons(s) responsible for the independent review should not currently be involved in these activities in order to maintain independence, but clearly do need to have appropriate skills and experience to be able to effectively review and challenge the evidence provided.

By way of example, the chief actuary (or equivalent) might take responsibility for the production and collation of evidence and the chief risk officer (CRO) might take responsibility for the independent review and reporting of the results to the board (or sub-committee). Alternatively, both individuals could potentially report into the CRO, depending on the insurance company's organisational structure and size, and where responsibility for development and maintenance of the economic capital model rests.

Both of the configurations described above are consistent with Articles 44 and 48 of Directive 2009/138/EC, which indicates that the development, maintenance and validation of the internal model are the responsibility of the risk management function, but that the actuarial function may contribute to these activities.

PRODUCTION AND COLLATION OF EVIDENCE

The clearly defined set of common requirements should be sufficient to demonstrate that:

- ❑ the model is fit for the purposes for which it is being used;
- ❑ the controls surrounding the operation of the model are adequate;
- ❑ changes to the model are subject to appropriate governance and testing; and
- ❑ the users of the model understand its weaknesses and limitations.

In particular, the requirements should ensure that Articles 120 to 125 of Solvency II are fulfilled if the insurance company is using its economic capital model to calculate the SCR under Solvency II.

The policy should require that the person responsible for the production and collation of evidence should also be responsible for defining the set of common requirements and providing a clear mapping from the evidence back to those requirements. The requirements should be broken down into a series of components, such as governance, systems and IT, methodology, data, assumptions and use, to make the process more manageable and facilitate more granular allocation of responsibilities.

The policy should require the adequacy of the common requirements to be considered as part of the independent review, as well as the evidence provided and designed to meet those requirements. This approach ensures that accountability for the maintenance and development of the model is not diluted and that the independence of the review is preserved.

DEFINING THE SET OF COMMON REQUIREMENTS

When defining the set of common requirements, a clear link needs to be established with existing processes and procedures. It should not simply be a set of abstract requirements, but also indicate how each requirement can be achieved in practice by the insurance company, and how existing documentation and controls can be used to meet that requirement. For example, with respect to governance requirements regarding model changes and data, the documentation and controls developed to meet policies dealing with these subjects should be used.

Similarly, with respect to internal reporting requirements, existing risk reporting to senior management and the board (or sub-committee) should be used as far as possible. In practice, it is unlikely that the contents of one single report will be able to demonstrate that all reporting requirements are met, but rather a number of different sections of different reports will need to be referenced.

The advantages of this approach are that it ensures that as far as possible the production and collation of evidence is embedded in business-as-usual activity, and utilises tried and tested documentation and controls. It also reduces the risk that new documentation is produced that duplicates existing materials, as this is not only inefficient but also creates the risk that the materials produced specifically for model validation purposes just end up sitting on a shelf not being looked at, or new controls are introduced that are redundant and therefore again simply become a box-ticking compliance exercise.

To establish and maintain a clear link from the common requirements to existing processes and procedures requires an investment of time and resources upfront to map existing processes and procedures to specific requirements. In addition, it requires really effective communication with a wide range of people in the organisation who are responsible for producing these documents and performing these controls. Those individuals need to be aware how the documents and controls they are responsible for help to demonstrate that model validation requirements are met to ensure that they consider this when making changes to these documents or controls over time.

For relatively static documents, such as documentation describing the functionality of specific aspects of the internal model, this should be relatively straightforward, but for more dynamic documents – particularly those related to regular reporting processes – the dynamic nature of these activities makes keeping track of changes and ensuring that model validation requirements are still evidenced by these documents more challenging.

QUANTITATIVE MODEL VALIDATION TOOLS

Given the above, it is important that the upfront mapping exercise is seen as an opportunity to review and challenge existing processes and procedures, and rationalise or enhance them as appropriate in order to make it as straightforward as possible to track production and collation of evidence over time. As part of this review, particular attention should be paid to the use of these specific quantitative validation tools:

- stress and scenario testing;
- sensitivity and stability testing;
- profit and loss attribution;
- backtesting;
- analysis of change; and
- benchmarking.

One would expect all these tools to be used by the person(s) responsible for the maintenance and development of the economic capital model to demonstrate that it is fit for the purposes for which it is being used. The results arising from the use of these tools, as well as how they are used, needs to be clearly documented. In particular, the documentation needs to demonstrate how the results and use of these tools provides the board (or sub-committee) and other model users with comfort that the overall results of the economic capital model are reasonable.

USE TEST

As part of the upfront mapping exercise, how the use of the outputs of the model in decision-making is documented should also be reviewed. This is to make sure that the use of the outputs of the model in decision-making is sufficiently transparent to an external third party. In this regard, it is also important that, where changes are made to the model as a result of a request from the board (or sub-committee) or other key model users, this is documented to help evidence that there is an effective feedback loop in place that results in improvements and enhancements being made to the model over time. This, in turn, works to ensure it remains fit for the purposes for which it is being used.

In addition to the above, to evidence that the key weaknesses and limitations of the model are well understood and taken into account when the use of the outputs of the model are used in decision-making, it may also be helpful periodically to interview some of key model users. These interviews could be conducted as part of the process of producing and collating evidence, or as part of independent review test plan (see "Independent Review", 1.13).

EXPERT JUDGEMENT

As well as the use of specific quantitative validation tools, an area that should be reviewed as part of the upfront mapping exercise is the application of expert judgement. The application of expert judgement is not restricted to determination of the key parametric assumptions used in the economic capital model, but are made in all parts of the modelling process. For example, expert judgement is applied when choosing the data sources to be used in the economic capital model, as well as in the process for determining how those data sources should be adjusted. Expert judgement is also applied when making key methodological choices.

To ensure that the application of expert judgement is subject to appropriate controls throughout the economic capital modelling process, an expert judgement framework should be put in place. Such a framework should cover expert judgements irrespective as to which part of the economic capital modelling process they are applied. The framework should require that expert judgements are identified and recorded, along with a brief justification for the judgement and the name of the expert. In addition, the materiality of the judgement should be assessed and documented. The materiality assessment should be split into two parts: first, an assessment of the uncertainty surrounding the judgement should be made, and second, there should be an assessment of the potential impact of the output of the economic capital model to the judgement.

The assessment of uncertainty should be based on the potential range of credible alternatives. By its nature, this assessment is necessarily qualitative. The assessment of the impact should be based on an assessment of the potential impact on the output of the economic capital model if different judgements from the range of credible alternatives were chosen. In order to make sure the process of assessing the materiality of judgements is not unduly onerous, expert judgements should be grouped together for the purposes of assessing the uncertainty surrounding the judgements and their potential impact. While in theory this assessment is quantitative in nature, it depends upon the necessarily qualitative identification of the range of credible alternatives. Furthermore, in practice the information regarding the potential impact on the output of the economic capital model may not be readily available, particularly with respect to the impact of choosing different data sources or different methodological choices.

On the basis of this materiality assessment, the key expert judgements should be identified and a more detailed rationale for these key judgements provided, including why they have been chosen over other credible alternatives. These key judgements and their rationale should be subjected to explicit review and challenge. The points raised by the reviewers and any actions taken as a result should be documented. In addition, the circumstances under which the judgement would be considered false should be recorded, along with identification of events that would trigger the judgement to be reviewed. The biographies of all experts involved in making or reviewing these key judgements should be maintained. These biographies should clearly indicate the individuals' expertise and experience with respect to the key judgements that they have been involved in making or reviewing.

INDEPENDENT REVIEW

The person responsible for the independent review should be responsible for development and maintenance of a joint assurance plan for the independent review of the economic capital model. That plan should be reviewed at least annually, and should take into account:

- weaknesses and limitations identified in previous reviews;
- changes made to the model since the last review;
- planned future developments to the model;
- changes in risk profile, business mix or systems, and controls of the insurance company since the last review; and
- changes in the external environment since the last review.

The joint assurance plan should break down the independent review activity using the same component structure as used for the production and collation of evidence to make it straightforward to identify relevant evidence. The joint assurance plan should also indicate for each component whether the review is to be performed by the risk management function, by internal or external audit, or by another third party.

Whoever is tasked with conducting the independent review of each component, the approaches adopted should be consistent so that the results of the activity can be consolidated and an overall opinion provided. In particular, the independent reviewer must have the appropriate skills and experience to review and challenge whether the evidence provided is sufficient.

The reviewer should first produce a test plan to perform the review. This plan should describe the list of tests that will be performed by the reviewer. The results of each test should be recorded and, where tests are not met, a weakness or limitation should be raised.

For the avoidance of doubt, when referring to a test plan in the context of the independent review, this is not a list of tests that should be performed by the individual(s) responsible for the development and maintenance of the economic capital model, including its methodology and assumptions. Rather, it is the description of the activities that will be performed by the independent reviewer to check whether the evidence produced by the individual(s) responsible for the development and maintenance of the economic capital model demonstrates that:

- the model is fit for the purposes for which they are being used;
- the controls surrounding the operation of the model are adequate;
- changes to the model are subject to appropriate governance and testing; and
- the users of the model understand its weaknesses and limitations.

The test plan may require some independent testing of the calculations to be performed by the independent reviewer. However, if those responsible for the development and maintenance of the economic capital model already have controls in place that require the calculations to be checked by individuals who have not been involved in that part of the model, then the test plan should not require the independent reviewer to duplicate this activity.

Instead, in this case, the test plan should focus on checking that those controls are adequate and have been effectively implemented. If, following that check, the independent reviewer identifies that some further specific tests need to be performed to complete their test plan (eg, a different goodness of fit test), then the independent reviewer may either perform those tests themselves or ask those responsible for the development and maintenance of the economic capital model to perform those tests on their behalf.

WEAKNESSES AND LIMITATIONS

Weaknesses and limitations should be subject to a qualification process before being recorded in a single weaknesses and limitations log, and a common approach to rating the criticality of issues developed. The precise details of any rating system will necessarily need to be tailored to the specific circumstances of each insurance company. In particular, the more aligned the rating system used for model validation is with rating systems used by other internal controls processes, the more straightforward it will be to place reliance on those existing processes.

Nevertheless, whatever the precise details of the rating scheme adopted, it should differentiate between the following types of weakness and limitation in order to help facilitate an overall assessment of the economic capital model's fitness for purpose.

- ❑ Category 1: Weaknesses and limitations that on their own could result in the model not being fit for the purposes for which it is being used.
- ❑ Category 2: Weaknesses and limitations that on their own would not result in the model not being fit for the purposes for which is being used, but in conjunction with other weaknesses and limitations could do so.
- ❑ Category 3: Weaknesses and limitations that would not result in the model not being fit for the purposes for which it is being used, even in conjunction with other weaknesses and limitations.

While many weaknesses and limitations will be qualitative in nature, the impact of some will be quantifiable. Quantitative limits should be established for these to differentiate quantifiable weaknesses and limitations along the lines above. Again, the precise details of any rating system will necessarily need to be tailored to the specific circumstances of each insurance company. However, as a rule of thumb, for weaknesses and limitations to be classified as a Category 1 weakness and limitation, then the quantitative impact on the outputs of the model should be sufficiently large that on their own they could influence the decision-making or judgement of the users of the outputs of the model, in particular the board (or sub-committee). Again, as a rule of thumb, the quantitative impact of a Category 3 weakness and limitation should be less than the simulation error of the economic capital models' calculation – eg, two-sided 95% confidence level of the economic capital model's 99.5% one-year value-at-risk (VaR) estimate.

The weaknesses and limitations arising from the independent review should only form a subset of all the weaknesses and limitations recorded on the log. In addition to this, the weaknesses and limitations identified by the individuals responsible for the development and maintenance of the model as part of the provision and collation of evidence and model change process should also be included in the same log to ensure that these processes are integrated.

The qualification process is important to make sure that remediation activity can be efficiently tracked and monitored over time. First, individuals responsible for the production and collation of relevant evidence should have the opportunity to comment on the weakness and limitation identified so that they are clear as to the reason for the weakness and limitation being raised, and do not believe that there is additional evidence that may address the point or there are mitigating controls in place.

Second, the individual responsible for the independent review should check to ensure that the weakness and limitation is new and does not duplicate previously identified issues, otherwise there is a risk of proliferation of weaknesses and limitations identifying the same or similar points. As far as possible, in these cases issues should be amalgamated to facilitate the tracking and monitoring of remediation activity.

In particular, where a weakness or limitation has been identified by those responsible for the development and maintenance of the model, a new weakness or limitation should not be raised by the independent reviewer. Finally, a consistency check should also be performed with respect to the criticality rating to make sure it is consistent with the rating of other issues so that there is appropriate prioritisation of remediation activity.

To permit clear accountability for the remediation of weaknesses and limitations on the log, a person responsible for the development and maintenance of the model should also be identified as responsible for remediating the issue, regardless of whether it was raised by them originally or by the independent reviewer. The adequacy of remediation activity should be reviewed as part of the next independent review, and if that finds the remediation activity to be unsatisfactory, should either result in the weakness and limitation being re-opened or a new weakness and limitation being raised.

The weakness and limitation log and associated remediation activity should be fully aligned with the future model development plan, and should help explain how the improvements to the model will make the outputs more appropriate for the decision-making processes they are already used for, or enable them to be used more widely in decision-making. The future development plan should set out a clear timetable for proposed improvements and enhancements to the economic capital model. The plan should be widely communicated and agreed by the model's users, developers, independent reviewers and budget holders, and the board (or sub-committee) to ensure that:

- the key weaknesses and limitations are being addressed within appropriate timescales;
- appropriate cost/benefit analysis has been conducted on planned improvements;
- adequate resources are in place to make the enhancements;
- adequate resources are in place to update model documentation;
- adequate resources are in place to independently review major model changes; and
- the joint assurance plan has been updated to cover major model changes.

It is not the case that one would expect all weaknesses and limitations to appear on the future development plan, either because they are not deemed to materially impact the model's fitness for purpose or because there are existing mitigating controls in place. However, in these cases it is still important that changes in the external environment, the risk profile, business mix or systems and controls of the insurance company are monitored to make sure that they do not result in this weakness and limitation becoming material or render the mitigating controls ineffective. Once an improvement has been made, this should be recorded on the model change log and the associated weaknesses and limitations should be closed.

MODEL VALIDATION REPORTING

Before the board (or sub-committee) approves a major model change and the new release of the model is put into production, the individual responsible for the independent review activity or the CRO should submit a report to the board (or sub-committee). The report should set out the independent review activity conducted with respect to the model change as part of the joint assurance plan, along with a summary of the weaknesses and limitations closed as a result of the improvements made to the model, as well as any new weaknesses and limitations identified.

At least annually, a report should also be provided to the board (or sub-committee) by the individual responsible for the independent review or the CRO summarising the independent review activity conducted over the period as part of the joint assurance plan, along with a summary of the new weaknesses and limitations identified as a result of this activity and a status update of efforts to improve previously identified weaknesses and limitations. This report should include an overall opinion as to whether the model remains fit for the purposes for which it is being used, and the controls surrounding the model are adequate taking into account any outstanding weaknesses and limitations. The report should also set out any limitations with respect to the independent review itself, in particular any issues that limited the scope of the review or its independence.

SCOPE OF MODEL VALIDATION

The scope of model validation and the overall opinion as to whether the economic capital model remains fit for the purposes for which it is being used and that the controls surrounding the model are adequate should cover the end-to-end process with respect to the calculation of economic capital metrics using the economic capital model. In addition, the scope of model validation should cover both valuation of the base balance sheet and valuation of the stressed balance sheet as, ultimately, required economic capital is simply the difference between these two numbers. Furthermore, the valuation of the base balance sheet is the figure that the required economic capital is compared to in order to determine the solvency ratio or solvency surplus. However, with respect to the determination of the valuation of the base balance sheet, one would expect that it would be possible to place considerable reliance on existing controls, and consequently the focus of incremental model validation activity should be on the valuation of the stressed balance sheet.

Given the broad scope of model validation, it is important that a proportionate approach is taken when considering the evidence requirements and the frequency of independent review. To facilitate this approach, as a minimum, core parts of the economic capital calculation process should be identified and subjected to regular independent review. Non-core elements should be subject to sample or exception-based review. Adoption of this type of proportionate approach to model validation requires a mapping exercise of the economic capital calculation process in order to break it into separate parts, with each part being assessed as to whether it is a core part of the model or not.

When arriving at an overall opinion as to whether the model remains fit for the purposes for which it is being used and the controls surrounding the model are adequate, the primary focus should be on Category 1 – weaknesses and limitations related to core parts of the model. One would generally not expect weaknesses and limitations related to non-core parts of the model to receive a Category 1 criticality rating, but if this did occur, then these should be taken into consideration as well. In addition, consideration should be given to the potential for an accumulation of Category 2 – weaknesses and limitations that may in aggregate result in the model no longer being fit for the purposes for which it is being used.

MODEL VALIDATION: GROUP-SPECIFIC ASPECTS

When looking at model validation in the context of an economic capital model being used by an insurance group, consideration needs to be given to the co-ordination of activity at group and business unit level. In these cases, it is important that individuals responsible for the production and collation of evidence and independent review are identified at business unit level, as well as at group level. Generally speaking, one would expect the person responsible for the independent review at the business unit level to be the business unit CRO. The responsible individuals at group and business unit level should work together to agree which evidence is most appropriately produced at group level and which is most appropriately produced at business unit level. Group will require evidence from business units to demonstrate that the model is fit for purpose at group level. Similarly, business units will require evidence from group to demonstrate that the model is fit for purpose at business unit level. Group and business units should use the same set of common requirements and components in order to facilitate the co-ordination and split of responsibilities with respect to the production and collation of evidence.

The joint assurance plan for the independent view should cover group and business units, and the individuals responsible for the independent review at both group and business unit level should be involved in the development and maintenance of the joint assurance plan, while weaknesses and limitations should be recorded and managed in a single group-wide log. Generally speaking, one would expect that the split of responsibilities between group and business units with respect to the independent review of evidence would follow the same split of responsibilities agreed with respect to the production and collation of evidence, although this does not always have to be the case. In the context of an insurance group, consideration also needs to be given to reporting to local boards as well as to the group board (or sub-committee), particularly as a change of a business unit-specific aspect of the model may represent a major model change locally, but not at group level. In these cases, a report would need to be prepared for the local board, but not necessarily the group board (or sub-committee).

CONCLUSION

The option for insurers to use their own internal economic capital model for regulatory purposes under Solvency II poses a number of challenges for both insurance companies and insurance supervisors. Insurance supervisors need to have a good understanding of the risk profile of the insurer, as well as the design and implementation of the internal model, in order to gain comfort that it is fit for the purposes for which it is being used, in particular the calculation of the SCR. They also need to understand how the model is being used in decision-making, and that the governance arrangements put in place to oversee changes to the model are adequate.

Firms not only need to assure themselves that their economic capital calculation is robust, but convince insurance supervisors as well. Depending on the approach adopted by insurance supervisors, this may require firms to put additional controls in place above and beyond what is required for internal purposes to make sure that their processes and controls are not only effective, but are sufficiently transparent to be seen to be effective by an external third party who is not as close to, or as familiar with, its business or internal systems and controls.

In this chapter, we have set out one way in which the regular cycle of model validation could be organised in practice to ensure the model validation process is implemented pragmatically, and adds real value from an insurance company perspective. This should be achieved while also adhering to the regulatory requirements and ensuring that the processes and controls are sufficiently transparent to be seen to be effective by an external third party who is not necessarily as close to, or as familiar with, its business or its internal systems and controls.

The level of control, or "validation", required by the insurance supervisor to be put in place to ensure that the economic capital model is robust and fit for the purposes for which it is being used above and beyond what the firm itself would deem necessary will be an important factor in determining whether the benefits outweigh the costs for insurers in applying to use their internal models to calculate the SCR rather than using the standard formula. It is likely that this will become even more important going forward as, in the wake of the financial crisis, regulators have increasingly looked to use crude indicators to second guess the output of companies' economic capital models and thus undermine the true benefit of model approval, which is to be subject to regulatory capital requirements that are truly risk sensitive and aligned to the way the insurance company identifies, measures, manages, monitors and reports its risks internally.

The views expressed in this chapter are the author's own and do not necessarily represent those of any third party with whom he is or may be associated.

1 European Parliament and the Council of the European Union, 2009, "Directive 2009/138/EC of the European Parliament and of the Council of 25 November 2009 on the Taking-up and Pursuit of the Business of Insurance and Reinsurance (Solvency II) (recast)", p.1.

2 EIOPA, 2013, "EIOPA Final Report on Public Consultations No. 13/011 on the Proposal for Guidelines on the Pre-application for Internal Models", September.

13

Solvency II Internal Model Documentation Requirements

Dermot Marron

Allied Risk Management

Successive industry surveys have shown documentation to be among the greatest challenges for undertakings in relation to internal models. In 2009, a Staple Inn Actuarial Society survey (Austin *et al*, 2009) indicated that 75% of firms had not even commenced the process of updating their model documentation to meet the Solvency II standard. One comment in the survey was "Our current documentation standards are high, but the approvals process appears to require much more than this". In the EIOPA guidelines (EIOPA, 2013b), the feedback was summarised as "Some stakeholders consider documentation requirements as burdensome". Stronger views have been expressed in the intervening period, but the consistent message has been that the documentation standards are high and the requirements many. This is perhaps a fair reflection of the requirements; however, when one considers the reason for the documentation requirements in the first place, the requirements make more sense and, rather than being burdensome, they should be seen as good risk management.

This chapter will draws on the author's experience of constructing and reviewing models as a chief actuary, regulator and consultant, and also from his time on the EIOPA Internal Models Committee; the chapter is also informed by industry surveys (including Austin *et al*, 2009; Anzsar *et al*, 2012) and commentary.

The chapter opens with an outline of the legal requirements and regulatory guidelines. We then consider how these apply in practice, in terms of the scope and form of internal model documentation. The next section presents some practical comments regarding the review of documentation from a supervisory perspective. There follows some comments and observations on the documentation of outputs, methodologies, expert judgement and validation, before some examples of poor documentation are provided. After looking at the contents of applications, the chapter closes with a discussion of external models and modelling platforms.

LEVEL 1 REQUIREMENTS

The requirements of the Solvency II Level 1 directive (see European Parliament and the Council of the European Union, 2009) are as follows.

> "Article 125
> Documentation standards
>
> Insurance and reinsurance undertakings shall document the design and operational details of their internal model.
>
> The documentation shall demonstrate compliance with Articles 120 to 124.
>
> The documentation shall provide a detailed outline of the theory, assumptions, and mathematical and empirical bases underlying the internal model.
>
> The documentation shall indicate any circumstances under which the internal model does not work effectively.
>
> Insurance and reinsurance undertakings shall document all major changes to their internal model, as set out in Article 115."

The above all appear sensible and practical; the main aims of the documentation are to:

- ❑ eliminate key person risk;
- ❑ facilitate supervisory review and approval of the model;
- ❑ facilitate senior management understanding; and
- ❑ based on the lessons learned from the global financial crisis, recognise the weaknesses of the model.

However, in practice, the above are demanding requirements, particularly the requirement that the documentation demonstrates compliance with Articles 120–124. These are:

- ❏ Article 120 – use test;
- ❏ Article 121 – statistical quality standards;
- ❏ Article 122 – calibration standards;
- ❏ Article 123 – profit and loss attribution; and
- ❏ Article 124 – validation standards.

Also, Article 126 should be noted.

> "Article 126
> External models and data
>
> The use of a model or data obtained from a third party shall not be considered to be a justification for exemption from any of the requirements for the internal model set out in Articles 120 to 125."

That is, the requirements of Article 125 apply equally to external models (such as catastrophe models and economic scenario generators). This has proved one of the most debated aspects of internal model documentation, with the catastrophe modelling providers being particularly protective of their proprietary rights and cautious about opening up their model to both users and supervisors through the documentation. This is treated in more detail below.

LEVEL 2 REQUIREMENTS

The Level 2 requirements (European Commission, 2014) expand on the above, providing more detail on the standard required. It is not proposed to repeat them here. However, particularly challenging and somewhat contentious, are the following general provisions:

> "(1) The Documentation of the internal model . . . shall be sufficient to ensure that any independent knowledgeable third party would be able to understand the design and operational details of the internal model and form a sound judgement as to its compliance with Articles 11, 112, 120 to 124 and 126 of the Level 1 Directive"
>
> . . .
>
> (3). . . . Outputs of the internal model shall in principle be reproducible using the internal model documentation and all of the inputs into the internal model."

These are at the same time both imprecise and challenging. The aims are clear – to facilitate supervisory review and approval of the model, and to mitigate key person risk. It is a subjective judgement as to whether the requirements above are met. However, in my experience as a supervisor, I have replicated parts of models and achieved similar results purely on the basis of the documentation. In this case, the second requirement above was clearly met. Likewise, if a supervisory authority is in a position to approve a model for use to calculate the solvency capital requirement (SCR), by definition the supervisory authority has satisfied itself that the model complies with the relevant articles of the Level 1 directive, and it is very difficult to see how this could be achieved without the model meeting the first requirement above.

The Level 2 requirements also detail the minimum content of the documentation, including:

- ❏ detail of the internal model governance (policy for model change, policies, controls, roles and responsibilities);
- ❏ description of IT platforms used and contingency plans;
- ❏ all relevant assumptions and how they were derived;
- ❏ data directory and data policy;
- ❏ risk mitigation effects allowed for in the model, how their impact is quantified and how secondary risks arising from use of risk mitigation techniques are captured in the model; and
- ❏ use of external models and data, and the reasons for their use.

The remaining draft Level 2 provisions specify considerable detail to be given in documenting circumstances under which the internal model does not work effectively, including:

- ❏ risks not covered;
- ❏ limitations in risk modelling;
- ❏ nature, degree and sources of uncertainty connected with the results of the internal model;
- ❏ sensitivity of the results to key assumptions;
- ❏ risks arising out of using external models and data;
- ❏ IT limitations; and
- ❏ limitations of internal model governance;

In addition, the documentation of minor and major changes to the model should include:

- ❏ a description of each change;
- ❏ the impact of each major change on the design and operation of the model; and

- for changes that have a material impact on the model results, a quantitative and qualitative comparison of the outputs of the model before and after implementation of the change.

Reviewing the above, it is understandable how undertakings view the documentation requirements as burdensome. However, when taken in the context of the aims of the documentation outlined above, each requirement on its own makes sense. Indeed, a good suite of documentation for a genuinely used internal model will already meet most or all of these requirements before cross-referencing against the Solvency II requirements.

SCOPE OF INTERNAL MODEL DOCUMENTATION

It is the scope of internal model documentation that has perhaps given rise to most concern regarding the extent of the internal model documentation requirements. It might be useful here to consider two elements of documentation: (i) that of the internal model (explanatory guides, user manuals, description of the methodological bases, etc); and (ii) the wider documentation is that necessary to support the application and meet the requirements of Article 125 of the Level 1 directive. Quite clearly, the documentation referred to in Article 125 refers to the latter of these two elements, while the everyday interpretation of the documentation of an internal model refers more typically to the former. This confusion in terms of the scope of the documentation is the source of much of the dissatisfaction that has been expressed regarding the volume and extent of the documentation required.

For example, Article 125 of the Level 1 directive requires that documentation demonstrate compliance with Articles 120–124. Taking the first of these (Article 120 – Use Test), the evidence an undertaking would provide to demonstrate compliance with the use test would be very wide-ranging: such as board minutes, risk committee minutes, use of the catastrophe model output in designing the reinsurance programme and model outputs in product design and pricing. Each of these could be strong evidence points in demonstrating compliance with the use test, while none would be regarded as part of the internal model documentation in the former (everyday) interpretation above.

Making the above distinction assists in any discussion of

documentation as it relates to the internal model. Distinction should be drawn between the internal model documentation and the application pack; in general usage, the internal model documentation relates to the former, whereas the documentation required for a complete application would include both the former and the latter.

FORM OF THE DOCUMENTATION

Documentation in paper form can be unwieldy and perhaps not the best format for updating and reviewing. The draft Level 2 implementing measures require an inventory of all the documents that form part of the documentation. Hyperlinks from this inventory to the actual documents then comprise the application pack (whether this is acceptable will depend on the approach of the relevant supervisory authority, as some may require the full application in paper form). However, "nested" hyperlinks (ie, hyperlinks within hyperlinked documents) are not user-friendly and create difficulties with version control, and should be avoided or kept to a minimum. Undertakings should be wary of inundating supervisors with documentation, and supervisory authorities do not wish to see vans full of documentation pulling up outside their premises!

Version control is very important, especially where there are different levels of documentation that cross-reference each other. There are various documentation management software packages available commercially to support the cataloguing of documentation and version control that are used to varying degrees across organisations; in the author's experience, the use of such packages has been less widespread than would have been expected.

DOCUMENTATION REVIEW

Experience from Basel II model reviews and early experiences of Solvency II internal model pre-application have shown that documentation reviews are not the best use of (sometimes limited) supervisory resources. Documentation is very time-consuming, both for firms to produce and supervisors to review. Even allowing for the work that can be done during the pre-application period, supervisory authorities have limited time in which to approve a model for use to calculate an undertaking's SCR.

Desktop reviews are no substitute for on-site reviews and for seeing a model in action (although one rarely sees a model in action as such, and indeed there is no physical model to see). A balance has to be found between desktop review and on-site inspections; how the model is operated in practice can, and sometimes does, differ from how it is described in the documentation.

An example of this from the author's experience is a model where the documentation mentioned, in passing, the facility to exclude outliers, as if this was only to be done in exceptional circumstances. The on-site review showed that this was actually done much more frequently than anticipated in the documentation; technically, the input files (where the outliers are excluded) form part of the documentation and, as such, this could have been picked-up in a desktop review, but an on-site review – which included interviews with the model users – was a much quicker and more effective way of discovering this information.

Supervisors are human too, and hundreds of hours of documentation review are unlikely to appeal to, or attract, the best supervisory talent! Achieving the correct balance between desktop and on-site review is important not only in achieving optimal supervisory outcomes, but also in maintaining interest and motivation among supervisory staff.

Therefore, a practical approach to documentation review is recommended. Many models are built in a modular way, with each risk being modelled in its own module and the results aggregated in a so-called calculation kernel. Even for models that do not take this approach (eg, risk driver models), the impact of each risk driver on the SCR can be reviewed in turn rather than in a holistic review of the whole model. Rather than reviewing the whole documentation of a model at once, when reviewing each module if the documentation meets the required standard then it will facilitate the approval of that module. A review for completeness to verify that the required documentation is all in place is then required to approve the model's conformance with Article 125 of the Level 1 directive.

DOCUMENTATION OF OUTPUTS

The outputs of an internal model form part of its documentation. For large, complex models the size of the output file can be very large. Cost of data storage is not the issue it once was, so there are not the same storage constraints on saving model outputs as might have been the case. However, there is limited value in saving the output of every model run. It is recommended that the full output for the run used to calculate the SCR is retained. This allows audit by supervisory authorities, internal audit and model validation teams, and also can allow the model to be re-run to assess the impact of changes in parameterisation, calibration or modelling approach. (Random numbers and/or random number seeds can be retained to replicate model runs at future dates, thus precisely measuring the impact of changes by eliminating random variation.)

There can also be considerable value in analysing simulation outputs. Most models use algorithms to allocate capital by risk type based on the simulation output (eg, averaging the contribution by risk type of, say, the 100 simulations either side of the "key" percentile, such as the 99.5th percentile). However, by analysing individual scenarios undertakings can learn more about their business and/or their model. For example, if an individual scenario shows a risk "spike" that is not evident from the capital allocation, then perhaps more attention should be paid to that particular risk, perhaps the model is not accurately reflecting that particular risk or it could be that the capital allocation methodology needs to be reviewed.

The above describes a model where the capital calculation is the result of a single simulation model. In practice, many models are more "modular" in form, with output from several modules being used as input for a capital calculation model. In such cases, the output of runs of the individual modules used for the SCR calculation should also be retained in full, for the reasons outlined above. In many cases, the input for the capital calculation model dispenses with much of the detail of the output of the individual module – this is not necessarily a fault in the model and is often necessary to keep models manageable and run times down; also, particularly for large and/or multinational organisations, the capital management function may not be particularly interested in the risk profile of individual territories or business lines. Where this is the case, the undertaking should take care that key features of the risks that are captured by the risk module that should be captured in the capital allocation model are not being lost in the transfer process.

Presentation of the model results is a key component of model documentation. While model developers and risk managers tend to be of a numeric bent, the model results are being presented to senior management and boards whose members typically will have a range of personality types. Therefore, while a model developer will review a table of results in the same way as they might read a page of prose, to some personality types this presentation style is not as intuitive. This means a range of presentation methods should be employed – graphic, tabular, high-level and detailed – as different personality types will be more or less receptive to different presentation styles. Much has been written on the communication of risk; however, although it is not proposed to repeat this here (the interested reader is referred to Gardner, 2008, and Evans, 2012), some basic principles hold:

- return periods are more intuitive than percentiles;
- cumulative distribution function graphs are typically less easily interpreted than probability distribution function graphs; and
- how risk is framed can have a considerable influence over management decisions (see Thaler and Sunstein, 2009).

The design of the risk dashboard as a presentation tool for the model output is critical to the success of the model, and in particular meeting the use test. A model can succeed or fail depending on how its results are presented to senior management and boards. The importance of the presentation of results cannot be understated; the aim should not be to meet the minimum requirements of the use test, but rather to maximise the effectiveness of the model (and its limitations) throughout the organisation based on effective communication.

DOCUMENTATION OF METHODOLOGIES

A particular challenge for undertakings and supervisors alike is the documentation of the methodologies used in a model. In many cases, this is an area where documentation is weakest: the description of the methodology fails to explain why the methodology adequately models the undertaking's business. This explanation is vital to facilitating supervisory authority with the model and evidencing conformance with the statistical quality standards.

In some instances, the documentation of methodologies can be very technical, with few individuals possessing the expertise to completely understand the methodology used; this in itself creates challenges in terms of the use test, and there is a balancing act between having a model that is sufficiently sophisticated to adequately model a risk and one that can be sufficiently understood by management and staff. A "plain English" description of the methodology is desirable, and this should be the aim at the outset. If such a description is not achievable, this does not mean that the model methodology should be dispensed with, but the undertaking should then be aware of the challenges of achieving senior management understanding – not solely for meeting this requirement of the use test but, more importantly, because senior management understanding is an important aspect of the model being an effective tool in running the business.

Many models – for example, econometric models and aggregation methodologies – are derived from academic research. While reference to academic papers are often useful and sometimes necessary in documenting methodologies, alone they would not be considered sufficient documentation of a methodology. A number of reasons for this are detailed below.

- One purpose of the documentation (see above) is to facilitate supervisory authority approval of the model. Where statistical quality standards are concerned, an academic paper alone will probably not be sufficient in this regard. Additionally, the staff of a supervisory authority may not have the expertise in all areas, which can be quite specialised and esoteric, and further explanation will often be necessary.
- Likewise, it is unlikely that an academic paper will be sufficient to enable senior management understanding to meet the use test (or to use the model effectively in the business).
- It is important that the subject matter experts themselves can evidence sufficient understanding of the model and the methodology used.
- Good documentation of methodologies is vital in mitigating "key person" risk in respect of a model. Therefore, reliance on third-party documentation is insufficient in this regard.

When developing a model, a number of approaches are often considered before one approach is developed. It can be very useful to retain the work done using other approaches/methodologies to facilitate supervisory understanding of the methodology, and show why it is the most appropriate approach for an undertaking. It can be very frustrating for a supervisor reviewing a model to see a methodology "drop out of the ether" with no history of its development or background information as to why the undertaking considers it the most appropriate for their business. Moreover, much of the value of a model is from the enhanced understanding of the risks faced by an undertaking learned through the modelling process as much as the actual output of the model. However, models that have been developed over a period of time, particularly those with a long history of use in an undertaking, will not always have this background information.

DOCUMENTATION OF EXPERT JUDGEMENT

Expert judgement is used throughout an internal model – indeed, the model itself is an exercise in expert judgement. Clearly then, there is a requirement for undertakings to properly document the use of expert judgement wherever it is used in the model.

The requirements regarding documentation of expert judgement are outlined in EIOPA's guidelines (EIOPA, 2013b), and it was expected that more detailed requirements would be included when the Level 3 guidance was published. Reviews of documentation of expert judgement have shown some poor practices, with little justification documented. In particular, where outliers are considered unrepresentative this is not a reason in itself for exclusion, and justification should be given for any exclusions bearing in mind that the model is intended to capture the full range of possible outcomes.

Where a methodology produces a number of results, the final choice and reasons for making that choice should be clearly documented. For example, if non-life reserve risk is measured using both paid and incurred triangles, and a number of different methods (eg, bootstrap and Mack), there will be a range of results from which the ultimate choice of parameter will be made.

Where expert judgement is used, the thought process and justification for the application of expert judgement should be documented, as well as an assessment of the impact (this is in the Level 3 guidance). Although onerous, when one considers these requirements in the context of the aims of the documentation, they make sense.

In cases such as those described above, it can be useful for those engaged in the parameterisation exercise to have a template for the exercise where expert judgement can be documented and recorded. This is an important part of internal model governance, and also provides a useful audit trail for supervisors or validation teams.

DOCUMENTATION OF VALIDATION AND VALIDATION OF DOCUMENTATION

The documentation of the validation should include the validation policy, techniques and results and is covered elsewhere; however, this in itself forms part of the internal model documentation. Given the requirement for validation of the internal model to be independent from development of the model, this area of the documentation may be beyond the control of those responsible for the remainder of the internal model documentation (depending on the internal model governance structure in the undertaking). Therefore, it is important that those responsible for the validation are aware of the documentation standards required.

Furthermore, the validation process and report are important tools to facilitate model approval. Given the required scope of the validation exercise, it can achieve a better level of insight and review at a greater level of granularity than the supervisory model review. Moreover, the validation process is required to include validation of the documentation. Validation of the documentation is a useful exercise, as it provides comfort to an undertaking that its documentation fulfils the requirements and, more importantly, is fit for purpose.

The documentation of the validation of external models raises the same issues in respect of documentation of external models generally (see below). Therefore, where an undertaking relies (to a greater or lesser extent) on the validation performed by the external model provider, this must be adequately documented with the documentation freely available to the undertaking and supervisory authorities.

THE GOOD, THE BAD AND THE UGLY

Good documentation has many levels: comprehensive, well-written summaries for board members; similar, but more detailed summaries for senior executives and users of the model output (eg, underwriters); detailed technical documentation for model users and subject matter experts (this should fulfil the requirement of providing a detailed outline of the theory, assumptions and mathematical and empirical bases underlying the internal model); and a user manual for each part of the model.

The documentation should be written with the intended reader in mind. For example, a detailed technical description of the mathematical bases underlying a model is unlikely to be appropriate for an independent non-executive director; the challenge in this case is to impart the necessary information effectively. On the other hand, a detailed step-by-step user manual is necessary to document the operation of the model for model users.

Below are some examples of poor documentation from the author's experience.

- The supervisor version: Documentation that appeared written with the supervisor in mind. In this particular case, throughout the documentation it explained how the model took a prudent approach (in particular, wherever there was uncertainty or a weakness in the model). At times, the documentation barely described the methodology but rather explained that the number was going to be higher than the "true" number. While from a supervisory perspective this may be desirable, the tone was such that any user would lose faith in the model. Thus, the use test would not be met in this case.
- The cookbook: The documentation presented was a detailed step-by-step user manual. While this is an important requirement (to mitigate key person risk), it is not in itself sufficient documentation of the internal model to allow approval by the supervisory authority. There was no description of the methodology and no justification as to why it adequately captured the risk.
- Lost in translation: This is not an example from supervisory experience. A company had invested several hundred thousand euros in employing consultants to build a model. The delivery day arrived and the consultants presented the model to the underwriters. The model measured volatility around the average loss ratio for each treaty – the "expected loss ratio" in the words of the consultants (which to them was simply the mean of the distribution of loss ratio outcomes for each treaty). However, a room of underwriters (for many of whom English was not their first language) quite reasonably interpreted "expected loss ratio" as the loss ratio they expect for a treaty when they write it (or the

"loss ratio expected" as one might put it); this number would be several points lower than the "expected loss ratio" for what was a class of business with a particularly skewed loss ratio distribution. As the discussion proceeded on two different tracks, the model was effectively rejected by the underwriters, and it took several months before they would use the model (mainly by tying remuneration to the model return on capital). In this case, the developers and the underwriters were literally speaking the same words in different languages.

CONTENTS OF APPLICATION

The draft Level 2 implementing measures include a list of the minimum documentation to be provided to supervisory authorities as part of the internal model application. The Level 3 guidance includes the additional requirement to involve a summary of limitations of the internal model and circumstances when it does not work effectively.

The contents of application is not an exhaustive list, and in practice more documentation will be required to facilitate approval of the model – eg, evidence of meeting the use test. Also, the level of granularity in the documentation to be submitted is not clear. For example "all relevant assumptions referred to in paragraph 2 of Article TSIM9 (information and assumptions concerning the methods used for the calculation of probability distribution forecast)" – could encompass every single piece of data and every single application of expert judgement in the each module of the model. It is not practical to include this level of detail in the application pack, and undertakings and supervisors should adopt a practical approach in terms of what is expected.

EXTERNAL MODELS

As noted above, the area of documentation of external models has been somewhat controversial, particularly with regard to catastrophe models. Generally, economic scenario generator providers have being more forthcoming with their model documentation – in many cases, the models are openly available (often published by academics), with the providers delivering information on the implementation of the chosen model and advice and assistance about its calibration.

There has been considerable dialogue between supervisors and the catastrophe modelling companies in this regard. Some supervisory authorities took the step of signing non-disclosure agreements with the catastrophe modelling providers to facilitate pre-application, while others have been reluctant to do so.

Generally speaking, external models are a good thing: it is better to have a team of experts employed by a modelling company dedicated to developing a specialist model rather than a smaller team of generalists employed by an insurance company developing the model. (Although, in general terms, there are other issues to be considered, not least of which are – from an industry point of view – the "herding" of insurance companies, where all use the same model,[1] and – from an individual company's point of view – leverage of the external model providers where their systems are integrated into the insurance company's system so that the insurance company is increasingly dependent on them.) However, Article 126 of the Level 1 directive requires that external models meet all the requirements of Articles 120–125.

In respect of documentation, this means that the external model's documentation meets the Level 2 requirement that "Outputs of the internal model shall in principle be reproducible using the internal model documentation and all of the inputs into the internal model." It is understandable that modelling companies are concerned by this requirement – it effectively requires the documentation provided to be such that users of their model could replicate the model based on the documentation. They also view it as a Catch 22 situation: if they fail to provide the documentation their product cannot be used for Solvency II internal models, but if they do provide the documentation then clients could build the model for themselves. However, this author's view is that the concerns are overstated. The client bases of the major catastrophe modelling companies are such that the development costs are spread among a large number of users. For an individual company to replicate the model based on the documentation would still be a huge undertaking and a considerable cost – probably a cost of many times the annual licensing fee for the software. Also, the company would still have to undertake and document the validation of the model. In addition, there is a level of comfort to be taken from the acceptance testing that the commercially available catastrophe models have undergone. Therefore, unless the cost of the model is not justified by the development cost incurred (in which case, market forces will eventually take effect) from an economic and practical point of view, insurance companies are (in my opinion) unlikely to seek to build their own catastrophe models.

Providers of economic scenario generators have generally taken a different approach. In many cases, the underlying mathematical models are freely available: the provider builds the software platform and provides expert input into the calibration of the model. The fact that insurance companies are still paying for the services of providers of economic scenario generators bears out the point that companies would be unlikely to build their own catastrophe model, even with full documentation available.

Modelling platforms

It is not clear where one draws the line regarding model documentation with regard to modelling platforms. While it is unlikely that one will see a full model in Microsoft Excel, much parameterisation work is done in the format. In this author's view, it is neither practical nor sensible to require the documentation for MS Excel to be included in the internal model documentation. However, many models use commercial software platforms such as Remetrica, Igloo or Risk Explorer, and others use bespoke software platforms. Again, in this author's view, it is neither practical nor sensible to require the code for such platforms to constitute part of the model documentation. Typically, such software platforms have been extensively tested both in production and in user acceptance testing; however, many firms do use bespoke platforms. What is the required level of use and user acceptance testing before a newly developed platform without a track record can be considered robust, and so its documentation is not required? Should full code and documentation therefore be required for all modelling platforms? Is supervisor review of documentation of an extensively used and tested modelling platform a good use of limited supervisory resources? Do supervisory authorities possess the expertise to detect flaws or weaknesses in a modelling platform through a review of its documentation?

The question of computer code is also of interest. It could easily be argued that this forms part of the documentation of the model. However, to require millions of lines of code to be held by undertakings and open to review by supervisors is neither feasible nor practical. Instead, one should look to the purposes of the documentation outlined above – facilitating model approval, evidencing conformation with model standards, mitigating key person risk, enabling senior management understanding, etc.

Clearly, reviewing thousands of lines of code will do little to enhance senior management understanding, and it is hard to claim that reviewing the code is an effective way of enhancing a supervisor's understanding of the model and unlikely that supervisory authorities have the expertise or desire to do this in any case. Errors in the code are more likely to be discovered in user acceptance testing, validation and supervisory review of the model. For widely used, well-supported platforms or external models, the user base is sufficiently large that if the provider ceases to exist, there is value in continuing to support the user base, and the intellectual property inherent in the code will have a value that can be sold on, ensuring continuity of service. For bespoke software, one solution is to hold the code in escrow such that the user gains access to the code and documentation should the software provider fail or cease to exist.

CONCLUSION

Adequate and complete documentation of internal models is a challenge: "burdensome" is perhaps a fair characterisation. However, when one considers the requirements in the context of the aims of the documentation, it is seen as necessary and the reasons for the requirements become clearer. Thus, documentation is produced with a purpose in mind rather than undertakings producing or supervisors requiring documentation for documentation's sake. The documentation that is required is that which should be in place in any case to achieve these aims.

In the author's opinion, a practical approach should be taken by both undertakings and the supervisory authorities in the production and review of documentation. To use an old teacher's maxim, the aim should be quality, not quantity. Documentation reviews can be time-consuming drudgery, and supervisory authorities should find a balance to optimise the use of resources and keep supervisors' work interesting.

The documentation of outputs and, in particular, presentation of result are very important areas. Clear, well-presented results can enhance the value of a model, whereas poorly presented results can severely reduce the value of even the best models.

Documentation of methodologies should aim to be clear and readable; it is not always possible to give a "plain English" description, but the aim should be to have the description as accessible as possible. A record of the development of the methodology, and any alternative approaches considered, is useful for supervisory authorities, validation teams and future model development.

The application of expert judgement should be documented at every step; application should not simply be recorded, but justified. The materiality threshold may be lower than undertakings are contemplating. A template for recording application of expert judgement can be useful in this regard.

Documentation of validation is in the scope of the documentation of the internal model. As this is typically undertaken by a different team, care is required to ensure that the same standards apply to the documentation of the validation.

External models raise particular challenges. However, the position taken by providers is hard to understand – ultimately, if undertakings cannot use external models in their Solvency II models, then the market for their products will cease to exist.

1 This concern is perhaps overstated for catastrophe models, given the binary nature of the risk. If a model is "wrong", the loss might never be realised in any case. On the other hand, if a large event happens, its occurrence is not a reflection of the accuracy or otherwise of the model – it would take many, many years to establish whether a model was wrong (that it had underestimated the probability of an event) or that quite simply a low-probability, large event had occurred.

REFERENCES

Anzsar, J., J. Armstrong, R. Austin, A. Bartliff, C. Bird, M. Cairns, C. Chan, G. Chavez-Lopez, A. Dee, G. Dunkerley, S. Latchman, D. Menezes, S. Robertson-Dunn, M. Strudwick and B. Truong, 2012, "Practical Issues in the Solvency II Internal Model Approval Process (IMAP) for General Insurance Actuaries" GIRO Working Party (available at http://www.actuaries.org.uk/sites/all/files/documents/pdf/practical-issues-solvency-ii.pdf).

Austin, R., M. Ashcroft, C. Dick, S. Morgan, A. Macpherson, A. McBride, I. Marshall, and R. Taylor, 2009, "Practical Implementation Challenges of Internal Models under Solvency II" (available at http://www.sias.org.uk/data/meetings/October2009/attachment/at_download).

EIOPA, 2013a, "Final Report on Public Consultations No. 13/011 on the Proposal for Guidelines on the Pre-application for Internal Models" (available at https://eiopa.europa.eu/fileadmin/tx_dam/files/consultations/consultationpapers/CP11–13/EIOPA-13–416_Final_Report_on_CP11.pdf).

EIOPA, 2013b, "Guidelines on Pre-Application of Internal Models" (available at https://eiopa.europa.eu/publications/eiopa-guidelines/index.html).

European Commission, 2014, "Level 2 Delegated Acts".

European Parliament and the Council of the European Union, 2009, "Directive 2009/138/EC of the European Parliament and of the Council of 25 November 2009 on the Taking-up and Pursuit of the Business of Insurance and Reinsurance (Solvency II) (recast)" (available at http://eur-lex.europa.eu/LexUriServ/LexUriServ.do?uri=OJ:L:2009:335:0001:0155:en:PDF).

Evans, Dylan, 2012, *Risk Intelligence: How to Live with Uncertainty* (New York, NY: Free Press).

Gardner, Dan, 2008, *Risk: The Science and Politics of Fear* (Toronto: McClelland & Stewart).

Thaler, R. H. and C. R. Sunstein, 2009, *Nudge: Improving Decisions about Health, Wealth, and Happiness* (New York, NY: Penguin Books).

14

How to Review External Models and Data Embedded in the Modelling Framework

Åsa Larson

Finansinspektionen

As we know, an internal model is a tool that a firm uses for risk management, risk control and risk measurement.[1] After the supervisor's review and approval, this model can also be used for the calculation of the solvency capital requirement (SCR). What is an "external" model, then? It should be noted that there is no clear definition of the term "external model" in the Solvency II directive (see European Parliament and the Council of the European Union, 2009). Only the wording in Article 126 suggests that a model or data obtained from a third party could be used as an internal model or form part of an internal model.

This chapter will deal with external models and data in this sense – ie, models and/or data from an external third party – and compare the use of external models to the use of purely internal models, ie, models and data developed and run in-house by a firm. The Solvency II requirements that a firm and a model need to meet to qualify as the tool for the calculation of the SCR, including the fulfilment of these requirements when external models are used, will be discussed throughout the chapter. Emphasis is put on the planning of the order of the review steps in the process.

The next section sets the scene by explaining a number of important concepts and terms, before the distinction between external data and internal data is drawn, followed by a comparison of principles for model's reviews using external and internal data, respectively. The chapter then covers the requirements on external models, as well as challenges for reviewers, finishing with a description of, and discussion about, the interface between internal and external models.

EXTERNAL MODELS' TAXONOMY AND PROFESSIONAL SECRECY

Taxonomy: Models, components, platforms

A practical way of looking at the concept of external models is to start with its characteristics: external models stem from a source outside the insurance firm. In most cases, they are developed and provided by external vendors, in some others they are available in the public domain. There are for example some open source tools that can be found that are free to use.

One possible definition of an external model is that external models and data cover systems and databases used in the internal model, including risk, data or business logic and/or strategy, which are used as input into the internal model and are provided by sources outside the firm.

A platform can be defined as a computer system or programming language/tool underlying the firm's internal model. Common examples are software such as Excel, SAS, Igloo and MatLab. Note that platforms should not automatically be seen as external models, although some have built-in functions that could count as external models.

However, external models – simulation models, random number generators, black-box formulas and complex calculations provided by an external source – do generate operational risks and need to be scrutinised and questioned. The biggest and most common external models are economic scenario generators (ESGs) and natural catastrophe models (nat cat). An ESG is a simulation model where a variety of economic scenarios are generated as a basis for the evaluation of all financial situations the portfolio can end up in. Market risks are in focus (the asset side of the balance sheet) and possibly financial contracts with options and/or guarantees (liability side). ESG models are developed externally and most commonly run internally – ie, the firm has a licence to use the model, which is owned and developed by the vendor.

Catastrophe (cat) models, on the other hand, are risk models handling geographies and perils that cover lines of business and their characteristics – eg, characteristics such as products sold to individuals or to enterprises. The type of coverage is also important. For instance, does the model handle only property damage or are other types of cover such as business interruption included? For cat models, outsourcing agreements are often set up where two or more models are licensed and run by a third party, usually a reinsurance broker. There is an agreement between the firm and the broker – ie, the broker has licences to use the models, which are owned and developed by the vendors.

Professional secrecy

When a firm buys an external model, the technical documentation can often be incomplete or unclear. Consequently, technical documentation on an external model provided by the firm to the supervisor during a review process can often also be insufficient. The reason for this is easily understood. For a vendor, the model represents an important intellectual property and, although it is not easy to quickly reproduce an advanced model, the vendor is typically reluctant to share all technical details with the firm to the extent required by the Solvency II framework. The technical documentation is something the reviewer needs to form an opinion on. The obvious starting point for this opinion would be: no information given, then sorry, no approval should be expected either!

In most cases, however, a good general understanding of the model and the technical details are fairly easy to get for a reviewer, since vendors are often willing to send documents and communicate with supervisory authorities directly as long as secrecy can be reasonably kept.

In some countries, such as Sweden, the need to maintain professional secrecy could be an issue in the sense that all documents registered in an authority's registry, at least in theory, are accessible to the public. The principle of public access is a long-established democratic principle enshrined in a fundamental law, the Freedom of the Press Act and the Public Access to Information and Secrecy Act (2009:400). All decisions by Swedish authorities are subject to the principle of public access. This means that, as far as possible and subject to the secrecy provisions, all decisions and underlying documents are public.

Documentation from firms and vendors should always be handled with great care and consideration, but even more so with the secrecy in mind. Information received as a part of an application, and therefore subject to confidentiality, must be kept private throughout the process.

When reviewing internal models, there is always a conflict between theoretical requirements and the practical applications of checking that the requirements are fulfilled. For external models and data, this conflict between theory and practice is clearly one of the key points to bear in mind. Due to the fact that ownership and the right to use and run the models are split between two or more parties, aspects of professional secrecy such as the right to share knowledge and documentation need to be considered.

DATA USED

When reviewing data to be used in the internal model, no matter whether it is internal or external data, there are three overarching requirements that need to be fulfilled: it should be accurate, appropriate and complete. Those three words are unfortunately neither very exact nor clear, but offer a wide range of interpretation. General guidance on the data quality is given in Article 35 of the Solvency II directive, where it is said that information (data) to be provided for supervisory purposes must:

- reflect the nature, scale and complexity of the business of the firm concerned and, in particular, the risks inherent in that business;
- be accessible, complete in all material respects, comparable and consistent over time; and
- be relevant, reliable and comprehensible.

Further description of the data quality requirements is likely to be given in the overall set of Solvency II regulations. For instance, drafts of implementing measures explain that, in order for the data to be considered accurate, appropriate and complete, it should also be free from material errors, be recorded and used in a consistent manner, as well as being sufficiently granular.

However, it is also obvious that emphasis should be on the quality of the data, and that it is not really a box-ticking exercise for a reviewer to check the compliance.[2] In the following section, the practical meaning of the data requirements will be discussed.

Principles for reviewing data in the internal model

Here, some practical areas for reviewing data will be described.

IT infrastructure

The IT architecture constitutes a reference point for the reviewer to understand the data usage and environment. The IT infrastructure describes the data sources and IT tools for the firm's business lines and products, including client services and outsourced services. The application portfolio summarises the applications, spreadsheets and/or external services used in terms of platforms, programming languages and other tools. The structure should also be described in an application map showing how applications and services are related, and how information is exchanged between applications and services. A key element in this description is the complexity of the IT structure. A presentation from the firm supported by an application map showing the complexity and structure of the IT system, a process map explaining the way the systems are used, including controls defined and references to supporting documentation, is a good way of getting to understand the overall IT environment.

Data directory

The purpose of the data directory is to ensure the high standards of control that the Solvency II rules aim to achieve. Each data item should be described with its corresponding source, important characteristics and intended usage. Traceability back to the source should be obtained. A data item can also be the result of a calculation from data at a more granular level. It should then be evident in the data directory what items the calculated data item consists of, either by way of a formula or as a narrative.

The data directory is a reference point for all data owners, contributors and users of the internal model. As such, it can take the form of a database, a spreadsheet, an intranet catalogue or any other solution that makes it informative, accessible and manageable. External data is thus also included.

The next review area to consider is data governance, including the governance documentation and data policy. There are quite a few requirements set for the data policy, which is here split into documentation and risk and process control.

Data policy documentation

The firm's principles and internal requirements for data quality should be addressed in the data policy. The review of data quality is closely connected to the appropriateness of data used when the SCR is calculated. This is why data quality is an integral part of a review of an internal model.

Examples of high-level requirements for the data policy contents are the internal rules and principles for data management and data quality assessment. For a more detailed description of the practical use of the principles, there should be process documentation and instructions providing the firm's granular definitions of data quality and how data quality assessment is performed.

Other items to be included in the data policy are the principles for the frequency of updates of different types of data and the possible reasons for updates. This should include both *ad hoc* updates and updates due to developments of the internal model. Ownership and responsibilities should be clearly expressed in the policy.

A description of the documentation structure with reference to the different requirements is imperative for the reviewer to be able to conduct a time-effective desktop review of the documentation prior to an on-site inspection. The purpose of the on-site inspection is to assess to what extent the data policy is implemented in the firm's processes.

Data policy risk control and process control

Strengths and weaknesses in business processes point out the necessary controls, and the instructions for risk assessments and data quality judgement. The methodology used for describing and controlling data risks needs to be considered. There are at least two different sources for data risks: operational risks in the processes and more specific data control risks in the data flows. These controls can be addressed in the validation of the SCR calculation process, as well as in the assessment of how the data policy is monitored. A risk and control matrix per risk area may be a good way of achieving a holistic view of data risks and consequences/losses to be aware of in case of incidents.

In summary, a practical walk-through of the data used in the internal model can be described as asking a firm to:

- ❑ show the relevant elements;
- ❑ show the principles used;
- ❑ show the documentation; and
- ❑ walk through an example.

Principles for reviewing external data in the internal model

The overarching review principles – appropriate, accurate and complete – apply in the same way to external data sources as to internal sources. The important message that should be underlined is that, where external data and/or external models are used, full responsibility is kept by the firm. Irrespective of what outsourcing agreements are in place, the understanding of the data and the models needs to be in-house. In addition, it needs to be shown by the firm in the internal model's governance and documentation that the data and models are understood.

A practical way of verifying external data compliance with the requirements is to structure the review, addressing the issues below.

- ❑ Appropriate: How does a firm come to the conclusion that data from an external source are suitable for its business and its purposes, and that the risk profile is properly reflected? Perhaps only limited parts of the external database – instead of the whole purchased register – should be used to ensure a better fit with the business?
- ❑ Accurate and complete: How can a firm ensure that data stemming from an external part is accurate and complete? To lean on data from an external part does not lift the responsibility for the data quality from the firm's shoulders. The firm is still in charge!
- ❑ Verify data: Do no forget that data and the use of data should be part of the model validation. Traceability and controls focusing on data quality (accurate, appropriate and complete) are therefore central when dealing with data, regardless of the data source used, but especially when reviewing the use of external data. The reason is that if the review of the external data validation (eg, in assumption setting) shows non-compliance with the

requirements, it is possible that more non-compliance could be found around the use of external models and data.

- Classify and register data: All data, whether internal and external, used when running the internal model should be classified and registered in the data directory. Source, characteristics and usage are three key words when classifying data.

Proportionality/materiality should also be considered in model reviews. For instance, providing protection for cat risk does not represent the main business for many firms. This portfolio is most often reinsured with the effect that the cat risk does not represent the biggest chunk of the SCR, but mainly the risk of losing the retention. This is why materiality considerations can apply when deciding from where to start the cat risk model review. In this case, for example, the reviewer may consider not starting the cat model review by scrutinising all details set out in the statistical tests and standards, but by making sure there is an overall understanding of the external model and its characteristics.

Let us look at a simplified (and fictitious) example of a cat model process. Three different cat models are run based on a commercial database for the relevant geographical area. It would have been possible to use the firm's own portfolio of insurance contracts as the basis for the exposure, but the firm has chosen not to. The main reason for choosing an external database instead of the firm's own portfolio is an insufficient level of detail in the records of the insurance contracts. For example, head office's address and postcode may be the only geographical details recorded in the portfolio, not the postcodes where the underlying risks are located. On running the external models, the worst-case effect might be that exposures for certain geographical areas risk being neglected had the company's own portfolio been the basis for the evaluation of the risks. Therefore, the firm has chosen to use a commercial comprehensive nat cat loss database as the evaluation basis. To estimate the exposures and the probability distribution forecast for the firm to be used in the SCR calculation, the results are scaled down using a local index, such as market share in a geographic area or similar indexes.

First, it should be noted that this process has clear potential for future improvement! For instance, the requirement to use only data that is appropriate, accurate and complete is obviously not fulfilled. While a commercial database might be considered complete (all risk exposures are surely covered), the fulfilment of the appropriateness and/or accurateness criteria is more questionable (ie, how is the database's reflection of the business' risk profile verified?). Also, the process step where results from a calculation on the risk sensitivity of an external database are scaled down and used as an estimate of the firm's risk profile clearly could benefit from some clarification – and not only the scaling itself (eg, what criteria are used when choosing the indexes? Are the same indexes used every time or chosen as to reduce the SCR results?), but also some governance around the scaling could be expected by a reviewer (what is the planned frequency of updates of assumptions made? Is a four-eyes-principle or a challenge process required?).

Second, for the supervisor reviewing the model and the process, it is important to consider the materiality of this process of evaluating cat risks and the solvency capital needed to cover this risk. Should this issue, if found in a review, be treated in a proportionate way (ie, more or less accepted) or should it be considered as a showstopper? There is no straightforward answer to this question, as it really depends on the materiality and complexity of the cat business. What is the importance of catastrophe risk with respect to the firm's business, to its risk profile and to its SCR? As highlighted earlier, for many firms cat risk is reinsured and the net risk corresponds only to a small part of the SCR. If this is the case – eg, cat risks are less material in a firms' risk profile – a process of running the external model as described in the example is far more acceptable than with respect to a firm where cat risk is the main risk driver.

REQUIREMENTS AND CHALLENGES FROM A SUPERVISORY PERSPECTIVE

Article 126 of the Solvency II directive[3] states that "The use of a model or data obtained from a third party shall not be considered to be a justification for exemption from any of the requirements set out in Articles 120 to 125." To express this more clearly, all requirements for internal models and internal data also apply for external models and external data.

Articles 120–125 cover these high-level areas:

- ❏ Article 120 – use test;
- ❏ Article 121 – statistical quality standards;
- ❏ Article 122 – calibration;
- ❏ Article 123 – profit and loss distribution;
- ❏ Article 124 – validation; and
- ❏ Article 125 – documentation.

In addition to the specific model's requirements, there are also other areas for the firm to comply with. One worth mentioning here is the requirement to have appropriate internal model governance in place.

Use test, governance

The purpose of the use test is to show that the internal model is used as a tool when managing the firm's business. The use test covers a handful of different requirements. The firm should demonstrate not only that the internal model is used in the management of the business, but that the model is appropriate/fit to the business, that senior managers understand the model and its limitations, that the model is integrated with the risk management and how frequently the model results are updated. Regarding the appropriateness/fit-to-purpose requirement[4] for the business performed, the firm needs to initiate a dialogue with the vendor (and, in the case of a cat model, with the broker).

The basic reason for checking the use test requirement at an early stage of the review is as follows. If a firm does not trust its model sufficiently to use it, how can the supervisory authority have any comfort in it? Or, put the other way round: if a firm does trust the internal model and really uses it not only for the solvency capital calculations, but also as input in decision-making; if the model is frequently run and members of the board and the senior management are able to understand and describe the model, and the model and its output are commonly referred to in board minutes; this should clearly evidence that the firm relies on the internal model. The supervisor can thus have more overall comfort in the model and the way it is used.

The same can be said about the model governance requirements. A firm demonstrating a sound and effective governance around the internal (and external) model can be trusted to have put a lot of thinking and effort into setting up model processes for developing, validating and running the model. This is especially important in cases where models or parts of the models are developed and/or handled outside the firm.

Statistical quality standards, calibration, profit and loss distribution

Among the technical requirements under the statistical quality standards heading are areas such as probability distribution forecast, risk ranking, diversification effects, coverage of all material risks, risk mitigation techniques, future management actions and expert judgement. An internal model should be calibrated in such a way that policyholders are provided with protection on the same level as the level of protection used in the standard formula. For modelling reasons, if the firm has chosen a different time period than one year and/or a different risk measure than value-at-risk (VaR), the choices and the calibration should be justified. Also, the profit and loss distribution for the time period modelled should be presented.

Generally, these requirements should be evidenced not only for internal models, but also for any parts of the model that are modelled externally. Anyhow, due to reasons connected to the fact that the model is developed externally, it is a good idea to leave the question of detailed compliance with these requirements to a later stage of the review, and not check the technical details until compliance with the use test, the governance requirements and also some of the validation requirements is assured.

Validation

In Article 124 of the Solvency II directive,[5] requirements on the validation process for an internal model and requirements on the validation tools used can be found. A walk-through of the validation process for external models and data should easily show whether the firm has enough knowledge and control of the external model itself and the usage of the model.

The validation can hardly be considered independent if carried out by the vendor. However, information and documentation, including technical validation documentation from the vendor, may be used as a basis for the firm's validation of the external model, although the validation needs to be performed by the firm itself.

Some extra review focus could be placed on the validation of the process of running the external models, including governance and ownership of this process. The review should include checking the assumption setting process when choosing data to be used as input in the external model and validation of the treatment of the outputs from the external model, often used as input, either in the SCR calculation or in other parts of the internal model.

Documentation

This article (Article 125 in the Solvency II directive) sets the standard for the documentation and provides the requirements on the form and the contents (eg, control procedures, methodology) of the documentation. Documentation of the output of the model is mentioned here, and the article also requires documentation on changes to the model and circumstances under which the model does not work effectively, as well as documentation on software and modelling platforms.

When using an external model, it is evident that the documentation should include details that easily identify the model – for instance, vendor, name of product purchased and version or date of purchase. A dialogue between the firm and vendor is needed in order to get the right granularity of this type of documentation. A high standard is set, particularly around certain areas of documentation. When reviewing documentation, however, it is important not to let requirements on form and process lead the review at the expense of substance and structure.

A good piece of practical advice for conducting a review of an external model would be to start with the requirements on the use test and governance. The board and management's high-level knowledge of the model's coverage regarding risk categories, business units, lines of business and products affected, including their materiality in the overall risk universe of the firm, is easily checked. The focus areas for the use test are clearly expressed in Article 120 of the Solvency II directive and can easily be checked. Model management, including ownership, steering, development and usage of the external model, is likely to show if the firm has created a sound process or not. Not until after having concluded that the process is sound based on documentation provided on governance of the external model and the interaction between external and internal model parts and taking the characteristics of external models into consideration, is it time to proceed with the other review areas.

As experienced by reviewers, the request alone to see the governance and documentation of the process of running the models seems in some cases to have strengthened the governance of the external model and the process of running it. Policies and routine descriptions have to be compliant with the overall requirements as set out in the firm's corporate manual, as have the principles for scenarios and input data to use. Last, but not least, the expectations on the deliveries from the external model and management of the output after running the external models have to be compliant with requirements set out in the firm's documentation governing the rest of the internal model.

The documentation of the internal model should be sufficient to ensure that any independent knowledgeable third party would be able to understand its design and operational details, and form a sound judgement as to its compliance with Articles 101, 112, 120–124 and 126 of Directive 2009/138/EC.[6] The documentation should be appropriately structured, detailed and complete, and also be kept up to date. Outputs of the internal model should in principle be reproducible using the internal model documentation and all of the inputs into the internal model.

This also means that the level of detail of the documentation has to be so granular that an independent skilled person should be able to reproduce the internal model's results by using the documentation, the data inputs and the tools alone. It is quite a burdensome task for a firm to produce this well-structured and understandable documentation, even for parts modelled by in-house experts!

With the complexity of these two requirements – understanding the model, being able to reproduce the outputs – it is hard to choose what to focus on when going through and ticking off the compliance. Again, the use test principle is a good way into this process – the documentation should not be intended primarily to satisfy the supervisor, but to satisfy the needs of the business to have a tool for understanding the model that is independent of the person using it. A tool that is used is one that the firm relies on, meaning that supervisors should be able to consider it of a higher standard than a mere description with no further purpose than being read by a reviewer.

INTERFACE BETWEEN INTERNAL AND EXTERNAL MODELS

When developing an internal model, there are a number of logical steps to take:

- specification of the problem to be solved and other objectives;
- preparations, such as literature review, market good practice, expert knowledge, earlier experience and data collection; and
- model building comprising a couple of building blocks, such as initial data analysis, model design, model estimation and model validation.

When buying and later using an external model, possibly as a part of the internal model, the same steps need to be taken. Objectives must be set, preparatory activities considered and initial data analysis, as well as a high-level model design, needs to be planned before going out in the market and buying a model. Otherwise, there is a big risk that the external model will not be able to produce the expected results.

A key area when reviewing external models has turned out to be the interface between the external model and the rest of the internal model. The statistical quality standards require that assumptions used in the internal model should be appropriate and verified. It needs to be checked whether that can be said of the treatment of the external models results when serving as inputs in other parts of the internal model.

Some examples of useful questions concerning the links between external and internal models are:

- how is the external model integrated within the internal model?
- what are the outputs of the external model and what are they used for? (as inputs in the internal model? what controls are made?)
- are any adjustments done to the external model results – for instance, scaling or exclusions of some scenarios or results?
- are there tools such as process maps, governance documentation and outsourcing agreements to identify all model changes of the external model?
- are requirements for the inputs consistent to inputs in the rest of the internal model?

- will it be possible to use in-house data or is the use of external data compulsory and, if so, why?
- what is the scope of the external model compared to the overall scope of the internal model?
- is there consistency between expectations on external and internal parts of the internal model? and
- is the external model run with the same frequency as the internal model?

The simplified example below shows where it is obvious that data (ie, output from the external model) is neither complete nor accurate, and that this model needs refinement. In other situations, it is not always that obvious. A big number of ESG simulations are run. When drawing the conclusions of the round of simulations only those simulations where the markets are going down are included, apparently because "when markets are going up everything is fine!" This choice of only parts of the ESG output turns out to have a very positive effect on the SCR. The model then describes a significantly lower SCR figure than if all output were used.

CONCLUSION

To conclude, it is important to remember that firms are dealing with models, although trying to mirror their risk reality. This is even truer when reviewing external models where the models are developed and owned somewhere else. A simpler but understandable external model may be a better tool for risk management and risk control than a sophisticated external black box model! This needs to be taken into account in the review.

Note that there are no other or easier requirements to fulfil for a firm using external models than for a firm using purely internal models. All the requirements on the use test, statistical standards, validation, documentation, etc, apply to an external model user just as to an internal model user. Also, the overarching data review principles – appropriate, accurate and complete – apply in the same way for both external and internal data sources.

Therefore, where external data and/or external models are being used, the key message of this chapter is that full responsibility has to be retained by the firm. Regardless of what outsourcing agreements are in place, the understanding of the models and the data need to be in-house. In addition, the fact that data and models are understood by the firm need to be shown in the internal model's governance and documentation.

The views expressed in this chapter are those of the author and not necessarily those of Finansinspektionen

1 For further details about the definition of an internal model, see Chapter 1.
2 For further details about data and data reviews, see Chapter 8.
3 For further details, see European Parliament and the Council of the European Union (2009).
4 For further details, see Chapter 6.
5 For further details, see European Parliament and the Council of the European Union (2009).
6 For further details, see European Parliament and the Council of the European Union (2009).

REFERENCES

European Parliament and the Council of the European Union, 2009, "Directive 2009/138/EC of the European Parliament and of the Council of 25 November 2009 on the Taking-up and Pursuit of the Business of Insurance and Reinsurance (Solvency II) (recast)".

15

The Limitations of Internal Models and the Supervisory Review Process

Paolo Cadoni and Christian Kerfriden

Prudential Regulation Authority, Bank of England

To paraphrase the famous quote by George Box, "all models are wrong, but some are useful",[1] no matter how much effort and skilled resources are dedicated to the development and implementation of an internal model, it will still suffer from limitations. This is not necessarily an issue: a model may have limitations, but it can still be appropriate. However, ignoring model limitations will certainly lead to problems in the future. Acknowledging promptly the internal model limitations within the firm allows the organisation to monitor their materiality and plan for corrective actions to improve, where possible, the functioning of the model.

This chapter will introduce a paradigm to deal with internal model's limitations, providing an illustration of the typical sources of limitations and stresses, and the importance of a good governance framework to identify potential issues and manage them appropriately. It will examine the ongoing monitoring of internal model performance and, more specifically, highlight that while both firms and supervisory authorities are working to prepare and review the internal model's pre-application and application submissions, they also need to look ahead and start developing a toolkit that enables them to monitor the internal models' performance over time. The chapter will then explain those instances, post-approval, where the use of the internal models stops satisfying the Solvency II requirements. Finally, an illustration of the internal models supervisory reporting and public disclosures requirements will be presented.

INTERNAL MODEL'S LIMITATIONS

When thinking about model limitations, a useful paradigm by Philipp Keller[2] builds on the Ronald Rumsfeld quote: "There are known knowns. These are things that we know. There are known unknowns. That is to say, there are things that we know we don't know. But there are also unknown unknowns. There are things that we don't know we don't know."[3]

More specifically, when developing, implementing, reviewing and monitoring internal model activities, there are:

- things that are known;
- things that are known to be unknown;
- things that are believed to be known but are actually unknown;
- things that are preferred to stay unknown; and
- things that are unknown to be unknown.

In practice, the main focus of risk management and supervision is often on things that are known (eg, high frequency–low impact risk) and things that are known to be unknown (eg, the impact of the next financial market bubble, natural catastrophes, terrorist events). However, in many cases, companies become financially distressed by things that are believed to be known but are actually unknown (eg, operational risk), things that are preferred to stay unknown (eg, risks that would force a change to the firm's business model) and things that are unknown to be unknown. The most dangerous are actually the third and fourth situations above: the things that are believed to be known but are actually unknown lead to overconfidence, and a belief that risks are monitored and under control. Things that are preferred to stay unknown are the sign of an inappropriate firm's risk culture, and are likely to emerge in the future by causing most financial problems.

It is certainly true that, in some cases, senior management prefers that certain risks stay unknown and not quantified. Not knowing about risks can allow management to continue with its existing business strategy (eg, investing heavily in sub-prime risks or selling long-duration performance guarantees). The chief risk officer (CRO) and actuaries might be pressured or replaced with more malleable ones who conform to the wishes of management. The board and supervisors have to be able to identify instances when management behaves in such a way and take remedial action. CROs and actuaries need to also have the courage to confront senior management with unpalatable truths.

Sources of model limitations

All models are a simplified representation of a more complex reality, and almost by definition have material limitations. The primary sources of model limitations are data, choice of methodology, uncertainty around assumptions and simplifications.

As data are used to inform the choice of methodologies around which the calculation engine (kernel) of the internal model is built, data limitations will result in limitations to the internal model. Moreover, even when available data cover a broad range of possible future events, they will not be able to cover an exhaustive set of future events. For instance, when claims data are used to select a statistical distribution for possible loss amounts, the data limitations impact on the appropriateness of the statistical distribution chosen. This distribution might give too much weight to the claims included in the estimation sample and underestimate the probability of different type of claims not included in the estimation sample. In particular, this may affect the estimation of low frequency and high severity events. An out-of-sample test – ie, testing the performance of the model with observation data not used during the development of the model – is a useful way to assess the sensitivity of the outputs of the model to the data used in its development.

The choices of methodology, sometimes driven by the available data, will also result in limitations to the internal model. A multitude of choices are made when building the internal model, which are often based on data and complemented by expert judgement. For example, the choice of a statistical distribution to characterise a population of claims assumes that the claims modelled using a single distribution exhibit some homogeneity. In reality, using a single distribution for the possible amount of claims is a simplification, as claims are driven by a set of heterogeneous risks and exposures.

The uncertainty around the internal models' assumptions also results in limitations to that model – eg, the uncertainty related to the estimation of parameters for the statistical distributions chosen. The accumulation and interaction of different sources of uncertainty in the calculation of the probability distribution forecast all contribute to the limitation of the internal model developed. An inappropriate use of expert judgement also creates uncertainty that impacts the result of the internal model.

Acknowledging the internal model limitations and internal model governance

As stated, acknowledging the internal model limitations within the firm allows the organisation to monitor them and plan for future developments/improvements to the model. For example, if limitations in the modelling of operational risk are identified and acknowledged (eg, due to limitations in available data), a plan to address data shortcomings can be defined. This may involve enlarging the existing data sample through the pooling of industry data.

The prompt identification and acknowledgement of model limitations help to mitigate the risk of overreliance on the internal model. It provides firms with an opportunity to communicate with both decision-makers and other stakeholders during the key stages/decision points of model development. For example, due to limitations in data available, the firm can propose to model two different portfolios jointly. Later on, once the model is implemented and embedded in the firm's risk management framework, acknowledging the model limitations allows it to communicate more effectively with internal stakeholders and decision-makers. For example, modelling market risk based on its risk drivers (interest rates, equity, etc) is likely to include assumptions on the dependency of the risk drivers. In this case, scarcity of data observed under stressed conditions will create limitations to the model. Recognising the limitations and testing different alternative assumptions – as part of the validation of the internal model in particular – provides decisions-makers with valuable information and reinforces their understanding and confidence in the internal model framework.

A firm's culture that encourages the communication of limitations increases the credibility of the internal modelling framework. This is not only because some limitations are expected, but also because limitations and strengths are identified. An appropriate internal modelling governance framework helps to deal with the limitations of the model. An important component of the internal model's governance framework is the regular cycle of validation prescribed by Article 124 of the Solvency II directive. In fact, the validation should identify the substantial limitations of the internal model and test the model sensitivity to the key assumptions. These validation activities contribute significantly to monitoring the internal model limitations.

A second relevant component of the internal model's governance framework is the policy for changing the model (Article 115 of the Solvency II directive). This policy should set out the framework to identify the need for changes to the internal model (eg, internal triggers and thresholds), the internal process to classify them into major and minor, and identifying when supervisory approval is required.

MONITORING THE ONGOING APPROPRIATENESS OF INTERNAL MODELS' PERFORMANCE

The internal model's activities of the firm and supervisory authority do not come to an end with the approval of the internal model to calculate the solvency capital requirement (SCR). Following good practice, firms are expected to monitor and update their internal models regularly to continue reflecting appropriately their risk profile. Moreover, according to Solvency II, firms are responsible for ensuring the ongoing appropriateness of the internal model by ensuring that it meets the tests and standards, and reflects the insurance firms' risk profile on an ongoing basis. To this end, insurance firms should also ensure that the SCR is calibrated and corresponds to the value-at-risk (VaR) of the basic own funds of the insurance firms subject to a confidence level of 99.5% over a one-year period. This means that supervisory authorities need to be assured that insurance firms have in place systems to ensure that the internal model operates properly on a continuous basis. Supervisory authorities also need to be confident that the controls put in place are adequate and effective at all times.

However, anecdotal evidence from banking suggests that both firms and supervisors put significant effort into the internal model approval process without adequate attention given to monitoring the ongoing appropriateness. This leads to risks that solvency standards deteriorate over time. It is important that these aspects are not overlooked in Solvency II and steps are taken within the firms to ensure that the internal model continues to produce appropriate and meaningful results over time. Similarly, insurance supervisors should not underestimate the resources and efforts required to monitor the use of internal models, and the benefit of putting in place systems and tools to monitor the performances of the internal models post-approval.

Responsibility of the firm's administrative, management or supervisory body

According to Article 116 of the Solvency II directive, the firm's administrative, management or supervisory body (AMSB) is responsible for "putting in place systems which ensure that the internal model operates properly on a continuous basis". This includes, among other things, ensuring an appropriate and regular cycle of internal model validation (Article 124 of the Solvency II directive), and that changes to the internal model are made in accordance with the approved model change policy (Article 115 of the Solvency II directive). The responsibility of the AMSB also includes the internal processes to ensure that the model is appropriate to play an important role in the risk management system and decision-making.

For instance, the frequency of calculation – including the use of appropriate simplified calculations – should be determined consistently with the relevant risk management and decision-making cycles in order for the model to play an important role in risk management and other decision processes. In a group context, this requires consideration when the internal model is used to calculate not only the group SCR, but also the solo SCRs, for some of the group entities.

The internal systems implemented by the firm might include a set of tools and indicators to monitor the performance of the internal model, and might be used to trigger additional validation or other actions – eg, assessing the need for a change to the model. For example, the analysis of changes of the internal model results (eg, changes in risks or lines of business contribution to the SCR) can be used to trigger additional validation. Moreover, the use of management information, external and independent from the model, can assist the identification of needs for changes to the model (eg, report of loss or combined ratio).

The supervisory review process

Article 36 of the Solvency II directive provides for a supervisory review process (SRP) to review firm's compliance with the laws, regulations and administrative provisions adopted in application of the Solvency II directive. The SRP covers also the calculation of the capital requirement. This includes the use of internal models for the calculation of the SCR.

Each supervisory authority is required to develop and implement its own SRP, but the level of harmonisation introduced by Solvency II aims to support convergence in the supervisory practices of insurance firms across the European Economic Area (EEA). Both the Solvency II directive and the actions of the European Insurance and Occupational Pensions Authority (EIOPA) aim to promote a risk-based, proportionate and forward-looking supervisory approach supported by adequate supervisory judgements.

As explained, after an internal model has been approved for use, the supervisory authority needs to attain comfort that it remains appropriate and, in particular, that the SCR calculated using the internal model is not underestimated. To this end, and to support a consistent SRP, it is important that supervisors put in place processes to monitor the use of approved internal models, and develop a suite of tools to ensure that, after approval, internal models and the SCR calculation remain appropriate on an ongoing basis.

It is often the case that supervisory authorities will not be able to dedicate the same amount of resources to the review of internal models as during the pre-application and application phase. To increase efficiency and effectiveness in their use of limited resources, supervisory authorities leverage tools and processes developed during the preparation and (pre-) application phase of the internal models to support the assessment of the model application (eg, analysis tools of internal models inputs and outputs). At the same time, it is also important that the supervisory authorities look ahead to how it would be possible to use the knowledge and information acquired during the model review to develop some other more specific systems and tools to enable them to monitor the ongoing appropriateness of firms' internal model post-approval.

Some of these tools and processes aim to analyse the performance of the internal models in a consistent way across different models and firms. For instance, mathematical methods to analyse the tail correlation between the outputs of different internal model's components could be embedded within an analytical tool. This tool could then be used systematically against models results in a frequency established on objective criteria.

Some other tools may help prioritise *ad hoc* reviews or other supervisory actions when their outputs give rise to concern. This might include simple indicators that compare the internal model outputs with independent metrics that are reasonably expected to move in congruence with the model's outputs. For instance, supervisory authorities may use simplified models or model components whose outputs are expected to change in relation with the change of the outputs of the internal model. Another example is the use of simplified metrics based on volume measures or other relevant measures. Another tool useful to prioritise specific reviews is the analysis of changes in the internal model outputs. Supervisory authorities – and firms – can use indicators based on the analysis of change and objective thresholds to trigger specific in-depth reviews of approved internal models.

These governance processes are important to ensure that, at both an insurance firm and system level, the firms' internal models continue to deliver outputs that are consistent with the requirements of the Solvency II directive. When developing these processes, supervisory authorities need to take into account the specificities of the firms, including their risk profile. For instance, supervisory authorities may decide on the frequency of reviews based on the nature, scale and complexity of the firm's business and modelling, but also taking into account any specific concern that may arise from the SRP of the firm or any other information deemed relevant.

For example, when deciding on the frequency of model's reviews, supervisory authorities may leverage on the activities performed as part of the assessment of any major change to the model. In practice, supervisory authorities may decide that the more frequent the application for major changes, the fewer additional review activities need be performed.

Internal models ongoing appropriateness indicators are therefore crucial. To facilitate the supervisory review of authorised insurance firms, supervisory authorities might use different tools, such as the analysis of the information regularly provided by firms (eg, the report to supervisors, RTS, as discussed later in the chapter), the request of additional specific information deemed relevant, the interview of employees from the regulated firms, on-site inspections and the collection and review of any other relevant information.

However, as described, supervisory authorities might also develop quantitative tools/indicators to help monitor the internal models. These tools might be run as part of the SRP on a regular or *ad hoc* basis.

What tools/indicators should be developed?[

Ideally, the supervisory toolbox should contain at least a suite of (early warning) indicators that target:

- ❏ the overall capital requirement (top-level indicators) – these indicators should help supervisors detect if the overall SCR as calculated by the internal model has been materially underestimated;
- ❏ the material risks borne by the firm – these indicators should help supervisors detect anomalies in the firm's estimates of specific risks (market risk, credit risk, underwriting risks, etc);
- ❏ the relative change in SCR – these indicators could monitor changes in the SCR (calculated using an internal model) relative to changes in underlying risks;
- ❏ the valuation of assets and liabilities – these indicators should capture anomalies in the valuation of assets and liabilities that feeds into the internal model calculations; and
- ❏ the economic and business environment – and, more generally, change in the external environment of the firms that should impact the SCR.

What should these tools/indicators target?

Should these indicators target the deterioration of a firm's financial conditions or a deterioration of its internal model? As an inappropriate internal model may lead to inappropriate decisions that in turn may lead to a deterioration of its financial condition, it is not always possible to disentangle these two issues.

It is, however, important to identify those situations where an internal model no longer reflects the Solvency II 99.5% calibration standard. Therefore, some of the tools and indicators may take the form of simple and independent tools to estimate a range or a lower bound for – under a simplified set of assumptions – the capital requirement calculated using the internal model. While not capturing the finest details of the firm's risk profile, these tools are powerful as a safeguard against an unintended drift of the internal model results due to unexpected behaviour of the complex relationships of risks within the internal model. For example, the correlation between risks or risk drivers might be modelled and calibrated appropriately for a specific balance of the firm's portfolio at a specific point in time. As the balance between risks in the portfolio changes over time, so does the contribution from the different risks or lines of business to the capital requirement. Therefore, the dependency structure or its calibration might not be appropriate for the new balance of the portfolio.

Another possible source for a downward drift over time of the model output is the selection bias for the improvements made to the model. Firms have more incentives to dedicate greater resources to reduce the uncertainties in those areas of modelling where they have applied conservatisms or prudence. While reducing the uncertainty might result in more accurate and appropriate modelling, over time this selection bias might result in the overall output of the internal model, and the SCR in particular, to drift significantly downwards. This might happen because changes reducing prudence are prioritised and implemented by firms, while other changes that should have been considered and that would increase the SCR are ignored and therefore not implemented. As one would expect, supervisory authorities are particularly concerned if such situation occurs and if a firm leans toward the selection bias without the protection of any internal safeguard, as this could result in – and also be a symptom of – weaknesses in the risk management system or the broader governance of the firm.

Supervisory authorities might also develop different types of simple indicators that estimate the capital requirement by focusing on some individual indicators of potential solvency weaknesses that are captured in the modelling using more complex and more fragmented possible contributors to these weaknesses. The best known of those indicators is probably the leverage ratio used under Basel III as part of the supervisory regime for banks and other credit institutions. The leverage ratio for banks supplements the more complex capital requirement calculation based on an individual set of risks and, while it might not be seen as a fundamental underlying risk, it is an indicator of overall weakness. For insurance firms, the leverage ratio is less relevant, but other simple indicators of weakness could also be developed to supplement a more complex capital requirement calculation. For instance, some indicators could be developed based on measures of the mismatches between assets and liabilities.

What ideal properties should these tools/indicators have?
These indicators should be characterised by being:

- independent from the insurance firms' internal model calculations – ie, they should not be agnostic to risks, but try to capture risks from a different perspective;
- simple to operate;
- transparent;
- appropriate with respect to a specific risk profile and specific internal model components;
- forward-looking – ie, they should be able to capture potential development of risks over the next 12 months; and
- fit for purpose, that is:
  - able to identify movements in the firm's risk profile;
  - contributing to the identification of the source of the movement in the firm's risk profile; and
  - minimising false positives.

Indicators that are independent from model's calculations are key to avoiding missing phenomena or risks as they develop and that are not necessarily captured, or appropriately captured, by the model. These indicators aim to identify instances where the model outcome diverges from reality.

Nevertheless, some indicators that monitor metrics produced by the model over time are also useful to monitor the performances of the model. In particular, they may help identify unexpected changes that could trigger further analysis or additional validation.

Examples
- Early warning indicators (EWIs) from the Prudential Regulation Authority (PRA). These indicators are based on the ratio between a firm's modelled SCR and the Solvency II pre-corridor

minimum capital requirement (pMCR). The PRA is developing thresholds for different industry segments below which the EWIs would trigger supervisory intervention to assess whether firms' modelled capital requirements are drifting downwards.

- Benchmark portfolios used to assess the calibration of models over time and across a sample of firms. These are more appropriate for homogenous risks to which firms are exposed – for instance, the use of benchmark portfolios is more appropriate for market risks (eg, equity risk) than for some insurance risks. The use of a benchmark portfolio allows for comparing over time the model's results and focusing on change in the assessment of the risk by removing the impact of the change in risk profile. For example, a benchmark portfolio can be designed as a simplified/stylised portfolio of assets reflecting the risk drivers. Alternatively, they can be designed to be portfolio-specific with respect to a firm at a given point in time, which is then used as a reference point.
- Percentiles of risk distributions and ratio of the tracked percentiles to the expected value of the distribution or to a relevant volume measure. Monitored over time, these indicators might show a strengthening or weakening of the calibration of the internal model – for instance, the result of an update of data used to estimate some parameters. Indeed, even a robust and objective process to estimate parameters based on observations might lead to unintended consequences where the observation period is shorter than an existing cycle in the data. This is the case for the insurance underwriting cycle, where the stochastic nature of the phenomenon leads to a deviation from a regular pattern – eg, some years of benign observations might lead mechanically to a reduction of the calibration that does not reflect a long-term change in the underlying risk.
- Trend of a split of the SCR calculated by the internal model according to the risk drivers. Such indicators are more likely to be internal to the model and will not identify developing phenomena not captured by the internal model, but will nonetheless provide useful information to monitor the performances and behaviours of the internal model over time.
- Track the movement over time of technical provisions (TPs) or SCR for business in the scope of the internal model as a propor-

tion of the total TP or SCR. Such indicators can be used to monitor the most complex and less transparent feature of capital models – ie, the interaction between risks. The complexity of this interaction depends on the model specification. For instance, for stochastic models using risk drivers correlated together, the resulting interactions of components of the business or some insurance products can be difficult to understand. Obviously, some changes in the firm's risk profile will lead to changes in the proportion tracked and will be anticipated, but changes that are not anticipated or properly explained should at least trigger further investigation or validation.

- Market indicators can be used to build indicators that compare model performances with observed market information. For instance, if a market phenomenon can be identified by the internal model, the indicator is able to monitor the frequency of such an event according to the internal model. Market observations can also be compared with outputs of the model where specific event cannot be identified, but the severity of the observed events and the severity of the model outputs can be connected – eg, changes in asset prices.
- Latest internal model SCR recalculated using the dependency (correlation, etc) assumptions from the calculation of the previous internal model SCR. As mentioned, interactions between risks are, for some types of capital modelling (eg, stochastic models), an area of complexity and opacity for the user. In addition, the parameterisation of the dependency structures (eg, copula) is dependent on a high degree of expert judgement. Therefore, monitoring the change in the SCR for the same parameters of the model dependency structure allows the impact of the changes in the dependency parameters to be isolated. Some related indicators can also be chosen depending on the structure of the internal model; for stochastic models using copulas, it is possible to identify the respective percentile of the different components or modules of the model that contribute to the SCR. Monitoring this information might be useful in informing the validation cycle.

NON-COMPLIANCE WITH SOLVENCY II INTERNAL MODEL REQUIREMENTS

When a firm has received supervisory approval to use an internal model to calculate the SCR, it cannot revert to calculating the whole or any part of the SCR with the standard formula, except in exceptional circumstances and subject to the approval of the supervisor (see Article 117 of the Solvency II directive). Nonetheless, it is critical that the internal model continues to produce outputs that are appropriate and, in particular, a SCR that is not mis-stated. The internal model governance framework and especially the validation and model change policy, but also the broader risk management system harnessed through the use test, provide tools to help ensure ongoing compliance.

Another important tool provided by the Solvency II framework is the own risk and solvency assessment (ORSA) process. The ORSA should include, in addition to the assessment of the own solvency needs and compliance with the capital requirement, an assessment of the potential significant deviation of the firm's risk profile with the assumptions underlying the calculation of the SCR.

Changes to the model and capital add-ons (Article 118)

As mentioned earlier, the firm (and, ultimately, its AMSB) are responsible for ensuring that the internal model continues to comply with the relevant Solvency II requirements and, in particular, the internal model tests and standards set out in Articles 120–125 of the Solvency II directive. Two aspects of non-compliance are relevant for this discussion:

- ❑ non-compliance with the internal model requirements; and
- ❑ deviation of the firm's risk profile from the underlying assumptions of the SCR.

An example of the first type of non-compliance is a failure of the validation process or nonfulfillment of the use test that jeopardises the robustness of the internal model and, more broadly, weakens the risk management system. An example of the second type of non-compliance is a failure to adapt the internal model to a change of the business that results in the internal model outputs misrepresenting the firm's risk profile. Both cases would require changes to the internal model or internal modelling framework to remedy the deficiency identified.

When the firm identifies a non-compliance it should promptly notify the relevant supervisory authority and submit a plan to restore compliance within a reasonable timeframe, or demonstrate that the impact of non-compliance is immaterial. When compliance cannot be restored in a reasonable timeframe, supervisory authorities need to ensure that the SCR continues to provide the policyholders with the appropriate level of protection. Following the SRP, when the supervisory authority has determined that the use of an internal model has been ineffective, they might decide to restore compliance with the SCR by setting a capital add-on (see Article 37 of the Solvency II directive). In some other cases, the supervisory authority may require the insurance firm to revert to the use of the standard formula for the calculation of the SCR (Article 118 of the Solvency II directive).

The standard formula appropriateness (Article 119)

As explained in Chapter 1, the use of an internal model is one of the options available to firms to calculate the SCR. This requires compliance with all the internal model's requirements and prior supervisory approval. However, when the firm's risk profile deviates significantly from the underlying assumptions of the standard formula, the internal modelling route may be the only suitable option.

Indeed, the standard formula design and calibration cannot provide for the diversity of insurance firms. For instance, the standard formula may not be well suited to capture non-traditional insurance risks or complex products embedding sophisticated options and guarantees. Similarly, some idiosyncratic risk profile, even if resulting from traditional insurance business, such as natural catastrophe risk, might not be adequately captured by the standard formula.

The firm is responsible for the calculation of its SCR in accordance with the Solvency II specifications – ie, VaR of the basic own funds with a confidence level of 99.5% over one year – in order to ensure the required level of protection to its policyholders. In particular, when using the standard formula, the firm should, through the ORSA process, assess that its risk profile does not deviate significantly from the assumptions underlying the standard formula.

If an insurance firm proposes to use the standard formula when it is not appropriate for the calculation of its SCR, its supervisor can require the development and use of an internal model. Obviously, the development and use of an internal model is not straightforward: it requires an appropriate firm culture, involves significant risk management activities and, above all, requires the firm to invest a significant amount of resources. However, the use of an internal model when embedded in an appropriate risk management framework should encourage the innovation of risk measurement and a continuous improvement of management methodologies, leading to an enhanced assessment of the (re)insurance firm's risk profile and capital allocation. Therefore, the development and use of an internal model is a risk management tool that results in more benefits for the firm than the mere calculation of the SCR.

SUPERVISORY REPORTING AND PUBLIC DISCLOSURES[4]

"Pillar III" covers the supervisory reporting (RTS) and public disclosure (solvency and financial conditions report, SFCR) aspects of the regime. This is the information firms are required to report to the supervisory authority and the information to be publicly disclosed to the market. Supervisory reporting requirements aim to support the risk-oriented approach to insurance supervision, while public disclosure requirements aim to reinforce market mechanisms and market discipline by acting as a strong incentive to firms to conduct their business in a sound and efficient manner, including the incentive to maintain an adequate capital position that can act as a cushion against potential losses arising from risk exposures.

Both the RTS and SFCR should contain a qualitative report, including quantitative data where necessary, and quantitative reporting templates. Both reports should be designed as stand-alone documents and follow a similar structure.

Solvency II requires firms to submit to the supervisory authorities' information:

- at predefined periods (regular basis);
- upon occurrence of predefined events; and
- during enquiries regarding the situation of the firm.[5]

Figure 15.1 Information to be received by the supervisory authority

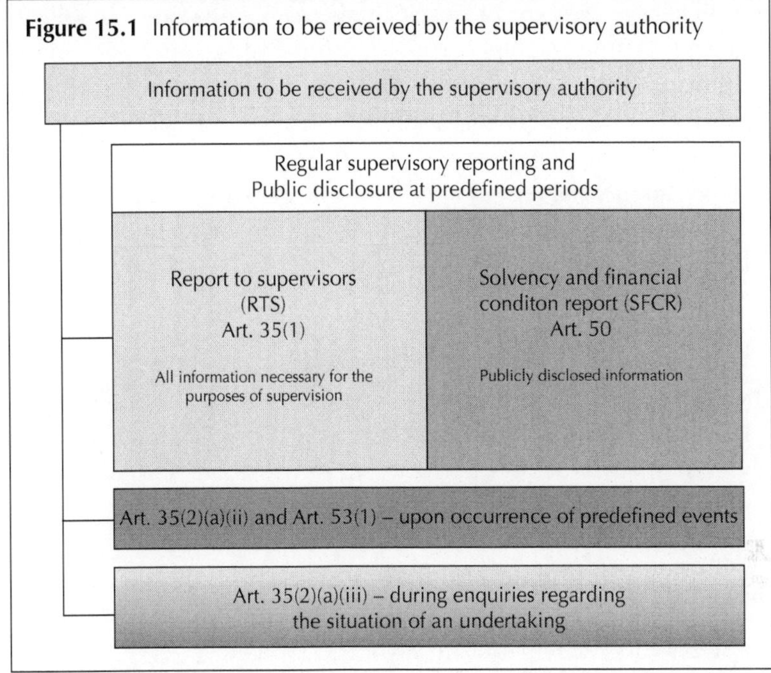

Public disclosure and SFCR

Solvency II sets out the minimum content of information that firms are required to publicly disclose, and establishes requirements on the updates to be provided on the disclosed information following major developments. As there are various ways an internal model can be constructed, implemented and operated, public disclosure requirements on internal models are to the extent possible based on principles with regard to the harmonisation of reporting and comparability issues between firms.

To enable different market participants to assess the internal model and make use of the information, the level and depth of information to be publicly disclosed is based on the principle that a knowledgeable person can achieve a reasonably good understanding of the design and operational details of the internal model, as well as to the reliability of the internal model – for example, disclosure of information related to the purpose, results and key decisions taken as a result of the use of its internal model.

Public disclosure is not required to the extent that information on internal models would prejudice to an unreasonable degree the commercial interest of the firm, or if there are obligations to policyholders or other counterparties that bind the firm to secrecy or confidentiality. However, where the non-disclosure of information is permitted by the supervisory authority, firms should state this in the SFCR and explain its reasons.

When an internal model is used for calculating the SCR, the information contained in the SFCR should be divided into qualitative and quantitative information. For example:

- qualitative information:
  - governance and risk management;
  - use;
  - scope and model coverage;
  - risk measure, confidence level, time horizon and basic own funds;
  - methodologies, including assumptions and aggregation;
  - data;
  - risk mitigation activities;
  - operational performance; and
  - validation activities; and
  - documentation.
- quantitative information:
  - solvency capital requirement;
  - comparison and reconciliation; and
  - validation analyses.

Supervisory reporting and RTS

The RTS should contain all the information necessary for the purposes of supervision. The information should be specifically aimed at the supervisor, including all elements set out in the SFCR (although at a more granular level). The RTS should follow a pre-set structure and template to facilitate its review and understanding.[6] (Re)insurers using an approved internal model are also subject to further requirements, including the reporting of:

- activities performed during the year to verify the ongoing compliance with regulatory requirements for internal models;
- analysis of the comparison and reconciliation of the previous year's results, including explanations for any material changes in the SCR;

- causes and sources of profits and losses;
- plans for future development of steps for the internal model;
- overall solvency needs;
- the information on how capital allocation is done, both for regulatory capital and economic capital;
- the reconciliation between economic capital and the SCR for firms using different time periods or risk measures than VaR 99.5% over a one-year horizon; and
- the information about future management actions used in the SCR calculation.

The quantitative information covered by the RTS, in addition to that required by the SFCR, should at least contain:

i) the SCR as calculated by the internal model;
ii) an estimate of the SCR according to the standard formula (if applicable);
iii) the split of undiversified capital charges and any adjustment for the loss absorbing capacity of technical provisions and deferred taxes;
iv) any capital add-on;
v) the economic capital;
vi) the comparison and reconciliation with last year results forecasts; and
vii) the summary report of the validation results performed during the year.

The information required by points (i), (iii), (iv), (v) and (vi) has to be provided to the lowest level of granularity at which the model is used. Group internal models have also to provide this information by legal entity. In some cases, the supervisory authorities may also require firms to present the information in point (ii) at a more granular level.

CONCLUSION

Even when approved for use by the supervisory authorities, internal models are likely to present limitations and weaknesses that offer sufficient reasons for ongoing monitoring. In addition, changes in the environment and the firm itself can create a need for monitoring the internal model's appropriateness.

The Solvency II internal model requirements, and in particular the regular cycle of validation, the model change policy and the use test, provide the framework for robust governance of the internal model. It is the responsibility of the firm, up to its higher governance body, to ensure that the internal model continues to operate properly on an ongoing basis.

Supervisory authorities also have the duty to monitor the ongoing appropriateness of the internal models and that will form part of the SRP.

The views expressed in this chapter are those of the authors and not necessarily those of the PRA, Bank of England

1 For further details, see Box (2007).
2 For further details, see Philipp Keller (2009).
3 The quote refers to a verbal answer to a question at a US Department of Defense News Briefing made by Donald Rumsfeld while serving as US Secretary of Defense in February 2002.
4 For further details, see CEIOPS (2009).
5 This may encompass any other information that supervisory authorities might deem necessary during the supervisory review process, using a wide range of methods and formats (eg, questionnaires, request for further information on a specific issue, relevant documents during on-site inspections).
6 For further detail, see Annex 1.

REFERENCES

Box, G. E. P. and N. Draper, 2007, *Response Surfaces, Mixtures, and Ridge Analyses (2e)* (Hoboken, NJ: Wiley).

Cadoni, P., 2009, "Using Internal Models to Determine the Solvency Capital Requirement: The Regulatory View", in Marcelo Cruz (Ed), *The Solvency II Handbook* (London: Risk Books), pp 75–112.

Cadoni, P. and P. Sharma, 2010, "Solvency II: A New Regulatory Frontier" in C. Kempler, M. Flamée, C. Yang and P. Windels (Eds), *Global Perspective on Insurance Today: A Look at National Interest Versus Globalization* (New York, NY: Palgrave Macmillan), pp 53–68.

CEIOPS, 2009, "Draft CEIOPS Advice for Level 2 Implementing Measures on Solvency II: Supervisory Reporting and Public Disclosure Requirements", Consultation Paper 58.

European Parliament and the Council of the European Union, 2009, "Directive 2009/138/EC of the European Parliament and of the Council of 25 November 2009 on the Taking-up and Pursuit of the Business of Insurance and Reinsurance (Solvency II) (recast)".

Keller, P., 2009, "Internal Model Review", presentation to the CEIOPS Internal Model Expert Group, January.

Index

(page numbers in italic type refer to figures and tables)